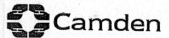 **Camden**

Libraries

You may return this book to any Camden library.
For a full list please see www.camden.gov.uk

3/2018		

For terms and conditions of library membership
www.camden.gov.uk/libraries

For 24 hour renewals
www.camden.gov.uk/libraries and click renew
(library card and pin number needed)

Tel: 020 7974 4444 for all library enquiries

Enrico Dandolo & the Rise of Venice

THE JOHNS HOPKINS UNIVERSITY PRESS

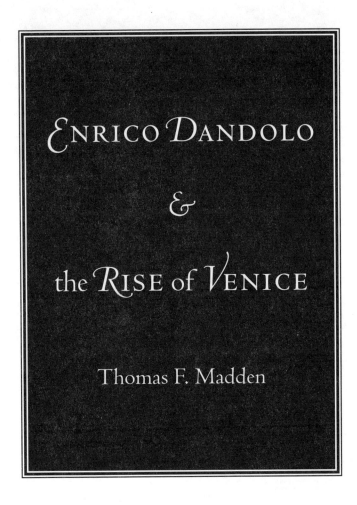

Enrico Dandolo

&

the Rise of Venice

Thomas F. Madden

THE JOHNS HOPKINS UNIVERSITY PRESS

Baltimore & London

This book was brought to publication with the generous assistance of the Gladys Krieble Delmas Foundation.

© 2003 The Johns Hopkins University Press
All rights reserved. Published 2003
Printed in the United States of America on acid-free paper

2 4 6 8 9 7 5 3 1

The Johns Hopkins University Press
2715 North Charles Street
Baltimore, Maryland 21218–4363
www.press.jhu.edu

Library of Congress Cataloging-in-Publication Data
Madden, Thomas F.
Enrico Dandolo and the rise of Venice / Thomas F. Madden.
p. cm.
Includes bibliographical references and index.
ISBN 0-8018-7317-7 (hardcover : alk. paper)
1. Dandolo, Enrico, 1108–1205.   2. Heads of state—Italy—Venice—Biography.
3. Venice (Italy)—History—697–1508.   I. Title.
DG677.64 .M33 2003
945'.3104'092—dc21
2002013623

A catalog record for this book is available from the British Library.

For my wife,

Page Andrea Ettle

Contents

Figures

Acknowledgments

n the decade since I began this project I have accumulated many debts—more than I can ever list or truly even remember. Nevertheless, there are persons who deserve special mention. First and foremost I thank my friend and mentor, the late Donald E. Queller. It was he who first suggested a doctoral dissertation on "the life and times of Enrico Dandolo," and then, inch by inch, brought me over to the study of Venice. It would be hard to imagine a more supportive advisor. Although this book is very different from the dissertation he directed, my hope is that it would still merit his approval. Don's former classmate, Louise Buenger Robbert, also deserves thanks. Her abiding love for Venice and its medieval past is infectious. Like Don and every other Venetianist whom I have ever met, Louise has always been generous with her time and expertise. Over the years she has never failed to pass on references and other bits of information that might be of interest to me. I am very grateful for her kindnesses and warm collegiality.

I would also like to thank my good friend Alfred J. Andrea, a fellow student of the Fourth Crusade. More than once he has double-checked the accuracy of my Latin translations and, in a few instances, suggested alternate wording. He was also kind enough to read chapters 7 and 8 in draft form, and he made many excellent comments. I have also benefitted from the observations, advice, and assistance of many, many others, especially John Barker, Thomas E. Dale, Robert C. Davis, Blake De Maria, David Jacoby, John H. Pryor, Juergen Schulz, and Alan M. Stahl.

The staff and archivists of the Archivio di Stato di Venezia merit warm thanks. They must certainly be the friendliest and most helpful people in any European archive—or at least very close to it. I am also grateful for the hard work of those in the interlibrary loan department of the Saint Louis University Pius XII Library. They bent rules and moved mountains to accommodate my odd requests.

I am extremely grateful to my financial benefactors, without whom this research could not have been undertaken. The Mellon Faculty Development Fund allowed me to take several research trips as well as time off from teaching duties. The Gladys Krieble Delmas Foundation generously funded two extended stays in Venice. I thank them both.

Lastly, I would like to thank my wife, Page. While many academic spouses suffer through years of hearing about the same project that never seems to end, few must do so while managing two children under the age of three in Venice. It was no small feat keeping them happy, clean, fed, and out of the canals. She did it, though, and so much more while I serenely spent my days, weeks, and months in the archives. Words cannot express my love and admiration for her. I offer this book to her, then, not only as the culmination of my work but also as a sign that our time with the "old doge" has indeed finally come to an end.

Introduction

ith the exception of Marco Polo, Doge Enrico Dandolo (1192–1205) is the best-known Venetian of the Middle Ages—and with good reason. He stood at the center of events that transformed the Republic of St. Mark into a maritime empire and fundamentally altered the Mediterranean world. He was also blessed with a colorful character. When elected to the dogeship he was already in his eighties and completely blind. Nevertheless, he remained a man of vigor with a sharp intelligence and plenty of practical wisdom. Historians have long employed other terms to describe him, as well, including *wily, clever, rascally, shrewd,* and *crafty.* In other words, Enrico Dandolo was a typical Venetian of the Middle Ages.

But was he? My interest in Dandolo grew out of my work on the Fourth Crusade (1201–4), that strange expedition that set out to conquer Muslim Egypt and ended by destroying Christian Byzantium. As the leader of the Venetians on the crusade, the doge played a crucial role in its course and outcome. I was struck early on, though, by the strong emphasis often placed on Enrico Dandolo's character. Based on the events of the crusade and eyewitness descriptions of him, one could certainly conclude that he was a man of probity, prudence, sturdy patriotism, and pragmatic sense. Yet a great many interpretations of the crusade rest squarely on much darker depictions of the man. He is cast as a beguiling trickster who ensnared the naive crusaders in a web of deceit, a confidence man who found in the feudal knights the perfect mark. With little or no interest in religion, Dandolo is said to have hatched a secret plan to pervert the crusade, turning it from its holy mission in the East into a war of personal vengeance against Byzantium.

Given such detailed characterizations, one would think that a great deal is known about Enrico Dandolo. As I soon discovered, however, the opposite is true. Aside from his role in the Fourth Crusade, very little scholarly attention had ever been paid to the life of the doge, or to his family, or even to the political and social environment in which he lived. Instead, the nefarious portrayals of Dandolo rest ultimately on two main foundations: uninformed medieval anti-Venetian bigotry and the early modern "countermyth" of Venice. The myth of early modern Venice is well known and much studied. It holds that Venetians belonged to a serene republic devoid of factionalism in which honor, honesty, and selfless devotion to the common good were plentiful virtues. The countermyth, which was favored by Venice's critics and enemies, portrayed the republic as a place of dark intrigue, clandestine designs, and cynical motives. Moved by patriotism and profit, Venetians were said to be "Venetians first, Christians afterward." It is this myth that has been most often projected back on Venice's medieval past. In short, what I learned was that the rich personality so often attributed to Enrico Dandolo was not his at all, but Venice's. Encrusted with centuries of historical narrative, the doge has become a Venetian Everyman, adorned with characteristics that *all* Venetians, both medieval and early modern, are often thought to share. Enrico Dandolo was not so much a man of his times as a manikin dressed up in a myth.

Although I came to study Enrico Dandolo to better understand the Fourth Crusade, I soon realized that to challenge the myth of Dandolo was to do the same for that of medieval Venice. Indeed, the life of the doge, which spanned the twelfth century, is an ideal tool for better understanding the medieval Republic. Dandolo and his family were in the thick of the profound changes that transformed Venice in the eleventh, twelfth, and early thirteenth centuries. They provide, therefore, a useful way to examine events and larger trends while remaining grounded in the lives of real people. Of course, we must not mistakenly assume that all Venetians were like the Dandolo. But all, or at least most, were affected by the same factors and dynamics that altered Venice itself, albeit in different ways.

It is not my intention to replace the old myth of medieval Venice with a new one. Venetians, like all people, were a diverse group, most of whom held common ideas and beliefs that bound them together, but otherwise differed in many respects. There is, however, one thing that I am convinced can be said of all medieval Venetians: They were medieval. Simply because Venetians were capitalists, for example, we should not assume that they were modern and therefore cynical in their outlook. Thousands of parchments in the Venetian archives attest to the heartfelt and very medieval piety of these people. Venetians built churches and monasteries at an extraordinary rate, showered them with pious gifts, and carefully looked after their spiritual health and well-being. Medieval

Venetians paid close attention to the papacy, in many ways closer than other Europeans since it was their only clear and abiding attachment to the West. They were early and enthusiastic supporters of papal initiatives, including Gregorian reform and the crusades. Indeed, as I was surprised to discover, until the Fourth Crusade relations between Venice and Rome had been exceptionally good. This work, therefore, is revisionist—in the best sense of that word, I hope, remaining grounded in clear reasoning and a sober analysis of the sources.

Misconceptions about medieval Venice are in part due to the relatively scant scholarly attention it has received. Although legions of scholars have enhanced our understanding of the majestic early modern Republic, only a handful now work on the medieval city of wood, stone, and mud. While it is true that archival materials in Venice are much more plentiful after the mid-thirteenth century, and do not really explode until the fourteenth century, thousands of documents are preserved from the eleventh and twelfth centuries and earlier. Most of these are from monastic archives and, therefore, not organized into neat topical categories—unless, that is, one is interested in the history of a particular monastery. But, with the help of a computer and a willingness to spend long hours in the Venetian state archives, it is possible to piece together some of these jumbled fragments of medieval Venetian lives. Only in this way can the underbrush be cleared away and a new history of Venice in the Middle Ages be written, one based on the firm foundation of documentary evidence. Indeed, it has already begun, led by modern pioneers like Irmgard Fees, Gerhard Rösch, Elisabeth Crouzet-Pavan, Daniela Rando, Marco Pozza, Andrea Castagnetti, Juergen Schulz, Louise Buenger Robbert, and others. Much more work remains to be done.

For the present study I have utilized my own database of several thousand documents before 1220 as well as the thousands more that have been published in collections. Together these form my main source for the reconstruction of the Dandolo family and the events in the life of Enrico Dandolo before the crusade. Throughout, I have treated literary sources written after Andrea Dandolo's *Chronica per extensum descripta* with great caution. Andrea Dandolo was doge with access to state documents that have since perished. His chronicle is judicious, sober, and frank, even when dealing with events embarrassing to his family. Venetian chronicles proliferated in the fifteenth and sixteenth centuries, yet few of their authors had access to more information about the eleventh and twelfth centuries than did Andrea Dandolo. Most of these later writers were prone to the patrician puffery characteristic of Renaissance Venice. This is especially true in the various genealogies of noble families that sought to bolster the pedigrees of the ruling elite. Very little in these works concerning eleventh- and twelfth-century families can be accepted without corroboration from contemporary sources.

Venetian archival documents, chronicles, and genealogies all have one unfortunate trait in common during this period: They virtually ignore women. Indeed, a glance at the genealogy at the end of this book might lead one to suppose that the Dandolo men spontaneously generated. There are a few exceptions. Primera Polani, Enrico Dandolo's sister-in-law, is visible and active in several surviving documents. His wife, Contessa, also makes a brief appearance. Yet, aside from these, virtually nothing is known about the women of the Dandolo family. By necessity, therefore, this book is decidedly one-sided, focusing almost exclusively on the activities of the Dandolo in the public sphere.

Although this study sheds new light on many aspects of Enrico Dandolo's life, the documentation is still too fragmentary to produce a biography in the modern sense of that word. I have therefore focused not only on the specifics of the doge's life but also on its context, particularly as it relates to his family. The first chapter describes the political, economic, and social factors in the tenth and eleventh centuries that allowed the Dandolo and other new families to acquire great wealth and then to seek political and social status commensurate with it. These same dynamics fueled similar shifts in power in other fledgling communes in Italy. However, in Venice, where circumstances are always unique, this took the form not of revolution against existing authority but of a gradual move toward power sharing that retained the basic components of traditional government. The Dandolo made their fortune in overseas trade and by the mid-eleventh century were sufficiently established to help found a new parish, San Luca, and to undertake service to the state. Like others of their social class, they would play a conspicuous role in Venice's relations with Byzantium as well as the city's crusading efforts.

The early twelfth century was a time of great uncertainty for the Dandolo family. Chapter 2 examines the career of Patriarch Enrico Dandolo of Grado, the uncle of the doge. Like his predecessors, Patriarch Dandolo became an ardent proponent of Gregorian reform in the Veneto. Contrary to myth, church reform was warmly received in Venice, chiefly because the Venetian church, which lacked feudal ties, simply required less reform. Patriarch Dandolo ran afoul of the doge when he began to tread on traditional prerogatives. A dispute over the election of the abbess of San Zaccaria soured relations between the two, while a disagreement over an alliance against the Normans caused a complete break. The Dandolo family, which had no stake in the quarrel, was punished for it. In

1147, Patriarch Dandolo, his supporters, and his entire family were exiled. The houses of the Dandolo were leveled. Thrust into a struggle between church and state, the family had no choice but to wait it out. A few years later, after successful negotiations between the pope and a new doge, the Dandolo were restored. The episode was an important turning point for the family, and it also serves to illuminate the otherwise poorly understood relationship between the ecclesiastical and political spheres in medieval Venice.

Rising out of the ashes of their family compound, the Dandolo moved quickly back into the ranks of the elite. A new doge, Vitale II Michiel (1155–72), was eager to patch up relations with the patriarch and, by extension, his family. Chapter 3 focuses on the pater familias, Vitale Dandolo, who became a regular official in the ducal court and one of the doge's closest advisors. Indeed, Vitale Dandolo soon became a powerful man in his own right, achieving a reputation for fairness and judicial probity across the lagoon. Like his brother, the patriarch, Vitale lived a very long life. He was in his eighties and had already retired from court when Emperor Manuel I Comnenus ordered the seizure of all Venetians and their goods in the Byzantine Empire. Nevertheless, he remained active. He sent his son, Enrico, the future doge, to accompany Michiel on a retaliatory expedition in 1172, which ended in complete failure and the murder of the doge. The expedition had been the brainchild of the people, almost certainly opposed by Vitale Dandolo and his son, as well as Michiel. The catastrophe led to a fundamental restructuring of the Venetian constitution, which is described in some detail. This transformation had the effect of concentrating power into the hands of a conservative oligarchy determined to bring order and stability to Venice and its relations with foreign powers. Their challenge was to temper the rashness of popular will with reasoned judgment and cautious actions.

Enrico Dandolo, the future doge, attempted to follow the example of his famous father. He, too, served on embassies to Constantinople and, contrary to common opinion, was a promoter of peace with Byzantium. However, sometime between 1174 and 1176, probably while on a voyage to the East, he received a blow to the head that damaged the occipital lobe of his brain. Within a few years he was completely blind. Chapter 4 begins with a detailed examination of Dandolo's blindness, the importance of which far transcends a simple life experience. Despite his failing eyesight, Enrico Dandolo apparently continued to serve in the court of Doge Sebastiano Ziani until the latter's death in 1178. He took part in the pageantry and problems of the Peace of Venice of 1177, an event of enormous importance for the increasingly self-confident Venetians as well as a cornerstone in the evolving myth of Venice. This chapter also examines the last years of Patriarch Dandolo's life.

Chapter 5 utilizes the ducal election of Enrico Dandolo in 1192 in order to examine the changing nature of the dogeship itself. Dandolo's oath of office, the earliest such oath to survive, is closely examined not only for what it tells us about Dandolo's own authority but also for the clues it gives concerning the history of the dogeship in the twelfth century. In addition, Chapter 5 focuses on the increasingly complex and regularized government of the commune. Building on these findings, Chapter 6 then describes the major events of the first decade of Dandolo's reign. These include a number of far-reaching domestic reforms, such as Venice's first civil code of law and the minting of Venice's first pure silver coin. Attention is also paid to Venetian foreign affairs at this time.

It is in Chapter 7 that this study meets the vast historiography of the Fourth Crusade. Yet, as much as possible, this book remains a history of Venice. The life of Enrico Dandolo, which served as a guide for understanding the medieval Republic, is put into similar service in an attempt to comprehend the Venetian perspective on and role within the crusade. Among the subjects examined in this chapter are Venice's changing relationship with the papacy, the decisions of Venetians within the context of recent governmental reforms, and the sheer enormity of the Venetian effort to prepare the crusade fleet. Chapter 8 then looks at how it all went wrong. By late summer 1202, Enrico Dandolo had a large and angry foreign army in the lagoon that could not pay its bills. As the chief proponent of the crusade, he was caught between his people and the crusaders, both of whom believed they had been wronged. The reforms begun in 1172 were now put to their greatest test. Attempting to manage the risk, the oligarchy had meticulously planned and confirmed every aspect of the crusade. When reality was different, the government was called upon to avoid a rash and costly popular reaction, like that of 1171, and seek out a prudent and fair resolution to the problem. The imperfect solution was the conquest of Zara. This allowed the crusade to get under way but convinced Pope Innocent III that Dandolo and the Venetians had hijacked the holy enterprise. This chapter also examines the effects in the Adriatic of the conquest of Zara and the subsequent departure of the crusade armada.

More than half of Venice's men and nearly all of its sea power were engaged in the Fourth Crusade, which was the focus of attention for all Venetians, including those left behind to manage things at home. Chapters 9 and 10 mirror this shift, looking closely at Dandolo and the Venetian crusaders' perspective on the conquest of Constantinople and the foundation of the Latin Empire.

Scholars have tended to take for granted that Venetians desired and even worked toward the destruction of Byzantium. These chapters demonstrate that the situation was much more complex. Stability and order were their primary goals. Doge Dandolo's challenge was to manage events largely outside of his control, maneuvering as best he could toward a sustainable and stable environment for the Venetians of Byzantium. This he did within the constitutional framework forged by his father. Throughout the crusade Dandolo acted as the leader of the Venetian crusaders, not as the doge of Venice—an important distinction. Ducal authority rested with his son, the Vice-Doge Ranieri Dandolo, who remained in Venice. In all his agreements throughout the crusade, Enrico carefully avoided committing the communal government to anything.

Yet matters remained beyond Dandolo's control. Despite his attempts to craft a stable government at Constantinople, the rest of the Byzantine Empire was in chaos. The epilogue briefly examines the immediate effects of the Fourth Crusade and the death of Enrico Dandolo on Venice. The complicated relationship between the commune and the Venetians of the Latin Empire is also explored. It is generally, and incorrectly, assumed that the Venetians seized the opportunity to gobble up the ruined pieces of Byzantium. Yet this chaotic state of affairs was precisely what the oligarchic Great Council had wanted to avoid. Its members were not at all sanguine about the achievements of the crusade. Indeed, they approached the whole matter with a great deal of trepidation. They feared the implications of a powerful Patriarch of Constantinople, even if he was a Venetian, and they balked at the cost and risk of capturing Byzantine lands. Although Enrico Dandolo would long be remembered as a hero in Venice, not everything he accomplished was welcomed or wanted at the time. In the end the enormity of events would force the Venetian government to extend its reach into the Aegean, thus transforming Venice once again, now into a maritime empire.

By any reckoning Enrico Dandolo was an extraordinary man. He was not the quintessential Venetian. Nevertheless, the study of his life and his world is a fruitful way to begin to better understand the rich history of the medieval Republic of St. Mark.

Enrico Dandolo & the Rise of Venice

ONE

RISE of the NEW FAMILIES

enice confronts the modern visitor with an intricate and compelling composition of stone and water. Tightly packed buildings crowd around narrow *calli* and seem to float on flowing canals. Soil and vegetation have little part in this splendor, tucked away in small private gardens and the Giardini Pubblici that Napoleon laid upon the Republic's corpse. Artists and tourists come to Venice to marvel at its artificial grandeur, a unique beauty made more so by the reflections of water and variations of light.

In the eleventh century Venice was a different place. Dirt and mud abounded. A boat ride down the Grand Canal was anything but spectacular. Venice's central waterway was flanked, not by towering *palazzi*, but by piers buzzing with workers loading and unloading merchant vessels, wooden buildings ranging from large warehouses to tiny hovels, and, most of all, land.[1] Yes, open areas were still quite plentiful in Venice. A traveler on the Grand Canal could watch farmers cultivating vegetables, fishermen netting their catch in closed-off rivers, and men and women tending vines and inspecting their grapes.[2] Many Venetians also scratched out a living in the lagoon's plentiful saltworks. The city's landscape was dotted with marshes crossed by tributaries flowing out of the Grand Canal. On the banks of the canal, where one day masterpieces of architecture would stand, cows grazed and pigs ate at the trough.

Merchant ships tended to cluster at the first bend in the Grand Canal. The area had no special name, so the inhabitants referred to it simply by the name they used for all of the islands in that part of the lagoon: *Rivoalto*, or Rialto. Stalls and piers set up by private landholders or merchants rose haphazardly around this area during the early centuries, but by the eleventh century, the Venetian state had taken over a good section of the market. There was still no bridge, yet there was an enormous amount of activity—even more so than today: Venetian merchants arriving from faraway ports sailed to the piers, unloaded their vessels, and argued over prices; notaries rushed with parchment and quill to stalls and ships to record business transactions; priests sprinkled holy water on vessels. Busy Rialto was the economic engine that drove medieval Venice.[3]

The most heavily built-up area of the city was the stretch between Rialto and the governmental center at San Marco; the area today called the Merceria.[4] At the end of this gnarled route stood the ducal church of San Marco and the palace of the doge. The structure of the church in 1100 appeared much as it does today, although there were considerable differences in decoration.[5] Much of the ornamentation still lay in the future, but the Byzantine-style church was nonetheless stunning. The nearby ducal palace was probably still a fortress. The Piazza San Marco did not yet exist, at least not the one we know today. Instead, there were two islands. The one to the east had the ducal palace and church on its eastern side and an L-shaped open field stretching a short distance to the west to a canal called the Rio Batario and to the south to the Bacino San Marco. Both the eastern and western islands were rimmed with the houses of wealthy families and shops. The western island had two churches and a hospice for pilgrims to the Holy Land.[6] A short distance east of San Marco was the wealthy convent of San Zaccaria, and about a mile further the island of Castello (formerly Olivolo), home to San Pietro, the cathedral church of Venice.

It is not certain when or how Enrico Dandolo's ancestors came to the Venetian lagoon. Most early modern patrician families boasted long histories stretching back to an original emigration of Romans from the mainland in the wake of the invasion of the Huns or the Goths. The stories were seldom true. The Renaissance passion for things Roman stirred Venetian families to manufacture tales of their ancestors' flight from barbarism to pioneer a new republic of the lagoons, and the Dandolo were not immune from that temptation. In time it would be maintained that a Dandolo from Padua led Roman refugees in the fifth century to the Rialtine islands and there founded Venice.[7] The truth is less spectacular, less Roman, and less certain. The name *Dandolo* is probably derived from the Lombard *Dand*,[8] which suggests a later arrival in the lagoon for the clan. The earliest Venetian histories, that of John the Deacon and the *Chronicon Altinate*, both written in the early to mid-eleventh century, mention no Dandolo.[9] None appears in any extant state or private documents until the tenth century. It was not until the fourteenth century that the Dandolo family became one of Venice's founders. According to the *Venetiarum Historia* (the so-called Giustinian Chronicle), written around the 1360s, the Dandolo were among the original refugees who fled Altino in circa 638 (where they had been tribunes and members of the *consilium sapientium*) to the island of Torcello.[10] However, Doge Andrea Dandolo, who wrote his *Chronica per extensum descripta* at least a decade before the *Venetiarum Historia*, attributes no such antiquity to his family.

According to the sixteenth-century genealogist and historian Marco Barbaro, one Antonio Dandolo served as Procurator of San Marco in 842.[11] If true, he was among the first to hold that position. The procuratorship was probably established shortly after the removal of the body of St. Mark from Alexandria in 829 and the subsequent construction of the ducal chapel to house it. Procurators of San Marco do not appear in the existing documentary record until 1152.[12] While it is true that Barbaro had access to materials that no longer survive, he was by no means immune from errors.

The Dandolo family does not really come into view until the late tenth century. Like many new families, the Dandolo appear to have taken advantage of the factional strife that rocked Venice at that time to assert themselves into expanding circles of political authority. The factions broke down along pro-Byzantine and pro-German lines, led by the Morosini and Coloprini families, respectively. The dispute was inherently destructive, leading to civil unrest and the murder of a doge and tearing at the fabric of Venice's social organization. Families that had long held power disappeared from the ducal court, while others took their place.[13] The Dandolo were among the latter. It is impossible to know on which side of the dispute they stood. They were merchants who did business in the East, so they may have favored the Byzantine party. In 978 or 979 a group of men in the court of Doge Vitale Candiano swore that the doge had requested and received a levy of funds, just as his predecessor had. One of those men was Orso Dandolo, the first member of the family to appear in the extant documentary record.[14]

As both sides scrambled for supporters, families who had come to moderate wealth through commercial success were welcomed into the ranks of the elite. The Dandolo were not the only family that benefitted.[15] The factional struggle gave new families an additional opportunity to enter into Venetian politics. Before the *Serrata* of 1297, when the ranks of the ruling class were closed, the membrane of Venetian nobility was permeable. Indeed, nobility in the sense of a group of families with a hereditary claim to political authority did not exist at all. In Venice wealth, not land, defined nobility; commercial skill, not military prowess. The events of the late tenth century failed to produce a revolution in the hierarchical structure because those families that were on the losing side remained wealthy.[16]

Doge Tribuno Menio (979–91) sought to heal the rift, initially favoring neither side. The earliest document that can be dated with certainty to his reign is the donation of the island south of the ducal palace to Abbot Giovanni Morosini, the brother of the murdered Domenico, for the foundation of the Benedictine monastery of San Giorgio.[17] The document, dated December 20, 982, was signed by the doge, three bishops, and 131 other leading citizens. First among the signers were the leaders of the two factions, Stefano Coloprino and Domenico Morosini. Further down the list, 42nd of 131, appears one Vitale Dandolo, the only member of his family to sign.[18] This document provides an important and rare snapshot of the power structure in Venice at this crucial period. The number of new families—indeed, the sheer number of families new or old—confirms the impact of the factional struggle in expanding the base of participating citizens. Henceforth, this body of "good men" or "faithful ones," as they were interchangeably called, would become a permanent part of the ducal court. Because of their wealth, these elites had the interest and the time to concern themselves with matters of government. Initially they were to represent the "people of Venice," yet they were clearly a new political force just beginning to carve out their own place between the doge and the people.[19] From this loose, ad hoc group of aristocrats would evolve the essential components of the Venetian commune, including the Great Council.

As for the Dandolo, although they had cracked open the door of Venetian politics, they were still minor players. The truly powerful men, those at the top of the signatory list, were the Morosini and Coloprini. Although Doge Menio seems to have tried initially to deal evenhandedly with the factions, after the murder of young Domenico Morosini he began to favor the pro-Byzantine party. The shift in power is evident in this document, which confirms with its signatories that both factions retained considerable authority but demonstrates with its text that the Morosini, particularly Abbot Giovanni Morosini, were moving into important positions.[20]

Venice's fortunes changed dramatically with Doge Pietro II Orseolo (991–1008). The factional strife withered under a doge who cultivated excellent relations with both German and Byzantine emperors. Otto III was a personal friend of the doge, even coming to Venice in 1001.[21] For his part, the Byzantine emperor, Basil II, issued a chrysobull in 992 that defined Venetian merchants' rights and privileges and reduced the tolls and tariffs they paid while doing business in Greek ports.[22] It is an important document for understanding the changing state of relations between Venice and Byzantium. The emperor referred to the Venetians not as subjects, but as "outsiders" (*extraneos*) who had proven themselves to be steadfastly loyal allies, always coming to the aid of imperial operations in Italian waters.[23] In 1000, Doge Orseolo led a war fleet against Croatian pirates based in Dalmatia. In short order the fleet suppressed the privateers and extracted oaths of loyalty from the Dalmatian towns. Orseolo promptly added to his title *dux Dalmatiae*.[24] Whether by coincidence or design, the Venetian military action assisted Basil II in his war against the Bulgarians by weakening their allies the Serbs and Croats.[25] Four years later, when Bari was besieged by Arab forces from Sicily, Venice again demonstrated its usefulness to Byzantium. In that instance, the doge personally led the Venetian warships that broke the siege.[26] The conquest of Dalmatia and victory over the Arabs brought prestige and wealth to the lagoon. Venice had a momentum that was complimented by its partnership with Byzantium and its friendship with Germany. Greater prosperity at home insured that the extension of political power to new families like the Dandolo would remain permanent. According to Barbaro, a Lucio Dandolo served as Procurator of San Marco in 992 and a Carlo Dandolo took the same office in 1033.[27] Ducal acts continued to have increasingly larger and more diverse groups of signers, signifying the wider avenues of authority now available to those with new money.[28]

As in most new families, the wealth of the Dandolo flowed primarily from shipping and trade. By the early eleventh century the family owned at least one vessel and was doing business in eastern ports. The leader of the clan, Domenico Dandolo, can be seen conducting business in Constantinople sometime between 1018 and 1025.[29] No commercial records survive, but one of his voyages was long remembered in Venice for its return cargo. A few Venetian merchants and priests learned of the presence of the body of St. Tarasius in a monastery near Constantinople.[30] After a difficult search, they discovered the relic and, in the accepted medieval tradition of *furta sacra*, stole it.[31] They carried it three miles to the ship of Domenico Dandolo. According to the fourteenth-century chronicler and doge Andrea Dandolo, Domenico was a "noble and devout man . . . who . . . received the holy body with reverence. From this man would descend two doges, namely Enrico Dandolo and we [Andrea] who are writing this now."[32] When Domenico arrived in Venice, he was greeted with abundant joy. Solemn ceremonies accompanied the transport of the saintly body from the merchant vessel to its resting place in the convent of San Zaccaria.[33] Andrea Dandolo's assertion that this Domenico was the root from which the famous branch of the Dandolo family had sprung is supported by Barbaro's genealogy—although the latter may be using the former as its source.[34]

By the mid-eleventh century the Dandolo were sufficiently well established among Venice's elite that they began to undertake service to the state. In 1055

Bono Dandolo, a son of the merchant captain Domenico, was appointed by Doge Domenico Contarini (1043–70) as one of two ambassadors to Henry III of Germany. Bono and his colleague, the future doge Domenico Silvio, met with the emperor and negotiated a confirmation of trading privileges in the German Empire.[35] In less than a century the Dandolo had gone from relative obscurity to a modest level of political prestige. The rescue of the body of St. Tarasius had undoubtedly added to the family's visibility.

The most conspicuous act a family could undertake to assert its status in the Venetian lagoon was to found a parish dedicated to its patron saint.[36] As the eleventh century began, Venice was still only on the cusp of its transformation from an archipelago of independent family enclaves into a unified city. The earliest families had built the first Rialtine compounds in the ninth century. Each had an open field (*campo*), a church, the family house, loading docks, and rental properties. As the power of these families grew, so too did their compounds. Adjacent areas were drained or filled to provide additional land on which to build. The focus, however, remained the church and the campo, not the larger community of islands. The remnants of that world are still visible today in the numerous *campi* scattered across Venice. In the tenth and eleventh centuries, as new families rivaled the old in wealth, they followed this same example, forming their own compounds and founding new churches to identify and bless them. The Dandolo probably settled on the northern outskirts of San Paternian parish.[37] Originally founded by the Andreaardi around 850, San Paternian grew into a region crowded with merchants doing business at the nearby Rialto markets.[38] In the tenth century, as these merchants grew wealthier, they showered their largess on San Paternian.[39] The parish ceased to be a compound controlled by one noble family, becoming instead a community of merchants. As the Dandolo grew in prosperity and prestige, they naturally sought to distinguish themselves from the crowd. They apparently joined forces with the Pizzamano, and perhaps other new families, to establish the church of San Luca (St. Luke) just north of San Paternian.[40]

The date of the foundation of San Luca is not clear. Traditionally it has been placed in the twelfth century; however, a document of 1072 mentions a priest of the church.[41] More recently that has become a standard date for the parish foundation, although it is probably too late. Given the paucity of surviving non-monastic materials from the tenth and eleventh centuries, a parish church could have existed for a long time before appearing in the extant documentary record. Since the Dandolo family is always credited with the foundation of San Luca,[42] it stands to reason that the church and compound were built when the family was sufficiently prominent to undertake so defining a project. A reasonable hypothesis, then, would place the foundation of the parish in the 1020s or 1030s—after the famous voyage of Domenico Dandolo but before the embassy of Bono Dandolo.[43]

The modern church of San Luca has only its site in common with the original wooden structure. To its south and east was a small and muddy campo. The original Dandolo house was probably farther south, facing the Rio di San Luca.[44] It was likely across a canal from San Luca and therefore part of San Paternian parish.[45] If so, the Dandolo may have switched parishes without moving at all, simply by filling in a canal. This would have changed the physical focus of the area, centering it on the new church and campo and away from the old. Small rental properties around the campo housed artisans, fishermen, and laborers.[46] Open land to the east of the compound may have been cultivated or used as a shipyard.[47]

But the days of insular parish life were ending. The Dandolo were not the only families building new structures. By the late eleventh century, Venice had a population of fifty thousand or more, making it one of the largest cities in western Europe. Within a century that number would double.[48] To sustain such growth in a lagoon, additional land was a necessity. As *rii* (rivers) were filled in, marshes drained, and bridges built, parish boundaries came to separate neighborhoods only, not independent communities.[49] Although Venetians would retain their parish identity, their various patron saints, once a sign of prestige and independence, were displaced by devotion to St. Mark, the patron of the doge and the state. The ducal chapel was rebuilt on a monumental scale in the late eleventh century, modeled on the Church of the Holy Apostles in Constantinople. It was a potent symbol of independence from and affinity with Byzantium. Venice was becoming one entity: the Republic of St. Mark.[50]

Venice's rising prosperity was built on a peaceful Adriatic and profitable trade in the East; the former was essential for the latter. After the campaigns of Pietro II Orseolo a safe Adriatic had become the joint responsibility of Venice in Dalmatia and Byzantium in Italy, but the partnership was short-lived, shattered by crushing blows to the Byzantine Empire in the eleventh century. The defeat of the Byzantine army at Manzikert in 1071 and the subsequent Turkish invasion of Asia Minor was a serious problem. Menacing from the west were the Normans, who conquered Sicily and southern Italy, once and for all ejecting the eastern Romans from the birthplace of their empire. These two enemies had the same ultimate objective: Constantinople. The seat of imperial power and the richest city in the Western world, Constantinople seemed like the burial goods of a dying world. For the Norman leader, Robert Guiscard, the way was clear. He would cross the Adriatic and capture the city of Durazzo. From there the ancient via Egnatia led directly to the capital.[51]

Venetians looked on the Norman invasion of Byzantium with apprehension and dismay. Normans were wild and warlike; in other words, bad for business. It was not long before Norman freebooters were actively disrupting Venetian shipping in the Adriatic. In 1074 Count Amico of Giovinazzo even attacked Dalmatian cities under Venetian control. At once, Doge Domenico Silvio (1070–85) led a war fleet against the Norman privateer, defeated him, and reasserted Venetian dominance in the area.[52] Reeling from external attacks and torn by internal unrest, the Byzantines were no longer able to take part in the policing of the Adriatic. Silvio's campaign made clear that control of the sea had passed from Byzantium to Venice.

Robert Guiscard launched his attack against Durazzo in the summer of 1081.[53] The new emperor, Alexius I Comnenus (1081–1118), dispatched envoys to Venice, promising rich rewards in return for military aid.[54] Doge Silvio needed little convincing. If Robert Guiscard were successful at Durazzo he would hold strongpoints on both sides of the mouth of the Adriatic. From there he could cripple or halt Venetian overseas trade altogether. The Venetians quickly assembled an impressive war fleet and Doge Silvio took command.[55] The subsequent war would last four years, costing the lives of thousands of Venetians and ultimately toppling the doge. Yet in the end the Norman threat was neutralized. Byzantium was saved.[56]

Alexius I had promised great rewards for Venetian aid and he made good on his promise. In a chrysobull he conceded the honorary title of *protosebastos* (first of the venerable) to the doge, annual stipends for the doge and Patriarch of Grado, annual tithes for Venetian churches, a church in Durazzo, and substantial buildings and properties in Constantinople—the last would form the nucleus of Constantinople's Venetian Quarter. Most importantly, the emperor granted Venetian merchants the right to trade free of taxation in Byzantine ports.[57] A few years later Domenico Dandolo, the leader of the clan and grandson of the merchant who transported St. Tarasius, served as an ambassador to Constantinople and accepted another reward for the doge, namely, titled jurisdiction over Dalmatia and Croatia. Henceforth Venetian doges were referred to as "doge of Venice, Dalmatia and Croatia and also imperial *protesbastos.*"[58]

The chrysobull of Alexius I forever changed relations between Venice and Byzantium. Most important was the tax exemption, which gave Venetian merchants a sizeable advantage over their Genoese, Pisan, and even Greek competitors. In effect, Venetian wharves in Byzantine ports became duty-free zones. Merchants from the lagoon flocked to the empire to take advantage of their privileged status and, in short order, many of them became rich. Alexius could not see it yet, but the new and conspicuous wealth of Venetian merchants and residents in Constantinople and elsewhere would transform Byzantine popular attitudes toward their old allies from gratitude into envy and resentment. From the Byzantine perspective, Venetians had always been the poor cousins of the empire: not quite barbarians, but almost as crude, poorly educated, and ill-mannered as all the other western Europeans. Now, as the nouveau riche, the Venetians were boorish, as well. It was galling to see these rough sailors flaunting their wealth in the streets of Constantinople, wealth that had come from the generosity of the emperor and at the expense of the Byzantine people.[59] These sentiments would fuel decades of rancor between the two peoples, leading ultimately to the tragedy of Constantinople's conquest in 1204.

We may assume that for the Dandolo being newly rich was not an insult but a badge of honor, which they wore proudly in Venice and hoped to acquire in Constantinople. They were not alone. Extant commercial documents make clear that around 1088 Venetian merchants began aiming their vessels for Byzantium in large numbers.[60] Nowhere else could they reap profits so large. Wealth poured into the pockets of Venice's new families, thus accelerating the process of expanded political authority.[61]

However, all news was not good for the Dandolo. In September 1084 or 1085 a powerful earthquake shook portions of Venice.[62] Hardest hit was the parish of San Angelo, where the church campanile was shaken into a slouching position.[63] Earthquakes are doubly destructive in Venice, for what the tremor does not tear down the high waves cover. Crops were destroyed and animals drowned, so many died of starvation in the months that followed. The doge, who had the resources to feed the hungry, did nothing.[64] While the well-off Dandolo surely did not starve, their homes, buildings, and perhaps vessels were likely harmed by the earthquake. Because of its proximity to San Luca, the force that rocked the campanile of San Angelo must have damaged the structures of the Dandolo compound. Did this have a lasting effect on the family? We cannot know for certain, but a clue is provided by Doge Vitale Falier's summoning of Venice's leading citizens to confirm his donation of properties in Constantinople to the monastery of San Giorgio Maggiore in 1090. Among the 133 signers of the document no Dandolo appears, not even Domenico, the ambassador to Alexius I.[65] Similarly, four years later, in October 1094, and eight years later, in March 1098, the Dandolo failed to appear among signers of public acts.[66]

The future of Venice and the Dandolo family was fundamentally altered in November 1095 when Pope Urban II made his appeal at Clermont for what would become the First Crusade. Europeans responded with a wave of pious enthusiasm that swept knights and commoners alike to the distant lands of the East. The Italian maritime cities were not immune to these sentiments. Indeed, they shared them, just as they shared their Catholic faith with their northern neighbors. Genoese merchants put together a small fleet of thirteen vessels, which set sail in 1097. Venice and Pisa, though, had much grander visions. They were the only two states in Europe to take up the cross.[67] In France, Britain, and Germany, monarchs stood aloof from the seemingly impossible project while their vassals prepared for departure. In contrast, the governments in Venice and Pisa put enormous resources into the crusade from the start. A Pisan fleet of some one hundred twenty vessels was ready for departure in 1098.[68] The Venetians, however, were not.

Venice has often been criticized for its tardy assumption of the cross, for waiting, as it is said, until after the crusaders' victory at Jerusalem in 1099 to join the enterprise.[69] The criticism is not altogether fair. By the time word reached Venice of the call to arms, Doge Vitale Falier was close to death. Infirmity may have kept him from embracing the crusade, or he may simply have shared the skepticism of his royal counterparts in England, France, and Germany. Protosebastos Falier was also unwilling to risk Venice's lucrative privileges in Byzantium by lending aid to an expedition that Alexius I viewed with suspicion.[70] But, in December 1096, as the various armies of the First Crusade were beginning to depart, Falier died.[71] When the Venetians assembled to choose a new doge, they turned to Vitale Michiel (1096–1101), one of Venice's most enthusiastic proponents of the crusade. Immediately after his accession, Michiel sent word to the towns on the Dalmatian coast to prepare for a great and glorious enterprise to free the land of Christ.[72] In the lagoon, shipwrights began work on war galleys while merchant vessels were pressed into service as supply transports. It was a large and time-consuming task. One year later, when Pisa launched its imposing fleet, Venice was still preparing its forces. In the spring of 1099 it was ready: a mighty armada of some two hundred vessels, the largest single contribution to the First Crusade.[73]

Doge Vitale Michiel called the citizens of Venice together and, much like Urban at Clermont, exhorted them to leave their families and country to take up the cross of Christ. He did not fail to point out the great spiritual and material benefits they could win in their holy enterprise. The people assented wholeheartedly, with thousands taking the cross that very day. The bishop of Castello, Enrico Contarini, was made spiritual head of the crusade, and Giovanni Michiel, the doge's son, took command of the fleet. In an emotional ceremony, the Patriarch of Grado, Pietro Badoer, gave Bishop Contarini a banner emblazoned with a large cross. Likewise, the doge gave his son the banner of St. Mark.[74] With some nine thousand Venetian crusaders on board, the fleet left the lagoon and the Adriatic in July 1099.[75] Thus began a tradition emblazoned permanently on the Venetian civic character of grand expeditions in the service of the faith. It would be replayed frequently, during the Venetian Crusade of 1122, the Fourth Crusade, and a host of other crusades throughout the centuries. In this case, although the Venetians could not know it at the time, within a few days or weeks of their departure from home the object of the enterprise, Jerusalem, had fallen into Christian hands.

The crusade fleet sailed to Rhodes, where the Venetians prepared to winter. Shortly after their arrival they received a message from Alexius I threatening to revoke their commercial privileges if they insisted on fighting for the Latin enemies of the emperor, but promising rich rewards if they would abandon the crusade. Bishop Contarini warned his countrymen that if they turned their backs on the cross of Christ for worldly gains they risked not only shame before men but the wrath of God as well.[76] A little later a Pisan fleet of fifty-odd vessels landed at Rhodes, probably with the intention of securing the island for themselves. The Venetians attacked, capturing more than half of their vessels and taking many prisoners. Most of the prisoners were later released, having sworn never again to attack Christians, unless in service of the Holy Sepulcher, and never again to conduct business in the Byzantine Empire.[77]

In the spring the Venetian crusaders set sail for the Holy Land, making one stop on the way. On May 27 they landed at Myra, made holy by the life of its bishop St. Nicholas, the patron saint of sailors. Thirteen years earlier Venetians had planned to steal the body of St. Nicholas to place in their new church dedicated to him on the Lido. But the men of Bari had similar ideas and got there first, capturing the relic in 1087. This remained a sore point for Venetians, who now had a church with a conspicuously vacant altar. And so, in 1100, they decided to investigate Myra, just to be certain. The local clergy insisted, even under torture, that the body of St. Nicholas was gone. In an attempt to appease them, the clergy directed their tormentors to the body of the saint's uncle and namesake, which the Venetians took. Then came the "saintly odor" that holy relics often emanated to catch the attention of medieval men. Thus, with great rejoicing the Venetians discovered the "true" body of St. Nicholas and placed it aboard ship.[78] The Bariense, of course, were not persuaded of its authenticity.

The fleet arrived at Jaffa in June 1100. There the Venetians met the remnants of the Frankish crusading army. Godfrey of Bouillon praised God for the Venetians' arrival, not least because he had only a thousand men, while the crusaders from the lagoon were nine times that number.[79] On the coast, the Franks held only Jaffa, and they sorely needed to conquer the rest. Heavily defended Acre was the key. In return for concessions in the captured city, the Venetians agreed to assist Godfrey in a large-scale siege of the city. But Godfrey's subsequent death caused a change in plan. Instead of Acre, Michiel agreed to assist Tancred in the capture of Haifa. The siege lasted more than a month before the city fell, on August 20, 1100. Haifa was no Acre. It lacked the population, wealth, ports, and markets of its much larger neighbor. Instead of property and riches, the Venetian crusaders returned home with almost nothing. Like most crusaders, they had hoped for both salvation and wealth but were disappointed in the latter.[80]

Beginning in the early twelfth century, the Dandolo family achieved a higher level of visibility not only among their fellow countrymen but also among modern historians searching the documentary record. It is in this century of rapid growth for the Republic that the lives of the Dandolo become clearer and their strategies for success more distinct. The leader of the Dandolo of San Luca, Domenico Dandolo, had at least four sons: Pietro, Bono, Vitale, and Enrico (uncle of the future doge).[81] In June 1107, Domenico twice served as a witness to large pious donations made to San Giorgio Maggiore. The second witness for one of these donations was Domenico's son Vitale.[82] In September of the same year, Doge Ordelafo Falier (1101–18) gave to the Patriarch of Grado properties in Constantinople that included bakeries, workshops, and the church of St. Acyndinus, where the Venetian weights and measures were kept. The revenue from these properties was to provide a stable source of income for the prelate. As with the ducal donation to San Giorgio Maggiore in July 1090, the *fideles* (faithful ones) of the court signed with the doge. We find on this list not only Domenico Dandolo but also two of his sons, Vitale and Pietro.[83]

Taking a broad view of the documentary evidence, Domenico Dandolo seems to have directed some of his sons toward civic and legal duties at home and others to business ventures abroad. Pietro Dandolo, the great-great-great grandfather of Doge Andrea Dandolo, appears only in documents made in Venice. After signing the ducal concession of 1107 with his brother and father, he served as a witness to a document in January 1112.[84] In February 1113, he witnessed a thirty-day loan of 130 lire to Bona Kecii and her married daughter Matilda. The women were unable to repay, so in April 1113, Pietro also witnessed the foreclosure and seizure of their property in San Salvatore parish.[85] Vitale Dandolo also appears solely in documents made in Venice.[86] It was around this time, traditionally ascribed to 1107, that Vitale's wife bore him a son, Enrico—a child who would one day ascend the ducal throne.[87]

The seafaring member of the Dandolo family appears to have been Bono. He was in Constantinople when Venetians once again brazenly pilfered a relic from the Greeks, further adding to the tensions on the street. In 1107 or 1108, Pietro, a monk of San Giorgio Maggiore, went to Constantinople to become prior over a church owned by the monastery. Almost immediately, Pietro struck up a friendship with a Byzantine monk at a nearby basilica. The prior suspected that the Greek church harbored a great relic, and he was right. After long discussions and much cajoling, Pietro's new friend revealed to him the location of the body of the first martyr, St. Stephen. Soon after, the two men entered the church and approached an altar from which the saintly odor began to issue. With great effort they destroyed a stone arch that concealed the coffin of the saint. Rejoicing, Pietro took the relic back to his own church in the Venetian Quarter. It was his plan to send it to San Giorgio Maggiore in Venice, but once the theft had been discovered that was no longer possible. The Byzantines would not violate the sanctuary of the Venetian church and the Venetians could not send the body home without risking its loss or further enraging the Greeks. So it remained where it was. After a year or so, tempers cooled and other problems pushed aside the matter of the protomartyr. A Venetian boat was prepared and St. Stephen was quietly placed on board.[88] Accompanying him were seventy-two Venetian notables, all eager to be part of the historic voyage.[89] Among the group was Bono Dandolo.[90] Also on board was an Orio Dandolo of San Luca parish, who may have been Bono's cousin or perhaps his brother.[91] Once the vessel set sail the passengers drafted a document creating a religious fraternity devoted to the saint. The undersigned committed themselves to an annual procession and veneration of the body, financial support of the saint's shrine, and pious works.[92] When the ship arrived in Venice on June 7, 1109 or 1110, it was greeted with every honor.[93] The doge bore the relics himself and deposited them in the monastery of San Giorgio Maggiore,[94] thus beginning a tradition of annual veneration that would continue for centuries—indeed, until the last days of the Republic.[95]

After 1107, Domenico and his son Vitale appear in no extant documents until 1122. Indeed, the only Dandolo who are discernable in that period are Pietro, in the documents of 1112 and 1113 discussed above, and Orio, who appears as a signer to a ducal charter in 1112.[96] The gap may be an accident of the sources. Nevertheless, if Domenico and Vitale were attempting to attach themselves to political power at home, they may have accompanied Doge Falier on a new Venetian crusade to Palestine. The Venetians in 1110 dispersed a Fatimid fleet attempting to relieve Sidon, which Baldwin of Jerusalem was about to reclaim.[97] Perhaps Domenico and Vitale also took part in the doge's siege and capture of Zara in 1116 or in the failed attempt to defend the city against Hungary in 1118. Lacking evidence, however, this remains conjecture.

In 1119, when the future doge, Enrico Dandolo, was about twelve years old, King Baldwin II of Jerusalem wrote to the pope and to Venice begging for assistance against his Muslim enemies. Calixtus II, preoccupied with the Investiture Controversy, passed the request on to the Republic of St. Mark. In 1120 ten papal legates arrived in the lagoon with a letter from the pope imploring the Venetians to come to the aid of the Holy Land. The high drama that once again played itself out in Venice over the next few months must have made an impression on the young Enrico Dandolo. Doge Domenico Michiel (1118–29) accompanied the papal legates to San Marco, where he summoned the people to hear the Holy Father's letter. An accomplished orator, Michiel then gave a stirring speech, concluding, "Venetians, what splendid renown and immortal glory will you receive through this? What rewards will you receive from God? You will earn the admiration of Europe and Asia; the standard of St. Mark will fly triumphantly over those distant lands: new profits, new sources of greatness will come to this most noble country. . . . Enthused with the holy zeal of religion, moved by the suffering of your brethren, excited by the example of all Europe, prepare your arms, think on the honors, think on your triumphs, and be guided to the blessings of heaven."[98] The response was tremendous. With the acclamation of the assembled, the doge himself took the cross, leaving his son Leachim and another kinsman, also named Domenico, as vice-doges.[99] The pattern established in 1099 was followed again, just as it would be on a similarly grand scale in 1202.

The remainder of 1120 and part of 1121 were spent building and outfitting the large crusading fleet. Michiel ordered all Venetians engaged in overseas commerce to return to Venice and assist with the crusading effort.[100] The forces of the Venetian Crusade appear to have consisted of a fleet of approximately one hundred twenty vessels and more than fifteen thousand men.[101] In a manner similar to that of later crusading monarchs, Doge Domenico Michiel planned to make use of the assembled host to advance state interests on the way to the Levant. During the first year of Michiel's dogeship the aged Emperor Alexius I Comnenus died and was succeeded by his eldest son, John II (1118–43). The new emperor was born two years after the war with Robert Guiscard. John and his generation had not experienced Venice's service to Byzantium, but only the effects of Venice's reward. By virtue of the chrysobull of 1082 Venetians were richer and

more numerous in the eastern empire than ever before. They were contemptu-
ous of Byzantine officials, many of whom, because of Alexius's chrysobull, had
no power over them anyway.[102] The freedom that some Venetians felt in flaunting Byzantine law is evident in their cavalier thefts of the relics of St. Stephen
and St. Nicholas. Behind all of this Venetian impetuousness, John believed, was
his father's chrysobull. He refused to renew it.[103] From the Venetian perspective,
this was the height of ingratitude. Yet at the time, aside from sending ambassadors with complaints, there was little that Michiel could do. Now, as he looked
across the Bacino San Marco at the brightly colored war fleet at his command—
a fleet not unlike the one Domenico Silvio had led to Byzantium's defense in
1081—the doge saw a new and more persuasive instrument of diplomacy. The
memory of the Venetian dead in that war against the Normans was still powerful in the lagoon. They had fought long and hard and had paid a heavy price to
protect the Byzantine Empire. They would not now be dismissed out of hand
by this young emperor. If John II would not honor his father's promises, then
let him lose Corfu, which the blood of Venetians had purchased. The doge and
his council made plans to capture the island on the way to the Holy Land.[104]

It was not only John II who had something to fear from the Venetian crusading fleet. Dalmatian rebels could expect swift punishment before the Republic
departed with most of its military force. Further south, the citizens of Bari were
also more than a little wary. There was, after all, the delicate matter of the body
of St. Nicholas. The Venetians might well be tempted to use their crusade fleet
as they had at Myra, capturing another body of the saint to accompany them on
their journey. That would certainly put an end to the competing claims of the
two cities. But Michiel wanted no trouble with Bari. If the Bariense believed they
were in danger, their ships could pose a threat to the Venetian fleet and its operations at Corfu. Therefore, in May 1122, three months before the fleet's departure, the doge issued a solemn oath that no Venetian would harm the property,
life, or limb of the citizens of Bari. The document was signed by the doge as
well as 372 of the greater men who had taken the cross.[105] Among the signatories was Domenico Dandolo and two of his sons, Vitale and Enrico. By 1122
Domenico Dandolo must have been in his fifties or sixties.[106] Vitale, who had a
son around fifteen years of age, was probably in his late thirties or early forties.
Enrico, likely the youngest of Domenico's sons, could not have been older than
his early twenties when he joined his brother and father on the crusade.[107]

The fleet set sail on August 8, 1122. Having received supplies and men from
the Dalmatian towns, Michiel led the armada to Corfu, where they besieged the
Byzantine citadel. The siege lasted through the winter. In early spring of 1123,

messengers from the Kingdom of Jerusalem urged the doge to set aside his quarrel with the emperor and sail immediately to the Holy Land. He agreed. When the fleet arrived at Acre in May, Michiel discovered that the Egyptian fleet blockading Jaffa had moved to its base at Ascalon. Swiftly the doge ordered a small group of Venetian merchant vessels to lure the Egyptians into battle. Once the engagement began, the Republic's warships surrounded and destroyed the Fatimids. Michiel, we are told, led his own ship against the opposing Egyptian flagship and sunk her. The victory was total: hardly a Muslim vessel survived the engagement.[108] The following year the doge led the Venetians against Tyre, assisting a Frankish attack on the city. After a difficult siege, the city fell in July of that year.[109] The Venetians were well rewarded. The Republic received in every city in the Kingdom of Jerusalem a street, bakery, bath, and church, freedom from all tolls and customs, and the right to use their own weights and measures. They also received one-third of Tyre.[110]

The events of 1119 to 1124, occurring as they did in Enrico Dandolo's teenage years, could not have failed to impress him. The figure of Domenico Michiel was immense in Venetian eyes and would have been greater for the men who served under him on crusade. He became one of medieval Venice's most important heroes. We can well imagine that the young Enrico Dandolo heard the stories of his crusading grandfather, father, and uncle and later drew upon them, when he himself sat on the ducal throne. The young man already came from a family of merchants and statesmen. After 1124, he was also the product of two generations of crusaders.

Enrico's uncle of the same name, Enrico Dandolo the elder, left the Levant sometime before the doge and the fleet. He may have felt, perhaps like others, that the destruction of the Egyptian fleet and subsequent winter in Jerusalem was sufficient to complete his vow. He may also have remained for the siege of Tyre, which began in February 1124, and perhaps was still there when the city fell, on July 7. Whatever the case, Enrico was in Venice in October 1124 acting as an advocate in the ducal court for a Petronia, widow of Pietro Encio, against San Giorgio Maggiore.[111] He lost the case. Petronia had argued that a saltworks in Chioggia that her husband had left to the monastery was in fact three separate properties, albeit under one roof. The monastery, she argued, was entitled to only one. Vice-Doge Domenico Michiel went to Chioggia with his ducal judges to discover the truth and ruled against her claim.[112]

Vitale Dandolo appears to have remained with the crusader fleet.[113] Shortly after the fall of Tyre, Doge Domenico Michiel bade farewell to his allies. There remained, however, the pressing problem of John II's refusal to honor the promises of his father to Venice's merchants. The doge was still determined to change the emperor's mind. In October 1124 the Venetians raided the island of Rhodes, then wintered at Chios, where they snatched the body of St. Isidore. Then they spent the spring of 1125 raiding and plundering various Greek islands before returning to the Adriatic. There the doge used his armada to restore Venetian control over several Dalmatian towns that had taken advantage of the fleet's absence to rebel in favor of the king of Hungary. When the crusade fleet finally returned home it was met with joyful acclamations. In one voyage Doge Michiel had dealt a blow to three of Venice's enemies: the Muslims, the Byzantines, and the Hungarians. Yet John II still held out. It is said that the doge was so angered at the emperor's recalcitrance that he decreed that henceforth all Venetian men must remain clean-shaven, lest they be mistaken for Byzantines. Early in 1126 he ordered a fleet of vessels to attack the island of Cephalonia. John II may have expected that the Venetian attacks would end with the crusade. When he discovered that the doge remained determined, he agreed to their demands. In August 1126 he renewed the trading privileges.[114]

Orio and Bono Dandolo, who did not join the crusade, were in Venice in April 1127, when they, along with Vitale Dandolo, witnessed the sale of a saltworks in Chioggia.[115] The notary, Pietro Flabianico, was a member of the clergy at San Luca, so he may simply have gathered the three men to serve as witnesses on his way to executing the document. Bono, who appears to have been the member of the family most involved with overseas trade, was also active in the supply of other Venetian merchants. In 1131 he rented an anchor to three men for a roundtrip voyage to Acta.[116]

The fate of Domenico, the pater familias, is more elusive, since his name drops out of any later documents. In a copyist's addition to Dandolo's *Chronica per extensum descripta*, an 1130 entry refers to the elder *"Henricus Dandulo ex patre Dominico."*[117] The absence of a *"quondam"* may suggest that he was still alive by that date. In a document dated July 1131 there is a reference to *"Bonus Dandulus f. Dominici Dandulo iudicis de confinio S. Lucie* [sic]."[118] Again, the lack of *quondam* in the manuscript suggests that Domenico was still alive in the summer of 1131.[119] It is also interesting that he is referred to as a judge, a question I will return to in the next chapter. In any case, by 1131 Domenico, who had been an ambassador forty-six years earlier and had signed documents with grown sons twenty-four years before, must have been in his late sixties or early seventies, at least. As we shall see, Dandolo males regularly lived into their seventies, eighties, and beyond, and they remained vigorous up to their deaths. The fact that Domenico drops out of the documentary record after 1131 suggests, therefore, that he died shortly thereafter.

As the generation of Domenico Dandolo passed away, the new one was in a favorable position to enhance its own wealth and political power. Vitale Dandolo would take his father's place as leader of the San Luca clan and far surpass his achievements. And yet, another member of the family was rising to power even more rapidly, and his career would fundamentally complicate, promote, and endanger the family's new position in Venetian society.

TWO

PATRIARCH ENRICO DANDOLO
&
the REFORM of the VENETIAN CHURCH

 n 1129 the Crusader-Doge Domenico Michiel fell ill. Knowing that his time was short, he resigned the dogeship and took monastic vows. The newly tonsured hero was borne to the monastery of San Giorgio Maggiore where he spent the last months of his life. His tomb, modest and inconspicuous, was placed in a small passageway leading from the church to the monastery. Yet the Venetians did not forget him. More than a decade later an inscription was added: "Here lies the terror of the Greeks and the glory of the Venetians, Domenico Michiel whom Manuel fears; a doge honorable and strong, whom all the world cherished; prudent in counsel and consummate in intellect. His manly deeds are declared by the capture of Tyre, the destruction of Syria, and the anguish of Hungary; he made the Venetians to live in peace and tranquility, for while he flourished his country was safe from all harm. You who come to look on this beautiful sepulchre, bow low before God because of him."[1]

When the Venetians sought a successor it was natural to look to Michiel's own family. Yet the days of ducal dynasties had ended with the death of Otto Orseolo in 1032. Venice was a different place. Population was expanding at a rapid rate, and the success of Venetian merchants brought healthy infusions of wealth into the lagoon, prompting increasing numbers of new families to demand political authority commensurate with their economic standing. It was in their interest to expand the avenues of power, restraining any one family from gaining too tight a grip on the dogeship. Their desire to honor Michiel and their determination to avoid tyranny were satisfied in their final choice.

Pietro Polani (1129–48) was a member of the Michiel family, but only by virtue of his marriage to the doge's daughter. He came from a very new family, one that even the Dandolo could consider an upstart. There is no mention of the Polani in the *Origo* or in Andrea Dandolo's history before the dogeship of Pietro. The family, originally from Pola, appears to have settled first in Chioggia, migrating to Rialto only in the eleventh century.[2] The first member of the family to appear in any extant document is a Vitale Polani, who was among the signers of a ducal act in 1074.[3] No other member of the family appears in the documentary record until 1098,[4] but the family was not idle. Taking advantage of the chrysobull of Alexius I, the Polani, like other Venetian families, undertook extensive voyages to the East. There, in the market stalls of Byzantium, they made a fortune.[5] When Venetian merchants in Constantinople spirited away the body of St. Stephen in 1110, Domenico Polani and his son (and future doge) Pietro were on board. But Domenico was more than just a successful merchant: he bore the highly coveted imperial title *protonobelissimos*.[6] For a foreigner of such modest station, this was a remarkable honor suggesting some extraordinary service rendered to the Byzantine state.[7] Two years later he loaned 900 lire, a very large sum of money, to Venice to prosecute the war in Dalmatia.[8] His son Pietro and a Stefano Polani were among those who took the cross in the Venetian Crusade of 1122.[9] A Domenico Polani, probably not the protonobelissimos, was doing business in Acre in 1128.[10] Pinia, the widow of Stefano Polani, invested money in a commercial voyage in 1131.[11]

The elevation of Pietro Polani to the ducal throne was good news for Enrico Dandolo and his family, who had achieved economic and political prominence relatively recently and in much the same way as the Polani. Despite his marriage to old blood, Pietro Polani was still a new man. As fellow merchants with shared interests, the Polani and the Dandolo were no strangers. Indeed, they were neighbors—the doge and his family were residents of the small parish of San Luca.[12] Not only did the new doge know many Dandolo, it appears that he grew up with them.

Early in his reign, Pietro Polani chose the leader of the Dandolo clan, Domenico, to be a judge in the ducal court.[13] This was a position of great importance, in power and prestige second only to the dogeship itself. As the old tribunes passed away, ducal judges replaced them.[14] The first are visible in the late tenth and early eleventh centuries, but they do not appear as distinct members of the court until the late eleventh century.[15] Henceforth they were indispensable participants in all of the doge's legal activities. In a city without a defined nobility, judges were as close as one could come.[16] In court, they were the doge's peers, and yet, just as with the dogeship itself, power flowed from the office, not the officeholder. Judgeships were not hereditary, nor were they often held for more than a year or two at a time. Once having served, however, one could retain the honorific title for life.[17] Judgeships were filled and vacated regularly at the doge's discretion.[18] Depending on the occasion, one could find at this time anywhere from two to five judges in court; the doge could not conduct business without them.[19] By the mid-twelfth century the road to the ducal throne invariably passed through the judiciary.[20] Domenico's appointment, therefore, was as close to the ducal court as any Dandolo had come. With the help of their neighbor, the family had at last broken into the highest ranks of the Venetian political hierarchy.

Pietro Polani brought several other new families into the ducal court, but he did not stop there. Among the most notable events of his reign was the institution of the Venetian commune. Reflecting prevailing fashion in other Italian towns, the change in terminology also recognized political and social changes at work in Venice for more than a century. Power was shifting incrementally away from the doge and into the hands of an expanded ducal court, which now included the *consilium sapientium*, a body of influential men who advised the doge. Under Polani, constitutional dynamics were set in place that would later give birth to the Great Council. The nature and implications of the commune will be discussed more fully in Chapter 5. In time the Dandolo would reap the benefits of these reforms, but, as we shall see, this was not the time.

Polani took the throne during troubled times in western Europe. Although the Concordat of Worms (1122) had brought a legal end to the Investiture Controversy, substantial rifts on both sides of the conflict persisted. When Henry V died childless in 1125 the German princes passed over the house of Hohenstaufen, electing instead the duke of Saxony, Lothar of Supplinburg, as their king. An enemy of the Hohenstaufen, Lothar had long been the most visible supporter of the papacy in Germany. Pope Honorius II (1124–30) confirmed the election, and the German church warmly supported the new king. But the Hohenstaufen were not so easily brushed aside. Lothar's enemies separated themselves and proceeded to elect Conrad of Hohenstaufen as king. There was no support for Conrad among the German bishops, who excommunicated the pretender in 1128. Pope Honorius did the same a few months later. Conrad did have support, though, in southern Germany and northern Italy. Gathering his forces, he invaded Lombardy and peacefully entered Milan, where Archbishop Anselm crowned him king of Italy.[21]

Honorius II was not at all pleased by the Lombard clergy's response to Conrad. In addition to Anselm of Milan, it appears that Gerhard, the patriarch of

Aquileia, and Giovanni Gradenigo, the patriarch of Grado, also supported the antiking.[22] In 1129 the pope's legate excommunicated the archbishop of Milan and deposed both patriarchs of the Veneto.[23] A few months later Honorius died. The Roman curia was for some time divided by factions that disagreed over the papacy's relations with Germany and the Normans, as well as issues concerning the Concordat of Worms. A schism had barely been avoided after Honorius's election in 1124. On February 14, 1130, the members of his faction, still a minority in the curia, convened and elected Innocent II. A few hours later, the opposing faction elected Anacletus II. With two popes, the Church was as divided as the empire. Although Innocent was not accepted in Rome, he had significant support in Europe's reforming circles. St. Bernard of Clairvaux ardently championed Innocent's papacy, leading to his acceptance in France, England, Spain, and among most of the bishops in Germany. With the support of the German bishops, the allegiance of Lothar III was never in doubt.[24] On March 21, 1131, Lothar met Innocent at Liège, where he led the papal horse. The king promised to use his temporal power to defend the Church against the Anacletan schismatics. Meanwhile, Anacletus II had won the support of the Norman leader, Roger of Hauteville, but at the price of papal recognition of the Norman kingdom. The pope traveled to Palermo, where, on Christmas Day 1130, he crowned Roger king of Sicily, Calabria, and Apulia.[25]

Venice had a keen interest in these matters. There were at least two Venetian cardinals in Rome during the pontificate of Honorius II, both members of the party that had elected Anacletus II.[26] Venetians in general were not overly enthusiastic about Innocent II. It was his faction, after all, that had deposed the patriarch of Grado as well as other leading Venetian clergy.[27] But the alternative appeared worse. Anacletus's creation of a Norman kingdom could only embolden those seafaring ruffians from whom Venice had had nothing but trouble. As a result, sympathies in Venice began to lean toward Innocent. When Innocent convened a synod at Piacenza in 1132, the attendees included the bishop of Cittanova and the abbot of San Giorgio Maggiore.[28] Nevertheless, Doge Polani continued to keep quiet about the schism. He sent forward no nomination for a successor to Patriarch Gradenigo because the very act of doing so would force him to recognize the authority of one of the popes.

But he could only play that game for so long. In Constantinople, John II Comnenus was enraged when he learned of Roger's coronation. Now that difficulties between Byzantium and Venice had been resolved, John sent envoys to the doge requesting an alliance against the Normans. Polani readily agreed. Venetian envoys were added to the mission and sent to the court of Lothar to enlist

German support. They arrived in August 1135. The German and Byzantine emperors agreed that the Normans must be removed from imperial lands—although just who was a Roman emperor and who was not remained a sore point. To paper over the problem they promised a marriage of their heirs in the hope of a reunited empire. Venice's intentions were less grandiose; she just wanted the Norman freebooters out of her waters.[29]

As far as the papal schism was concerned, Venice played her hand when she joined the alliance against the Normans. Now a partisan of Innocent II, the doge was at last free to turn his attention to the long vacant see of Grado. The highest ecclesiastic office in the lagoon, the patriarchate of Grado had metropolitan jurisdiction over six dioceses: Torcello, Malamocco, Jesolo, Caorle, Cittanova (Eraclea), and Venice's own diocese of Castello. Although the bishops were responsible for electing the patriarch, as elsewhere in Europe the ruler still exerted a powerful influence over the decision, including the right of nomination. Final confirmation, of course, would have to come from the pope.

The patriarch of Grado did not wield the kind of political power in the lagoon that other European bishops and archbishops had in their domains. Venice's lack of feudal institutions, as well as the continuation of Byzantine traditions, meant that religious leaders remained subordinate to their secular counterparts.[30] The great church of San Marco, which stood at the center of Venetian civic life, was the doge's chapel. The bishop's cathedral was tucked away on the island of Castello on the far outskirts of town. The patriarch of Grado's church was even farther away, at the edge of the Veneto. This does not mean, as many have assumed, that the Venetian church was simply an arm of the state. In feudal Europe the relationship between Church and State was bedeviled by the power held by ecclesiastical lords and the desire of secular authorities to manage that power. In Venice those dynamics did not exist. A Venetian bishop or abbot received neither lands nor anything else from the doge for which he owed military service. Instead, the clergy of Venice lived on tithes, gifts, and the occasional business deal. When they owned land at all they did not hold it in fief to a lord, but instead rented it out as a means of income. When considering the medieval Venetian church it is important to remember this crucial distinction. By comparison to their counterparts in the rest of Europe, the Venetian clergy were poor and weak. On the other hand, because they were also not responsible for raising troops, defending territory, or governing people, their duties were limited to the spiritual welfare of Venice.

The unique nature of the Venetian church meant that the reform movement of the eleventh and twelfth centuries had a very different effect in the lagoon

than it did on the continent. The clerical abuses that led to reform, chiefly simony and clerical marriage, were rare in Venice. Simony flourished across Europe because the wealth and power of an episcopal see made it worth purchasing. Likewise, simony stocked the episcopate with men of little or no piety who
allowed clerical discipline to founder. Since a bishop in Venice had a meager income and authority only over his clergy, the job tended to attract the genuinely
pious.[31] It is true that the doge sometimes played a role in the election of bishops, abbots, or abbesses, but this was merely a customary right with no practical effect on the doge's political authority.[32]

Although the stakes were lower for the doge than for his continental counterparts, the selection of a new patriarch of Grado remained a weighty matter.
As it happened, Pietro Polani did not have a particularly difficult choice to make.
The doge was himself a supporter of Gregorian reform, although he probably
had no appetite for a radical.[33] He would also naturally favor someone with a
healthy respect for the rights of his kinsman, Giovanni Polani, who was the
bishop of Castello.[34] Like any ruler, Polani wanted a prelate whom he could trust
and with whom he could feel comfortable. He nominated Enrico Dandolo, the
son of Domenico.[35] Enrico Dandolo, the uncle of the famous doge, was a young
man when he became patriarch of Grado around 1134.[36] Most chroniclers remark
as much on his youth as his piety. He does not appear to have been a member
of the clergy before his elevation. In 1122 he took part in the Venetian Crusade
and went on to serve as a legal advocate in 1124.[37] By 1134 he must have been in
his early thirties, making him about the same age as the doge.[38] As neighbors in
the small parish of San Luca, Pietro Polani and Enrico Dandolo must have
known each other since boyhood.

As patriarch-elect, Enrico Dandolo was immediately thrust into the centuries-
long conflict between Grado and Aquileia. Both patriarchates claimed to be the
successor of the ancient see of Aquileia, and they had been feuding over jurisdictions for centuries, although in recent decades the popes had favored Grado.
When the Concordat of Worms restored peace between the papacy and the empire in 1122, the prelates of Aquileia began working to restore papal recognition
of their metropolitan authority. The schism of 1130 gave them an excellent opportunity on that front. While the doge of Venice bided his time, withholding
the nomination of a new patriarch of Grado, Peregrin of Aquileia raced to the
pope's synod at Piacenza in 1132, proclaiming his support for Innocent II and
Lothar III. In gratitude, the pope granted Peregrin all the privileges that Aquileia
had long ago lost: the patriarchal title, the pallium, and the processional cross.
More importantly, he confirmed Aquileia's metropolitan authority over its tra-

ditional episcopates, including those of Istria. When Enrico Dandolo arrived at the Council of Pisa in June 1135 he was presented with a fait accompli. Grado had ceased to be "New Aquileia" and was now merely the metropolitan see of the lagoon. Innocent confirmed Grado's traditional rights and privileges, including the pallium and processional cross, but that was all.[39]

St. Bernard of Clairvaux also attended the Council of Pisa. A strong and passionate advocate of reform, he preached the monastic discipline of the Cistercian order as well as the need for the purification of Christian society. He had a powerful presence and considerable influence over popes and kings. Perhaps, as Daniela Rando suggested, he had the same effect on the young Enrico Dandolo.[40] We cannot know with certainty what, if any, relationship existed between Bernard and Dandolo. What is certain, however, is that the new patriarch of Grado soon embraced the ideas and methods of the reformers. Shortly after his return to Venice, Dandolo introduced the first chapter of Cistercians into the lagoon at the monastery of S. Giorgio di Pineto.[41] Throughout his long patriarchate, Dandolo would consistently cultivate close ties to the papal court, and, as we shall see, he remained a strident defender of the rights and freedom of the Church. Whether he knew him personally or not, Enrico Dandolo worked all of his life for the ideas that St. Bernard preached.

Like Bernard, Patriarch Dandolo was also interested in reforming the secular clergy along monastic lines through the promotion of the canons regular. The term *canons regular*, as Giles Constable noted, is both redundant and confusing.[42] Generally speaking, canons were those who reformed themselves into a community of clergy living in common under the rule of St. Augustine. Some lived in a monastery, while others embraced the discipline and poverty of the common life in a parish setting.[43] A community of canons regular was inherently less susceptible to influence from family or government and was therefore a useful tool of reform. Popes had been actively supporting the canons regular for almost a century.[44] Not surprisingly, many of the chapters had direct ties to Rome, and some were exempt from local control. The canons regular had only recently made their appearance in Venice with the foundation of S. Maria della Carità. Pope Calixtus II (1119–24) sent a cornerstone for it in 1121, although the church was not completed until 1132.[45]

It was one thing to bring reform clergy into the city, but Dandolo sought also to convert existing parish clergy into communities of canons regular. With his support and encouragement, the clergy of San Salvatore, an ancient church in the heart of Venice, announced in 1139 that they were taking the habit and the rule of St. Augustine.[46] The newly elected prior, Bonofilio Michiel, received Patriarch Dandolo's support for the decision.[47] Dandolo had met with a cardinal in Verona at about this time, so he may have been able to convey the support of the Holy See as well.[48] But the clergy of San Salvatore did not have the support of their bishop, and that was a problem. The bishop of Castello, Giovanni Polani, had direct jurisdiction over the parishes of Venice. He was outraged when he learned that the Patriarch of Grado had plotted behind his back to reform clergy from his diocese.[49] Like all bishops of Castello, Polani remained vigilant against any patriarchal infringement of his rights. The reform of San Salvatore struck him as a power grab, an attempt to take control of an important parish;[50] many prominent members of the parish saw it that way, too.[51] With their support Bishop Polani placed San Salvatore under interdict.[52] Patriarch Dandolo responded by putting the church under his metropolitan protection.[53]

Not all parishioners of San Salvatore opposed the clergy donning the habit of the canons. Among their supporters was the powerful and prominent Badoer clan. Aside from their antiquity and prestige, the Badoer were widely known for their piety and generosity to the Church.[54] Since the days of Pietro Badoer, Patriarch of Grado from 1092 to 1104, the family had been champions of Gregorian reform in Venice. In 1109, they donated their private church, S. Croce di Luprio, to the first Cluniac community in Venice.[55] It is quite possible that members of the Badoer family in San Salvatore were the first to urge the clergy there toward reform; they would likely have had more influence than the patriarch. What is certain is that the Badoer soon became one of the canons' most generous benefactors.[56]

Since there is a marked tendency in modern scholarship to assume that medieval Venetians were unencumbered by piety or selfless impulse, it can be surprising to learn of a Venetian family that favored ecclesiastical reform. Venetians, it is commonly asserted, were allergic to Gregorian ideas and determined to keep reform clergy like the canons regular, Cluniacs, or Cistercians out of the lagoon.[57] According to this point of view, the Church was merely a tool in Venetian family struggles. The doge and bishop opposed the reform of San Salvatore because it sapped power from their own family, created a reformed religious community with direct ties to Rome, and enhanced the position of the Dandolo family.[58] This interpretation ignores, however, the ecclesiastical nature of this dispute. In truth, Bishop Polani was not opposed to the introduction of reform clergy into Venice—indeed, he actively supported it. In 1138 he gave the parish church of San Danielle and all of its incomes to the monks of Fruttuaria to support a monastery they had built near the cathedral of Castello.[59] The Fruttuarians were reformed Benedictines akin to the Cistercians, although more willing to live under episcopal jurisdiction than the latter.[60] The bishop's donation of San Danielle demonstrates in deed rather than words his position on reform clergy: He favored and supported them, provided that their arrival did not affect his own jurisdiction or rights. The new monks of San Danielle dutifully swore to respect and render tithes to the bishop.[61] The canons of San Salvatore did not, and their eagerness to take their case to the patriarch suggested their attitude toward episcopal authority. For his part, the patriarch's willingness to become involved suggested an attempt to usurp episcopal rights in Venice. For these reasons alone the bishop of Castello opposed the conversion.

The attitude of Doge Pietro Polani toward the dispute over San Salvatore is less certain. Like his kinsman, the doge was a supporter of the reform orders. In June 1132, lands belonging to him and his mother were donated to the canons regular at Santa Maria della Carità.[62] This was by no means unusual; indeed, support of ecclesiastic reform was quite popular within the Venetian ruling class at this time.[63] Yet it is still possible that the patriarch's infringement on his kinsman's authority irritated the doge; if so, however, he did not take it out on the Dandolo or Badoer families. In February 1143, Pietro Badoer was one of only four lay signers of the doge's constitution for the procession of the Purification of the Virgin.[64] In April 1144, the doge made a pious donation of lands in Chioggia to the Cluniac monastery of San Cipriano di Murano. The doge, three judges, and thirty leading citizens signed the document in the ducal court. Third on the list of signers was a Giovanni Badoer. Two other Badoer (both also named Giovanni) signed as well. Vitale Dandolo, the brother of the patriarch, signed sixth on the list.[65] Domenico Badoer served as a judge in September 1145.[66] Both the Dandolo and Badoer, therefore, were apparently still in ducal favor long after the controversy over San Salvatore had been settled. There is, furthermore, little evidence to suggest that relations between the doge and patriarch were harmed by the dispute.[67] It was, after all, a matter of ecclesiastical, not secular, jurisdiction.

With matters at a stalemate, Patriarch Dandolo took his case to Rome.[68] Innocent II was uneasy about the jurisdictional dispute, but there was never any question that he would support the conversion of the clergy. His consistent promotion of the Augustinian rule led to a lively expansion of the canons regular during his pontificate.[69] On May 13, 1141, the pope formally placed San Salvatore under his protection and lifted the bishop's interdict.[70] Innocent also sent two canons from Rome to instruct the new congregation in the observance of the rule.[71]

While the controversy over San Salvatore was bubbling, Dandolo pursued still other opportunities to promote the canons regular in Venice. He identified a wealthy donor, Pietro Gattilesso, whose nickname, "the Robber," suggests that he had many sins for which to atone. With Dandolo's urging, Gattilesso put up the money to build a church and pilgrims' hostel dedicated to San Clemente on the island that would henceforth bear that name. In 1141, Dandolo placed and blessed the first stone of the complex, which would for centuries be an important way-station for pilgrims bound for the Holy Land. From the start San Clemente belonged to the canons regular. It had also been Gattilesso's intention that the island fall under the jurisdiction of the patriarch of Grado, but this would remain for many years another bone of contention between Dandolo and the bishop of Castello.[72]

Relations between the bishop and the patriarch degenerated so rapidly that in August 1143 cardinal-priest Goizo of Santa Cecilia traveled to Venice, apparently in an attempt to ease the tension.[73] Part of the problem was that by the twelfth century patriarchs of Grado spent virtually no time in Grado itself, but rather resided in San Silvestro, a Venetian church near Rialto that had been patriarchal property since 989.[74] This arrangement strained canon law, since one prelate was not supposed to reside within the jurisdiction of another. It may have been Goizo's report that led Pope Lucius II (1144–45) to issue two privileges within ten days of each other to the bishop of Castello and the patriarch of Grado. Both clearly defined the jurisdictions of the respective sees, but neither effectively addressed the fundamental problem of the patriarchal "visitor" in the diocese of Castello.[75]

The smoldering rancor between the patriarch and bishop soon erupted into a flame that would tear across Venice's political landscape. The new spark was struck sometime between 1141 and 1145 with the death of Nella Michiel, the abbess of the convent of San Zaccaria.[76] As was customary, the doge nominated the new abbess.[77] It may well be, as Cessi has suggested, that he selected one of his own kinswomen,[78] as the abbesses of San Zaccaria routinely came from the family of the doge.[79] Polani's nominee was forwarded to the nuns of San Zaccaria, who promptly elected her. However, before the doge was able to invest the abbess-elect, the patriarch of Grado condemned the election and the investment. With classic Gregorian arguments, Dandolo insisted that the sisters of San Zaccaria must hold a free election without lay interference; under no circumstances should the abbess receive her office from the hands of the doge. Pietro Polani was outraged. It was one thing for the patriarch to squabble with the bishop over ecclesiastical jurisdiction, but quite another for him to deny the doge's right to nominate and invest the abbess of the wealthiest and most pow-

erful convent in Venice. With no obvious way to resolve the dispute, the patriarch took his case to Rome.[80]

On January 2, 1146, two cardinals met with Dandolo in Verona.[81] The location and timing suggests that the purpose of the visit was to discuss the controversy. Unfortunately, at this point in the story the trail of evidence grows cold.
It is not possible to say with certainty who prevailed in the quarrel. What is
certain is that the matter dragged out over many months and perhaps years.
Throughout the year 1145 there was no abbess of San Zaccaria to conduct the
convent's business.[82] The pope did not send a confirmation of privileges to a
new abbess until September 26, 1151, suggesting that the position remained vacant for a long time.[83] The new abbess in 1151, Giseldrude, was not a member of
any of Venice's leading families—indeed, she was probably not even Venetian.[84]

In his zeal to promote reform, Patriarch Dandolo managed to anger two of
the most important men in Venice. But matters were about to get worse. During the summer of 1147 a fleet of Normans sailed across the Adriatic and captured the Byzantine island of Corfu, and from there they proceeded to plunder
the Greek coast, with little opposition. Once again the Normans were poised
to invade the empire, and once again the emperor turned to Venice for assistance.
There was never any question that Venice would oblige. Venetian merchant families, like the Dandolo and Polani, had an enormous interest in a stable and peaceful Byzantine Empire. A Norman conquest of Greece or Constantinople would
be economically and strategically cataclysmic for Venice. Emperor Manuel I
Comnenus (1143–80) hastily sent off a chrysobull in October 1147 confirming all
of Venice's privileges. It probably arrived in the lagoon in November. If he had
not done so already, Doge Pietro Polani announced to the Venetians that they
were once again to wage war against the invading Normans, calling upon everyone to help prepare a fleet to sail in the spring.[85]

Although the Dandolo family had every reason to favor the defense of their
commercial interests in Byzantium, the good of the clan no longer carried much
weight with the patriarch of Grado. His eyes were no longer on his earthly family
but on the welfare of the Church of Rome. He had become the standard-bearer
of Gregorian reform in the lagoon. When he learned of Venice's alliance with
Byzantium, he strongly denounced it. Calling together an assembly of clergy and
laity, he rebuked the doge and his policy. Faithful Christians, Dandolo and his
supporters asserted, should not come to the aid of the unrepentant schismatics
of the Byzantine Empire.[86] The patriarch's opposition party was small, but determined. It included many reform-minded clergy, including the canons of San

Salvatore, as well as prominent members of the Badoer clan, who had defended the patriarch's actions since at least 1145.[87] With this controversy Dandolo introduced into Venice the most expansive elements of Gregorian reform. Already a defender of the Church against lay interference, Dandolo took the next step, asserting his right to overrule secular leaders when their decisions threatened the Church or the spiritual well-being of the faithful.

Although in keeping with reform thought, Dandolo's decision to oppose the alliance with Byzantium is an odd one, suggesting that he and his supporters had become overly zealous in their goals. Having already captured Thessalonica, the Normans were gunning for Constantinople itself. It was in everyone's interest, both in Venice and in Rome, to stop them. Control of Corfu already gave the Normans an opportunity to close off the Adriatic Sea, thus strangling Venice's access to eastern markets. Few Venetians could accept such a state of affairs, least of all the Dandolo, who derived much of their wealth from trade. The pope, too, would not have supported the patriarch's position. The papacy and the Normans were in a technical state of war, although at the time under a seven-year truce. Manuel Comnenus, on the other hand, was in the process of giving material assistance to the armies of the Second Crusade. The Norman attack on Byzantium was calculated to occur while the emperor was distracted with that holy mission. The pope could not have condoned it. Enrico Dandolo himself had an enormous stake in Constantinople, since virtually all of his income came from patriarchal properties there. By opposing the Venetian alliance with Byzantium, then, Dandolo was working against the interests of the patriarchate, the state, his family, and the Church.

It would be interesting to know with certainty how the doge viewed the Dandolo family's role in this latest controversy. It seems unlikely that he believed that his old neighbors were using the patriarchate to acquire power in Venice at his expense, as is often argued. The doge had enough experience with the Dandolo family to know that the patriarch was now beyond their reach. In any event, Enrico sought authority for Grado and the papacy, not the Dandolo. Perhaps, fearing retribution, some of the Dandolo fled to the open arms of the Badoer, who clearly did support the patriarch. This would naturally have led the doge to count them among his enemies. More likely, though, Polani took advantage of the family's relatively weak position in Venice by threatening to destroy them if the patriarch did not relent. What is certain is that the members of the Dandolo clan were not direct players in this quarrel. No source, not even late or defective ones, casts the patriarch's family as anything but a victim of the dispute.[88]

Doge Polani's patience with the patriarch had reached its limit. He would not have churchmen dictate Venetian foreign policy. He must also have felt a sense of betrayal, attacked as he was by the patriarch, whom he had long known, and the Badoer family, whom he had favored in his court. It is difficult not to notice the parallels between the early career of Patriarch Dandolo and that of his contemporary, St. Thomas à Becket, archbishop of Canterbury. Like Dandolo, Becket was chosen to fill the highest ecclesiastical office by a ruler who was sure he could be trusted. Both prelates soon ran afoul of those leaders by zealously defending the rights of the Church. The anger and sense of betrayal felt by Henry II of England, therefore, may well have found an earlier echo in the heart of Doge Pietro Polani.

In late 1147 or early 1148, while the war fleet was still in preparation, Pietro Polani lashed out at his enemies. He ordered the exile of Patriarch Dandolo, his supporters in the clergy, and the members of the Badoer and Dandolo families. For his old neighbors in San Luca, though, the doge had an additional punishment: Once the Dandolo had been removed from the city, Polani ordered their homes to be leveled.[89] That the Dandolo were singled out for this extreme measure lends further weight to the hypothesis that the doge had previously issued an ultimatum to the patriarch, threatening to destroy his family if he did not relent. By ducal order all that the Dandolo of San Luca had labored to build for more than a century was demolished. They were simply erased from Venice.[90]

At one time the struggle between Patriarch Enrico Dandolo and Doge Pietro Polani was viewed as a manifestation of the Gregorian reform movement that continued to shake church-state relations in Europe throughout the twelfth century. In 1905 the great historian of Venice Heinrich Kretschmayr even went so far as to label the incident the "Venetian Investiture Controversy."[91] A sharp change occurred in the 1920s with two publications. In a 1926 essay on the medieval Venetian nobility, Margarete Merores stated briefly and in passing that the Investiture Controversy manifested itself in Venice not as a struggle between church and state but as a family struggle between the Michiel and Polani, on one side, and the Dandolo and Badoer, on the other.[92] The following year, Paul F. Kehr, in his influential essay "Rom und Venedig," criticized Kretschmayr for overgeneralizing a local political dispute into a facet of a larger trend. Patriarch Dandolo, Kehr maintained, was a political animal whose only interest in religious matters was as cover for his own designs. The dispute between the doge and patriarch, Kehr insisted, was not between two men but between two families and their political supporters.[93] From this perspective, the questions of ecclesiastical jurisdictions and Gregorian reform become crude weapons wielded by a clever patriarch, his family, and his allies. In essence, this remained the prevalent view of historians for the next seventy years.[94] Recent studies, though, have begun to question this interpretation. Giorgio Cracco, while insisting that the cause of the dispute was primarily family rivalry and a power-hungry patriarch, nevertheless allows that Enrico Dandolo may have been a pious man with some interest in church reform.[95] In a well-researched study, Daniela Rando points out that support for the reform clergy transcended politics, becoming a favorite cause of Venice's elite. Enrico Dandolo, she believes, was a sincere albeit zealous reformer. The argument between doge and patriarch, therefore, was not about reform but about ecclesiastical jurisdiction and was further enflamed by political family rivalry.[96]

It is important to note that the earliest descriptions of this controversy make no mention of family strife, describing it merely as a quarrel between the doge and the patriarch.[97] The first reference to any tension between families appears in the fourteenth century, when Andrea Dandolo wrote his schematic, first-draft work known as the *Chronica brevis*. There Dandolo recorded that Patriarch Enrico Dandolo and the Badoer family opposed the election of Pietro Polani in 1129. Once elected, however, the new doge wisely reconciled the families with a marriage.[98] This does not appear in the *Chronica per extensum descripta*. There, Andrea Dandolo recorded that the patriarch and his supporters spoke out against the alliance with the Normans, prompting the doge to exile him, his family, and the Badoer family. Later in the work, he noted that during the dogeship of Domenico Morosini, peace was sealed with a marriage between a Dandolo and a Polani.[99]

Whenever the *Chronica brevis* and *Chronica per extensum descripta* disagree it is better to favor the latter. The *Chronica brevis* is riddled with factual errors. In this case, the error is plainly evident. Patriarch Dandolo could not have opposed the election of Doge Polani in 1129 because he did not become patriarch until around 1134.[100] The opposition of the patriarch and the Badoer family is clearly placed under the wrong dogeship—a common error in this work. It belongs during, not before, the reign of Polani, as Dandolo correctly recorded in the *Chronica per extensum descripta*. Likewise, the marriage that brought peace between the families belongs just after the election of Polani's successor, not the election of Polani himself. The testimony of the *Chronica per extensum descripta* on these matters is corroborated by numerous contemporary documents,[101] whereas no contemporary evidence supports the version in the *Chronica brevis*.

The erroneous passage in the *Chronica brevis* should have been ignored by later Venetian chroniclers, but it was not. This was largely the fault of a copyist of the *Chronica per extensum descripta* who expunged the entire episode from the history, apparently to save embarrassment to the Dandolo family.[102] Subsequent chroniclers who used the sanitized version turned to the *Chronica brevis* to explain the strife between doge and patriarch.[103] Unfortunately, the repair of the *Chronica per extensum descripta* has done little to change the general view of the events. It is still commonly said that the Dandolo and Badoer clans, having opposed the election of Pietro Polani, connived to harm him, his family, and his dogeship.[104] Enrico Dandolo then cynically used the patriarchate to wage political war on the Polani, both bishop and doge. Dandolo, therefore, became the focal point of an out-of-power faction seeking to destroy its enemies and ultimately to seize power in Venice.[105]

With the testimony of the *Chronica brevis* discredited on this point, the central support for the political nature of the controversy is removed.[106] The rest of the story collapses from its own internal contradictions. The patriarch of Grado could not have opposed the election of Pietro Polani in 1129 because there was no patriarch. Enrico Dandolo came to the throne several years later, and he was Pietro Polani's nominee, not his enemy. For their part, the Badoer were not opponents of the doge, but trusted members of his inner circle for more than a decade. Real trouble did not begin until 1144 or 1145, when the death of the abbess of San Zaccaria led the patriarch and prominent members of the Badoer family to support the rights of the Church over the customary rights of the doge. Their vocal opposition to the alliance with Byzantium a few years later was the final straw. The Dandolo family paid the highest price and yet had nothing to gain. They had not the slightest interest in the nature of the clergy of San Salvatore or the investiture of the abbess of San Zaccaria. When Enrico Dandolo denounced the Byzantine alliance he argued not only against his own interests but against those of his family as well.

After his expulsion, Patriarch Dandolo traveled to Rome for justice. He found a sympathetic ear in an angry Pope Eugenius III (1145–53), who immediately excommunicated the doge and placed Venice under interdict.[107] Pietro Polani was unmoved. All his attention was directed at the preparation of the Venetian war fleet, which was ready to sail by the spring of 1148. A grateful Manuel Comnenus significantly expanded the Venetian Quarter in Constantinople in return for the promise of Venetian assistance in September. When the Venetians sailed for Corfu, the doge himself took command of the fleet. That summer, though, Pietro Polani became ill, and he died shortly thereafter.[108] Under the command of his brother and son, the Venetians joined with the Byzantines in the siege of Corfu. The citadel held out for one year, finally surrendering in the summer of 1149.[109]

The death of Pietro Polani was, of course, good news for all those he had exiled. The new doge, Domenico Morosini (1148–55), at once rescinded the exile orders. The canons of San Salvatore returned to their church almost immediately,[110] and Badoer family members began to return, as well.[111] But for the Dandolo the situation was more complex. The patriarch could not return until Venice had made peace with the Church, and the rest of his family had no homes to return to. With their hopes for restitution in the negotiations between Rome and Venice, the Dandolo of San Luca remained in exile. Some probably stayed with the patriarch in Rome. Others may have followed the example of Giovanni Badoer, a resident of San Salvatore parish, who went to Constantinople.[112]

Domenico Morosini did not pursue peace with the Church until the war with the Normans had ended. This must have been a deliberate decision. Although eager for a resolution to the problem, Morosini knew that negotiations would go nowhere while Venice was still engaged in the war that the patriarch had condemned. In late 1149, with the war no longer an issue, doge, patriarch, and pope turned their attention to the problems of Church and State in Venice. In an instant, Morosini ended the "Venetian Investiture Controversy" by agreeing to the Church's terms. The doge took an oath that he and his successors would preserve the liberty of the Church, ensuring that lay powers would have no influence on ecclesiastical government or elections in Venice.[113] These were not mere words. Henceforth, doges stayed out of Church business in Venice. The earliest surviving oaths of office confirm the doge's duty to protect the rights of the Church while avoiding any interference.[114] Dandolo's victory, however, was a double-edged sword. Secular powers no longer took part in ecclesiastical appointments, it is true, but by the same token, prelates no longer played any role in Venetian government.[115] The slow disappearance of the clergy from state documents had begun earlier, but after 1149 it was complete. The two spheres of power were separate. In 1175, when once again a dispute erupted over the election of the abbess of San Zaccaria, it was the Church courts, not the State, that settled the matter.[116] In the same way, the Venetian Church played no part in dealing with the problems presented to the State by the Fourth Crusade in 1202.

Before the pope lifted the interdict there remained the matter of the Dandolo family to consider. Doge Morosini agreed to restore the Dandolo to their properties in San Luca and to rebuild their houses at state expense. But the doge was understandably concerned about relations between the Dandolo and Polani. Bitter rancor between the two families of San Luca could be poisonous to the political well-being and general peace of the commune. To forestall the possibility of vendetta and factionalism, Morosini insisted that a marriage between the two families be arranged. And so it was that Andrea Dandolo, a nephew of the patriarch and brother of the future doge, married Primera Polani, a niece of Doge Pietro Polani.[117] With that settled, the papal interdict was lifted and the Dandolo returned to Venice, in 1150 or 1151.[118] The Venetian government's willingness to accede to all of Rome's demands ushered in a new era of warm relations between the commune and the papacy. Peace with the Church would remain a high priority for the Venetian state and the Venetian faithful, one that at times required great sacrifice.[119]

The canons of San Salvatore found a tense situation when they returned to Venice. Although the Badoer continued to support them, the canons remained bitterly unpopular in their parish. They suffered several violent attacks in the narrow streets near their church; Prior Bonofilio Michiel may have been killed in one such attack.[120] Some of the greater families shifted their allegiance and tithes to nearby San Bartolomeo, undoubtedly leaving San Salvatore in financial difficulties. The church itself was in such poor repair that the canons were forced to petition the pope to direct Bishop Polani to spend a portion of their episcopal tithe on restorations.[121] As time passed, however, tempers cooled and, under the watchful eye of Enrico Dandolo, the canons prospered. The patriarch forced wayward houses to return to San Salvatore and even expanded the parish at the expense of its neighbor—so much so that in 1198 San Bartolomeo came under the control of the canons.[122] Many priors of San Salvatore went on to become bishops. Patriarch Dandolo naturally retained a fondness for the canons whose reform he had championed and who later shared in his exile. He never forgot them.

Dandolo also did not forget the convent of San Zaccaria. The wealthy and prominent house probably lacked an abbess since the deadlock between doge and patriarch, when it had become the battlefield of ecclesiastical liberty in Venice. With the battle won, Dandolo presided over fundamental changes in the convent. The sisters formally announced their intention to convert to a Cluniac monastery, thus adding significantly to the strength of reform orders in the lagoon. They likewise broke with tradition by failing to elect an abbess from one of Venice's elite families. Instead, their choice fell upon Giseldrude, a woman with no surname and a very un-Venetian Christian name,[123] who had likely been sent from another Cluniac house. Thus Dandolo succeeded in securing freedom from lay interference for San Zaccaria and in leading the wealthiest religious house in Venice to join the reform orders.

The patriarch pressed his advantage against Bishop Giovanni Polani of Castello as well. In January 1153, he presided over a provincial synod in Venice to consider a dispute between the clergy of San Stefano and Santa Maria, both of Murano.[124] The dispute was real, but the decision to hold the synod at Rialto rather than the patriarchal church at Grado was clearly designed to put the bishop of Castello in his place. Dandolo also prevailed upon the pope to settle in his favor the jurisdictional dispute between himself and Bishop Polani over San Clemente. In October 1156 the bishop was forced to relinquish all claim to the island church.[125] The clearest demonstration of Dandolo's victory over Polani, however, was his decision in 1156 to build the first permanent patriarchal palace at San Silvestro.[126] Situated directly on the Grand Canal, the palace was only a short walk from the Rialto markets and, coincidentally, directly across from the Dandolo compound in San Luca. It made an imposing and unmistakable statement that the patriarch of Grado was in Venice—indeed, the very heart of Venice—to stay.

Dandolo's authority outside of the lagoon also grew in the aftermath of his victory. The expansion of Venetian power into Dalmatia had led previous patriarchs of Grado to seek jurisdiction over the episcopates there to mirror the secular control of the doges. The recent Hungarian conquest of southern Dalmatia now made that possible. With the metropolitan city of Spalato under Hungarian control, the archbishop was cut off from his northern suffragans in Venetian-dominated areas. Therefore, on October 17, 1154, Pope Anastasius IV (1153–54) elevated the city of Zara to metropolitan status and placed the northern dioceses of Ossero, Veglia, Arbe, and Fara under its authority.[127] A few months later, on February 22, 1155, Pope Hadrian IV (1154–59), after commending Enrico Dandolo's honesty, prudence, and sincere devotion, consecrated him "Primate of Dalmatia" with jurisdiction over the archbishop of Zara. Dandolo was given authority to consecrate not only the bishops of the archdiocese but even the archbishop himself.[128] This was a remarkable move. By elevating one metropolitan over another, Hadrian had at last made Grado a true patriarchate: the only one of its kind in western Europe besides Rome. The pope did so, as Innocent III later wrote, "so that your Church would clearly possess the patriarchal dignity not only in name but also in full right."[129]

In June 1157, Hadrian added further to Dandolo's power, giving him the right to ordain Latin bishops in Constantinople and any other Byzantine city in which Venetians had churches.[130] With these decrees, the pope attempted to bring the ecclesiastical authority of Venice's prelate into line with the expansion of the Republic's power and influence in the East. In the same month Hadrian wrote a letter to the people of Venice and the new doge, Vitale II Michiel (1155–72), reporting that in his presence the archbishop of Zara had taken a vow of obedience to Dandolo. He enjoined all Venetians to regard the patriarch of Grado as their spiritual father, offering him every honor and devotion.[131] Many Venetians were

Figure 1. *Reception of the Relics of Saint Mark.* Choir Chapter of San Clemente, San Marco.
(Photo from author's collection.)

now glad to do so. The tensions of the last decade, deriving from an ambiguous
delineation of ecclesiastical and political spheres of power in Venice, were now
subsiding. With these spheres better defined, Venetians could again take pride in
the majesty of their patriarchate with less fear of clerical meddling in the government of the commune. Just as the doge no longer dictated the outcome of
ecclesiastical elections, so too the prelates no longer influenced the ducal court.

The new state of affairs was graphically represented in the doge's own church
of San Marco. In the Choir Chapel of San Clemente, just to the right of the
main altar, two mosaic groups depicting the patriarch of Grado were executed
around 1155.[132] Pope Pelagius II and Patriarch Helias of Grado are portrayed
standing in an archway between the chapel and the presbytery. In his hand Pelagius holds a scroll confirming the patriarch as metropolitan of Venice, Istria, and
Dalmatia. The Pelagian privilege depicted here was taken from a widely known
concession (itself a forgery), yet the addition of Dalmatia was new, prompted
by the patriarch's recent elevation.[133] Within the chapel the *Reception of the Relics
of St. Mark* in Venice depicts the arrival of Venetian merchants bearing the body
of the evangelist. In the original text of the ninth-century *Translatio* and in the

enamel representation of the Reception in the much older Pala d'Oro, Bishop Ursus of Castello alone received the relics. In this new mosaic, however, two groups receive the holy body. To the right is the earliest mosaic representation of the doge of Venice, accompanied by his judges and a sword bearer (see fig. 1). To the left is the patriarch of Grado, surrounded by his suffragan bishops, who ceremoniously support the patriarch's hands, a gesture denoting his ecclesiastical authority.[134] The mosaic depicts seven bishops, six with croziers and one on the far left bearing a cross. As Thomas E. Dale argued, the seventh figure probably represents the archbishop of Zara.[135]

The mosaic depicts both clergy and laity receiving the legitimizing authority of St. Mark, yet in different ways. For the patriarch the presence of the body confirmed his right to the apostolic authority once vested in Aquileia and now expanded to include Istria and Dalmatia. For the doge, the relics represented a foundational component of his secular authority. Investment of the dogeship was performed in the name of St. Mark, and coins depicted the doge receiving the symbols of his office directly from the evangelist. In this mosaic the clergy and laity share the benefits of the arriving relics, yet the two groups remain distinct and separate.[136] In a snapshot of sorts we see the secular and ecclesiastical institutions of Venice not at the arrival of the body of St. Mark but at the return of Enrico Dandolo of Grado.

As the presence of these mosaics in the ducal church suggests, relations between Patriarch Enrico Dandolo and Doge Vitale II Michiel were favorable from the start.[137] The same can be said of the families of the patriarch and the doge. The Dandolo had risen to a modest level of prominence under the dogeship of Domenico Michiel and entered the ducal court for the first time under his son-in-law, Pietro Polani. The quarrel between Polani and the patriarch caused the Dandolo to be removed from the ducal palace, but it does not appear to have affected their relations with the Michiel.[138] Indeed, the families became quite close. Once again the ducal court was opened to the Dandolo. They would need to work quickly to restore their political power even as they hurried to rebuild their demolished homes.

By the actions of the patriarch of Grado, the Dandolo family, like the Badoer before them, acquired a reputation as reformers. In the twelfth century that was a good thing. While Enrico Dandolo continued his reform of the Church, his brother, Vitale Dandolo, would play a prominent role in the reform of the state.

THREE

VITALE DANDOLO

$\mathcal{E}$

the REFORM of the VENETIAN STATE

atriarch Enrico Dandolo returned to Venice bedecked with victory and adorned with honor and authority. His nephew Enrico and the rest of his family did not. When their vessels rounded the canal bend of Rialto, the Dandolo of San Luca were faced with a heartbreaking sight: Charred wood and rubble were all that remained of their homes. As they disembarked, friends undoubtedly welcomed them and related events in the parish since their exile. Others, particularly those who had profited from their expulsion, averted their eyes, grumbled, or worse. In nearby San Salvatore the returning canons of the church were violently attacked by their enemies.[1] There is no evidence that members of the Dandolo family were similarly persecuted, but relations with some of their neighbors must have been tense. We cannot know to what extent the marriage of Andrea Dandolo and Primera Polani healed the rift between the two families. It is worth noting, however, that after the return of the Dandolo the political status of the Polani rapidly declined.[2]

The rebuilding of the Dandolo homes provides an opportunity to assess the nature of their properties as well as the extent of their losses. Because of the fragmentary nature of the evidence, it is difficult to piece together a family compound in twelfth-century Venice. For most families it simply cannot be done. Building on the work of Juergen Schulz, however, there is much that can be said of the Dandolo compound before and after the expulsion.[3] The family patriarch, Domenico Dandolo, seems to have owned a sizable amount of property in the heart of San Luca parish, extending from the Grand Canal to the parish church and including property south of the church up to the boundary of San

Paternian parish.[4] The church of San Luca and its small campo were flanked by Domenico's properties, lending further support to the tradition that the Dandolo founded the parish. In the early twelfth century much of this land remained vacant. The family also owned quays and workshops along the Grand Canal, as well as several rental properties scattered across the area.[5] It appears that Domenico owned a large house situated just south of the Campiello San Luca facing the Rio di San Luca. The dwelling probably had its own courtyard with a wellhead.[6]

According to Venetian law all legitimate sons had a right to an equal share in their father's property. When Domenico Dandolo died he left four sons: Enrico, Bono, Pietro, and Vitale. Enrico became patriarch of Grado and therefore had no further claim on his father's property. Bono, who was a merchant, appears to have died childless sometime in the 1130s, about the same time as his father.[7] Pietro and Vitale, therefore, inherited the family compound. As was customary, they held the properties together until all of their father's bequests had been paid out; they then divided the remaining property. Unlike Italians in other northern towns, who worked hard to hold family property together in enclaves, Venetians regularly divided patrimonies between sons. A family compound in medieval Venice was merely a location in which many members of an extended family lived near one another. Each property was separate and could be bought and sold at will, although family members naturally received preference as buyers.[8] As Venice grew from a collection of island communities into a unified city, the family compound linked closely to a parish church became a thing of the past. By the thirteenth century, Venetians were trading real estate on the open market the way they traded any other commodity. As a result, extended families fragmented and family compounds splintered.

Pietro Dandolo received his father's property south of the parish church, where, it seems likely, the family's main house stood. His brother, Vitale, took the more sparsely settled properties to the north of the church, which included the shops and quays along the Grand Canal (see fig. 2).[9] Vitale received no grand house, only areas of open space and several simple dwellings, where he and his family could pursue their merchant activities.[10] Because of the scattered nature of his properties, Vitale must have suffered less from the hammers and axes of 1147. Doge Polani had ordered the destruction of the Dandolo homes, but presumably not the various buildings they rented out. Since Vitale's home was modest, so too would have been his losses. Upon his return, rental income and profit from overseas trade probably began to come in. He also owned other income properties outside of Venice.[11] All in all, then, Vitale Dandolo was harmed, but not gravely so, and the reparation money quickly healed his financial wounds.

Pietro Dandolo and his grown son, Marco, were in a much more difficult bind. Their house on the Rio di San Luca had been completely destroyed.[12] The cost of rebuilding created some difficulties for the government, but the doge and his council hit upon an effective and ironic solution. In March 1148, in gratitude for assistance in the war against the Normans, Manuel I Comnenus had expanded the Venetian Quarter in Constantinople. Pietro Polani granted a four-year lease of the new properties to seven men, each of whom would pay the commune 100 hyperpers (a Byzantine currency) at the end of the lease. Shortly after Dandolo's return to Venice, Doge Morosini and his court, declaring that the destruction of their houses had been unwarranted, transferred the right to collect these lease payments to Pietro and Marco Dandolo. In 1156 the two men collected the 700 hyperpers (1,400 lire).[13] And so it was that the fruits of the war that led to the exile of the Dandolo also paid for their restoration. Marco and Pietro Dandolo built a very large house filling the entire parcel of land. From the building's courtyard, which survives, portions of the new structure's portico columns are still visible.[14]

Although his brother, Pietro, received the big house, Vitale did better for himself in almost every other respect. Vitale Dandolo was born sometime in the 1080s and married while in his early twenties. He had a son of his own by 1110.[15] Along with Pietro and their father, Domenico, Vitale was one of the citizens who ratified Doge Ordelafo Falier's concession of property in Constantinople to the Patriarch of Grado in September 1107.[16] He took the cross in 1122 and sailed with his father and brother to the Holy Land, where, along with the other Venetian crusaders, he took part in the conquest of Tyre.[17] After the death of his father around 1131, Vitale prepared to take his place in Venetian society. Unfortunately, few court documents survive from this period to tell us about his early political career. The first document to have a signatory list during Pietro Polani's reign was executed in April 1144. After the signature of the doge, Vitale Dandolo signed sixth of thirty, suggesting that he was a man of some importance.[18] It does not appear, however, that he served as a judge before he and his family were exiled.[19]

Not surprisingly, Vitale Dandolo's political and social standing suffered as a result of his family's expulsion from Venice.[20] Yet it quickly recovered—so quickly, in fact, that it is hard not to see the hand of his brother, Patriarch Enrico Dandolo. The prelate had become a powerful man, in a position to assist kin harmed by his feud with the former doge. Sometime in 1152 or 1153 Vitale Dandolo became a judge, thus bringing him into the company of Venice's highest elites.[21] About the same time the new abbess of San Zaccaria appointed Vitale

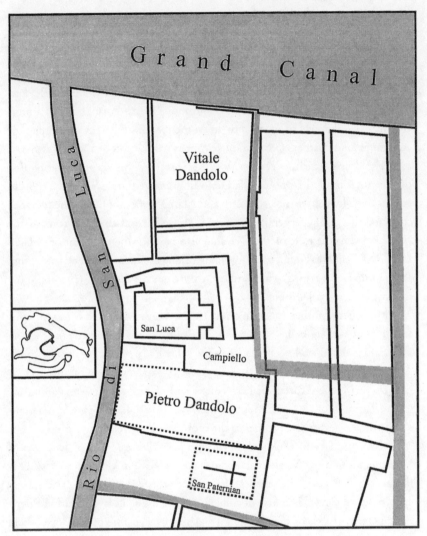

Figure 2. Dandolo Compound, ca. 1155. Black square in the inset represents
Dandolo Compound. (Based on Schulz, "Houses of the Dandolo.")

advocate of the convent[22]—a position of great prestige. Advocates in medieval
Venice served as lawyers of sorts for religious houses or, in some cases, widows.
Since law remained largely customary, legal training was not required; one needed
only a good reputation, basic literacy, and some experience in a public forum.[23]
San Zaccaria selected advocates only from Venice's most illustrious men.[24] As its
recent conversion into a Cluniac house demonstrates, the convent was strongly

under the influence of Enrico Dandolo. The appointment of the patriarch's brother, then, is hardly surprising.

By the time of Doge Domenico Morosini's death in February 1155, the Dandolo fortunes had been stunningly reversed. Patriarch Dandolo had contended with Venice's bishop and doge and had bested both. No patriarch of Grado before him had greater control over his see. In addition, he was primate of Dalmatia. For his part, Vitale Dandolo emerged as the "lay patriarch" of the family, with a position in the ducal court and in the affairs of San Zaccaria.[25]

Nothing is known about the election of Morosini's successor, Vitale II Michiel (1155–72). After so much internal strife in Venice, the decision to return to the house of Michiel suggests a desire to restore peace and stability to the lagoon. It also recalled the greatness of Venice's crusading doges, Vitale I and Domenico Michiel. Although Doge Pietro Polani was married to a Michiel woman, it appears that her family never supported the doge's campaign against the patriarch and the Dandolo family. Indeed, since the prior of San Salvatore, who had defied Bishop Polani by reforming his parish clergy, was himself a Michiel, members of the family may actually have supported the patriarch. Whatever the case, there can be no doubt that Vitale II Michiel warmly favored Patriarch Dandolo. As we have seen, when the doge commissioned new mosaics for San Marco, he depicted Patriarch Dandolo, flanked by his bishops, receiving the relics of St. Mark. Substituting the patriarch of Grado for the bishop of Castello in this crucial episode in Venetian history speaks volumes about the doge's attitude toward Enrico Dandolo as well as Bishop Giovanni Polani. It also demonstrates the doge's view of the patriarch's recent elevation to primate of Dalmatia. Michiel saw Dandolo's ecclesiastical jurisdiction as complimentary to his own political control over the Dalmatian towns. When the archbishop of Zara subsequently rebelled against the patriarch of Grado, the doge immediately declared war on the city. When it was subdued in 1159, Michiel required all Zarans over the age of twelve to take loyalty oaths to himself and the patriarch. Both doge and patriarch had a strong interest in maintaining and expanding their mutual authority along the Adriatic coast.[26]

Michiel favored not only the patriarch but other members of the Dandolo family as well. It is clear from subsequent events that the Michiel and Dandolo families were becoming quite close. Vitale Dandolo immediately took his place as a judge in Michiel's court. In the earliest surviving court document, dated March 1156, the three judges were Domenico Querini, Sebastiano Ziani (the future doge), and Vitale Dandolo.[27] In the next extant court document, executed in August 1158, the three judges were Sebastiano Ziani, Orio Mastropiero (also a future doge), and Vitale Dandolo.[28] This trio would remain the doge's favored judges for many years.[29] They appear in most of the court documents from Michiel's reign. All three were from new families that had come to prominence with wealth earned in commercial ventures. Indeed, Ziani and Mastropiero were the richest men in Venice at the time.[30]

When Ziani, Mastropiero, and Dandolo did not serve in the ducal court, their absence alone suggests that one or all of them may have been away from the city. In April 1159 the doge heard a case with only one ducal judge in attendance, Vitale Dandolo.[31] Likewise, none of the three was present for proceedings in May 1160 and March 1161.[32] We cannot know with certainty why they were absent, but it may have had something to do with events in Lombardy. In preparation for his conquest of Italy, the German emperor, Frederick I Barbarossa, demanded from the Lombard cities what in theory they owed him all along—obedience, support, and money. With the urging of Pope Hadrian IV, most of the cities refused. When Hadrian died on September 1, 1159, the College of Cardinals split along pro- and anti-imperial lines. The latter group elected Alexander III; the former, Victor IV. In February 1160 Barbarossa called a meeting at Pavia to sort out the schism. Envoys from across the empire attended, although Alexander III and his legates were not among them. Venice surely sent representatives to this gathering, which proclaimed itself both a Church council and a diet of the empire. It is possible that those representatives were the doge's trusted men, Ziani, Mastropiero, and Dandolo. Not surprisingly, given the presence of the emperor, the synod recognized Victor as pope and excommunicated Alexander. In response, Alexander excommunicated Victor and Barbarossa and dissolved all bonds of allegiance to both. He then fled to France, where he remained for the next three years. Frederick turned his attention to the ringleader of the rebellious Lombard towns: wealthy and populous Milan. He laid siege to the city throughout 1160 and 1161, finally capturing and destroying it on March 1, 1162.

Venice usually took only a passing interest in events in Lombardy or Germany, but the violence of Frederick Barbarossa and the papal schism made this a different matter. Venetians could not condone Barbarossa's plan to capture Italy, a plan that would not only harm their friends, the Byzantines, but would also jeopardize Venetian independence and authority in the Adriatic. Doge Michiel and Patriarch Dandolo were quick to voice their support for Alexander III, and the pope was very glad to have it.[33] Thereafter, Venice served as both a conduit to the East for Alexander and his partisans and a safe haven for Italian clergy seeking to escape from the German "tyranny." Indeed, during the 1160s Venice was awash in refugees from all over Lombardy. So important was the Republic to Alexander that he sent the Apostolic Vicar, Cardinal-Legate Hildebrand Crasso, to Venice, where he remained from 1161 to 1168.[34]

Vitale Dandolo was back in the ducal court along with Sebastiano Ziani and the doge in July 1161, when they heard a case concerning an inheritance dispute.[35] At about the same time Dandolo received yet another honor when he was named advocate of the wealthy monastery of San Cipriano di Murano. In August 1161 he pled a case for that religious house before the ducal court;[36] his being a regular member of the court was apparently not considered a conflict of interest.[37] In the next surviving court document, dated August 1163, Ziani, Mastropiero, and Dandolo were once again the three judges.[38]

The summer of 1164 was a busy one for Vitale Dandolo. In June, he represented the convent of San Zaccaria before an ecclesiastical court. Presiding was Cardinal-Legate Hildebrand and Vitale's brother, Patriarch Dandolo. Marco, prior of the canons regular of Santa Maria di Lispida near Padua, made the charge that the abbess of San Zaccaria had seized his goods and evicted him from a house in Venice. Speaking for the abbess, Vitale Dandolo explained to the court that the prior was a refugee from the desolation wrought by Frederick Barbarossa nearly three years earlier. Expelled from his church, he had come to Venice, where the abbess took pity on him, promising to give him a home and necessities for up to three years. Over the course of those three years, however, Marco had consumed far more than expected or promised. When his time was up the abbess had ordered Marco out of the house and confiscated some of his goods to make up for her losses. Vitale Dandolo may have offered an eloquent defense, but he was speaking to a cardinal who was himself a refugee and therefore had a natural sympathy for Marco. Hildebrand ordered the abbess to return all the goods she had taken and to pay Marco 100 soldi. For his part, Marco was to affirm in writing that his dealings with the convent were at an end.[39]

Vitale Dandolo remained active in the ducal court throughout that summer. In June he served as a judge for a voluntary state loan. A group of leading citizens rendered to the commune 1,150 silver marks in return for shares in the government's markets at Rialto over the next eleven years.[40] In August, along with Sebastiano Ziani and Orio Mastropiero, Vitale signed a ducal concession to San Marco at Tyre.[41] About the same time he also served as a judge in an unusual property dispute, one that sheds some light on his position and reputation in Venice. In his will, Orso Badoer had left a vineyard in Chioggia to the church of San Salvatore. After his death, someone, probably a kinsman, contested the extent of the bequest, claiming that the land invested to the church was in fact three vineyards, only one of which Badoer had intended the canons to have. Doge

Michiel ordered his judges to cross over to Chioggia and investigate the matter. There the three summoned Chioggian judges, as well as several old men, all of whom testified that the land in question was one parcel, not three. The document that records the case is an affidavit made in Venice shortly thereafter by two witnesses to the proceedings. It is interesting that, although the doge sent all of his judges, the witnesses reported that after the evidence had been presented, "Lord Vitale Dandolo, who was a judge, immediately said that by law and judgement all of the aforesaid vineyard should be invested to the name of the church of San Salvatore as one vineyard alone."[42] Not only did Vitale Dandolo decide the case without consulting the doge, he appears not even to have consulted with his fellow judges. It was highly unusual, almost unheard of in Venice, for a judge to decide a case on his own.[43] This suggests that Vitale not only had the doge's confidence but he had also acquired a wide reputation for fairness.

While obviously vigorous, Vitale was an old man. If he was twenty when his son Enrico was born, around 1107, he would have been in his mid- to late seventies in 1164. The evidence suggests that it was around this time that Vitale retired from the ducal court. In May 1165 he was not present when the doge invested his son, Leonardo Michiel, with the office of count of Zara.[44] Nor does Vitale appear as a ducal judge in any subsequent court document. He remained, nevertheless, among the most important men in Venice. On June 28, 1166, the doge issued a decree concerning the jurisdiction and authority of the count of Arbe. The document was signed first by the doge, then by Patriarch Dandolo, who had ecclesiastical jurisdiction over the island, then by Sebastiano Ziani, Vitale Dandolo, and a long list of leading citizens.[45] Neither Ziani nor Dandolo signed as judges, since their participation was apparently not required for a privilege of this sort.[46] Vitale's signature immediately after that of the doge, the patriarch, and the richest man in Venice succinctly describes his social and political position after his retirement from the court's daily affairs.

In October 1166 Vitale Dandolo turned his attention to the hereafter, bestowing a large gift of lands in Pellestrina to the monastery of San Cipriano di Murano for the benefit of his soul and those of his family.[47] But he still had much to do in this life. On December 15, 1167, a fire broke out in the church of San Salvatore and spread quickly across the city. The Dandolo compound was directly in its path. The parish church of San Luca was destroyed, as must have been the newly restored house of Marco Dandolo. Given the extent of the blaze, it is impossible that Vitale Dandolo's properties escaped undamaged.[48] For the second time in his life Vitale was forced to reconstruct the homes of his family—this time, of course, without government assistance.

Because of his reputation for judicial probity, Vitale continued to be in demand. Interestingly, in 1168 he was asked to settle a dispute between two monasteries, San Cipriano di Murano and San Giorgio di Fossone. Both houses had for a number of years wrangled over a property in Plebis. Stefano Corner had bequeathed it to San Cipriano, and even the monks of San Giorgio admitted that San Cipriano had possessed it for a long time. The abbot of San Giorgio contested the ownership when he discovered in his archives a parchment stating that his predecessor, Pietro, had purchased the property from two residents of Plebis. Litigation between the two houses became fierce, sometimes played out in the courts of Padua, sometimes elsewhere. A lasting solution was hindered, in the words of the abbot of San Giorgio, by the "constant waiving of parchments around." And so it was that in 1168 both monasteries decided to abandon the courts and select an arbiter to examine the records and make a binding decision. Both abbots agreed upon Vitale Dandolo, even though Vitale had served for years as advocate to San Cipriano and had just recently bestowed lands on that monastery. That the abbot of San Giorgio would accept Vitale in spite of this relationship says much about the judge's reputation in the lagoon. Dandolo collected all relevant documents and scrutinized the legal basis for the various arguments. In the end he concluded that both houses had good claims to the property and thus devised a compromise. San Cipriano, he ruled, would keep the property but pay San Giorgio an annual tithe as well as a one-time payment for the restoration of San Giorgio's hospital. The bill of sale, which the abbot of San Giorgio had discovered in the archives, was to be surrendered to the abbot of San Cipriano. As they had promised, both sides accepted the decision.[49]

Passing from his seventies into his eighties, Vitale Dandolo continued to remain active as an advocate of San Zaccaria and a counselor to the doge.[50] Still, he knew that he could not live forever and must therefore have been considering his political legacy to his three sons: Enrico (the future doge), Andrea, and Giovanni. We have already met Andrea, whose marriage to Primera Polani around 1151 sealed the peace between the doge and the patriarch and allowed the lifting of the papal interdict on Venice. Giovanni Dandolo is trickier to identify as there was another Giovanni Dandolo of the San Polo branch alive at the same time, as well as others with the same name. What is clear, though, is that Giovanni, son of Vitale, regularly undertook business overseas. In August 1161 he was in Acre, where he made a business agreement with Romano Mairano for travel to Alexandria. The following February he was in Constantinople, where he collected his share of the profits from the voyage.[51] In October 1166, he witnessed his father's pious donation to San Cipriano di Murano.[52] Like his uncle, Bono Dandolo, Giovanni appears to have been the son who conducted the family's business in foreign ports.

Enrico Dandolo is scarce in the documentary record before 1172, appearing only as one of many signatories to the state loan made in June 1164.[53] Given his later election to the ducal throne and the long shadow he would cast over Venetian history, it has often perplexed historians that Enrico Dandolo should be so invisible during the first sixty years of his life. Some have suggested that he was not in Venice at all, but instead pursued profit in the markets of Constantinople, Tyre, and Alexandria.[54] If so, it is curious that none of these commercial documents survives. As the example of his brother Giovanni demonstrates, conducting overseas business tended to generate more parchment than simply remaining in Venice. The suggestion that Enrico Dandolo was busy overseas is based on later documents, which place him in Alexandria and Constantinople. As we shall see, he was not involved in commerce during those voyages. Indeed, there is no evidence that he ever conducted business overseas.

Enrico Dandolo is largely missing from the documentary record before 1172 for the same reason that his brothers also rarely appear: Their father was still alive. Enrico Dandolo may have been elderly in 1170, but his father was ancient. He was not emancipated, a legal act by which a son left the family, and therefore the power, of his father. A father could emancipate a son by giving to him his patrimonial inheritance, which then severed any legal bond between the two. Vitale Dandolo emancipated none of his sons.[55] Enrico and his brothers did, however, have a partial emancipation, called in Venice a filial subjection.[56] This permitted an adult son to enter contracts and conduct business for himself, but kept him within his father's family and under his father's control.[57] As elsewhere in northern Italy, the urban family had a corporate nature. While their father lived, Vitale's sons worked for the benefit of the family. Vitale represented the family and ruled it, so it is he who most often appears in official documents. In his final years, Vitale would naturally look to placing his sons in good positions to do well for themselves. It is for this reason that Enrico Dandolo appears in the documentary record only as his famous father approached death.

During the dogeship of Vitale II Michiel the Dandolo passed into a new phase of their history. No longer a second- or third-tier clan, they had become and would remain one of Venice's most powerful families—owing largely to the efforts of Vitale Dandolo. Although surely helped to power by his brother the patriarch, Vitale quickly made important political and personal connections with the doge and his fellow judges, connections that would in the coming years permanently shape Venetian history. Vitale Dandolo was not as rich as Orio

Mastropiero and Sebastiano Ziani (although he was by no means poor), but he enjoyed a wealth of respect in the city for wisdom and fairness. In his eighties, Vitale was justified in scaling back his activities and letting his sons find their place in Venetian politics. Yet he would get no rest. The Republic of St. Mark was about to receive a vigorous shaking, and Vitale and his family would be called on to play crucial roles in the unfolding tragedies of the early 1170s. Patriarch Dandolo led the reform of the Venetian church. His brother, Vitale, would do the same for the Venetian state.

The political waters of Europe remained extremely treacherous in the 1160s. With fire and sword, Frederick Barbarossa imposed his authority over the Lombard towns in 1162; Venice alone remained defiant. Relations between Venice and Frederick were so bad that at his instigation Verona, Padua, and Ferrara launched a naval attack on Capo d'Argine.[58] A Venetian fleet repulsed the attack, but the incident made clear that Frederick considered Venice a threat. In 1163 the doge and his council formed an alliance with Verona, Vicenza, and Padua. The four pledged mutual support and to render nothing to Frederick that their fathers had not given to all German emperors since Charlemagne. Having pried these towns from imperial control, Venice quickly sent funds to assist them in the defense of their freedom.

At the moment, Frederick had greater matters to attend to. In October 1163 he returned to Italy with fresh German troops, which he joined with Italian forces to conquer the peninsula. He had already signed a treaty with Venice's commercial rivals, Pisa and Genoa, who were to begin hostilities against the Norman kingdom on May 1, 1164. But over winter things began to unravel. Additional troops from Germany were slow in coming, and many of the Italians were having second thoughts. In the spring, when the invasion was scheduled to begin, Frederick was bedridden with illness. Meanwhile, Doge Michiel sent envoys to Constantinople to suggest to Manuel Comnenus that he lend financial support to Lombard independence. In 1165 a Byzantine embassy arrived in Venice delivering the emperor's promise of support for all Italian cities in rebellion.[59] There was even some discussion of the Lombards submitting to Byzantine rule if Manuel would defend them.[60] The doge pledged 100 Venetian galleys to support a Byzantine attack on Frederick in Italy.[61]

Venice remained at the eye of the storm, continuing to support and coordinate rebellion against Frederick, but remaining physically out of the struggle. After having failed to restore control over Verona in June 1164, the German emperor headed south during the winter of 1166–67. In his absence many of the Lombard towns began to rebel. Cremona, Mantua, Brescia, and Bergamo made a secret league against Frederick in spring 1167. Although they did not formally join the Verona league, they did alert them of their sympathies. The four sent troops to escort the exiled citizens of Milan back home and assist them with rebuilding their city and its defenses. By the summer, Piacenza, Lodi, and Parma had been brought into the growing rebellion. When Frederick returned with his plague-wracked army in August, he failed to recapture Piacenza and was forced to hole up in Pavia. With the emperor now on the defensive, the consuls of the eight cities met with the leaders of the Verona league, as well as consuls from Ferrara, Bologna, and Modena. On December 1, 1167, all agreed that they would stand as one against new imperial taxes. The Venetian delegates, however, were in a unique situation. Venetians had never paid taxes to Frederick, nor had he subjugated them. Venetians assisted with the rebellion, but they were not really part of it. The delegates agreed to continue to funnel Byzantine and Norman money to the Lombard towns.[62] But Venice asked for no military assistance against Frederick and offered none. The Lombard League was formed, but Venice was only a charter member.

While Venetians watched events in Italy from a distance, real trouble was brewing for them in the Byzantine Empire. Manuel Comnenus was not personally fond of Italian merchants, Venetians least of all. He had learned from his father the violent reaction they exhibited when their commercial rights were threatened, and, like most Byzantines, he chaffed at the haughtiness of these wealthy foreigners in the capital city.[63] Nevertheless, Venice remained an important ally, crucial to the emperor's activities in Italy. Manuel's most cherished goal was the restoration of Italy to Byzantine control. In 1166 he opened negotiations with the newly crowned King William II of Sicily, offering him the hand of his daughter and heir, Maria. Such a marriage offered an enticing opportunity to restore Constantinople's control over southern Italy. Yet negotiations soon broke down.[64]

The following year, Manuel scored a decisive military victory against King Stephen III of Hungary, opening the way for him to restore Byzantine control over Dalmatia and Croatia.[65] This impressive conquest led the emperor to reassess his relations with the Normans and to consider the possibility of a new military campaign against them in Italy. On December 10, 1167, three Byzantine envoys made a grand entrance into Venice. They came to speak of war. What they wanted from the doge was the "customary aid" of a Venetian war fleet to be put into Byzantine service. Michiel and his advisors knew well that such aid was customarily used against the Normans. In the past, Venice had always complied with these requests, since the Normans usually posed a threat to the Republic, too. But times had changed. The Normans were strong supporters of Alexander III and the Lombard towns. Indeed, the pope had been under Norman protection since he fled Rome in April. Like Byzantium, Venice had signed a treaty with William I promising to respect his lands and vessels. Were the Venetians to join in an attack on the Norman kingdom they would not only violate their treaty but also antagonize the pope and, by extension, the Lombards. In short, the Venetians would alienate everyone except Manuel, whom they had no reason to trust very much. The doge refused to give the emperor the requested aid.[66]

Manuel was outraged when he learned that there would be no Venetian fleet—without which he could not launch an invasion of Italy. Venice was now a hindrance to his aspirations and he treated her as such. The doge and his counselors recognized the change immediately, and they ordered Venetian merchants to avoid Byzantine ports lest they fall prey to the emperor's wrath.[67] The order may have been merely a warning, since it does not appear that anyone was ever prosecuted for doing business in Byzantium after 1168. Whatever the nature of the doge's words, they had little effect. The Venetian Quarter in Constantinople still teemed with commercial activity—little wonder, since Venetians continued to trade tax-free and with scant competition after the expulsion of the Genoese and Pisan merchants in 1162. Enormous profits made the doge's decree a dead letter. Although relations between the courts of Venice and Constantinople had soured, economic relations remained quite good.[68]

Sometime in 1169 or 1170 Doge Michiel sent envoys to Constantinople to smooth over any problems. Manuel Comnenus professed, probably sincerely, that he had no intention of harming Venetian residents and merchants in his empire. He promised to continue to abide by all treaties between the two states. With these assurances the doge lifted his largely symbolic trade embargo on Byzantium. Cautious Venetians who had kept out of the Byzantine markets for the past year or so now rushed in. To streamline the process, the doge sent two of his advisors, Sebastiano Ziani and Orio Mastropiero, to Constantinople to act as ducal legates for the Venetian community. In this way, property disputes, rental contracts, and other legal matters could be dealt with quickly and efficiently without having to send to Venice.[69] Vitale Dandolo remained in Venice with the doge.[70]

In 1169 the empress bore Manuel Comnenus a son and heir, which made his daughter Maria no longer so attractive a match. Almost immediately the emperor began offering her hand to various western leaders in an attempt to forge some sort of alliance. In 1171 he offered her to William II of Sicily, who accepted the following year. More important were Manuel's negotiations with Frederick Bar-barossa. In March 1168 the German emperor had returned north of the Alps, where he busied himself with gathering support for his struggle against the pope and the Lombard League. To that end, he opened lines of communication with Manuel Comnenus. In 1170, Frederick's minister, Archbishop Christian of Mainz, traveled to Constantinople to propose that Manuel and Frederick join forces to conquer Italy. Manuel could not have been more pleased. He sent a return embassy to Frederick to suggest that the German ruler's son Henry marry Maria to seal the alliance. William II of Sicily, to whom Maria had already been promised, was left waiting at the altar. The promises of Frederick rekindled Manuel's hopes for regaining his foothold in Italy. With German support, he no longer had any need of the Venetians. Indeed, given that the Venetians were the enemies of Frederick Barbarossa, Manuel's relationship with them had become a liability.[71]

Shortly after opening negotiations with Frederick, Manuel informed the Pisans and the Genoese, both of whom supported the German emperor, that he was willing to end his quarrel with them.[72] In 1170 merchants from both cities were restored to their quarters in Constantinople. It was fighting between Pisans and Genoese that had caused the emperor to expel them eight years earlier, so he gave stern warnings that the peace must be kept. Constantinople's Venetians were obviously not pleased to see the return of their rivals. Almost immediately a mob of them attacked and pillaged the newly restored Genoese Quarter. For Manuel this was the last straw. He sent secret messages to Byzantine officials across the empire ordering them to arrest, imprison, and confiscate the property of every Venetian in their jurisdiction on March 12, 1171. Amazingly, the messages re-mained secret, suggesting that Venice had very poor intelligence concerning ac-tivities in the Byzantine government.[73]

Shortly after the Venetian attack on the Genoese Quarter, the doge's legates in Constantinople, Orio Mastropiero and Sebastiano Ziani, went to see the em-peror. It is impossible to know what was said or even whether the legates were apologetic or defiant.[74] What is known is that Manuel assured them that all was well and that he would take no action against Venice. This they reported to their countrymen in Constantinople and to the doge when they returned home.[75] Venetians across the Mediterranean breathed a sigh of relief. The emperor's rea-sons for lying are clear enough: If he expressed outrage or promised punishment, Venetians would naturally flee his dominions before he was able to capture them; so he spoke soothing words to quiet their fears and lower their guard.

The arrests began at the appointed time, on March 12. In Constantinople and every other Byzantine port Venetian men, women, and children were thrown into prisons, and when the prisons were full, they were put into monasteries. Their houses, shops, and vessels were confiscated. A few escaped and a few others were able to negotiate their freedom, but the vast majority, well over ten thousand people, would remain in captivity for years.[76]

The obvious question is why Manuel Comnenus went to all the trouble and expense of incarcerating thousands of Venetians when he could much more easily and more profitably have confiscated their property and expelled them, just as he had done to the Genoese nine years earlier? The answer is equally obvious, yet little noticed. The Genoese were unable to harm Byzantium, particularly while the emperor could count on Venetian fleets to defend him. Venice, on the other hand, could gravely harm Byzantium, especially if she joined forces with the Normans. Manuel knew that the Venetians' natural response would be to launch a retaliatory force, just as they had done against his father five decades earlier. He hoped that by holding thousands of hostages he could check that impulse. Hostages would also give him a stronger position in subsequent negotiations.

No sooner had Orio Mastropiero and Sebastiano Ziani assured the doge of the emperor's friendship than news arrived of the coup against the Venetians. As one would expect, there was quite a bit of outrage in the ducal court, as well as some embarrassment on the part of the legates, who had been so completely taken in by Manuel. In so grave a matter the doge could act only with the support of his counselors, the sapientes. As we have seen, this group regularly included Orio Mastropiero, Sebastiano Ziani, and Vitale Dandolo. The counselors advised caution, because the report they had received seemed fantastic, almost unbelievable. They urged the doge to dispatch envoys to Constantinople to ascertain the facts on the ground. If the report was true, the envoys should assess the damage, inquire into Manuel's reasons for inflicting it, and demand the release of the hostages and the restoration of their property.[77]

Vitale Michiel's response to the advice of his counselors has been badly misunderstood. The doge is universally portrayed as rash and autocratic, a man who ignored the advice of the court by choosing to declare war on the Greeks.[78] There is, however, no evidence that Michiel ever acted without the support and advice of his counselors, particularly Ziani, Mastropiero, and Dandolo, who had served him since his election.[79] Indeed, in the new age of the commune it is difficult to see how he could have done so. In this case Michiel accepted the advice of his counselors and prepared to send envoys to Byzantium. What changed everything was the arrival in the lagoon of a convoy of Venetian vessels that had narrowly escaped capture on Halmyros. With great passion the sailors related their harrowing stories, and the word spread quickly across Venice. People poured out of their houses, enraged and eager for revenge. They gathered together, proba- bly outside the ducal palace.[80] The assembly of the people of Venice, the *arengo*, was the theoretical basis of all authority. It was this assembly that selected new doges and, in some cases, legislated directly.[81] Reacting to the widespread anger of the people it was the *comuni consilio*; in other words, the representatives of the people at the ducal court, that ordered the construction of a fleet of 120 and 20 transports for a punitive attack on Byzantium. In addition, they ordered Doge Michiel to take command of the strike force personally, leaving his son Leonardo to act as vice-doge in his absence.[82] It was not Michiel who ignored the advice of his counselors, but the people of Venice. Once they had decided to use force of arms, there was nothing the doge could do to resist.[83] The decision, in any event, was not irrational; a war fleet had, after all, persuaded Manuel's father to see things Venice's way when he crossed the Republic.

Venetians worked overtime to produce the new fleet, and less than four months later it was ready to sail. Michiel took with him several advisors, in- cluding Vitale Dandolo's son, Enrico. The fleet sailed down the coast of Dal- matia, quickly reinforcing Venetian control there. It then entered Greek waters, landing on the island of Negroponte (Euboea) and laying siege to the capital, Chalkis. The Byzantine governor met with the doge and his counselors, who made clear to him that they preferred a diplomatic solution to their quarrel with the emperor if one could be found. In return for the withdrawal of the Venetian forces, the governor agreed to send an envoy to Constantinople to urge the em- peror to release the hostages. The envoy was accompanied by a Venetian delega- tion made up of Manasse Badoer and Bishop Pasqualo of Jesolo.[84] The latter, whom Patriarch Dandolo had consecrated only one month earlier, could speak Greek.[85]

With high hopes for peace, the doge ordered the fleet to withdraw from Ne- groponte. They sailed to the island of Chios, where they spent the winter wait- ing for word from Constantinople. Manuel Comnenus, however, refused to re- ceive the envoys. As Michiel and his advisors had feared, the emperor would listen to no words of peace while the Venetians waged war in his empire. He did, how- ever, send back his own envoy, who held out hope for a negotiated settlement. On Chios, the doge and leading men listened to the optimistic words of the im- perial messenger, who urged them to send another embassy to Constantinople. Donald M. Nicol reasonably surmises that the Byzantine envoy's real objective was to spy on the Venetian forces. The request for an additional embassy makes clear that Manuel was also attempting to impede the progress of the fleet with diplomatic delays. By dangling the possibility of peace before the doge, the emperor hoped to forestall further attacks on his territories while he prepared his own forces to meet the Venetians. The ruse worked. The doge sent his envoys back to Constantinople along with Filipo Greco, another Venetian notable.[86]

Shortly after the embassy's departure, plague hit the Venetian camp. More than a thousand people died in the first days of the outbreak. Many blamed Byzantine agents, whom they believed had poisoned the wells, but there was also a good deal of grumbling against the doge, who was hardly dealing out swift vengeance against the Byzantines. In the only attack on a Greek city thus far, Michiel had withdrawn in order to pursue his preferred diplomatic strategy. Since then the Venetians had done little but wait—and die—on Chios. In March the fleet moved to the island of Panagia, but the plague followed. At the end of the month the delegation returning from Constantinople arrived and gave their report. It was no better than the last; again the envoys had been denied an imperial audience. But Manuel sent another envoy to the doge with a promise that if a third legation was sent, he would receive it.[87]

Doge Michiel's situation was dire. His armada was crippled and more of his men were dying every day. He had already received intelligence of a Byzantine plan to attack them on Chios or at sea, so he found it difficult to believe that peace was really on the emperor's mind.[88] But his options were limited. If he could shake off the plague, the Venetian fleet was still large enough to make trouble in the Aegean. Perhaps that threat, along with another embassy, would be enough to persuade Manuel to release the Venetian prisoners. It was, in any case, his only hope. Bishop Pasqualo was not available for another embassy, presumably having died of the plague.[89] So Michiel turned to Enrico Dandolo, sending him and Filippo Greco to the emperor's court.[90]

Enrico Dandolo's presence on this last desperate peace mission says much about his outlook on Byzantium and the events of 1171 and 1172. If he were the Byzantine-hating zealot some historians have made him out to be, it would have made little sense for the doge to send him to the emperor's court to negotiate peace.[91] We can assume that, like all Venetians, Dandolo was horrified at the seizure of his countrymen. But he must also have shared the view of his father and the doge that the decision to launch a retaliatory fleet was premature and dangerous.[92]

As it happened, Dandolo never did meet the emperor. He was in Constantinople only a short time before news arrived that the Venetian fleet was sailing home. The doge had again tried to shake off the plague, moving his forces first to Lesbos and then to Skyros. Nothing worked. As the numbers of dead mounted, it became depressingly clear that the fleet was no longer a threat to the emperor and was itself in grave danger. The men of Venice ordered their doge to take them home and so he did. Dandolo and Greco headed back to Venice having accomplished nothing.[93]

What was left of the retaliatory fleet sailed into the Venetian lagoon in late May 1172. Rather than revenge, Michiel brought home defeat, humiliation, and plague. Once again the people took matters into their own hands. A general meeting of some kind was held in the ducal palace on May 27, with the doge and his counselors present to discuss the tragedy with the assembled citizens. The meeting went badly from the start. Amid tears for fallen loved ones were angry cries of accusation. The people of Venice had given the doge the means and a mandate to retaliate against the emperor, yet he had done nothing of the kind. Instead, he used the fleet merely as a tool of diplomacy. Many of the survivors angrily denounced the doge, saying, "We were poorly led, and if we had not been betrayed by the doge dragging out matters with legates, then all of these troubles would not have overtaken us!" Among the crowd stones and knives began to appear. While Michiel attempted to reason with the people, his counselors began slipping out of the room; Vitale Dandolo may well have been among them. Finding himself alone, the doge made a break for the sanctuary of nearby San Zaccaria, but was stabbed and killed before getting that far.[94]

The popular act of regicide became bitterly unpopular after Michiel lay dead. A good man and a "lover of peace," he had been put into a difficult situation by the people themselves. Marco Casolo, the doge's assassin, became the scapegoat for the people's rage, but his execution did not wash away their guilt. After an emotional funeral and burial at San Zaccaria, the people assembled at nearby San Marco to choose Michiel's successor. Venetian chroniclers give sparse details about what happened next, but in the end the people elected not a new doge but an eleven-man commission charged with selecting a new doge.[95] What, then, induced the arengo to give away this important right?

The murder of Vitale II Michiel was a pivotal moment in Venetian history— everyone agrees on that. What historians have differed on is the meaning and impact of that moment. Roberto Cessi, who saw Michiel as an autocratic man, argued that killing the doge was an act of revolution. New families, like the Casolo, had come to power through the commune, yet the commune itself was endangered by this doge of the old aristocracy. They decided therefore to assassinate the tyrant.[96] Giorgio Cracco accepts Cessi's characterization of Michiel, yet believes that the division was not between social ranks but between economic classes. It was overseas merchants like Marco Casolo, harmed by the closing of trade with Byzantium, who lashed out at the landed aristocracy typified by Doge Michiel.[97] Responding to these arguments, Andrea Castagnetti has warned against grand conclusions about rank or class struggles in medieval Venice based on the evidence of one episode and the name of the assassin. He points out that the Casolo family was not all that active in overseas trade, while the Michiel family was. The delineations that Cracco makes, therefore, simply do not stand up. Instead, Castagnetti suggests that the rise of the commune and the continued presence of a powerful doge from an old family led to an impasse that only assassination could resolve.[98]

All these arguments accept the false premise that Michiel was a man of autocratic temperament whose family held a stranglehold on the dogeship. In addition, these attempts to explain Doge Michiel's assassination in terms of various social, economic, or political trends in Venice fail to take into account the passion of the moment. When the crippled fleet returned, Venice's citizens were not musing about constitutional dynamics; they were angry. Their hopes for the release of their loved ones had been dashed, and thousands were dead. In a most human response they looked for someone to blame, and they did not have to look far. But they blamed Michiel not for his bellicosity but for his lack of it. Words of regicide were uttered not out of a desire to establish governing councils but to avenge the fathers, sons, and brothers who lay dead on Greek islands. Knives were pulled on the doge not because he resisted the development of communal institutions but because "we were poorly led."

To understand the importance of 1172 we must bear in mind that the power of the sapientes grew at the expense not only of the doge but also of the people. The sapientes were conservative men who wanted to check both autocratic doges and also the volatile arengo. It was, after all, the people who had demanded the launching of the ill-fated fleet over the wishes of the doge and his counselors. Men like Vitale Dandolo could remind the weeping assembly that had their advice been heeded, many hundreds would still be alive and Venice would be that much closer to securing a release for the thousands still held overseas. The selection of a new doge was crucially important. Would it not be better to leave it to those same wise men? Unfortunately, we cannot know what arguments were made at this assembly, but we do know that when it was over the people had delegated away their authority to select the next doge. It was a moment of profound importance, a milestone in the creation of a new Venetian government. The last direct tie between doge and people had been severed.

The identity of the eleven men chosen to select the new doge confirms the people's desire to return to the wisdom of Michiel and his court. First among the eleven was Vitale Dandolo, joined, as usual, by Orio Mastropiero. Domenico Morosini, who had also served in Michiel's court, was another elector. Also on the committee was Leonardo Michiel, the late doge's son and a close friend of the younger Enrico Dandolo.[99] Filippo Greco, who had just returned from Constantinople with Enrico Dandolo, was also among the eleven, as was Manasse Badoer and Ranieri Zane, both of whom had accompanied the doge on his tragic mission to the East.[100] These were not revolutionaries who had opposed a tyrant, but the closest associates of the fallen doge. Conspicuously absent from the committee was Sebastiano Ziani, the richest man in Venice and a long-time member of the doge's court. Plainly, he was missing because he expected the committee to elect him, which it did after three days' deliberation. Sebastiano Ziani was seventy years old in 1172—venerable, but still younger than his colleague Vitale Dandolo.[101] The new doge had a clear mandate to pursue Michiel's original policy of peaceful diplomacy, which the fury of the people had overruled. When Ziani's election was announced the people of Venice approved it enthusiastically, shouting "Long live the doge, and may we be able to obtain peace through him!"[102]

It is impossible to adequately understand late-twelfth- and early-thirteenth-century Venice, including the course and outcome of the Fourth Crusade, without taking into account the lessons learned by the Venetians in their failed mission of vengeance. They learned that the fury of the mob was a poor substitute for the reasoned consideration of experienced statesmen. Those statesmen, the friends and counselors of Vitale II Michiel, became the new leaders of a reformed and reforming Republic. The next three doges were marked by their association with Michiel and probably elected for that very reason. They were men who knew first hand the importance of a doge's counselors and who feared rash actions, whether of the people or a doge. A fundamental shift was occurring in the history of Venetian government, as well as in the development of the later "myth of Venice." Venice, the republic where powerful doges ruled powerful people, was becoming an oligarchy, where a distinct body of elite, known for their wisdom and service to the state, began to draw into themselves the powers of both people and doge. Vitale Dandolo and his sons were important players in this reform of Venetian politics, although we can directly observe them only infrequently.

Doge Ziani's first and most important task was to negotiate the release of the Venetian hostages and, if possible, make peace with Constantinople. In 1173 he sent Vitale Dandolo to the emperor, accompanied by Manasse Badoer and Vitale Falier.[103] It must have been a difficult trip for Dandolo, who was close to ninety years old. His presence on the embassy clearly underscored the importance of its mission. Yet the ancient statesman had no better luck obtaining an audience than had his son a year earlier. After having been put off with various excuses and delays, Vitale and his companions at last concluded that Manuel would never see them. Just before leaving Constantinople the emperor sent envoys to accompany them back to Venice and negotiate peace with the doge in Venice. The mission seemed, therefore, at least a partial success.[104]

While Manuel Comnenus was ignoring Vitale Dandolo, his position in the West had begun to unravel. Frederick Barbarossa, it appears, had never really been interested in sharing Italy with Manuel, but rather wanted to prevent an alliance between the Byzantines and the Normans. In that he was successful. William II was incensed at being jilted. Doge Ziani and his court hoped that, with few friends left in the West, Manuel Comnenus would come to terms with Venice. To urge him in that direction, the doge made diplomatic overtures to the emperor's enemies. Given Venetian support for the Lombard towns, Ziani could hardly forge an alliance with the Germans, but he did send a fleet to assist them in an attack on Byzantine-friendly Ancona.[105] He also sent Enrico Dandolo and Giovanni Badoer to Sicily to discuss a treaty of friendship with William II.[106]

While Enrico Dandolo was traveling south to Sicily, he ran into his father, who was on his way back to Venice with Byzantine ambassadors. Enrico listened to the Greek diplomats, who spoke of peace and held out hope for the release of the Venetian prisoners. Enrico Dandolo and Giovanni Badoer knew well that the purpose of their embassy to Sicily was to pressure Manuel Comnenus to make amends with the Venetians. If the imperial envoys were correct in their assessment, there was no need for their embassy. Indeed, the mission could hinder the release of the hostages—a consideration that the Byzantine envoys no doubt brought to their attention. The fate of the captive Venetians, of course, trumped all. Enrico Dandolo and Giovanni Badoer, therefore, abandoned their mission and returned home.[107]

In Venice, negotiations with the new Byzantine envoys crept along, so slowly that many began to suspect that the emperor's purpose was merely to play for time. In an effort to keep things moving, Doge Ziani again sent Enrico Dandolo to the court of William II, this time accompanied by Manasse Badoer, who had served with Vitale Dandolo on his recent diplomatic mission to Constantinople. It is possible that this embassy was meant to be covert, since apparently no record of it was available to Andrea Dandolo in the fourteenth century. It can be pieced together, however, from a group of private documents. In July 1174 Enrico Dandolo's brother, Andrea, signed over to him power to collect from the merchant Romano Mairano money that was to be paid in Venice that Christmas.[108] Immediately thereafter, Enrico Dandolo and Manasse Badoer sailed for Alexandria, where they expected to find William II.[109] The Norman leader had recently left Sicily with a large fleet to assist King Amalric of Jerusalem in the capture of the Egyptian port. William arrived in August, but Amalric died along the way. The Normans prepared to besiege the city, but a sortie put them to flight, first to their ships and then back to Sicily.[110] Enrico Dandolo and Manasse Badoer arrived in Alexandria shortly thereafter, probably in September. They found no William II, although Romano Mairano was there, as Dandolo had expected.[111]

Enrico Dandolo's transaction in Alexandria with Romano Mairano is often interpreted as evidence of his career as a businessman, traveling among the ports of the Mediterranean in search of profit.[112] Yet, aside from this lone document, there is no evidence for his involvement in any commercial activity outside Venice. Sailing across the Mediterranean for his brother to collect money that would have been paid in person two months later is hardly a savvy business deal. Indeed, it is no deal at all—simply a transfer of authority to collect on a previous contract. Dandolo's brother would have had his money much sooner had he simply sat tight in Venice and waited for Mairano to sail into port.[113] He gave Enrico the authority to collect the money in Alexandria not because it was a more efficient way of collecting a debt (it was not), but because it was a safe means of providing funds for an overseas journey. It was not, however, the purpose of the journey. It strains credulity to believe that two men, Enrico Dandolo and Manasse Badoer, intimately involved in ongoing Venetian diplomacy, sailed to Alexandria while the Normans besieged it with no thought at all of meeting with William II. They must have come to talk.

Enrico Dandolo had twice attempted to negotiate with the Norman king and twice failed. It was rare, although not unheard of, for vessels to leave Egypt for the west in the late fall, which was one of the few times during the year when the strong northwest winds subsided enough to make the trip possible. Despite the winds' cooperative nature, the weather took on a foul mood, making navigation dicey in the Mediterranean from September to March.[114] Nevertheless, Romano Mairano risked it. His ship was safe in a Venetian dock that winter.[115] But there is no evidence that Enrico Dandolo accompanied him on the hazardous voyage. For Mairano, time was money; he had contracts to make and fulfill in Venice before the start of the next sailing season. Dandolo lacked that incentive. Indeed, he had good reasons to stay in Egypt. Saladin and his troops were in Alexandria for at least part of the winter. According to the *Historia ducum veneti-corum*, written in 1229, Venice concluded a *"pacem firmissimam"* with Saladin in

1175.[116] Venetian merchants were never as active in Egypt as their counterparts from Genoa and Pisa. However, with Byzantium's ports now off-limits, it made sense to open the Egyptian market, even just a crack. The Venetians may have been granted a *funduq* (a merchant hostel) in Alexandria at this time, but they had no colony in the city. Venetian merchants remained scarce in Egypt, coming and going rather quickly, even bringing their own notaries to record transactions.[117]

The failed Norman attack on the Egyptian city was an obvious topic of conversation in the streets, homes, and markets of Alexandria during the winter of 1174–75. From locals and fellow Venetians Dandolo could learn of the Normans' landing and of their retreat. Despite their great fleet strength, William's primary thrust was on land. The rout of his troops had occurred while his soldiers were busy constructing siege machinery. For the seafaring Venetians this must have seemed an inefficient means of attack. Although Alexandria's ports were heavily fortified, once breached the city had few defenses. What Dandolo learned in 1174 about Egyptian strengths and weaknesses added to his abilities as a commander in the Fourth Crusade, whose initial objective was Egypt. When he took the cross in 1202, proclaiming that no one could lead the Venetian crusaders as well as he could, he may have been thinking of Alexandria and the lessons he had learned there from Muslim victories and Norman mistakes.

Back in Venice negotiations with the Byzantine envoys had reached another stalemate. Still insisting that peace was at hand, the envoys urged the doge to send another legation to Constantinople. Ziani obliged in 1174, again sending Vitale Dandolo to the imperial court. The old judge departed, bidding farewell to his long-time friends and associates, Doge Ziani and Orio Mastropiero. He would never see them again. Accompanied by Enrico Navigaioso, Vitale Dandolo made the journey to Constantinople, where he presented his credentials and requested an imperial audience.[118] Manuel ignored the request, while his agents begged excuse for the delay. At the age of ninety or more, Vitale Dandolo had no more time to spend on patient diplomacy. There in Constantinople, still hoping to secure release for his captive countrymen, Vitale Dandolo died. Enrico Navigaioso oversaw his burial and then headed back to Venice. Manuel sent two imperial legates back with him.[119]

During his lifetime Vitale Dandolo witnessed enormous changes both for his family and for Venice; indeed, he had been at the center of many of them. Crusader, lawyer, judge, statesman, and diplomat, he served his country until the very last moments of his life. He had been instrumental in the political reforms that would engender a sober, conservative state at the expense of ducal and popular authority. His personal reputation for fairness, intelligence, and wisdom, as well as his political expertise, promised that his family would not sink back into political obscurity after his death. What the Dandolo later became, what Venice later became, was a direct result of Vitale Dandolo's efforts. Before he was the conqueror of Constantinople, Enrico Dandolo was better known as the son of Vitale.

FOUR

COMING of AGE

1175–1192

ews of his father's death may have reached Enrico Dandolo while he was still overseas. Assuming that he wintered in Egypt, the earliest that he could have taken ship was March 1175, when Venetian vessels began their eastward journey to the ports of Syria or Cyprus. There a ship's captain could conduct business and join a westbound convoy propelled by favorable winds. This circuitous route home was not only safer and more profitable, but during the summer it was the only way a large-capacity sailing vessel like a roundship could sail west.[1] Perhaps Dandolo visited the crusader port of Tyre, which had a sizable Venetian community, or Acre. The latter was less important to Venetian merchants, but the vice-count of the city was one of Enrico's kinsmen, a Giovanni Dandolo.[2]

Whether he learned of Vitale's death abroad or after his return to Venice, it is clear that Enrico Dandolo's world had changed. Already in his sixties, it was at last time for him to take his father's position as the clan's leader and political representative. While he and his father were absent on their respective diplomatic missions, it was Enrico's brother Andrea who had represented the family as a judge in the ducal court.[3] Upon his brother's return, Andrea stepped down, allowing Enrico to take his place at the doge's side. It appears that throughout the remainder of Sebastiano Ziani's reign Enrico Dandolo remained a conspicuous and regular member of the ducal court.[4]

Enrico Dandolo experienced another, and far more profound, shift in his world during his travels to the East in 1174 and 1175, for it was at this time that his eyesight began to fade. In later years his blindness would become one of his most noted characteristics, remarked upon by all medieval and modern writers. Then as now, observers attempted to reconcile Dandolo's lack of sight with his remarkable career. In some cases this led to flights of fancy. In 1204, for example, just after the conquest of Constantinople, a legend circulated in the streets of the city that Emperor Manuel I Comnenus had blinded Dandolo during his embassy of 1172. The rumor was recorded in the *Chronicle of Novgorod:* "Manuel blinded this doge; for many philosophers had begged the emperor: 'If you let this doge [sic] go whole, then he will do much harm to your empire.' And the emperor not wishing to kill him, he ordered his eyes to be blinded with glass; and his eyes were as if uninjured, but he saw nothing."[5] No other contemporary source mentions this story, not even the chatty Robert of Clari, who delighted in relating street legends and conspiracy theories. Although the rumor apparently did not last long in Constantinople, it did become part of family lore, surfacing again in Andrea Dandolo's fourteenth-century chronicle. In that version, however, the imperial fortune tellers are absent. Instead, Dandolo is partially blinded because he bravely defended Venice against Manuel Comnenus's insults. After his return to Venice, the story goes on, Enrico Dandolo carefully kept his poor vision a secret.[6]

Blaming Manuel Comnenus for Dandolo's blindness made for a colorful tale in the aftermath of the conquest of Constantinople, but it was just a story. In truth, Enrico Dandolo never had the opportunity to gainsay insults against Venice in 1172 because he never obtained an imperial audience.[7] As for the soothsayers, they somehow lack the ring of truth. In any event, there is solid evidence that Enrico Dandolo could still see long after 1172. According to the thirteenth-century *Historia ducum veneticorum,* Doge Sebastiano Ziani carefully verified that Dandolo and his colleague were unharmed when they returned to Venice.[8] Even more compelling is the evidence of Dandolo's surviving signatures. In Venice, as elsewhere, those who could not read were not allowed to sign or mark a document signifying their agreement, as the document could easily be contested on the grounds that the person had not been properly informed about what he or she was signing. Instead, a Venetian notary would read the document to the person and, after his or her assent, write "Signum N. qui hec fieri rogavit."[9] This rule extended from the lowest classes up to the doge himself. Indeed, Enrico Dandolo signed no documents during his tenure as doge because his blindness would have made his signature invalid. But he did sign documents twenty years earlier, after his return from Constantinople.

In September 1174, during his stay in Alexandria, Enrico Dandolo signed a commercial document. The signature is straight, clear, and legible (see fig. 3).[10] More importantly, it exists, proving that Dandolo could see well after his embassy to Manuel Comnenus. The Venetian shipboard notary would not have accepted the signature of a blind man, nor would the other party in the document, in this case the business-savvy Romano Mairano.

His next surviving signature is even more revealing. As noted previously, Dandolo served as a judge in the ducal court, a position that required literacy.[11] His presence in the court testifies that he could still see, but his signature suggests that his eyesight had already deteriorated. In a court document made in October 1176, Dandolo signed immediately after the doge, using the standard formulation, "+Ego Henricus Dand[ul]o iudex manu mea subscripsi." But the quality of the signature is very poor (see fig. 4). After a good start it begins to arc downward, while the individual letters for the most part remain vertically aligned; this is especially clear in the letters of "Dand[ul]o iudex."[12] A downward arc of this sort is not uncommon among those with poor eyesight. Although able to keep individual letters straight, when lifting the pen to make each subsequent letter the writer unconsciously moves his arm closer to the body, resulting in the downward arc. In Dandolo's case, the defect was so exaggerated that the other judge, Andrea Delfino, was forced to conform his own signature to Dandolo's stray one. While it is true that medieval Venetians were hardly known for careful penmanship, in the thousands of twelfth-century documents that I have examined I have never encountered a signature that trails so far from its proper place. Here on this ragged parchment, we appear to have an image of Enrico Dandolo's encroaching blindness.

Given just one troubled signature, it is impossible to say with certainty how much of his sight Dandolo had lost by October 1176. One assumes that the sapientes, notaries, and other members of the ducal court would have objected to a judge who could not recognize people or walk through a room unaided, so it is unlikely that he was yet completely blind. He probably retained sufficient sight not to arouse suspicion. Still, the doge at least would have noticed Dandolo's difficulty at the inkwell. No later documents from the court of Ziani survive. Yet from subsequent events it is clear that Dandolo remained an active member until the doge's death in 1178.[13] Perhaps Ziani ignored Dandolo's failing eyesight, provided that he could keep up appearances. If so, there may indeed be a kernel of truth in Andrea Dandolo's account of Enrico disguising his blindness.

What was the cause of this rapid degeneration of Dandolo's vision between September 1174 and October 1176? Twenty-five years later his friend, Geoffrey of Villehardouin, noted that, despite his blindness, Dandolo's eyes appeared to be quite healthy.[14] When asked about it, Dandolo said that he had lost his vision after a blow to the head.[15] This explanation fits well with the rest of the evidence. A severe blow to the back of the head can indeed cause partial or total

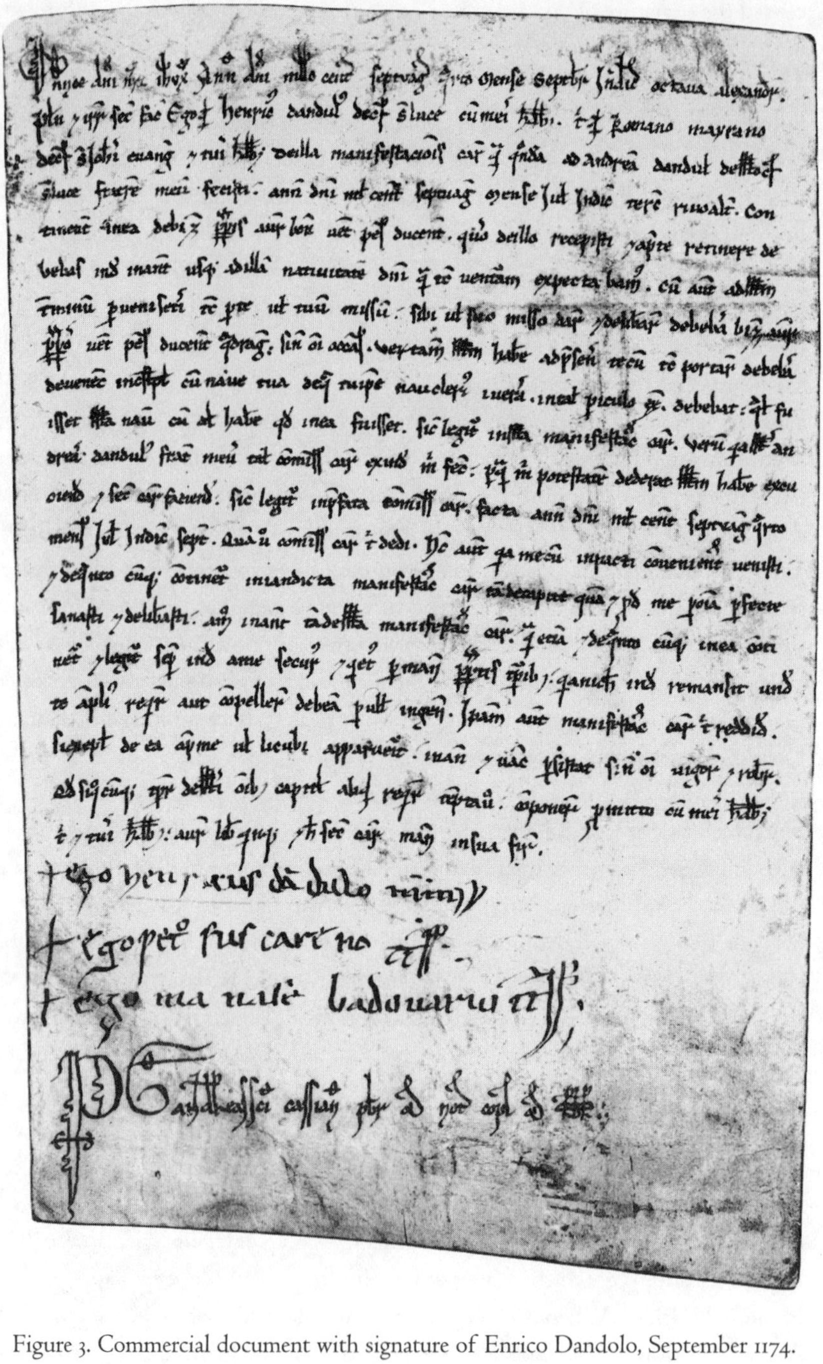

Figure 3. Commercial document with signature of Enrico Dandolo, September 1174.
(ASV, S. Zaccaria, B. 35 perg.)

loss of vision as a result of damage to the occipital lobe of the brain. Cortical blindness, as it is called, is not caused by a defect in the eyes, but in the processing of visual signals. Even today the effects of injuries to the brain are unpredictable. It is not unusual, however, for someone affected by damage to the occipital lobe to lose partial vision, including sometimes the ability to read and write. With children the brain is usually able to recover, but that is much less likely in adults. Since Enrico Dandolo was in his sixties in 1175, it is not surprising that his vision never improved. In fact, his blindness eventually became total.[16] Continued degeneration of vision can occur when the damaged occipital lobe is unable to process adequately the incoming signals from the eyes and therefore over time shuts down ocular reception completely.[17] While it is perilous to render a medical judgment on one who has been dead for eight centuries, the evidence does suggest that Enrico Dandolo suffered from cortical blindness caused by a blow to the back of the head. The quick degeneration of his eyesight in the space of two years, the continued degeneration over subsequent years, the apparent continued health of his eyes, and the evidence of his own testimony all point to that unhappy diagnosis.[18]

While the onset of blindness was naturally a matter of great importance to Enrico Dandolo, it has become a defining feature of the man in modern scholarship. Indeed, this one physical defect has been blamed by various authors for the generally poor relations between Byzantium and Venice in the late twelfth century, the diversion of the Fourth Crusade, and the conquest of Constantinople in 1204. This is all the more remarkable when we consider that there is no source for this link, either contemporary or late. It comes instead from a stitching together of the rumor of Manuel Comnenus's complicity in Dandolo's blindness and the unrelated testimony of Nicetas Choniates. The latter, a Byzan-

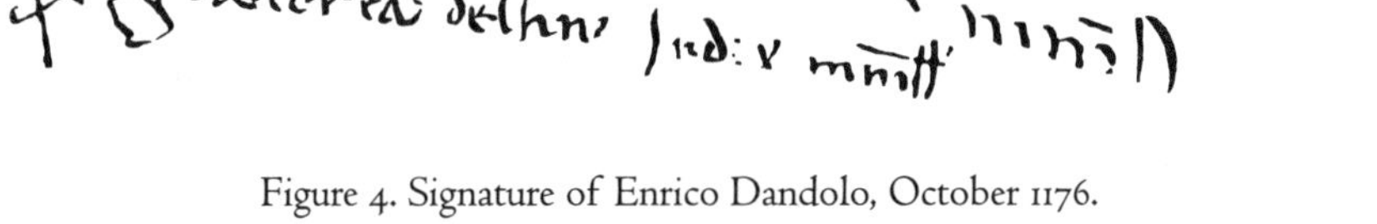

Figure 4. Signature of Enrico Dandolo, October 1176.
(ASV, S. Nicolò di Lido, b. 9, Proc. 77.)

tine senator and historian, lived through the events of the Fourth Crusade and fled Constantinople after its fall. Not surprisingly, Choniates had nothing good to say about Enrico Dandolo. Writing after Dandolo's death, Choniates contended that the Venetian leader bore a strong grudge against Greeks for the events of 1171. Dandolo, he wrote, considered it "nothing less than a death sentence not to exact vengeance from the Romans for their violence to his people," so he labored over "secret designs" to conquer Constantinople.[19] Of course, as a Byzantine refugee Nicetas Choniates had no way of knowing what was hidden in Enrico Dandolo's heart. Leaving that aside, it is important to note that, although the senator accurately recorded Dandolo's blindness, he did not blame the Byzantines for it.[20]

Putting all of this together, some have concluded that because the Byzantines were responsible for Dandolo's blindness (as the rumor contends) he harbored a deep desire for vengeance against them (as Choniates claims).[21] In other words, a false rumor is joined to an unfounded assertion. In the last century or so, although scholars have tended to discount the story of Manuel blinding the future doge, most have been reluctant to decouple Dandolo's blindness from his attitude toward Byzantium. As a result, despite the lack of evidence, many scholars still insist that Dandolo's blindness was linked to his hatred of Greeks, which subsequently contributed to the diversion of the Fourth Crusade.[22] In an unfortunate attempt to preserve this linkage Steven Runciman, in his *History of the Crusades*, reported that during Dandolo's embassy to Constantinople in 1172 he was blinded by a blow to the head suffered during a street brawl. As a result, Dandolo harbored great "bitterness" toward the Greeks.[23] Runciman's brawl was pure fabrication, but the popularity of his work has led to its uncritical acceptance by some authors.[24]

In reality, Enrico Dandolo's blindness had nothing to do with Byzantium. It occurred as a result of a head injury suffered at a time when Venetians were *banned* from the Byzantine Empire. Dandolo, therefore, did not blame Greeks for his loss of sight and consequently would not have nurtured a festering hatred of them because of it. History would require less thought if difficult problems could be explained with facile conspiracy theories, but that is rarely the case.

After burying Vitale Dandolo in Constantinople, Enrico Navigaioso returned to Venice with new Byzantine envoys in June 1175. Apparently negotiations did not go well, or perhaps Doge Ziani and his advisors were tired of being put off. The doge quite visibly dispatched a new embassy to Sicily, this one led by Orio Mastropiero.[25] Mastropiero's luck at rendezvousing with the Norman king was better than Enrico Dandolo's on his earlier missions. William II received the envoys graciously and quickly agreed to a new treaty of friendship between the two states.[26] This was not, however, an alliance, but a renewal of the treaty of 1154, which had affirmed Venice's rights in the Adriatic and pledged both powers to respect the other's citizens and spheres of influence. As we have seen, the primary purpose of Venice's embassies to the Norman kingdom was to provoke Manuel Comnenus into releasing the hostages and making peace with Venice. The treaty of 1175, therefore, was meant to capture the emperor's attention merely by its existence, not by its terms. Indeed, the Republic still retained a clause in the treaty exempting from its provisions Venetian warships defending the Byzantine Empire.[27]

When Orio Mastropiero and his colleagues returned to Venice they contrasted the friendly reception of William II with the cynical delays of Manuel Comnenus. With the approval of the people and a bit of fanfare, Doge Ziani expelled the Byzantine ambassadors from Venice, thus closing diplomatic channels that had, in four years, failed to produce any serious results.[28] This, too, was meant to attract the emperor's notice.

But Manuel Comnenus did not notice; his attention was hardly on Venice at all, consumed as he was with preparations for a crusade to the East. After the death of Nur ed-Din, the emperor began organizing a massive expedition aimed at conquering Muslim territories in Asia Minor and Egypt. It was to be the crowning achievement of his reign, an opportunity not only to reestablish Byzantine control over the eastern Mediterranean but also to position himself as the true defender of Christendom. These aspirations were extinguished, however, when a Turkish army crushed the Byzantine advance at the Battle of Myriocephalon, in 1176. This crippling defeat permanently removed Byzantium as a player in the affairs of western Europe and the Latin East. What Manuel Comnenus had striven so hard to build now crumbled around him.[29]

In Europe, both sides in the continuing struggle between pope and emperor could now safely ignore Constantinople. Manuel was isolated, with few friends, no allies, and eager enemies. For the moment the Normans of Sicily were involved in Italian matters, but when they again turned their attention to the conquest of Greece, Manuel could rely only on the unreliable Genoese for support. Faced with this calculus, it appears that Manuel made a goodwill gesture to the Venetians, releasing some of the hostages. The initiative apparently went nowhere, however, so the emperor focused his diplomatic efforts elsewhere.[30]

Although securing the release of their loved ones remained a priority for the Venetians, their gaze was also on the great struggle between Frederick Barbarossa and Pope Alexander III, now entering its final act. By mid-1176 it was clear even to Frederick that he could not defeat the alliance of the pope, the Lombard towns, and the Normans. Plans for a peace conference were made, but its location posed a problem. Ravenna and Bologna were suggested, yet neither was acceptable to both sides. With still no agreement on the location, Alexander III left the Norman kingdom in early 1177, sailing up the Adriatic toward Venice. After an eventful voyage he landed at Zara, on March 13.[31] The first pope ever to visit the city, Alexander received an enthusiastic welcome from its citizens. The ruler of Zara was its archbishop, Lampridus, a subordinate to Patriarch Dandolo. Lampridus did not in the least enjoy being the only archbishop in Christendom answerable to another metropolitan. The state of affairs had already led to armed rebellion, so it must have been a topic of conversation between the archbishop and the pope. Based on subsequent events, it is safe to assume that Lampridus found in Alexander a sympathetic ear, although at the moment there was little that the pope could do. Venice had played and would continue to play an important supporting role in Alexander's struggle with the emperor. This was not the time to anger the Patriarch of Grado.

On March 24, 1177, the pope's vessel landed at the Lido. The sons of Doge Ziani and a party of leading Venetians received him with honor. It is possible that Enrico Dandolo (the younger) was among this group. After spending the night at the monastery of San Nicolò, Alexander boarded a lavish state galley and was rowed to the Piazza San Marco, now jammed with thousands of people eager to see the pope and receive his blessing. As his galley approached the piazza Alexander was met by the doge, Patriarch Dandolo, and the Patriarch of Aquileia, Ulrich II of Treffen, all in their own ceremonial galleys. Moving to the doge's galley, the pope was seated between Ziani and Dandolo and then taken to the piazetta. The crowds parted as the pope, doge, patriarchs, and leading citizens processed to the church of San Marco. After hearing mass, the pope blessed the people in the church and the crowds in the piazza. He then boarded the doge's galley, which took him down the Grand Canal to the patriarch's palace near the Rialto market. Alexander would remain the houseguest of Patriarch Dandolo for the next two weeks.[32]

The arrival of the pope not only underscored Venice's growing importance in western European affairs but, within the city itself, also cast in stark relief the power and position of the new families that had come to prominence over the course of the twelfth century. The patriarch of Grado, the doge of Venice, and most of his court were from families that had scarcely been visible in the eleventh century. The Ziani family was particularly prominent, but so too were the Dandolo. It is striking that when Alexander III met with the secular and ecclesiastical leaders of Venice, prominent among both groups were elderly men named Enrico Dandolo.

After a full schedule of ceremonies and the showering of Venice with privileges, Alexander III left on April 9 bound for Ferrara. There he met with representatives of the Lombard towns and the German emperor in an attempt to settle on a place for a peace conference. The Lombards, who had begun to question the depth of the pope's commitment to them, insisted on Bologna, where they felt sure they could control matters. Not surprisingly, Frederick's agents objected to this choice, suggesting Ravenna, Pavia, or Venice. Frederick himself favored Venice, because it was neutral, trustworthy, and "subject to God alone"—which is precisely why the Lombards opposed it. Nevertheless, after much arm-twisting Alexander finally persuaded the Lombards to relent. To assuage their fears, the pope asked Frederick to remain outside Venetian territory until all sides had agreed upon a final peace. Frederick agreed. Envoys were then sent to the doge of Venice requesting oaths of safe passage, which were promptly granted.[33]

As anyone who has strolled through the Great Council Chamber in the Ducal Palace and seen there the sixteenth-century depictions of the Republic's history knows, the Peace of Venice was an epic moment in the developing Venetian self-image.[34] Subsequent centuries would profusely color it with civic pride, religious piety, and not a few apocryphal legends. The events of 1177 were well remembered because they both shaped and were shaped by the "myth of Venice," which extolled the Republic as an impregnable citadel of justice and an ardent defender of the faith.[35]

Frederick Barbarossa went to Ravenna, where he received regular reports from his agents. Pope Alexander celebrated Easter in Ferrara and then returned to Venice with his cardinals on May 10. Once again he was escorted grandly to San Marco and then to Patriarch Dandolo's palace, which became the headquarters for all subsequent negotiations. Twice a day, every day, the patriarch welcomed the various ambassadors to his palace for another session of talks. The building itself was filled to capacity with lodgers, including the pope, his cardinals, and other clerical envoys from across Italy. The Rialto area, always buzzing with activity, was now crawling with diplomats as well as merchants. In fact, all parts of Venice had their share of visitors as the city swelled with the thousands of dignitaries and churchmen hoping to affect the peace or gain favors from the emperor or pope.[36]

Negotiations dragged on for many weeks, but by the beginning of July it was clear that an agreement was close at hand. In order to minimize delays in the final negotiations, Frederick requested that he be allowed to relocate from Ravenna to Chioggia, on the outskirts of the lagoon. Sometime around July 6, Alexander gave his permission, provided that Frederick renew his promise not to enter Venice without papal permission. Shortly after Frederick's arrival at Chioggia a party of cardinals and German agents were sent to gain the emperor's approval on a final draft of the peace. If agreed to, it would end the schism and grant truce to the Lombards and Normans. At the patriarchal palace, all waited in hopeful expectation.[37]

At this point an interesting episode occurred that provides some insight into the doge's court and its relationship with the popular arengo. The only source for the incident is Archbishop Romuald of Salerno, an ambassador from King William II of Sicily who was staying at Patriarch Dandolo's palace with the pope. According to Romuald, a great crisis occurred when a body of sympathetic Venetians traveled to Chioggia to suggest to Frederick that he enter Venice without the pope's permission. Frederick, who had just been presented with the latest draft of the peace treaty, was interested but cautious. He told the group that if the doge and the people of Venice would agree to such a thing, he would be willing. Straightaway they went to the doge, while Frederick stalled the papal envoys. In a large assembly in San Marco, the group demanded that the doge immediately bring Frederick into Venice. They likewise stirred up the people into rebellion, claiming that Ziani had failed in his responsibility to see to the comfort of all participants in the conference. Frederick, they reported, was languishing at Chioggia, where the heat, flies, and gnats were intolerable. Surely, he would remember this insult and repay Venice for it. The doge responded, saying that he and his council had sworn oaths that they would not allow Frederick into Venice without Alexander's permission. The rebels were unmoved. After a day of argument, a few of the assembled were sent to the patriarchal palace, which they boldly entered, demanding that the pope be roused from bed and then requesting his permission for Frederick's entry into Venice. The startled pope responded that he would be glad to give that permission as soon as Frederick had sworn to the terms of the treaty before him. He expected his cardinals to return with word of Frederick's decision very soon. Until then, however, the emperor must not enter the city. Upset and angry, the delegation left.

The next day, according to Romuald, a rumor spread throughout Venice that the doge was preparing to bring Frederick into the city anyway. So frightened were the Lombard ambassadors that they fled to Treviso. The Normans readied galleys to take the pope out of Venice, but Alexander insisted that they wait to hear something definite from Chioggia. And so, filled with zeal, Romuald and the other Normans went to see the doge. Upon entering the ducal court, they rebuked

Ziani for failing to keep his oath, reminding him of the kindnesses that their lord, William II, had bestowed on him. The doge responded with soothing words, but the Normans were not placated. They returned to their galleys and, with great fanfare and the blowing of trumpets, prepared to leave the city, telling anyone who would listen that when they returned to Sicily they would report the faithlessness of the Venetians to the king. This sparked a popular uprising, particularly among those with family or assets in Norman ports. Angry mobs descended on the doge's palace and demanded an explanation. Ziani put the entire blame on the evil rebels and then sent a delegation to the pope to beg forgiveness. He also had it proclaimed throughout Venice that no one was to speak about Frederick coming to Venice before the pope commanded it. Therefore, as a result of the quick Norman response, a diplomatic and political crisis was averted. When Frederick learned of this he agreed immediately to the peace treaty.[38]

Much ink has been spilled (and more will be spilled here) attempting to assess the accuracy of this story and the identity of the various Venetian groups that Romuald describes.[39] We must, however, accept at the outset the limitations of our source. Romuald of Salerno had little experience with Venetian government or society. He is, therefore, a poor source on which to base an analysis of the class structure or political organization of the city, as some have tried to do. He describes, for example, the rebellious Venetians who favored bringing Frederick into the city as "common people" (*populares*); yet elsewhere has the doge address them as "lords" (*domini*) and later still discusses a mass uprising of commoners against the rebels. For the most part, Romuald is a sober source, although he naturally exaggerates both the importance of the Norman mission of which he was a part and the awe others had for the power and majesty of William II. However, his testimony cannot be taken at face value when he recounts conversations that he could not have heard and events he could not have witnessed, including the secret talks between the rebellious Venetians and Frederick, the meeting in San Marco between the doge and rebels, and the mass meeting of the citizens in response to the Norman threats. For these, he is relying either on hearsay or on his own belief about what was behind the events he witnessed. We can, however, take seriously Romuald's testimony for those events that he personally saw or took part in.

If we remember Romuald's limitations and factor in the political climate of the time, it is possible to come closer to an explanation of just what did happen. First, the story of Frederick's secret negotiations with the Venetian populares must be rejected. It is unlikely that the Holy Roman Emperor was in the habit of giving audience to commoners or taking seriously their grand plans to seize control of the conference. Even if we assume that the populares were the "do-mini" that Romuald later describes, it would make no sense on either side for Frederick to enter Venice without papal permission. The Venetians had no reason to embrace a partisanship that they had scrupulously avoided from the start. For his part, Frederick had already sworn to the German lords that he would obey the pope in this matter, remaining outside Venice until given leave to enter. He had nothing to gain and everything to lose by entering the city early.[40]

Although Romuald insists that the plan was to bring Frederick into the city so that he could take control of the conference, the actual events Romuald witnessed and the words he heard spoken tell a different story. Romuald reports that an assembly of Venetians was debating the question of Frederick's arrival for an entire day. However, he witnessed only the arrival at the patriarchal palace of a delegation demanding to see the pope. Romuald's description of what was said at the assembly is then contradicted by the words of the Venetian delegates, who came, after all, to request the pope's permission for the emperor's entry. If the court had decided to transport Frederick to Venice without papal approval, as Romuald reports, why were they seeking papal approval?

The best information for the dynamics in the ducal court comes from Romuald's description of his own visit there. At the beginning he notes the large number of people present, among whom may well have been Enrico Dandolo. He describes the legates' ultimatum to the doge, threatening to leave Venice and report his behavior to William II. Doge Ziani then responded "peacefully and kindly," saying that he was amazed at their agitation over the matter. Venice in no way wished to anger William II or his representatives. Ziani continued, "because we believed that peace had been established between him [William II] and the emperor, we desired that the lord king's peace be consummated here in our city, just like a very close friend. And because of this we will not give you permission to leave, but we affectionately ask for your prudence, so that in your houses, safe and without fear, you may await the arrival of the emperor."[41] According to the doge himself, therefore, there was a desire in the court for the final peace to be celebrated in Venice, as well as some confusion as to whether the emperor had yet agreed to that peace.

It appears, then, that the Normans simply overreacted to a rumor, which would explain why no other source took note of the incident. It is clear from the doge's words that he and his council feared that Frederick might conclude the peace elsewhere. Since Chioggia was likely as uncomfortable as Romuald reports, it is not surprising that some Venetians worried that the emperor would leave the lagoon as soon as possible. Ziani was under a great deal of pressure.

On the one hand, he did not want to lose the "Peace of Venice" to Ravenna or some other Italian town; on the other, he could not bring Frederick into the comforts of the ducal palace without the pope's approval. As the many depictions of the Peace of Venice attest, it was no small matter to the Venetians that their city host this historic event.

It also appears that the doge and his court received an erroneous report that the emperor had already accepted the peace terms in Chioggia. Why then, they wondered, had the pope not commanded them to bring Frederick into Venice at once? Since time was of the essence, a delegation was dispatched to the pope, rousing him from bed and requesting immediate permission to transport the emperor. The pope's response, which Romuald likely heard, was that Frederick had not yet agreed to the peace but that the cardinals would return with word very soon. The Venetian court's eagerness to transport Frederick to the palace as soon as possible, therefore, led to the rumors that Frederick and the Venetian leaders were conspiring together. Ziani was genuinely surprised at the anger of the Norman delegates because he and his court saw this as a matter of logistics, not an attempt to hijack the peace.

Of equal interest in this episode is the response of the people of Venice. When news spread that the Normans were departing, there was a groundswell of anger aimed at the doge. In this case, Romuald, who was lodged near the Rialto markets, was in a position to observe what he reports. And so it was that one rumor led to a counterrumor, both destructive to the peace. To put an end to the matter Ziani ordered that no one speak about Frederick entering Venice before the pope had given his permission. From the perspective of Venetian government, this episode makes clear that, despite the increasing concentration of power in the ducal court since 1172, the arengo of citizens still held considerable authority in Venice.

On July 21 and 22 all parties swore to the terms of the newly crafted peace treaty. The pope at once asked Doge Ziani to bring the prodigal son to him. The Venetians, of course, were quick to do so. The next day six rich galleys loaded with various important personages went to Chioggia to collect Frederick and transport him to the monastery of San Nicolò, on the Lido. Meanwhile, the citizens were busy preparing the Piazza San Marco for the arrival of the emperor and his meeting with the pope. Ships' masts were set up along the length of the piazzetta, each bearing long banners of St. Mark. In front of the church a dais was constructed for the pope's throne.[42]

The following day, July 24, was a Sunday. Alexander III woke early and went to San Marco, where he heard mass. He then dispatched four cardinals to the

Lido to receive Frederick's renunciation of the schism and his promise of obedience to Alexander. Once word of the emperor's absolution had reached San
Marco, Doge Ziani, Patriarch Dandolo, and several other Venetian notables
boarded the doge's galley for the Lido, where they greeted Frederick. The emperor boarded the doge's vessel and was seated between Ziani and Dandolo. The
galley, now filled to capacity with the cardinals and various Venetians, was rowed
to San Marco.[43] At 10 A.M. those on the galley disembarked and walked in procession down the center of the piazzetta to the church, where the pope was seated
on his throne surrounded by cardinals, archbishops, and bishops. Several Venetian notables, current judges or perhaps other members of the court, accompanied the doge in the procession. Enrico Dandolo (the younger) was among
them.[44] Patriarch Dandolo, who was also in the procession, took his place at the
pope's right hand.[45] The emperor approached Alexander, took off his purple
cloak, knelt, and kissed the pope's feet. With tears of joy, Alexander lifted Frederick up and gave him the kiss of peace. Bells rang and the people lifted their
voices in the *Te Deum.* It was a moment of high drama ending nearly two decades
of strife between pope and emperor.[46]

Alexander and Frederick remained in Venice for some time, giving them ample
opportunities to reward the Republic with privileges and other largesse. Patriarch Dandolo and the pope were both strong supporters of reform orders, particularly the canons regular. In April, during the pope's first visit to Venice,
Alexander had formally dedicated a new church of the canons regular, Santa
Maria della Carità.[47] Now, with the peace settled, Dandolo was in a position to
ask for favors. It appears that he directed the pope's attention to the church of
San Salvatore. Three decades earlier, the conversion of the clergy of this church
to the canons regular had precipitated the bitter struggle between Dandolo and
the bishop of Castello—a struggle that ultimately led to the exile of the patriarch and his family. Accompanied by Patriarch Dandolo and Frederick Barbarossa, Alexander dedicated the newly rebuilt church of San Salvatore. The previous structure had been destroyed in the same fire that wiped out the Dandolo
compound ten years earlier.[48] The pope blessed the high altar, bestowed a number of indulgences on various portions of the church, then celebrated the first
mass there.[49] It was a glorious ceremony, one that the canons of San Salvatore
would recount proudly for centuries;[50] for Patriarch Dandolo, it must have been
a gratifying moment.

Although the patriarch of Grado could look with pleasure on the pope's favor
toward San Salvatore, he did not fare so well in other matters. In the wake of the
Peace of Venice a new political landscape was conspiring against Dandolo's ju-

risdictional interests beyond the lagoon. Nowhere was this clearer than in the patriarch's long rivalry with nearby Aquileia. As long as Aquileia supported the imperial antipope, Grado had fared well with Alexander. That changed with the accession of Ulrich II of Treffen (1161–82), who began his patriarchate on a belligerent note, attacking the cathedral of Grado by force. Doge Vitale II Michiel led a counterattack that not only repulsed the invaders but also captured Ulrich and his twelve canons. As a condition of their release, Ulrich promised that he and his successors would henceforth send to the people of Venice on every Fat Tuesday a bull and twelve pigs, meant to represent the patriarch of Aquileia and his canons. Thus began one of the most enduring civic ceremonies in Venetian history. Each year for centuries the animals were solemnly brought to the Piazza San Marco, where, under the watchful eye of the doge and his council, they were tried and condemned to death. The revelers would then chase them around the piazza, capture, decapitate, roast, and eat them. The event was so popular that in the fifteenth century, when the patriarchate of Aquileia was merged with that of Grado, the Venetian government agreed to continue to provide the annual bull and pigs at public expense.[51]

When the antipope Victor IV died in 1164, Ulrich brought his church into communion with Alexander III. This put him in a unique position. He had come to the throne of Aquileia through his friendship with Frederick Barbarossa, but the growth of Venetian power on the mainland meant that Aquileia and its suffragans were increasingly under Venice's sphere of influence. With considerable political skill, Ulrich was able to retain his friendship with the emperor and recognize Alexander as pope, all the while enjoying the support of Venice. He used his position to act as an honest broker during the years of the struggle and, in 1169, was named a papal legate.[52] Now that the pope and the emperor were at peace, both men were eager to reward Ulrich for his services. Frederick extended the secular jurisdiction of the patriarchate of Aquileia.[53] Alexander confirmed the patriarch of Aquileia's right to wear the pallium and his jurisdiction over sixteen dioceses, including those in Istria claimed by the patriarch of Grado.[54]

It was probably also at this time that Alexander transferred control over the church of San Giorgio in Venice to the patriarch of Aquileia.[55] Since Venice had extended its authority across the lands of the patriarchate of Aquileia, Ulrich naturally wanted a place at the center of power. Just as the patriarchs of Grado had long ago begun spending time at San Silvestro in Venice, so the patriarch of Aquileia gravitated toward San Giorgio. The transfer of this church also tells us something about the Venetian government's willingness to allow the jurisdiction of the Istrian bishoprics to be lost to Grado at a time when Venice's leaders were in a position to request papal favors. As Otto Demus noted, Istria was now securely under Venice's military and economic control. As long as the patriarch of Aquileia remained in Venice's orbit, it no longer mattered which prelate claimed jurisdiction over those lands.[56]

Numerous other bones of contention between Grado and Aquileia remained, but pope, emperor, and doge were now united in their desire to settle things at last. In March 1179, Patriarch Dandolo and his bishops traveled to Rome to attend the Third Lateran Council. There, with the representatives of Patriarch Ulrich, the details of a settlement were finalized. On July 24, 1180, in the presence of Alexander III and nine cardinals, Patriarch Dandolo formally ended the ancient disputes between Grado and Aquileia. He ceded all rights over the disputed dioceses in Istria, as well as the treasures stolen from the cathedral of Grado by Popone at the beginning of the eleventh century. He also agreed to a redrawing of jurisdictions on the mainland.[57]

Despite these losses, Dandolo retained the jewel in the patriarchate's crown: primacy over the metropolitan of Zara. It was this authority that made Grado a patriarchate in more than just name. Yet, even here, it seems that the pope hoped eventually to defuse the explosive situation. On November 24, 1179, Alexander wrote to Theobald, the new archbishop of Zara, reminding him that he owed respect and obedience to the patriarch of Grado.[58] However, on April 14, 1182, when Pope Lucius III confirmed Grado's privileges, he conceded to the patriarch not the primacy but the *prioratum* over the archbishop of Zara, his bishops, churches, and goods.[59] This was not a mistake, for it was reiterated in Urban III's confirmation of privileges sent on May 31, 1186.[60] This naturally made the relationship between the two sees uncertain—as it was probably meant to do. The question of Grado's jurisdiction over Zara could not be settled as easily as that of the Istrian bishops, for Zara itself was not firmly under Venetian control. It would remain a nexus of resistance against Venice for many years.

At about the same time that Dandolo was negotiating the settlement with the patriarch of Aquileia, he seems also to have been attempting to better consolidate his authority at home. Perhaps as early as 1177 he suggested to Alexander III that the patriarchate of Grado and the episcopal see of Castello be merged. He also enlisted the aid of the doge, who wrote a letter to the pope in support of the idea.[61] The doge noted that the patriarchate of Grado was an anachronism; moving it to Venice would not only better reflect the political realities of the twelfth century but would also put an end to the jurisdictional disputes between the two sees. Alexander replied with a friendly letter in which he agreed with the doge on almost every point, noting that it was indeed unusual for a minor see like Venice to be home to so many ecclesiastical disputes. However, while supporting the plan in principle, Alexander insisted that this was not the time to undertake it. He pointed out that Patriarch Enrico Dandolo was a very old man who would be lucky to live even two more years. Better to wait, he said—presumably until Dandolo died and was replaced with a younger man. Then, the pope promised, he would move swiftly to grant the doge's request.[62]

But it was Alexander III, not Patriarch Dandolo, who died before two years were out. By putting off the proposed union of Grado and Castello, the pope lost a valuable opportunity, for indeed the time was ripe. Patriarch Dandolo still had a decade or more to live, and the bishop of Castello, Vitale Michiel, does not appear to have opposed the merger.[63] Several centuries of ecclesiastical headaches could have been avoided if Alexander had seized the day and combined the sees. For the moment, however, the proposal was shelved, where it would remain until the establishment of the patriarchate of Venice in 1451.

Soon the grand and glorious party in Venice was over and the people of the city began the business of getting back to normal—or as normal as things could be while thousands were still held hostage overseas. It was in the early months of 1178 that the aged Doge Ziani fell gravely ill. In the doge's court there was now an urgent discussion concerning the means of selecting his replacement. The "good men" of the court clearly wanted to retain the power to select the new doge given to them by the people in 1172. Yet had that authority been bestowed on the doge's council indefinitely or only in an ad hoc fashion during a time of emergency? That was, of course, the question. Like the members of his court, Ziani wanted to keep this important privilege out of the hands of the people. These men all had a natural desire to concentrate power into their own hands, but they also genuinely feared the recklessness of the arengo, which had led to the disaster of 1172 and the murder of the doge. Over the past decade, the doge's council had grown substantially in size and was beginning to resemble the Great Council, whose precursor it was.[64] In any governing body, size breeds factionalism. To minimize this dynamic, the council decided to select four men who would in turn choose forty from the council to serve as electors of the new doge. After swearing to act in the best interest of Venice, the forty would then make their decision by a simple majority vote.[65] The selection of the Four, more so than the Forty, was all important. Yet it is not clear how these four were chosen or even if they were presented to the people for approval.[66] Sixteenth-century chroniclers sometimes identified Enrico Dandolo (the younger) as one of the Four, but that is unlikely.[67]

After the selection of the Four, Doge Ziani retired to the monastery of San

Giorgio Maggiore, where he died, in early April 1178. Three days later the Four appeared in the packed church of San Marco and read off their list of forty electors for the people's approval. Surely someone among the assembled must have noticed that the people were no longer being asked to choose their new doge, as they had throughout Venetian history, or even to approve a doge chosen by someone else, as they had done just six years earlier. Instead, their approval was being sought for the electors of a doge. If anyone objected, however, it is not recorded. Those selected for the Forty were the most powerful and respected men in the city. Many of them were marked by their association with Vitale II Michiel, who still cast a long shadow over Venetian politics. Near the top of the list was Enrico Dandolo, further underscoring that he had indeed assumed his father's position in the court.[68] By 1178, Dandolo, like his father, had served as a judge, was regularly at the doge's side, and now was named a ducal elector. Despite his failing eyesight, he continued to follow the new Venetian *cursus honorum*.[69]

After the people of Venice had approved the forty electors, the latter discharged their duty quickly. They turned again to Vitale Michiel's inner circle, electing Orio Mastropiero (1178–92). With Sebastiano Ziani and Vitale Dandolo now dead, the new doge was the last surviving member of the three closest advisors of the murdered doge. Like Ziani and Dandolo, Mastropiero was a member of a relatively new family grown wealthy in commercial ventures and only recently having entered the highest levels of political power in Venice. Like his colleagues, he was a conservative man who valued prudence and moderation in all things, nowhere more so than in Venice's relationship with Byzantium. The highest order of business for Venice remained the release of the hostages.

The election of Orio Mastropiero brought Enrico Dandolo's tenure in the ducal court to a rather abrupt end. It seems unlikely that the new doge had anything against Dandolo or his family; indeed, he appears to have trusted and supported them.[70] Dandolo's disappearance from the ducal court, therefore, must be attributed to his failing eyesight. He already saw poorly in 1176. If Doge Ziani and the other members of the court did not have the heart to remove him from their number, the election of a new doge provided a useful opportunity to assemble a court without him. Enrico Dandolo would remain an important man in Venice, but his elimination from the court must have been a great disappointment to him. Old and blind, he looked like a man whose political career had come to an end.

After Vitale Dandolo's death in 1174, Enrico and his two brothers had retained their *fraterna*, a legal status that kept the family and its wealth unified. This made sense during the reign of Ziani, when Enrico Dandolo, as the pater familias, represented the family at court; now the arrangement was no longer so advantageous. Furthermore, all three brothers were of advanced ages and would naturally want to settle their patrimonial inheritance for the sake of their own children. The three, therefore, decided to divide the estate, creating three separate legal family units. Negotiations between the brothers and the paperwork necessary to insure that all Vitale Dandolo's bequests were settled likely took some time. Finally, however, on April 5, 1181, the fraterna was divided. It is possible from later documents to piece together some of the more important aspects of the division, thus giving an insight into the continued atomization of family property in Venice.

Because of the fragmentary nature of the evidence, it is not possible to say with certainty what Giovanni Dandolo received in the division. In later years the family compound properties appeared to have been divided evenly only between Enrico and Andrea. Yet as Schulz convincingly argued, Giovanni probably initially received one-third of the properties. After he died without sons, his holdings were divided between his two brothers, both of whom did have male offspring. Enrico and Andrea Dandolo ultimately split a parcel of land that lay between the church of San Luca and the Grand Canal. The area had wooden houses and workshops, but remained sparsely built up. Enrico's property corresponded to the present site of Palazzo Corner-Valmaran, while Andrea received the adjacent plot, the present site of the Palazzo Corner-Martinengo-Ravà (see fig. 5).[71] It is noteworthy that, despite his wealth and prominence, Vitale Dandolo never built a grand palazzo for his family. In fact, the era of palazzos, in which great stone structures facing the Grand Canal became symbols of affluence, was still some decades away. Neither Enrico Dandolo nor his brother would build one on their property, although Enrico's son, Ranieri, would do so.[72]

After his years in the ducal court Enrico Dandolo, like his father, turned his attention to diplomacy. For Enrico it was a return to diplomacy, for he had already served on several missions. The year that the Dandolo brothers divided their fraterna marked the tenth anniversary of Venice's hostage crisis and technical state of war with Byzantium. During that decade Venice had failed repeatedly to come to terms with Manuel Comnenus. There seems to have been a brief thawing of relations in 1175, when the emperor released a few hostages, probably in an attempt to forestall a Venetian alliance with the Normans. When no such alliance occurred, the releases stopped.[73] In 1177, the Peace of Venice left Manuel out in the cold in the West, and he likely blamed Venice for it. Depending now on Genoa, the emperor no longer had any reason to bother with Venice, particularly when his attention was consumed by other matters in the East.[74]

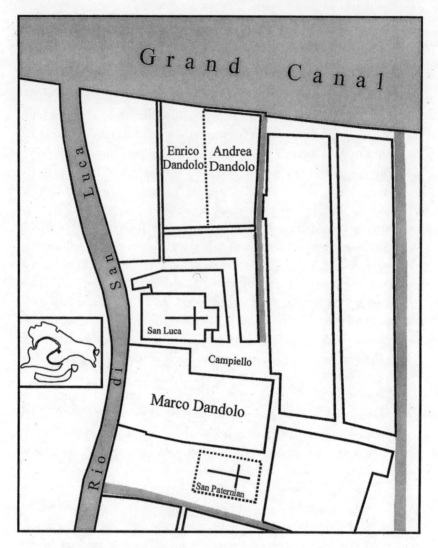

Figure 5. Dandolo Compound, ca. 1185. Black square in the inset represents Dandolo Compound. (Based on Schulz, "Houses of the Dandolo.")

It is commonly held that Byzantium and Venice struck a peace of some kind in 1179.[75] In truth, hostilities continued between the two powers well after that date.[76] When Emperor Manuel I Comnenus died on September 24, 1180, still at war with Venice, he left behind a twelve-year-old son, Alexius II. A series of rebellions ensued, tainted with the virulent anti-Latin hatred that ruled the streets of Constantinople. In 1182, the governor of Pontus, Andronicus Comnenus, took over the regency. To repay his supporters in Constantinople and begin with a clean slate regarding the Latin quarters, Andronicus signaled the citizens that they might give full vent to their hatred for their Latin neighbors. The massacre that ensued was brutally efficient. The Greek mobs poured into the Latin quarters along the Golden Horn, murdering, raping, and torturing their victims. The easiest targets were women, children, and the aged, who were cut down mercilessly. Latin clerics and monks were also massacred; the papal legate to Constantinople was decapitated and his head tied to the tail of a dog. The slaughter so embarrassed Nicetas Choniates that he simply omitted it from his history.[77]

Venice's alienation from Constantinople now seemed good fortune. The few Venetians living in the city in 1182 were by definition well connected and, therefore, probably had advance warning of the carnage. The only reference among Venetian sources to the massacre is tucked away in a commercial document made in Alexandria in June 1182. A Venetian merchant vessel bound for Constantinople was warned by other Venetians fleeing the city that "if you do not flee you are dead, because we and all the other Latins of Constantinople have been expelled."[78] Venetian chroniclers made no reference to the massacre and the Republic never requested restitution for damages from later emperors.[79] Indeed, if anything, the pogrom was a boon. With Pisa and Genoa now hostile to the empire and the Normans preparing to renew their attacks, Andronicus had little choice but to turn to Venice for support.

The specifics of the new regent's overtures are complex to reconstruct, as no treaty or record of negotiations has survived. Something, however, was ironed out. What Venetians wanted every Byzantine knew: their citizens released and their assets returned. These were not points for debate but minimum requirements for ending the state of war between the two powers. In short, there could be no meaningful negotiations until the emperor (or his regent) met these conditions. At once Andronicus released all Venetian hostages and promised to make installment payments on damage claims.[80] He also restored the Venetian Quarter to its owners.[81] Venetians who had been doing business in the empire before 1182 were probably the first to return. They were not the last. Venetian merchants flocked once more to the lucrative city on the Bosporus that they knew so well.[82] Back home, those with assets in Constantinople began in 1183 to administer their properties for the first time since 1171.[83] In the summer of 1183, Patriarch Enrico Dandolo gave his nephew Giovanni full power to rent out patriarchal property in Constantinople.[84] Newly released hostages began arriving in Venice by January 1183.[85] The first restitution payments, however, did not arrive until November 1185.[86]

In September 1183, Giovanni Dandolo was preparing to catch one of the last boats to Constantinople. He had a great deal of business to conduct for his uncle, who, as patriarch of Grado, was one of the largest Venetian landholders in Constantinople. Giovanni's brother Enrico joined him on the voyage.[87] Enrico Dandolo was selected by the doge and his court to be one of three ducal legates to the restored Venetian community in Constantinople. His two colleagues were Pietro Ziani and Domenico Sanudo.[88] As Venetians streamed into their old quarter in Byzantium they had their hands full with reclaiming old property, renegotiating contracts, and rebuilding an ordered and profitable life. In the past when legal disputes arose the practice had been for both parties to agree to an arbiter. When that was impossible cases were sent to the ducal court in Venice. By sending ducal legates to Constantinople, therefore, Mastropiero streamlined the process of resettling the quarter, allowing quick resolutions of the numerous legal disputes that were bound to arise.[89] It is interesting to note that, although Dandolo's blindness kept him out of the doge's court in Venice, it apparently did not bar him from acting as the doge's legate in Constantinople. This is consistent, of course, with the fact that Dandolo was not barred from the dogeship itself in 1192.

The three legates were probably given a diplomatic charge as well. Although peace between Venice and Constantinople was established with the release of the Venetian hostages and the emperor's promise to make good on their losses, it was a far cry from an alliance that would commit Venice to defending Byzantium. For that there would need to be hard negotiations not only for the terms of the alliance but also for the continued payment of reparations. Although Dandolo and his colleagues are commonly credited with brokering the peace between the two powers, their primary mission was predicated on peace already having been established.[90] In other words, had the emperor not released the hostages and restored the Venetian Quarter, there would have been no need for legates to assist with the resettlement. Nevertheless, the three probably did have a diplomatic function of some sort.[91]

Before leaving Venice, Enrico Dandolo delegated authority over his commercial and private affairs to his brother Andrea; his wife, Contessa; and Filippo Falier of San Tomà parish.[92] Given that he would be absent from the city for an extended period of time, it was prudent to designate proxies for his financial affairs. This document does, however, shed some faint light on several otherwise unseen aspects of Dandolo's personal life. Of paramount interest is the choice and identity of the three proxies. It is not surprising, of course, that he chose his brother Andrea to help manage his affairs. Given that their fraternal had been dissolved only two years earlier, Andrea would still be quite familiar with Enrico's properties. We can only assume that Filippo Falier was a trusted friend, yet aside from this proxy assignment, nothing else is known about his relationship with Enrico Dandolo. The earliest surviving reference to Falier places him in Constantinople in October 1170.[93] Fortunately for him, he left the city before the mass arrest of Venetians the following year.[94] Like Enrico Dandolo, Falier served in Sebastiano Ziani's court, so it may have been there that he and Dandolo formed their relationship.[95] Falier also served in various functions in the court of Orio Mastropiero, including that of *iudex comuni*.[96] He appears to have died sometime around 1190.[97]

The most intriguing piece of information that this document yields is the name of Enrico Dandolo's wife—or at least her first name. Because of the nature of the surviving materials, it is rare indeed to get a glimpse of a Dandolo woman. Unfortunately, this glimpse is a brief one, and there is nothing else known with certainty about Contessa Dandolo. In a weighty history of his family published in 1901, Demetrius Minotto claimed that this Contessa was a member of the Minotto family on the basis of a will drafted in September 1209 by an Ota Minotto, in which she left money to her two daughters: Maria, wife of Aurofino, and Contessa. Demetrius Minotto argued that since the name *Contessa* was rare in Venice, Contessa, daughter of Ota Minotto, must have been Contessa, wife of Enrico Dandolo.[98]

Throughout his book, Demetrius Minotto made assumptions that are often based on scant evidence or outright errors.[99] None of his conclusions can be taken at face value. Nevertheless, in this one case he may have had a point. The name *Contessa* was more than just rare in twelfth-century Venice; it may well have been unique.[100] Nevertheless, if these two Contessa's were one in the same, it seems odd that Contessa Minotto's mother did not identify her as the former *dogaressa*, while she did identify the commoner husband of her other daughter, Maria. Still, the naming practices in this document are generally terse; Ota Minotto did not even name her own husband. It may be that the notary in this case simply left out the names of dead husbands. If so, this would add further support to the identification, since in 1209 Enrico Dandolo had been four years in the grave. In short, despite sloppy methods, Demetrius Minotto may be correct. Although we cannot be certain, Contessa Minotto may indeed have been the wife of Enrico Dandolo. Of course, given his longevity, it is possible that Dandolo had more than just one wife.[101]

This simple document can tell us one more thing about Enrico Dandolo: he was blind when it was made. Here for the first time we have a document that the notary signed for him. Dandolo's previous signatures and his presence in the ducal court prove that he was literate. His failure to sign this document, therefore, provides a *terminus ad quem* for the onset of his blindness.[102] Dandolo never again signed a document himself. He was legally blind, no longer able to read for himself. But was his blindness total? Some have doubted it, arguing that a blind man could not have done all that is attributed to Enrico Dandolo during the course of the Fourth Crusade.[103] Yet to accept that Dandolo's eyesight was simply poor requires one to ignore a diverse array of contemporary sources that attest to his blindness.[104] In fact, Dandolo is never described as engaging in an activity that would be impossible for someone without sight.[105] Lacking a compelling reason, therefore, to disregard the testimony of so many witnesses, we must accept that Enrico Dandolo's blindness was indeed total.

Giorgio Cracco has argued that Dandolo's loss of vision was the reason for the proxy of 1183. Because of debilitating blindness, Cracco contends, Dandolo was forced to turn over permanently the management of his affairs to others.[106] Yet this cannot be. Far from being incapacitated, when Dandolo signed away these legal powers he was preparing to sail to Constantinople, where he would represent the doge himself. There are also several surviving records of Dandolo managing his own affairs after his return to Venice.[107] Clearly, then, he did not in 1183 relinquish power over his assets forever; nor does the document say that he did. Cracco appears to have become confused by the use of the phrase *in perpetuum*, which refers to Dandolo's acceptance of transactions made in his name by his proxies, not to the proxy itself. It was Dandolo's impending voyage to Constantinople that necessitated this document, not his blindness.

The two Dandolo brothers probably arrived in Constantinople by early October 1183. Both were familiar with the city and, like other Venetians, could not have been displeased by the absence of the Pisans and Genoese. The Byzantine mobs had done a good job scouring Constantinople of Venice's rivals. Giovanni Dandolo's task was straightforward, although not simple. He had to assess and reorganize the patriarchate's extensive properties in the city—no small matter, as almost all of Grado's revenues came from its Byzantine assets. It was not until February 1184 that Giovanni began closing deals. The first was the simplest: a one-year rental of two shops on a landing stage called Cacegalla in the Venetian Quarter. Annual rent was set at 12 hyperpers, which was paid up front.[108] The following month, Giovanni closed all the patriarchate's long-term rental agreements at one time; he had probably been negotiating them for months. Altogether, five have survived. All were for properties near the landing stages of the Venetian Quarter and all were twenty-five-year leases. All renters were entitled to build on the property and sell the buildings, provided the patriarch of Grado had the first opportunity to buy. The annual rents varied from 11 to 19 hyperpers.[109] Despite the rush of Venetians back to their old quarter, however, those who returned were not altogether sanguine about the future; in every one of these agreements the investors were freed from all responsibilities to the patriarch of Grado in the event of "violence of the lord Emperor."[110]

It was not unusual for renters, investors, or land speculators in Constantinople to demand a clause releasing them from some or all responsibilities in the event of fire. Fires were common, often appallingly destructive events in the massive city.[111] Giovanni conceded in the one-year rental and in four of the five twenty-five-year agreements a complete waiver of rents in the event of fire damage. It is instructive that these four long-term leases required payments of 16 to 19 hyperpers a year. In the one agreement in which there was no protection clause for fire damage, the lease payment amounted to 11 hyperpers annually.[112] Since the contracts are otherwise identical and the properties adjacent to one another and of equal size, one can infer that investors were willing to pay almost a fifty percent premium for a fire waiver—a further indication of the great danger these blazes posed.[113]

Giovanni Dandolo's brother, Enrico, was also busy. As noted earlier, he was probably engaged in negotiations of some sort with Andronicus I concerning reparation payments, although no record of these negotiations survives. His first known action as ducal legate was a simple one, although complicated by the times: He invested the monastery of San Nicolò at Embulo with certain lands and houses in the city. One landing stage and twelve houses included in the investment were still in dispute between the Venetian monks and various Greeks who had captured the property a decade earlier.[114] He presided over a more interesting case two months later, in May 1184. He had only Domenico Sanudo as a colleague, since Pietro Ziani pled the case for one of the parties: the Venetian monastery of San Giorgio in Constantinople. On the other side was Avorlino Pantaleo, advocate for Pinamonto Cupo. Ziani began the proceedings by demanding an explanation before the court for Cupo's seizure of a number of properties owned by San Giorgio and previously leased to Pietro Lambardi. Avorlino replied that Cupo had concession documents from the monastery giving him control over the properties. Ziani requested that the documents be shown to the court. Cupo presented to the civil judge, Vitale Staniario, one document that had been cut and was in very poor shape. Ziani then asserted that because of the mutilation the documents were worthless. Staniario agreed. Avorlino then requested an opportunity to prove that the abbot of the monastery had conceded the houses to his client. He was given the opportunity, but the court, unimpressed, ordered Cupo to evacuate the properties.[115]

Having done their part to put the Venetian Quarter back on its feet, Enrico and Giovanni Dandolo returned to Venice the following year. Almost immediately Enrico was named legal advocate for the monastery of San Cipriano di Murano, a position his father had also held. On December 16, 1185, he argued a case in Chioggia for the monks.[116] Little else is known about Enrico's activities over the next five years. He appears to have turned his attention to his own affairs. In November 1187 he made a medium-sized contribution of 150 lire to a voluntary state loan raising money to prosecute a war against Zara.[117] The following year, he purchased a saltworks in Chioggia.[118] As for his brothers, nothing more is known with certainty about Giovanni Dandolo; the presence of several other prominent men with the same name has hopelessly scattered his tracks. Andrea Dandolo was by this time firmly established as a leading member of the ducal court,[119] a position he would retain throughout Orio Mastropiero's reign. This was a time of continued change in the ducal court. The men of the council were forming into a governing unit—indeed, several governing units—with authority greater than that of the doge himself. I will return to this topic in the next chapter.

As the decade closed the most dramatic event to affect the Dandolo family, and indeed all of Venice, was the death of Patriarch Enrico Dandolo, sometime around 1188.[120] Patriarch of Grado for more than half a century, his tenure was characterized by both victories and defeats, but most of all by change. From the beginning, Dandolo had sought fully to reform the Venetian church along Gregorian lines. He successfully championed the introduction of a number of reform orders into the lagoon as well as the conversion of existing parishes and monasteries. As a result of his clash with Doge Pietro Polani, the Venetian state distanced itself from ecclesiastical elections, limiting itself to the role of protector of the church. Dandolo's attempt to overrule a decision of the doge and his council, however, was an utter failure—one that he never repeated. In the space of his career, Dandolo reformed not only the Venetian church but also its relationship with the Venetian state. It has even been suggested that his reforming vigor infected Venice's secular leaders, giving inspiration and impetus to the birth and growth of the Venetian commune.[121] In any case, Rando is certainly justified when she refers to these five decades as the "Epoch of Enrico Dandolo."[122]

The patriarch's nephew and namesake returned to state service in 1191. The council dispatched him and Pietro Foscarini to Ferrara to negotiate a new treaty with the formerly belligerent city. The agreement they hammered out was decidedly in Venice's favor. The Venetian government gained the right of justice over its own citizens in Ferrara, as well as the right to extradite criminals and escaped slaves.[123] According to Sanudo, Dandolo attempted to hide his blindness during the negotiations by placing a very small hair in his soup at dinner. He then made a loud protest, pointing out to the steward the almost invisible object. Sanudo insists that this fooled the Ferrarans.[124] Whether it did or not, the fact of the embassy makes clear that, despite his age and blindness, Enrico Dandolo remained highly valued in the ducal court. His success at Ferrara would speak well of him a few months later, when electors in Venice once again assembled to choose a new doge.

With the death of the patriarch, the last member of the previous generation of Dandolo men was gone. Vitale and Enrico Dandolo had taken part in the sweeping changes that altered their world, each one shaping and reforming Venice in his own way. Despite the solid accomplishments of the next generation—Enrico, Andrea, and Giovanni—they must have sometimes felt hidden in the shadows of these giants. In 1190 the three sons of Vitale Dandolo were no longer young. Indeed, they were old men. No one could then see it, because it was nowhere to be seen, but the younger Enrico Dandolo, now in his eighties, would soon be responsible for changes in Venice that would dwarf those of the twelfth century. While the previous generation of Dandolo had helped to reform Venice, the next would transform it.

ᴛʜᴇ ᴍᴇᴅɪᴇᴠᴀʟ ᴅᴏɢᴇsʜɪᴘ

&

the ᴇʟᴇᴄᴛɪᴏɴ of 1192

ot long after Enrico Dandolo's return from his embassy to Ferrara, the aged Doge Orio Mastropiero, the last surviving member of the trio of councilors who had advised Vitale II Michiel and helped to effect the dramatic changes in the Venetian government, fell ill. In May 1192, Mastropiero abdicated the throne and entered the monastery of San Croce, where, on June 13, he died. The doge's council sent word throughout the lagoon for the people to assemble and approve forty electors in what was now the "customary way" of choosing a doge.[1] In short order the Forty were ratified. Thirteen of them came from families represented in the election of the previous doge,[2] and the remaining twenty-seven came from a mix of ancient and relatively new families. There were, however, no electors chosen from families that had only recently entered the political arena.[3] The Dandolo were there—indeed, they were one of only four families who could boast a spot among every group of electors thus far.[4] In 1192 it was Marino Dandolo who served on the electoral commission. He was probably the son of Andrea Dandolo and nephew of Enrico Dandolo, and a man who would one day aspire to the ducal throne himself.[5]

On June 1, 1192, after due deliberation about which we are told nothing, the majority elected Enrico Dandolo to be the forty-first doge of Venice.[6] By any reckoning the selection was unusual. While Dandolo certainly came from an influential family and had rendered substantial service to the state, this was true of others as well. We must ask, then, why the electors chose a blind man in his eighties.

Until now the only scholar to address this question has been Giorgio Cracco,

who sees the election of Dandolo as a manifestation of larger social and political trends at work in medieval Venice. Cracco views Dandolo as a weak and relatively obscure man. The logical choice for the dogeship, he insists, was the son
of Doge Sebastiano Ziani, Pietro, who was "the only man wealthy enough and
with a sufficient number of clients to aspire to the dogeship." Ziani, however,
was an investor, not a merchant. He loaned money or acted as a *stans* (stay-at-
home investor) in overseas trade agreements, which, Cracco maintains, alienated
him from the seagoing bourgeoisie. He was also much too powerful in Venice,
which unnerved the nobility anxious to avoid another Vitale Michiel. Dandolo,
therefore, appealed to both sides of the political tug-of-war. The merchants saw
him as one of their own, someone who had done business in the Levant and
knew their problems in Byzantium. For the *grandi*, Dandolo's pedigree was sufficient to pass muster, and debilitating age and blindness assured them that he
would remain powerless.[7]

   Cracco is certainly correct that Dandolo's handicaps would not have escaped
the electors' notice. Yet in other respects his theory is flawed. As a frequent ambassador, a ducal legate, and a member of Ziani's court, Dandolo was anything
but obscure. Indeed, his recent success at Ferrara would have been fresh on everyone's mind as the electors convened. As for Pietro Ziani, it does not appear that
he was even a candidate for the dogeship in 1192, since we find him as a member
of the electoral committee itself.[8] There is also no evidence that seafaring merchants viewed Ziani with suspicion simply because he did not ply the waters himself. In fact, Ziani's rather heavy involvement in trade may well have made him
more attractive to merchants, since his own money was also at risk.[9] Venetian
merchants, after all, were not an oppressed working class, but thriving business-
men who had little reason to distrust or resent their investors. Pietro Ziani was
also no babe when it came to Byzantine affairs; he had been one of Dandolo's
colleagues in the legation to Constantinople in 1184.[10] Enrico Dandolo similarly
does not fit Cracco's mold. Although it is possible that he engaged in overseas
commerce, there is no evidence for it. The lone reference to any foreign commercial activity in his life comes from a trip to Alexandria in 1174, when he simply collected a debt for his brother Andrea.[11] Even that, as we have seen, was not
a commercial voyage.[12] In short, Ziani was no cloistered aristocrat and Dandolo
no seasoned sailor. The Venetians of the twelfth century simply do not fit into
tidy political and economic categories. If they did, and both sides of the struggle were set firmly against Pietro Ziani, one wonders how he went on to win the
dogeship in 1205.

   With no help at all from contemporary or even late sources, it is impossible to know the precise reasoning behind the decision of the Forty in 1192. Never-theless, we can identify various factors that must have influenced their choice. Given his family and his service to the state, Enrico Dandolo was clearly wor-thy of the dogeship. Although he was very old and blind, we know from con-temporary descriptions of him that he was wise, vigorous, and a natural leader of men.[13] These are qualities to be esteemed in a doge, and they would not have escaped the attention of the electors, who knew him well. There were a number of foreign affairs problems for Venice in 1192, in particular, tense relations with Constantinople. Dandolo was an experienced diplomat familiar with the Byzan-tine court, so these considerations alone would have made a compelling argu-ment for his election. But there may have been yet another, less tangible factor at work here: Enrico was the son of Vitale Dandolo. It is striking that in the two elections after the murder of Vitale II Michiel the electoral committees selected two of the three men who were most often at the slain leader's side. The third, Vitale Dandolo, had died in 1174. Perhaps in this election, then, there were those who saw it as Vitale's turn, casting their ballots for the son out of respect and gratitude to the father.

Whatever the weight of these various considerations, in the end each elector still had to make peace with Enrico Dandolo's age and blindness. Or did he? Just as some have doubted that Dandolo was really blind, so others have suggested that he was not really all that old. Marino Sanudo recorded that the new doge was eighty-five years of age in 1192.[14] Earlier chronicles and almost all contem-porary witnesses remark on Dandolo's very advanced age, but none is more spe-cific.[15] Most scholars, therefore, have accepted Sanudo's figure, since it is the only one available and it jibes with contemporary accounts. A few, however, have sug-gested that, considering Dandolo's actions on the Fourth Crusade, a decade or more should be shaved from his age.[16] And yet, there is no good reason to do so. An octogenarian leading a crusade army is only marginally more believable than a nonagenarian. Ninety or even 100-year-old men are not outside human experience. Indeed, in the Dandolo family great longevity was almost expected. Enrico Dandolo's father was probably in his nineties when he sailed to Con-stantinople to negotiate with the emperor in 1174. His uncle, the patriarch of Grado, lived into his eighties or perhaps nineties. Simply put, Enrico Dandolo had good genes. Without evidence to the contrary, then, there is no reason to disregard Sanudo's report of the doge's age.

Just how did the members of the Forty view Dandolo's advanced age and per-haps total blindness? As Cracco suggests, some of the electors may have favored Dandolo because they believed his handicaps would keep him from attempting to turn back the clock and restore the dogeship to a quasi-monarchy.[17] Yet it seems unlikely that these suspicions would dog someone who had been a member of the ducal court himself and whose family had been instrumental in strengthening the council and weakening ducal authority. What is certain, though, is that each elector must have anticipated that by selecting Enrico Dandolo there would be another election very soon. No one could have expected him to live for very much longer; surely no one anticipated his surviving another thirteen years. It is safe to say, then, that the electors made what they believed was a short-term choice. Without additional evidence, we cannot know why.

When Enrico Dandolo was led to the throne of St. Mark he took his place in a court and a government that had undergone significant change over the course of the previous century. It is worthwhile, therefore, briefly to review those changes. In its earliest days, the Venetian government was based ultimately on the doge and the people, who bore a nominal allegiance to Constantinople. In their assembly the people chose by acclamation a doge who then ruled. Yet a doge was quite unlike other medieval rulers. The theoretical basis of all power in Venice was the popular assembly, or arengo. As we have seen, during times of emergency the arengo could convene and take any action it chose, ranging from a declaration of war to direct legislation. Although doges did everything "with the approval of the people of Venice," in reality they acted alone or with church prelates unless and until something compelled the people to assemble. This began to change in the tenth century, as Venice, like other Italian cities, responded to its growing prosperity.

A new class of wealthy families, like the Dandolo, became increasingly interested in affairs of state, and they had the means and the leisure to work themselves into the political fabric of the city. These are the "good men" or "faithful ones" visible in ducal acts by the end of the tenth century. They did not constitute a formal body, but they were wealthy and respected men who wished to be present and to have their views heard on various matters before the doge. Because there was no official membership, their number fluctuated widely, from just a few to several hundred when matters of great importance were at stake. Their powers, too, were undefined. Not surprisingly, over time these fideles came to be seen as representatives of the people in the court of the doge.[18] Later, important attendees who were in ducal favor began to serve as judges and sapientes. The latter would often sign ducal acts for the larger body of fideles. In other words, they became representatives of the representatives. By the twelfth century ducal acts were routinely made in the name of the doge, his judges, and the people of Venice.[19]

Although the members of these newly wealthy families constituted a distinct class—indeed, a fledgling ruling class—they were not nobility in the European sense of that word. Before the *Serrata* of 1297, Venice had no nobility. Venetian elites enjoyed no legal privileges and were in close and constant contact with all segments of society.[20] A Venetian of the Middle Ages might be referred to in a document as a "noble man," but he was not a nobleman.[21] In so vibrant a capitalist society, status was almost as fluid as wealth. This was also true in other Italian commercial cities, despite the presence of landed nobility.[22] In Venice, new families like the Dandolo and Mastropiero, who were among the fideles of the late tenth century, and the Ziani, who did not make their appearance until the mid-eleventh century, were able to aspire to great power despite their lack of pedigree because of their substantial wealth. Ancient families were admired and respected for their history, but their political power ultimately rested on their wealth.[23] Such a society naturally confounds modern attempts to impose clear lines of social demarcation.[24]

During the dogeship of Pietro Polani an important milestone was reached with the advent of the *comune Veneciarum.* There is still considerable uncertainty whether this was an evolutionary or revolutionary change in Venetian government.[25] Responding to an immediate crisis, an ad hoc body, called the *consilium sapientium,* was established and then never disbanded. This council provided a permanent organ for elites to participate directly in Venetian government, thus allowing them to carve out for themselves a sphere of power between the doge and the people, sapping authority from both.[26] The council was also the essential element in the creation of the Venetian commune. The term *commune,* when applied to Italian cities, is confusing and resistant of simple definition. Yet aside from the term, which the Venetians clearly borrowed from their neighbors, the Venetian commune is hardly the image of its Italian counterparts. The purpose of the Venetian commune was not to unify political power or topple a leader or acquire local control in opposition to external authority. Venice had long been an independent state—in practical terms, since at least the eighth century. The dogeship, moreover, did not die with the birth of the commune.[27] Instead, the Venetian commune's initial purpose was simply to share political power with the doge and a council of elites, who saw themselves as the representatives of the people. The trend had begun more than a century earlier; the commune simply institutionalized it.[28]

During the dogeships of Domenico Morosini and Vitale II Michiel the ducal court was made up of the doge, his judges, the council, and assorted other functionaries and officers who appear and disappear in ducal acts.[29] When reading the documents of the court at this time one gets the distinct impression that the Venetians were still feeling their way along. There is very little consistency in the formulas or the groups who undersign. This fragile system was then given a vigorous shaking by the catastrophe of 1171. When Doge Michiel learned of the arrest of all Venetians in the Byzantine Empire, he was advised by his "wise men" to send envoys to Constantinople to discern the truth of the reports and the motives of the emperor. When the people assembled and demanded revenge, however, it was the council, responding to the people's wishes, that ordered the doge to lead a retaliatory strike against Byzantium. He obeyed.[30]

It was only after the decimation of the fleet and the murder of Michiel that the people of Venice saw the wisdom of the wise men. As a result, they allowed the councilors, rather than the arengo, to select Michiel's successor. Not surprisingly, the electors chose one of their own, Sebastiano Ziani. The events of 1172 led to a rapid increase in the power of the communal government at the expense of the doge and the arengo. This was not a march toward *Signoria*, characteristic of other Italian communes in the twelfth and thirteenth centuries, but it was an increasing concentration of power in the hands of an elite. The catalyst in Venice was the new electoral system, which gave the selection of subsequent doges to the sapientes and the council. In the same way that the Papal Election Decree in 1059 insured that all subsequent popes would be strong reformers, Venice's election reform of 1172 made it a certainty that subsequent doges would favor the expansion of the authority of the communal government. Those who did not could never be elected.

Precision is impossible when discussing the reforms enacted during the reigns of Ziani and Mastropiero. They are attested to only in the structure of official acts and are by no means consistent. It appears, however, that the council itself began to expand, perhaps to divide, and certainly to elect various officers. Both Ziani and Mastropiero may still have appointed their own judges, but even that prerogative was soon to perish.[31] By 1185 we find a reference to decisions made by a majority vote of the council.[32] Two years later, mention is made of two separate councils, one large and one small. This particular decree was enacted in the name of the doge "with the approval of the judges, the large and small councils, the advocates of the commune, and the people of Venice."[33] The large council corresponded to the *consilium sapientium* or *consilium communis*. Castagnetti is probably correct when he suggests that the small council was made up of the "councilors" who had very recently begun to appear among the signatories of ducal acts.[34]

Apart from control of the electoral process, the communal government had another safeguard against an autocratic doge—the *promissione*, or oath of office.

Oaths were a staple of Italian communes, sworn by the citizens to one another. In Venice, there was a long history of ducal oaths, usually sworn to the people on an ad hoc basis. Oaths of office had probably existed for several decades before the election of Enrico Dandolo in 1192, although none survives.[35] Dandolo's *promissione* is the first available, although in a somewhat damaged manuscript. Nevertheless, for the medieval historian of Venice it is a precious document, providing a snapshot of the legal and political framework of late-twelfth-century Venetian government and a precise definition of the powers that Dandolo received when he took the throne. Because of its importance, it is translated here in full.

These are the items that we, Enrico Dandolo, doge by the grace of God, are bound to observe as long as we live as doge.

1. We will assume administration of the country and we will watch over its government in good faith.

2. And we will be diligent as to equity and justice for all who seek it, and for those who have sought it, it will be produced in good faith without any delay and without fraud, unless it is stayed by a majority of the Council, or unless the matter falls under the jurisdiction . . . with regard to established laws and judgments passed by a decision of the judges, we will diligently bring it to completion in good faith and without fraud.

3. In the case of lawsuits that come before us, we will postpone nothing through any kind of fraud. If, perhaps, our judges appear at some time or other to disagree regarding a pronouncement of law, we then must decide the law, opting for the better faction [of judges], which seems to us to be in accord with custom. Where, in fact, custom fails us, we will, without fraud, render a decision according to our own conscience. We will accept no gift, nor will we allow such to be accepted either to aid or to harm any party or any person. And if for us anyone then accepts a gift on our behalf and informs us of it, we will have it returned in a timely fashion without fraud. We will also accept no gift nor will we allow one to be accepted for anyone . . . or on behalf of the commune of the Venetians.

4. Moreover, we will consider, attend to, and work for the honor and profit of the Venetians in good faith and without fraud.

5. Also all deliberations that we, along with the majority of the Council, command to be held secret, we will keep secret, according to our understanding of the situation.

6. And if in our tenure any of the assets, possessions, or funds of the commune of the Venetians shall be given or promised to any person or persons, we

will not hold firm that donation or promise unless it was first considered and confirmed by a majority of the Council.

7. In the matter of [commercial] goods that a majority of the Council will prohibit, we will give a seal to no person unless it is approved by a majority of the Council.

8. In the matter of all false documents that are shown to us, we will be diligent to render justice and to do so according to the custom of our country.

9. If our Mother Church, the patriarchate of Grado, should become vacant, we will leave the election of the new patriarch to the entire congregation of our clergy and people, from whom we must not seek any gift. Likewise, without exacting any gift, we relinquish power over the election of bishops to their filial clergy and people; in the same way, without gift, we relinquish electoral power over monastic churches that are subordinate to the bishops to the suffragan congregations themselves, along with their bishops.

10. In the matter of the fortieth and other assessments that the vicelords of our Commune have customarily collected and regarding those funds that come from the March of Quarnero, excepting the fruits of Lombardy, we ought to have two parts and the vicelords a third. We must not meddle with the fifth that comes by sea or the fifth that comes from Castelnovo through us, for this is done through its own efforts, or in the bestowal of a salt seal that has been obtained at Capo d'Argine. . . . we shall contribute at our expense ten ships armed for war, forty . . . and archers.

11. We will not dispatch legations and letters to the Roman Pontiff, to emperors, or to kings without [the consent] of the majority of the Council.

12. We will not appoint judges in our palace without election.

13. We will not appoint notaries without [the consent of] a majority of the Council and the approval of the people.

14. We will not undertake any inquiry regarding any offense against us without a decision from the judges.

15. In the matter, indeed, of communal transactions, we will oversee those that have been arranged by a majority of the Council, which will inform us [of them] by means of a writ of obligation.

16. In the matter of an issue that might especially concern the dogeship, we will discharge those concerning which all of the Councilors of the Small Council will agree with the majority of the Great Council, from which we will have been informed by a writ of obligation. Yet, if some member of the council was not bound to us by an obligation of fidelity before a decision is made and is needed by us, then when the decision on that issue is rendered, he should swear an oath of fidelity to us.

17. We will observe in good faith [and] without fraud each and every one of these items listed above in good faith without fraud while we live in our dogeship, with the exception that if there is someone who is not bound by fidelity to us . . . and who does not wish to render it to us.[36]

At first glance the oath appears to be almost entirely restrictive in nature. With the exception of promises to attend to the welfare of the Venetian state and administer justice to the people, the oath is primarily a list of things that the doge may *not* do. Without the approval of the council, Dandolo may not alienate state funds or property, divulge state secrets, permit prohibited exports, conduct foreign diplomacy, appoint notaries, or administer communal business. He is prohibited from meddling with customs duties, influencing ecclesiastical elections, presiding over cases against himself, or even appointing his own judges. In short, by 1192 the doge could do almost nothing without the approval of the council. The dogeship itself had become a component of the Venetian commune.

The strong limitations enunciated here make the analysis of Dandolo's role in his own dogeship problematic, at least before 1201, when we get eyewitness accounts of the man. Are actions attributed to him by later chroniclers his own or that of the council? The pace of achievements during Dandolo's tenure, as well as his vigorous participation in the Fourth Crusade, have led some to conclude that the old doge took command of the state in the same autocratic manner in which he led the Venetian crusaders.[37] Holding the opposite view, Cracco insists that it is impossible to believe that an old and blind man could do everything that is attributed to him in the years 1192 to 1201; nor could he have been the vigorous leader of the Fourth Crusade that contemporaries report. The former is simply a convention whereby Venetian chroniclers attributed to doges all of the initiatives of their reign; the latter is the laziness of Villehardouin, who transfers all Venetian actions to the doge himself.[38]

As is often the case, the reality lies somewhere in the middle. It is difficult to accept Cracco's argument, which is based on a characterization of Dandolo that is contradicted by all contemporary sources. Villehardouin repeatedly stressed that despite Dandolo's age and blindness, he was "very wise, brave, and vigorous."[39] Nicetas Choniates, who with good reason hated Dandolo, reported that he was "a sly cheat who called himself wiser than the wise and madly thirsting after glory as no other."[40] While thoroughly uncomplimentary, this is not the description of a doddering old man led to Constantinople by his countrymen.[41] On the other hand, Cracco is right to point out that Dandolo could not have personally done at home all that his dogeship is credited for. Executives can only lead their organizations, not undertake all of their responsibilities.

Dandolo and his successors were not simply figureheads with little or no real authority. As Dandolo's tenure and the subsequent history of Venice proves, doges remained extremely important. A doge may not have been free to conduct diplomacy without oversight, but it was still he who conducted the diplomacy. It was he and his advisors who crafted instructions to legates and drafted letters to monarchs, while the council simply acted to check initiatives that the majority did not support.[42] The same was true of all of the other activities described in the promissione that required the council's approval. Provided, therefore, that a doge retained the support of the majority of the council, he could be quite powerful. In all cases, however, the doge was and would remain the leader of Venice. As the ducal oath makes clear, he was also its servant.[43]

Dandolo's oath of office is in many respects a written constitution, one that would be rewritten with every subsequent doge. It is a product of the interests of the elites of the ducal court, those who were responsible for the doge's election and who were now in a position to make the rules for his dogeship. Lessons learned during the reign of one doge were transferred to the oath of the next. The organic growth of the document can be seen clearly when we compare Dandolo's oath to that taken by Giacomo Tiepolo in 1229.[44] The latter was built on the foundation of the former; indeed, the wording is often identical. In the same way, Tiepolo's successor, Marino Morosini, took an oath based on Tiepolo's. This repeated revision explains the seemingly disorganized nature of the ducal oath. Yet it is organized—not merely thematically, but chronologically.

Doge Tiepolo's oath begins with a prologue that may be lost in Dandolo's.[45] With one minor exception, the next twelve clauses follow Dandolo's first ten clauses very closely in both order and wording.[46] The only addition in these initial clauses is Tiepolo's promise to adhere to the party in the council that seems most reasonable. It is possible that this short clause was originally in Dandolo's oath, since that portion of the manuscript, between clauses 4 and 5, is effaced and illegible. Dandolo's clause 10, which discusses various taxes and tariffs, corresponds to Tiepolo's clause 12. As would be expected, many of these regulations had changed by 1229, requiring the addition of two clauses dealing with Chioggia and two for other fiscal matters. In this case, then, the authors of Tiepolo's oath inserted new clauses where they believed they were related to existing clauses. Like Dandolo, Tiepolo next swore not to conduct diplomacy without the council's approval, although this is expanded into two clauses. Both doges then promised in the next two clauses not to appoint judges or notaries, although again Tiepolo's oath provides more details, appropriate to the more mature government of his time. Next in Dandolo's oath comes his promise not to preside over cases that involve the dogeship. This is replaced in Tiepolo's oath by a group of clauses dealing with specifics of the doge's personal property, money, and kin. Here again, the promissione's authors followed the organizational model of the earlier oath, yet expanded on various themes.

Dandolo's oath of office ends with two clauses that attempt to close any loopholes left by the earlier enumerated promises. In clause 15, Dandolo swears to administer communal business only when he has been ordered to do so by the council. Clause 16 appears to deny him any of the traditional prerogatives of the doge unless they are confirmed by all members of the Minor Council and a majority of the Great Council. These two clauses were abandoned in Tiepolo's oath in favor of enumerating the specific prohibitions and responsibilities in sixteen new clauses. In other words, at the point that the previous doge's oath concluded, the authors added whatever additional clauses they wanted. When writing Tiepolo's oath, therefore, the practice was to revise and expand on previous themes while appending all substantive additions.

Since Tiepolo's oath is generally composed of older promises at the beginning and newer ones at the end, it seems likely that the same is true for Dandolo's oath. If so, the text of this document can provide clues to the structure of earlier lost oaths as well as the growth of Venetian communal government. There are additional reasons to assume that Dandolo's oath is ordered in a roughly chronological pattern. Until the end of the document the governing body is referred to simply as "the Council"; it is only in the last clause that a reference is made to a Great Council and a Small Council.[47] As we have seen, in 1192 the Small Council was of recent vintage, emerging only in the reign of Dandolo's predecessor, Orio Mastropiero. A distinction between the councils, therefore, would not appear in earlier oaths, just as it does not appear in the earlier clauses of Dandolo's oath.

The first four clauses of Dandolo's oath deal with the royal dignity, attention to the welfare of the Venetians, and the administration of justice: the traditional rights and responsibilities of Venetian doges. Except for one mention of the council, these four clauses could have been sworn by any doge since the mid-eleventh century.[48] It is only after clause 4 that real restrictions are placed on ducal authority. Perhaps some of these were added at the accession of Domenico Morosini. Clause 9, in which the doge promises to stay out of ecclesiastical elections, is the result of Morosini's settlement with Patriarch Enrico Dandolo, so it may have first appeared in the oath of his successor, Vitale II Michiel. Clause 11, which forbids the doge to conduct diplomacy without permission, could well have been a response to Michiel, who sent legates to Constantinople in violation of the council's order. It is difficult to know which of the next four clauses might have been added for Mastropiero and which for Dandolo. Clearly, though, clause 16 was newly added in 1192. Dandolo's oath of office, therefore, appears to provide us with a crude time-line for the slow assumption of ducal authority by the communal government. Just as the amendments to the American constitution provide a chronological record of issues important to those who enacted them, so too the growth of the doge's oath of office gives us a similar insight into the history of the early Venetian commune.

It is ironic that, after Dandolo's election to the ducal throne, when his name appears on hundreds of archival documents, it is more difficult to discover events in his personal and family life. A few surviving receipts attest to his ownership of saltworks in Chioggia and other investment properties on the terra firma, but the rest of his recorded activities involved the state.[49] It is only when the French crusaders arrive in Venice in 1201 that solid descriptions of Enrico Dandolo the man become available.

Nevertheless, it is possible to say a few things about Dandolo's family during his reign. As we have seen, the doge's brother Giovanni had already disappeared from the documentary record and may thus have been dead before 1192. His other sibling, Andrea, was still alive and remained an important person in the Great Council for a short time after his brother's election.[50] However, by late 1192 his name no longer appears in any court documents. Given his visibility during the reigns of Ziani and Mastropiero, Andrea Dandolo's sudden absence at court is ominous. Whatever the exact circumstances, however, he was certainly dead by February 1198, when his wife, Primera, is referred to as a widow.[51] As noted earlier, it appears that Andrea had a son, Marino, who served as one of the electors of his uncle.[52]

As far as Enrico Dandolo's children go, we can be certain of only one son. Ranieri Dandolo first appears in the documentary record in February 1198, when he witnessed the document made by his aunt, Primera, referred to above. By then he was already a wealthy man in his own right. On April 3, 1200, Ranieri purchased a vacant plot of land on the Grand Canal, adjoining the Dandolo compound in San Luca (see fig. 6). A *piscina*, or closed-off canal (now called Cavalli) separated the plot from the property of the late Andrea. The land, which Ranieri appears to have purchased from Patriarch Benedetto Falier,[53] was directly across the Grand Canal from the patriarchal palace. This was probably the shipyard that

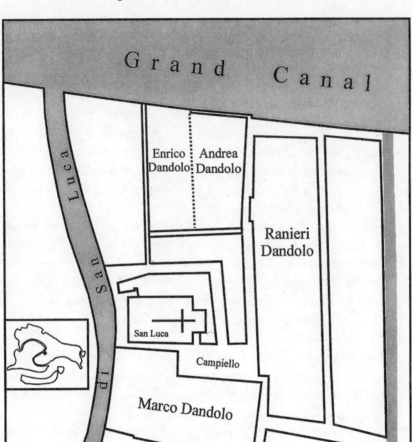

Figure 6. Dandolo Compound, ca. 1200. Black square in the inset represents
Dandolo Compound. (Based on Schulz, "Houses of the Dandolo.")

was active when Ranieri's great uncle, Enrico Dandolo, was patriarch.[54] It was a
large property, several times larger than his father's lands in San Luca parish.
Shortly after purchasing it, Ranieri began construction of a large stone palazzo
looking out over the Grand Canal. Now called the Ca' Farsetti and used as
Venice's city hall, Ranieri's palazzo is the earliest surviving example of the Gothic
style (see fig. 7). Ranieri was a product of his generation, responding to a new

Figure 7. Ca' Farsetti (*left*).
(Photo by the author.)

social environment among Venetian elites. For his father, the doge, the family house was a place to live and work whose focus largely remained on the parish community; for Ranieri, a family's palazzo was an emblem of its wealth and position.[55] No longer clustered around a parish campo, thirteenth-century palazzi stood imposingly on the banks of Venice's main canals. The city's most powerful families advertised their status by building along the city's greatest waterway, the Grand Canal.

It is unclear whether Enrico Dandolo had other children besides Ranieri. Later chroniclers and genealogists attributed a full brood to the old doge, yet none of these offspring can be confirmed by contemporary evidence and most are suspiciously related to the conquest of Constantinople. The earliest reference to other children appears in Sanudo's *Lives of the Doges*, where a Fantino Dandolo, son of the doge and second Latin patriarch of Constantinople is mentioned.[56] Although the election of the second patriarch in 1211 was disputed, neither of the candidates was a Dandolo.[57] Indeed, there never was a patriarch of Constantinople by that name in the history of the Latin Empire, nor is there any record of a Fantino Dandolo in Venice at that time. Sanudo also records that a daughter of Enrico Dandolo married Boniface of Montferrat, the titular leader of the Fourth Crusade.[58] In a thorough analysis of the marriages of Boniface,

Leopoldo Usseglio characterized this suggestion as "absolutely bizarre."[59] Although the marquis of Montferrat was a widower when he came to Venice in 1202, apart from Sanudo's claim there is no evidence that he married into the Dandolo family. He was unmarried in 1204, when he took as his wife Margaret of Hungary, the widow of Emperor Isaac II Angelus. He died, still married to Margaret, in September 1207.[60] The remainder of the children attributed to the doge are found in much later, and therefore much less reliable, seventeenth- and eighteenth-century sources.[61]

Although it is difficult to bring Enrico Dandolo into sharp relief before 1201, we should not conclude that he was a weak puppet of his council. As his diplomatic activities before his election and his heroic actions in the last years of his life demonstrate, Dandolo was a vigorous and perceptive man and a gifted leader. As Frederic Lane wisely wrote, "The way in which [Dandolo] dominated events showed that, although the doge of Venice could not go against the views of his councils, he could be as powerful a ruler as any king."[62] It was this interaction between a wise executive and a conservative council that had been constructed as a breakwater against the capriciousness of the arengo. It served to promote Venetian interests at home, lend coherence to Venetian diplomacy abroad, and stabilize Venetian society during times of crisis. In the following chapter I examine the effectiveness of the communal government during the first decade of the new dogeship—a period of calm before the storm of the Fourth Crusade would put all of the reforms to their ultimate test.

SIX

ENRICO DANDOLO'S DOGESHIP:
THE FIRST DECADE, 1192–1201

ven had Enrico Dandolo not been the conqueror of Constantinople, his reign would still be remembered as one of the more significant in Venetian history. During the decade in which he served in the ducal palace he and his council were responsible for sweeping reforms at home while vigorously pursuing Venetian interests abroad. Given the wide scope of his activities, it seems best to organize them into two subcategories: domestic and foreign.

A VENETIAN DOGE in the late twelfth century was not tucked away in his palace beyond the view of the people. Quite the opposite, he held public court on an almost daily basis. By far the most time-consuming task for a doge and his judges was the administration of justice. Every Venetian citizen—all hundred thousand of them—had a right to have his or her case heard by the doge.[1] Since there was not yet a division between civil and criminal law, the caseload for the court was immense.[2] In earlier centuries doges would simply pass judgment alone or in consultation with their judges. Dandolo's oath of office makes clear that those days were gone. Although he had to give his attention to each case, Dandolo rendered his own decision only when his judges were deadlocked. There is no evidence that this ever occurred. Given the relative inactivity of the doge in judicial matters one might imagine that he would simply stop showing up, allowing the court to process cases without him unless and until the judges were unable to agree. This is what happened in a few other Italian cities, most notably Naples. In Venice, however, the doge was absent from the court only when ill or abroad, and even then a vice-doge would take his place.[3] Even though he was seldom called on to make a decision, the doge was just as necessary to the administration of justice as were the judges themselves. As the leader of the people and the chosen of St. Mark, the doge's presence legitimized and sanctified the official proceedings. When a judgment was rendered it was the doge, not the judges, who delivered it. This was true for criminal trials as well as property transfers. As doge, Enrico Dandolo had the sacred authority to enact what the men of his court had decided. He was the conduit between human reason and divine approbation.

Because the state archives from this period do not survive, nothing is known about the day-to-day administration of criminal justice during Dandolo's reign. What does survive is a tiny percentage of the thousands of documents issued by the ducal court to parties in civil disputes or property transfers that were held by private citizens and later placed in family or monastic archives. They attest to the wide range of cases heard in Dandolo's court, from dowry disputes to property foreclosures. As such, they provide a useful glimpse into the daily routine of the court and the lives of the citizens.[4]

Most numerous among these court records are the property transfers. Living on water, Venetians took land very seriously. For that reason, when a property was transferred the doge would invest the new owner with the land *sine proprio*. This tentative ownership became part of the public record and initiated a period of time in which those who believed they had a better right to all or part of the property could bring their objections to the court, which would then issue a document informing all parties of the contest. Subsequently, both sides would argue their case in the ducal court. When a property transfer was not contested or when the contest was dismissed, the doge would invest the new owner with the land *ad proprium*. This imparted complete and irrevocable ownership of the property.[5]

In the realm of domestic affairs, Dandolo's dogeship was one of bold and sweeping reform, remarkable even during an age of reform in Venice. Dandolo and his court wasted no time. His first surviving decree, issued on August 16, 1192, was a comprehensive policy targeting recent arrivals to the lagoon. He ordered Venetian landlords to evict at once from their premises all foreigners who had lived in Venice for less than two years' time. In addition, Venetians were henceforth forbidden to offer new accommodations to foreigners who had resided in the city for fewer than three years. Penalties were stiff. Citizens in violation of the decree would be fined 50 lire, while foreigners would have all of their goods confiscated, with two-thirds going to the commune and one-third to whoever reported the landlord. Venetians were likewise forbidden to lend money to foreigners for more than fifteen days, with an exception for those from Umana or Ragusa.[6]

What prompted this rather draconian measure is unclear. The preamble of the decree, which simply cites Dandolo's duty to look after the well-being of the commune, is no help. Later Venetian chroniclers are silent on the subject. Cracco placed it into a landscape of class warfare in medieval Venice, arguing that the expulsion of the foreigners was a backlash of the old aristocracy against the merchants responsible for Dandolo's election.[7] It is not clear, though, how Cracco's aristocracy, who could not control the ducal election, was able to control the ducal court and the Great Council.

Rather than regard the decree as a weapon in a hypothetical struggle of the orders, it is more productive to examine it for what it was: a measure dealing with foreigners. As the Venetian economy boomed during the twelfth century, Venice became an extremely attractive place for foreigners of all stripes to relocate. This was not new. As a bustling merchant city, Venice had always hosted a sizeable foreign population.[8] What was new, apparently, was a recent large influx of foreigners into the city. Dandolo's decree had three practical effects: it expelled those who had only recently come to the lagoon, it closed off further immigration, and it put foreigners at a commercial disadvantage. What it did not do was cleanse Venice of foreigners.[9] Only newcomers were affected. Given the lack of evidence, we can only guess at the court's motives. They may have feared that in a city where space was at a premium additional outsiders could no longer be absorbed. Perhaps they also worried about foreigners claiming too great a share of Venetian merchant activity. Dandolo knew well the problems of large foreign populations in Constantinople and would, therefore, have had good reason to avoid similar problems in Venice. Any of these considerations would have provided ample reason for the doge and the court to act.

Interestingly, despite its broad scope, this first decree was delicately crafted. It had to be, for at that same time Venetian ambassadors were busy negotiating treaties with other states to establish reciprocal rights for expatriates. Indeed, treaties like the one that Dandolo negotiated with Ferrara in 1191 probably led to the increased foreign presence in Venice. Since many of these foreigners were untouchable, the doge's decree was addressed to Venetian citizens.[10] It is, therefore, not the commune that expelled the newly arrived foreigners, but their landlords. Since foreigners were forbidden to own real property in Venice, however, an eviction notice would have the same practical effect as an expulsion order.[11]

Over the next several years Dandolo and his court put considerable energy into the Venetian legal system. As Dandolo's oath of office makes clear, even in 1192 the administration of justice in Venice was based on customary law. The judges of the ducal court were men elected to their position for their wisdom and experience, not their understanding of Roman or Lombard law. Cases were therefore decided on the basis of custom, precedent, and reason. As Venice grew in size and wealth, this method became increasingly unsatisfactory. In the absence of a written legal code, the doge and his judges could be accused of administering justice capriciously—and probably were so accused by those who lost their cases. That is one reason why Dandolo's oath was peppered with clauses promising not to show favoritism or act in a fraudulent manner. An attempt to impose more uniformity on judicial decisions had been made during the reign of Dandolo's predecessor, Orio Mastropiero. In March 1181, Mastropiero swore to administer justice in accord with a long list of criminal and civil offenses and their associated penalties.[12] This *promissio malificorium* was poorly constructed. When Dandolo took the throne there appears to have been a desire to expand and better organize the oath—in effect, to lay the foundations for a Venetian code of law. In 1195 the reformed oath was published and Dandolo swore to uphold it. The oath itself has not survived, but the historian-doge Andrea Dandolo recorded that, with a few minor additions and changes, the oath of Enrico Dandolo was still in use during the fourteenth century.[13]

As the name suggests, the *promissio malificorium* addressed judicial cases, both criminal and civil, in which someone had transgressed the law. Yet these were only part of the cases that a doge and his court heard. As noted earlier, much of their time was spent sorting out civil disputes over property and assets. Not surprisingly, then, there arose a similar desire to produce a written body of law that would govern the court's decisions when resolving civil disputes. When completed, it consisted of seventy-four statutes organized topically. The first five statutes dealt with ecclesiastical property in Venice, forbidding priests, bishops, and metropolitans from alienating property without proper approval.[14] Statute 6 defined jurisdictions between civil and ecclesiastical courts, while 7 and 8 referred to the power of the ducal court to summon citizens. The next six statutes referred to the specifics of property investment and disputes. Statutes 16 through 24 addressed the property rights of women, which were similar to those of men, although complicated by the disposition of the dowry. The remaining fifty statutes prescribed civil laws governing foreigners, commercial transactions, inheritance, and the proving of documents.[15]

The civil code of Enrico Dandolo laid the cornerstone for what would become a complex superstructure of Venetian law. Nevertheless, not much more is known about it. Was Dandolo himself involved in the production of the code, or was it was imposed on him and his judges? Even the timing of the code is in question. Andrea Dandolo placed the publication of the statutes and the reform of the *promissio malificiorum* in 1195.[16] Later chroniclers, like Bertaldo and Sanudo, also affirmed that Dandolo was responsible for the first codification and reform of Venetian law.[17] The earliest surviving manuscript of the civil code is from the fourteenth century, in a legal compilation that includes statutes attributed to Ranieri Dandolo, the son of the doge who acted for his father after 1202, as well as Dandolo's successors, Pietro Ziani and Giacomo Tiepolo.[18] In this manuscript there are two civil codes attributed to Ranieri Dandolo. The first, however, appears to belong to Enrico Dandolo and therefore corresponds to the code referred to by the chroniclers. The second is a collection of new civil statutes published in 1204 by the vice-doge.[19]

Enrico Dandolo is also credited with a complete overhaul of Venetian coinage. When he was elected in 1192 Venice was minting only one unremarkable coin: a silver penny modeled on that of Verona. It was about 25 percent fine and weighed less than half a gram. During much of the twelfth century this coin or the Veronese one was the preferred currency for domestic transactions. Sometime around 1180, however, the Veronese penny was debased and its design changed, thus separating it from the Venetian currency. This was not the only currency problem that faced Venetians in the late twelfth century. In Italy, Germany, and England new coins of high value were threatening the baser coins. Among the most important was the British sterling, first introduced by Henry II in 1180. More important for Venice, though, was the collapse of Eastern high-value coinage. For most of the twelfth century Venetian merchants conducted trade with coins minted either by the crusader Kingdom of Jerusalem or the Byzantine Empire. As the crusader kingdom faltered, however, the coins that it minted were systematically debased. By the time Saladin captured Jerusalem in 1187 the new *saracenate bezants* had a gold content of only 68 percent fine.[20]

Matters were not much better for Byzantine coinage. Venetian merchants often stipulated sums in the Byzantine *hyperpyron*, a gold coin seven-eighths fine. Because *hyperpyra* were relatively rare, Venetians usually exchanged the *aspron trachy*, a coin originally worth one-third of a hyperpyron and composed of 30 percent gold, 60 percent silver, and 10 percent copper. This coin, more than any other, was the one most familiar to twelfth-century Venetian merchants. But economic and political problems in Byzantium took their toll on the aspron trachy. By the middle of the twelfth century, Manuel I Comnenus had debased it sufficiently that it was valued at four rather than three to the hyperpyron. Subsequent emperors debased it further, so by the time of Dandolo's election it took six aspron trachy to purchase one hyperpyron.[21]

These fluctuations in coinage at home and abroad were destabilizing to Venetian trade. Dandolo and his council, therefore, resolved to take matters into their own hands by producing a new, stable coinage. For reasons that are not altogether clear they discontinued production of the silver penny and replaced it with two new coins.[22] The first was the *bianco*, or half-penny, which weighed about half a gram and had a 5 percent silver content. With a cross on one side and a bust of St. Mark on the other, the coin was valued at one-half a Veronese penny.[23] The other new base coin was the *quartarolo*, or quarter-penny. With virtually no precious metal, this was the first token coin minted in Europe since ancient Rome.[24]

Although important domestically, neither of these coins solved the problem of the devalued trade currencies. It was in dealing with this problem that Enrico Dandolo and his council would make their mark on international currency for more than a century. They issued the *grosso*, the first high-value coin minted in western Europe in more than five centuries. The grosso weighed about 2.2 grams and had the purest silver content that medieval technology could produce: about 98.5 percent fine.[25] The design of the coin left no question that it was meant to replace Byzantine coins as a medium of trade. The aspron trachy was struck depicting an emperor and a saint both grasping a cross or a labarum on the front and an enthroned Christ on the back. In clear imitation, Dandolo's grosso depicted himself and St. Mark grasping the banner of St. Mark on one side with Christ enthroned on the reverse (see fig. 8).

As with the Dandolo's legal reform, there is some debate concerning the precise date of the introduction of the grosso. Martino Da Canal, a Venetian chronicler writing about 1275, recorded that the first grosso was issued during the reign of Enrico Dandolo and implied that it was introduced in 1201 as a means to pay shipwrights building the war fleet for the Fourth Crusade.[26] In the following century, Andrea Dandolo recorded that the grosso was first struck after Venice's second treaty with Verona (Oct. 4, 1193) and Dandolo's mediation in the dispute between Padua and Verona (1193).[27] Scholars have for some time attempted to resolve this conflict.[28] While the question is of some interest, we should remember that there is only a difference of eight years. Whether Dandolo issued the grosso in 1193 or 1201 is much less important than the fact that he did issue it and that it would one day become the dominant coin of Mediterranean commerce. That day was still years away, however, for it appears that the grosso took a while to gain widespread acceptance, particularly given the popularity of the sterling.[29] Horde and die studies suggest that the Dandolo grosso had a fairly anemic run.[30] If indeed it was first issued in 1193–94, then it must have been a scarce coin. Perhaps, as Lane and Mueller have suggested, it was only in 1201 and 1202, when large amounts of silver began pouring into Venice to pay

Figure 8. Enrico Dandolo *grosso.*
(American Numismatic Society Collection, New York. Used with permission.)

for the crusade fleet, that the grosso began to be minted in any quantity.[31] Whatever the case, the Dandolo grosso was an important numismatic innovation, which established Venice as a major player in European and Mediterranean currency markets.

ALTHOUGH BOLD REFORMS characterized Dandolo's domestic policy, the same cannot be said of his foreign relations. Instead, the doge and his council sought to stay the course, continuing the policies of their predecessors, as can be seen in several areas. Throughout his reign, Enrico Dandolo continued to pursue diplomatic initiatives to secure legal rights for Venetian merchants in foreign lands. Even as they were causing foreigners in Venice to be evicted from their homes, Dandolo and his council continued their efforts to support Venetians living abroad. On September 21, 1192, just one month after the decree targeting new foreigners, Venice signed a treaty with Verona stipulating specific rights for Venetian merchants there. In addition, Verona accepted responsibility for attacks on Venetian shipping on the Adige and promised to make reparations to the tune of 10,000 lire. Venetians were also granted exemption from tolls or duties on the Adige.[32] With other Lombard states like Ferrara falling into line, it behooved the Veronese to make peace with their sometime enemy, even if the peace was less than optimal. Pressing its advantage, Venice negotiated a second treaty with Verona, signed on October 4. In it, rules governing disputes between Venetian and Veronese citizens were more fully laid out, as well as new procedures for the return of criminals and debtors.[33] Again, the terms were decidedly in Venice's favor. At about the same time Venice successfully mediated a dispute between Verona and Padua, although it is not clear what the quarrel was about.[34]

Dandolo also continued his predecessors' policy toward rebellious Zara. As we have seen, the city had chafed under Venetian political and ecclesiastical control for many years. Rebellion after rebellion was put down until 1180, when the Zarans were at last successful. For the next two decades Zara would remain a lone holdout on the otherwise Venetian-controlled Dalmatian coast. It was a matter of great concern for Venetian merchants, who feared the pirates hidden along the crannied coast near Zara, as well as the state, which relied on Zara for supplies of oak. In 1187 Doge Orio Mastropiero borrowed money from the Republic's leading citizens to prosecute a war against Zara; Enrico Dandolo was among those who had chipped in. In response, the Zarans allied themselves with King Bela III of Hungary, who constructed a strong fortress to ward off the Venetians. As it happened, the war was short-lived. Almost immediately after the siege had begun, Pope Gregory VIII ordered a cessation of all hostilities in preparation for the Third Crusade. Venice complied, signing a two-year truce with the Zarans. In 1190, shortly after the truce had expired, Mastropiero dispatched another fleet against Zara. The result for Venice was disastrous. The Venetians failed not only to capture the city, but in the process they lost control of the islands of Pago, Ossero, and Arbe.[35] Once again a short truce was struck. Given the alacrity with which the Venetians assembled a new war fleet, Zara's defiance must have remained a pressing issue in Dandolo's court. In 1193, probably in September, Dandolo sent a strike force to Zara commanded by Domenico Michiel.[36] The lost islands were recaptured, but Zara remained defiant.[37]

Just as the latest war with Zara was ending, another conflict in the Adriatic was heating up. Relations between Pisa and Venice, both far-flung commercial powers with weighty interests in Constantinople, had never been cordial. The Latin Massacre of 1182 had profoundly injured Pisa and led to Byzantine concessions to Venice. Pisan ships turned to piracy, raiding Greek coastal cities and preying on Venetian merchants.[38] Hostilities between Venice and Pisa were officially ended in 1183, when the two cities signed a ten-year truce, but Pisan corsairs continued to exact a toll on Greece.[39] Emperor Isaac II Angelus made a series of attempts to restore relations with Pisa, but they were confounded by the Pisans' unwillingness to repay Byzantium for damages. In 1195, Isaac was deposed and blinded by his brother, Alexius III. The new emperor had risen to power on a wave of anti-Venetian sentiment in Constantinople. Once again the Byzantine pendulum of favor swung away from the Republic of St. Mark and toward her rivals, Genoa and Pisa. Alexius encouraged Pisans to attack Venetian vessels as well as the Venetian Quarter in Constantinople. He ordered Venetian goods and vessels in Byzantine ports to be taxed—something forbidden by the chrysobulls of Isaac II—and ceased all reparation payments to the Republic. Inasmuch as the elevation of Alexius III coincided with the expiration of the Veneto-Pisan treaty, the Pisans had no qualm about reopening hostilities with Venice.

If Pisans needed an excuse to enter the Adriatic, the Venetian attack on Zara provided it. Back in 1188 the Pisans had signed a loose treaty of "peace and friendship" with the Zarans, which committed them to nothing but provided a rationale for intervention, if necessary. In 1195 a Pisan fleet sailed first to Zara and then to the island of Pola, which surrendered without resistance. At once, Dandolo dispatched ten galleys and six transport vessels commanded by Giovanni Morosini and Ruggero Permarino to Pola. By the time the fleet arrived, the Pisans had already fled. Again, Pola offered almost no resistance. Morosini and Permarino destroyed Pola's sea walls and then headed south in pursuit of the Pisans.[40] At Modon, they came across six heavily laden Pisan vessels. Four escaped, but two were captured and returned as trophies to Venice.[41]

The following year Ruggero Permarino was again in command of a Venetian fleet, this one parked just off the Greek island of Abydos. His colleague in command was Giacomo Querini. The fleet's original orders are unclear, but they probably included harassing Pisan shipping and protecting Venetian vessels. Nevertheless, Enrico Dandolo considered the fleet's proximity to Constantinople overly provocative and ordered it back to Venice. The captains refused to obey. The problem became largely academic, however, when, in September 1196, Emperor Henry VI imposed another ten-year truce on Pisa and Venice.[42] Despite the truce, the two states remained enemies. In 1200 Pisan pirates operating with assistance from Brindisi attempted to close off the Adriatic, thus strangling Venetian trade. Dandolo dispatched a fleet under the command of Giovanni Basilio and Tomà Falier to shatter the blockade. Once again the Pisans fled. The Venetian fleet punished Brindisi for its complicity, but the resulting treaty imposed on them was lenient, stipulating only that Brindisi deny its port to Pisa or any of Venice's enemies.[43]

Venice's quarrel with Pisa was primarily over Byzantium. Pisan pirates had usurped Venice's role as the maritime defender of the eastern empire. While the war ended in the Adriatic, it continued in the streets of Constantinople. It was vital for Venetians not only to get the upper hand over Pisa in the East but also to regain their privileges and the promise of reparations. To those ends, Dandolo again traversed the rocky path of negotiations with the Greeks. Shortly after the truce with Pisa had been signed, the doge sent Marino Mastropiero, son of the previous doge, and Ranieri Zeno as ambassadors to Alexius III.[44] Zeno had considerable experience in Constantinople and the crusader states, and he had once been a business partner of the doge's kinsman Giacomo.[45] The two men were well received by Alexius, but there was no diplomatic breakthrough. It seems unlikely that Dandolo and his council gave the ambassadors authority to go much beyond insisting on the reconfirmation of the chrysobull of 1187. The emperor sent the Venetians back with his own ambassador, John Cataphloros.[46]

Back in Venice, Cataphloros worked with Dandolo and his court to draft a new treaty based on the earlier chrysobull. In 1197 the work was complete, and Cataphloros returned to Constantinople with two envoys, Enrico Navigaioso and Andrea Donà. A third envoy, Benedetto Grillioni (one of Dandolo's electors), was to join the embassy in Constantinople.[47] In what was probably common practice at the time, Dandolo wrote up detailed instructions for his ambassadors outlining their options and limitations. It is the only document of its kind to survive from this period, and as such it constitutes an important source for understanding the role of the doge in Venetian diplomacy. Dandolo's instructions are given in his own name, not that of the council, the judges, or even the people. According to his oath of office, the doge was forbidden to pursue diplomacy with foreign powers without the council's consent. However, these instructions make clear that once that approval had been given and as long as it was sustained, it was the doge himself who directed negotiations. This document has additional value, for it provides a unique opportunity to hear Dandolo speak in a frank and open voice to his own men.

> We, Enrico Dandolo, by the Grace of God doge of Venice, Dalmatia, and Croatia, enjoin you, Enrico Navigaioso and Andrea Donà, our legates, that, when you have greeted the Lord Emperor and presented our letters and made the preface of your speech from its beginning, just as your insight impels you, then you should come to the root of the embassy: If he wishes that the treaty should be confirmed just as it was made, let it be so. But if he puts in a word about the king of Sicily's clause, which is contained therein, and declares that that occasion has already past and he wishes to include in the wording that we ought to aid him against Sicily and Apulia: say that we have not thought of that problem and entrusted nothing to you in your commission, and so you can do nothing about it. But if he wishes it [the treaty] with the question of the status of Sicily and Apulia postponed, let it be so, but otherwise not. And if he does not desire it any other way, skillfully attempt to bring his envoys to us. If, moreover, he mentions the emperor of Germany's clause and wishes to remove it, say that we sent you clean-handed and honorably and did not intend this nor say anything to you of it; wherefore you cannot do otherwise than as stated. And if he will not have it unless that clause is removed, you cannot allow it, but try to bring his representatives to us. If, however, he assents and wishes it, just as it stands, do you and the other envoys, if they are there, and if not, you alone, pledge our word that we, as is customary, have been empowered by the Vene-

tians to swear to this treaty in good faith, and we will keep it. If he sends with you his envoys and thereby sends us his chrysobulls for this purpose, that we should have them specifying those things which the others we have specified, and gives you or otherwise sends by his messengers the four hundred pounds of hyperpers which we have been owed to receive for two years, and if he is unwilling to send or give four hundred but at least gives or sends two hundred, assent. Yet if he does not even wish to give or send those two hundred, but gives us chrysobulls to the effect that we ought to have them, this should not therefore be refused. Furthermore, we enjoin you that if it appears necessary to spend anything on the problem of the Pisans, with the advice of the wise men who are in Constantinople and who are bound by oath to investigate in good faith and honorably about that problem, spend what seems right to you and them from the revenue of old and new date. And if the question should be of a truce to be made between ourselves and them, in the presence of the captains of the fleet still in our service, by their advice and that of other wise men who have been bound by oath for that purpose, as many as seems good to you, you have the power of agreeing with them [the Pisans] on whatever seems right to you and the others. But if the captains have already departed and the question of making a truce arises, do what seems good to you and to those whom you have bound to your council.[48]

The instructions concern four problems that Dandolo anticipated might arise in the course of negotiations in Constantinople. The first two deal with the king of Sicily and the German emperor. Clearly, the treaty draft that the Venetians took to the emperor was closely akin to the one signed in 1187. In the previous chrysobull, Venice had pledged to defend the empire against all aggressors except the German emperor and the king of Sicily. The latter was left out in 1187 because Venice had earlier signed a peace treaty with William II which would not expire until 1194. In his instructions, therefore, Dandolo anticipated Alexius III objecting that the clause exempting Venice from supporting Byzantium from a Sicilian attack was no longer necessary because the peace treaty had expired. But the doge had no desire to omit it. Henry VI wore both crowns in 1197.[49] If the new emperor launched an attack on Byzantium, Dandolo wanted there to be no doubt where Venice would come down. The third matter concerns the reparation payments, which were, as usual, overdue. While it is clear that he wanted the money, Dandolo was not willing to lose the treaty over it. Finally, he instructed his envoys to make peace with the Pisans in Constantinople or those undertaking corsairial warfare nearby, as they saw fit.

The draft treaty was not acceptable to Alexius III. As Dandolo had requested, another imperial legate was dispatched to Venice. The sticking points were, as they had been in the negotiations leading up to the chrysobull of 1187, the exemptions for attacks by the Germans or Normans. The problem soon evaporated, though, when Henry VI died. A few months later his wife, Constance, also died, and the infant Frederick II came under the tutelage of the pope. Rome and Constantinople breathed a sigh of relief, and Venice joined them. In 1198 a new treaty between Venice and Byzantium was finally agreed to. In it, Venice dropped the offending clause concerning the king of Sicily and promised to aid the Byzantines if the German emperor attacked them—something he was unlikely to do while cutting his milk teeth. In return, Alexius granted Venice exemption from all taxes and tolls in a long list of Byzantine ports. He further agreed that Venetians in Constantinople should have their cases heard by Venetian judges in all matters except murder or riot.[50] Despite the careful specifics of the laboriously negotiated agreement, Alexius III continued to tax Venetian shipping, as he had before. Although Venetians increased their business in Byzantium somewhat, it remained at lower levels than it had stood during Isaac II's reign.[51]

With the new chrysobull in hand, Enrico Dandolo and his council again turned to relations with their neighbors. On August 11, 1198, Venice signed a treaty with Treviso that, like the treaties with Ferrara, Verona, and Constantinople, provided for mutual defense, protection of expatriates, and special judges to decide cases between Venetians and local parties.[52] In June 1200 Dandolo concluded a treaty with the Patriarch of Aquileia, which provided, among other things, for mutual defense and stipulated that the patriarch would make no separate peace with Treviso if Venice went to war with the latter.[53] In the same month, Dandolo put his 1191 treaty with Ferrara to the test, claiming that Ferraran merchants owed Venice a great deal of bread, wine, and two boars. Legates from Ferrara agreed to pay up.[54] Three months later, Venice signed a treaty with Brindisi as a result of continued hostilities with Pisa.[55] According to Romanin, Dandolo also made a treaty with the king of Armenia in 1201.[56]

DOMESTIC AND FOREIGN policy can never be strictly segregated, yet doing so here provides a clearer picture of the progress of various initiatives during Enrico Dandolo's reign. After 1201, however, it is no longer possible to separate the two spheres. Led by Dandolo, Venice was about to become involved in the largest crusading effort in its history. The massive preparations for the Fourth Crusade for a time fused Venetian foreign and domestic concerns and strained the fabric of the newly reformed state. The outcome of the crusade would change Venice forever.

ᴛHE ᴄRUCIBLE of the ᴄRUSADE

nrico Dandolo became Venice's most prominent doge, not for his various reforms, his diplomatic initiatives, or even his great age, but for his involvement in the Fourth Crusade. It is through this lens that scholars have judged him, focusing intently on the last few years of his long life. There are good reasons for this. The Fourth Crusade was an event of enormous importance, one that shaped the subsequent history of the Mediterranean as well as relations between the Latin West and the Greek East. It is also a good story, which has attracted legions of investigators over the centuries, many of whom have drawn very different conclusions about its causes, course, and effects.

It is not my purpose here to rehearse the long and complex history of the Fourth Crusade. Rather, my intention is to examine Venice within the context of the crusade. The life of Enrico Dandolo, which has served as a guide for understanding the development of Venice in the twelfth century, can also be used to illuminate the Venetian perspective on the campaign to the East. When it was launched, the Fourth Crusade was the largest and most expensive project in Venetian history. More than half of all Venetian men and nearly all of Venice's sea power would take part in the enterprise. By the time it was finished it would transform Venice from a merchant republic into a maritime empire. No event in the Middle Ages had so profound an impact on Venice. Because of its enormity, the Fourth Crusade casts a sharp light on Venice in general and Enrico Dandolo in particular. The numerous memoirs left by crusaders enable the historian to view the doge and his city through the eyes of outsiders, both friendly and unfriendly.

The Fourth Crusade also provides a context from which to view the reforms that had shaped Venetian political life for many decades. The conservative oligarchy of leading citizens, disastrously overruled by the people in 1171, had succeeded in building a new government that concentrated power in their hands. They were risk averse, and a crusade, particularly one of this magnitude, presented an enormous risk. The means by which they, working with the doge, managed that risk not only elucidates the internal dynamics of the communal government but also better explains the actions of the Venetians within the framework of the crusade. For Venice, the Fourth Crusade was not a side trip or careless adventure. It overshadowed everything, consuming virtually all Venetian energy and ultimately disrupting the ordered world of the Venetian elite. For a few momentous years the history of Venice and the Fourth Crusade became one.

A word should be said at the outset about the character of the doge. A great many accounts of the crusade rely heavily on the harsh words of Nicetas Choniates, a Byzantine senator who never met Enrico Dandolo.[1] To this is added the shopworn stereotype of "Venetians first; Christians afterward."[2] The result is a rather grotesque caricature of the doge, based on little knowledge of the man or his world, which is then pressed into service to explain the outcome of the crusade.[3] Dandolo in these accounts is portrayed as a conniving and clever trickster who beguiled the naive northerners into a web of confusion so as to pervert their pious crusade into a war of Venetian profit and revenge. He kept his designs secret, mulling them over in the dark recesses of his black heart, where they apparently can be discerned only by the sharp eyes of contemporaries who never met him and by various modern historians.[4]

Needless to say, this colorful character will not receive another airing here. Instead, my goal is to apply what is known about Enrico Dandolo and his Venice to the events of the crusade in order to illuminate both. For a start, it seems evident that Dandolo was no Byzantine-hating zealot or irreligious charlatan, but a man of his time. He was a member of a new political class, which valued prudence and reasoned deliberation in Venice's dealings with other powers. The doge and his family had long worked for a peaceful and profitable relationship with Byzantium. The Dandolo were known for their piety, distinguished not only by their association with the patriarchate of Grado but also by their liberal donations to reformed monastic houses.[5] They were also crusaders.[6] As for Enrico Dandolo's personality, Nicetas Choniates' uninformed assessment of him as "a sly cheat . . . madly thirsting after glory as no other" is contradicted by a diverse body of witnesses who either knew the doge personally or had the opportunity to observe him over months and years. Geoffrey of Villehardouin described Dandolo as "very wise, brave, and vigorous," while the poor knight, Robert of Clari, judged him a "most worthy man and wise."[7] The Cistercian abbot Martin of Pairis related that Dandolo was an "especially prudent man," "perceptive of mind," who "compensated for physical blindness with a lively intellect."[8] The powerful baron Hugh of St. Pol praised the doge, describing him as "prudent, discreet, and skilled in hard decision-making."[9] In short, the testimonies of eye-witnesses confirm what the course of Dandolo's life suggests: He was a man of intelligence, probity, and prudence.

The Fourth Crusade was the brainchild of a new pope, Innocent III (1198–1216). Young, brilliant, and determined, Innocent believed that his great-est charge was to restore the lost patrimony of Jesus Christ in the Holy Land. After the decisive Battle of Hattin in 1187, the Muslim leader Saladin had wiped away most of the crusader kingdom, capturing Jerusalem and the precious relic of the True Cross. These were events that all Christians pondered and lamented. The Third Crusade, led primarily by Richard I Lionheart, successfully restored most of the Syrian-Palestinian coast to Christian control. Yet Jerusalem remained in Muslim hands. After the death of Saladin, the Muslims split into warring fac-tions, providing a respite for the Christian states. The pope was determined to seize the moment.

Almost immediately after assuming the throne of St. Peter, Innocent issued a call for a new crusade. Simply calling, however, would not bring it into being. The kings of England and France were at war and a disputed royal election plagued Germany. From the start, the pope put his hopes in the knights of France, who had always formed the bulk of crusade armies. It was necessary, therefore, that peace be made between Richard and Philip II Augustus. Innocent probably hoped that the Lionheart would return to the Levant, yet whether he would or not, the end of the war would free up French warriors to do so. In an encyclical written on August 15, 1198, Innocent laid the groundwork for the new crusade. He had already assigned two papal legates to the holy enterprise: Soffredo, cardinal priest of Santa Prassede, and Peter Capuano, cardinal dea-con of Santa Maria in Vialata. These trusted and experienced men were also charged with making the crusade a reality. Peter Capuano was sent to the kings of England and France with a mission to forge a permanent peace between the two or, failing that, at least to arrange a five-year truce. Cardinal Soffredo was sent to Venice "in search of aid for the Holy Land."[10]

The pope's decision to send one of two crusade legates to Venice was an im-portant one. It suggests that, contrary to common opinion, Venice's role in the cru-sade was neither an afterthought nor something imposed on an unwilling pope.[11] Rather, it appears that from the start Innocent envisioned Venice playing a prominent role in the crusade. Unlike other legates later sent to Genoa and Pisa to make peace, Cardinal Soffredo was a legate to the forming crusade with a clear directive from the pope to enlist Venetian participation.[12] His mission, therefore, was reminiscent of the events of 1120, when ten papal legates were sent to Venice seeking aid for the Holy Land. Yet the situation in 1198 was rather different. Calixtus II had urged the Venetians to embark on their own crusade. Innocent did not, for his sights were set rather higher. Soffredo, it appears, was part of a two-pronged effort to marshal troops in France and vessels in Venice. In other words, like his colleague in France, the cardinal was in Venice to lay the groundwork for a new crusade.[13]

Soffredo did not get far with Enrico Dandolo, who refrained from making any commitment.[14] Instead, the doge sent two of his own trusted legates, Andrea Donà and Benedetto Grillioni, to Rome to speak directly with the pope about the matter.[15] These two had just returned from Constantinople, where they had negotiated with Alexius III according to Dandolo's written instructions.[16] No doubt the doge provided similar instructions for this mission, although they do not survive. We can surmise the crux of them, however, from Innocent's letter of reply. The legates arrived in Rome in November 1198.[17] They informed Innocent that Venice's ability to aid Jerusalem was, in fact, constrained by the pope himself. They pointed out that since 1187, when Pope Gregory VIII decreed that no Christian merchant was to have commerce with Muslims, Venice had paid a price in lost revenues for the good of the faith. They reminded Innocent that, unlike other Europeans, Venetians did not engage in agricultural production but relied instead on shipping and trade for their livelihood. As a result, the Venetian people had already shouldered the burden of crusade for many years. It is unlikely that the envoys committed Venice to anything, but they did imply that a lifting of the papal restriction would pave the way for Venetians once again to take up the cross.[18]

This was Innocent's first dealing with Enrico Dandolo, and it was not altogether to his liking. Nevertheless, the pope wanted Venetian participation in the crusade and, just as with the English and French, he was willing to make a deal to get it. In what Alfred J. Andrea called a "grudging" letter, Innocent granted Venetians a dispensation to trade in nonstrategic goods in Egyptian ports.[19] In return, the pope expressed the hope that Dandolo and his people would enthusiastically come to the aid of Jerusalem. He strongly warned the doge that anyone who abused the dispensation would be excommunicated.[20] Despite its tone, Innocent's letter reveals the importance he placed on a Venetian fleet as part of the new crusade. It was important enough to send one of two crusade legates to secure it and important enough to allow the Venetians to engage in limited trade with the infidel to support it.

Historians have sometimes charged Venetians with faithlessness for their desire to trade with the Muslims. Yet the reality is precisely the opposite. The Venetian government had been restricting its own trade with Muslims centuries before the papacy began doing so. In 827, the famous Venetian merchants who stole the body of St. Mark in Alexandria were there in violation of an edict prohibiting trade of any kind in Muslim ports.[21] In 971, in response to a request from the Byzantine emperor, Venice banned trade in strategic goods with Muslims;[22] this ban remained in effect throughout the eleventh and twelfth centuries. When the Third Lateran Council in 1179 forbade Christians to traffic in strategic goods with Muslims it simply duplicated existing Venetian law. Of course, not all Venetians followed the law. Still, Venetian commerce of any kind with Muslims was extremely limited. From 1150 to 1205 Egyptian destinations account for only 11 percent of all surviving Venetian commercial documents.[23] Merchants from other Christian ports, like Genoa and Pisa, routinely traded in Egypt despite papal prohibitions.[24] Venice alone sought a dispensation to do so. It was, then, a matter of some importance to the merchants of the lagoon that their livelihood not be in opposition to their faith. If Venetians cared nothing for papal directives, as is often asserted, they would simply have ignored them, as many others across Europe did, and not have bothered to plead for a limited privilege from a reluctant pope.

The next few weeks were good ones for Innocent and the new crusade. Venice had responded vaguely, but not unfavorably, to the idea of a crusade, and, after difficult negotiations, Philip and Richard had agreed to a truce.[25] The pope had reason to be hopeful. That all changed in March, when Richard was killed during a siege. The crusade foundered for months but was at last saved by Count Thibaut of Champagne. At a knightly tournament held at his castle at Ecry-sur-Aisne on November 28, 1199, Thibaut, his cousin, Count Louis of Blois, and many others attending the tournament took the vow of the cross.[26] This gave the crusade a foundation on which to build. Enthusiasm among the nobility swelled. In February 1200, the illustrious Count Baldwin of Flanders also took the cross and was joined by his wife, Marie, Thibaut's sister. Although they were not kings, Thibaut, Louis, and Baldwin were among the most powerful lords in France. All three were young men in their twenties, eager to finish the work of Richard I in the East.[27]

A council of the leading crusader barons met at Soissons in early 1200 to discuss the timetable and goals of the new crusade. They agreed not to venture down the land route across the Byzantine Empire but instead to follow Richard's example and travel by sea. Yet, unlike the king of England, they did not possess a large fleet. They decided, therefore, to contract vessels from a maritime port. Thibaut, Louis, and Baldwin each appointed two of their men to a six-man committee with full powers to make contracts in their names. These six were to travel to whatever port seemed best and make whatever arrangements they thought wise and prudent. One of the six was Geoffrey of Villehardouin, the marshal of Champagne, whose memoirs are one of the most valuable sources for the crusade. According to Villehardouin, the six headed for Venice because they believed that no city could better supply their needs. Whether they knew that the pope had already approached the Venetians about joining the crusade is not clear. In any event, the envoys' options were fairly limited given the state of war between Pisa and Genoa.[28]

The envoys arrived in Venice in mid-February 1201. Geoffrey of Villehardouin was deeply impressed by the city and the doge. His account of his stay in Venice offers a detailed description of the negotiations, providing a unique opportunity to view the medieval Venetian government in action. The envoys were first greeted by Enrico Dandolo alone, probably at their place of lodging. They presented their letters of credence from the three barons. To these letters were appended clauses giving the envoys full authority to commit their principals in all matters. They were to be treated as if they were the counts themselves.[29] Dandolo marveled at the letters, for it was not every day that men came into Venice with blank checks from powerful lords. He asked the six what it was all about. The envoys, however, must have known something about Venetian ways because they refused to state their business until they could do so before the doge and his Small Council. They asked Dandolo to assemble the council the next day. Dandolo responded that it would not be possible for four days. In the meantime, the doge ordered that the envoys be entertained and honored as befitted those who represented great men.[30]

Enrico Dandolo is sometimes criticized for making the envoys wait. This and subsequent delays are seen as negotiating ploys to put the Franks in their place or as plays for time to allow the doge to hatch his plans.[31] Yet, as we have seen, the ducal court was a very busy place. Many of the cases before it were time-sensitive and could not be pushed aside. Four days, therefore, was not an unreasonable amount of time to bring the matter before the court. Nevertheless, even given the caseload, it is impossible to believe that Dandolo did not soon discuss the matter with his councilors. Although the six envoys may have kept mum about their mission, it would take only a little thought to discern it. Across France a large crusade was forming led by the barons whose seals were affixed to the envoys' letters. What else could they be doing in Venice if not arranging for transportation?[32]

On the fourth day the Franks were brought to the ducal palace, which Ville-hardouin described as "very rich and beautiful," and ushered into a room where the doge and his Small Council of six were seated.[33] After dispensing with for-malities, the envoys got to the point of their mission. "Lord, we have come to you on behalf of the great barons of France, who have taken the sign of the cross to avenge the shame done to Jesus Christ and to conquer Jerusalem, if God per-mits. And because they know that no one has as great a power as you and your people, they beg you for the love of God to have pity on the land beyond the sea and on the shame done to Jesus Christ, and to consider how they can obtain ves-sels and a fleet."[34] Dandolo asked for clarification. Just what were the envoys ask-ing for? They responded that they wished the aid of Venice in whatever way the doge and his council proposed and advised, provided it was within their means. Dandolo noted that the envoys were asking for a very great thing. It was not pos-sible for him and his councilors to answer immediately. They would need some time to study and consider the matter. He asked, therefore, that they return in eight days, although Dandolo frankly admitted that it could take longer.[35]

Although Villehardouin does not mention any numbers at this point, he and his colleagues must have told the council the size of the army that would require transportation; they could hardly negotiate without that important bit of in-formation. Dandolo's characterization of the matter as "great" and the subse-quent week of deliberations seem to confirm that the envoys had delivered some kind of estimate to the ducal court.[36]

At this stage the envoys' request remained with the doge and his Small Coun-cil. It was their job, apparently, to assess what Venice could do for the crusaders and how much it would cost. This was no small thing, given that the Franks were asking for one of the largest fleets in medieval history. Dandolo and his coun-cilors had to consider how many vessels could be drafted into service from Venice's merchants and how many more would need to be constructed. There was also the question of Venice's own participation in the crusade, which had been more or less promised to the pope almost two years earlier. It was crucial that they get it all right. If they overextended the commune's resources or failed to ask for sufficient payment, the results could be catastrophic. On the other hand, if properly managed, the merchants of Venice, who had plenty of experi-ence transporting pilgrims to the Levant, could make a tidy sum while still dis-charging their duty to fight for the liberation of Jerusalem.

On the eighth day the Frankish envoys were summoned to the ducal palace, where they again met with the doge and his Small Council. According to Ville-hardouin, they had a long and wide-ranging discussion, although he provides no specifics. In the end, Dandolo presented the envoys with the fruits of their de-liberations. Before doing so, however, he made clear that this was not an offer of service, but only one possible plan that would have to be approved by the Great Council and the arengo of the people of Venice—provided, of course, that the envoys themselves found it acceptable. With that understood, he laid out the offer. Venice proposed to provide transport and provisions for one year for 4,500 knights and their horses, 9,000 squires, and 20,000 infantry. The cost would be four silver marks for each knight and each horse and two marks for each squire and foot soldier, for a total of 94,000 silver marks. This was a rea-sonable price, well in keeping with the going rate at other ports. In addition, Dandolo announced that the Venetians would themselves join the crusade, sup-plying fifty fully armed war galleys, provided that all booty was divided equally between the Frankish and Venetian crusaders.[37]

The envoys were clearly pleased by what they heard, but asked for a day to think it over. It appears that they were able to negotiate the price for each knight down to two silver marks, bringing the total price of the fleet to 85,000 silver marks payable in four installments over the course of the next year. The fleet was to be ready to sail on June 29, 1202, unless changed by common agreement.[38] With that settled, the envoys announced that they were willing to seal the deal. Dan-dolo responded that he would bring the proposal to his people for their approval.[39]

With perfect hindsight it is possible to discern the seeds of the crusade's trou-bles sown here in the grossly exaggerated estimate of the size of the crusader army. The Frankish envoys bear the blame for the blunder—particularly Ville-hardouin, who as marshal of Champagne was supposed to know how to assess military strength and force sizes. We should not, however, judge them too harshly. By any measure, this was guesswork. Recruits were still joining the crusade across France and Germany, and it was not unusual to hear rumors of hundreds of thousands taking the cross. Villehardouin and his companions may well have be-lieved that their estimate was conservative.[40]

Many scholars have blamed Enrico Dandolo for the overestimation of troops, contending that the doge knew full well that the French could never assemble an army of that size. He did not dissuade them, it is said, for two reasons. First, he wanted to make a lot of money at the expense of chivalry-soaked simpletons. Second, he wanted to divert the crusade for his own purposes and realized that by trapping the French into a contract that they could never fulfill he would possess them body and soul.[41] There are, however, rather profound problems with this oft-repeated construction of events. It assumes, first of all, that Enrico Dandolo was an expert on feudal warfare and Frankish troop mustering as well as levels of enthusiasm for crusading in France and Germany. In fact, Dandolo had no experience whatsoever with the care and upkeep of large armies; few Venetians did. What he and his advisors did know was the sea. They knew how many war galleys they could produce and man and how many transport vessels would be needed to accommodate an army of the projected size. But for the size itself Dandolo relied on the experts—namely, Villehardouin and his colleagues. That is all that he could do. It is equally absurd to believe that Dandolo would knowingly commit Venice to an enormously expensive endeavor with the full knowledge that the other party could not pay their bill. Historians must remember that massive fleets and tons of provisions do not materialize simply because we write about them.[42] They were real and they required real outlays from real people who faced real losses if the French defaulted on their contract. Of all ways to attempt to control a crusade, this would surely rank as the most expensive and foolhardy.

During the next few days Enrico Dandolo shepherded the proposed treaty through the new and increasingly complex Venetian system. He summoned the Great Council, which convened three days later. Villehardouin tells us that the body consisted of forty men. The round number suggests that membership was now regulated and probably elected.[43] Nevertheless, the old practice of simply summoning important men to support a particular action was not yet extinct. After winning the support of the Great Council with "wit and wisdom," Dandolo took the proposal before successively larger groups of leading citizens—first 100, then 200, then 1,000.[44] Clearly, the communal government was still in a transitional state in 1201, mixing standardized governing bodies with customary ad hoc assemblies—at least for a matter of this gravity.

With the assent of the majority of the Great Council as well as the other groups, Dandolo was ready to bring the matter before the arengo. As we have seen, the rapid growth of the aristocratic communal government had been achieved at the expense of the traditional rights of the doge and the assembled people. Nevertheless, while the doge was constricted by an ever-growing body of regulations, the people could be kept only at arm's length. If they truly opposed an action of their representatives, they might strike it down, as occurred in 1177, when they believed that the doge was preparing to bring Frederick Barbarossa into the city in violation of papal orders.[45] Despite the significant reforms of the twelfth century, it remained true that no doge or council could commit Venice to as large an undertaking as the Fourth Crusade without the approval of the people. Nevertheless, a clear shift in power was evident, for now it was the oligarchy that summoned the arengo, not the other way around. The popular assembly was being asked to ratify what the councils had already crafted and approved. The task of the government would be to insure that initiative and authority remained firmly with the councils.

It is important to remember that the question to be put before the people was not only whether to enter a business deal with the Franks but also whether Venice should once again take up the cross of Christ. In other words, this was a moment of religious as well as economic importance. For the first time in eighty years Venetians were faced with committing themselves as a people to the redemption of the Holy Land. Everywhere else in Europe crusading was an individual decision, made by each crusader, but not in Venice, because Venetians crusaded as a state. Their decision, therefore, was a corporate one. In part this was owing to the requirements of naval warfare, but it was also a product of a strong Venetian self-identity. The question before the people, therefore, was not simply whether they should don the cross themselves, but whether Venice itself should do so.[46]

Because it was a religious question, the people were summoned to San Marco to hear a Mass of the Holy Spirit and to pray for guidance. After mass, Dandolo invited the crusaders to address the assembly. Villehardouin later recalled how curiously the Venetians had stared at them. He spoke for the envoys, telling the crowd how the most powerful lords in France had sent them to Venice, knowing that no other city had such great power on the sea. He implored his hearers to have mercy on the Holy City and to avenge the shame done to Jesus Christ by the desecration of the Holy Places. After finishing his plea, Villehardouin was joined by the other envoys. They fell to their knees, weeping profusely and swearing that they would not rise until their request had been granted. Dandolo and his fellow Venetians, equally moved by the plight of the Holy Land, also wept and stretched their arms upward, crying, "We grant it! We grant it!" Thus spoke the arengo. When the church at last fell silent the aged doge climbed the steps to the lectern. He told his people how highly honored they were that the greatest men in the world had chosen them as their companions in this enterprise.[47]

The next day the treaty was officially redacted. Two copies, both in the name of the doge, survive.[48] It was in this document that the pious enthusiasm of the Venetian people was matched by the careful precision of their government. The post-1172 reforms bore fruit, producing a cautious and detailed agreement designed to launch a grand crusade while simultaneously managing the risks in-

volved. Despite its precision, however, the treaty did not name a specific destination, although the principals made a secret agreement that the crusade should
land in Egypt. Following the advice of Richard the Lionheart, the French lords
believed that the Holy Land could best be recovered by striking at the base of
Muslim power on the Nile rather than by a direct assault on Jerusalem.[49] Dandolo, who had spent time in Egypt and had had an opportunity to judge Alexandria's defenses in the wake of a failed Norman attack, probably found much to
praise in the French plan.[50]

It is at this point in some accounts of the Fourth Crusade that the reader is
treated to a tale of dark intrigue. Enrico Dandolo, it is said, was secretly opposed
to an attack on Egypt fearing it would disrupt Venice's profitable position there.
Some have even gone so far as to suggest that the doge was engaged in clandestine negotiations with the sultan of Egypt to divert the crusade away from his
lands. Dandolo made up his mind then and there, it is said, to find a way to direct the crusade to Constantinople.[51] Although the story remains popular, it is
wrong.[52] Not only is it unsupported by any credible evidence, but, like most in-
dictments of the doge, it is based on an impossible intimacy with Dandolo's
inner thoughts. It also makes no sense. Venice, in fact, did very little business
with Egypt, despite the recent papal indulgence. An attack on Egypt, therefore,
risked little for the Republic. In 1201, the lion's share of Venetian overseas commerce was conducted at Constantinople, not Alexandria. If Dandolo had been
concerned only with profit, he would have worked diligently to bring the crusade to Egypt and keep it as far away from Byzantium as possible.[53]

With the treaties redacted, the envoys came to the ducal palace to receive their
copies. The doge had assembled the Small and Great Councils, whose members
swore on relics that they would uphold the terms of the treaty. Dandolo fell to
his knees weeping and then he too took the same oath. Moved by the sight of
the ancient doge, the envoys and the members of the councils also wept. According to Villehardouin it was at this meeting that the envoys explained to the
councils that the crusade was bound for Egypt. Shortly thereafter they borrowed
2,000 silver marks as earnest money to begin the construction of the fleet.[54]

Villehardouin's careful description of these negotiations provides a unique
window into the operations of Venetian government. What is most striking is
the continued importance of the doge, despite the erosion of his power over the
preceding decades. Throughout their stay in the lagoon it was Dandolo alone
who negotiated with the envoys. He did not, of course, have a completely free
hand. Like most modern leaders, he was able to work with his advisors in ham-
mering out a treaty, yet he lacked the authority to ratify it. That power rested

with the representatives of the people in the Great Council and, in this case, with the people themselves in the arengo. What is also clear from Villehardouin's account is that this was very much Enrico Dandolo's crusade. He and his Small Council were responsible for the Venetian proposal, and it was he who championed the plan during every step of its ratification. Enrico Dandolo sold this crusade to the Venetians. His prestige, position, and perhaps even his life were on the line.

All that remained, then, was to acquire the pope's confirmation. Envoys representing the Franks and Venetians arrived in Rome with drafts of the treaty in early May 1201. The crusade appeared to be shaping up along the lines that Innocent had originally envisioned. He immediately confirmed the treaty and sent letters throughout Europe ordering all crusaders to assemble at Venice the following year.[55] On May 8, 1201, Innocent wrote a letter to the Venetian clergy urging them to assist in every way his "beloved sons," Enrico Dandolo and the people of Venice, as they prepared to avenge the injuries of Christ. He then imposed a clerical tithe on them to help finance the crusade.[56] As Tessier points out, this letter confirms that the pope remained enthusiastic about Venice's involvement in the crusade.[57]

There was, however, the seed of a problem—one that would grow and ultimately strangle the long friendship between Venice and Rome. It was Zara. With the active support of Bela III of Hungary, the rebellious town on the Dalmatian coast continued to defy Venetian control and plague her shipping in the Adriatic. Zarans had also struck up a friendship with Pisa, providing assistance and encouragement for Pisan vessels waging war against Venice in her own waters. The situation was intolerable. As we have seen, one of Dandolo's first acts as doge was to launch a fleet against Zara, which captured several islands but not the city itself.[58] Since then Venice's hands had been tied. In 1195 or 1196, Bela took the crusader's cross, thus conferring on his lands the protection of the Church. The king died with his vow unfulfilled, and Hungary was plunged into a civil war between his two sons, Andrew and Emeric. In the interim, Zara turned to Pisa for support, until 1200, when Emeric won the throne and took his father's vow. Although the new king of Hungary had no immediate intention of crusading, the Church's protection was useful for warding off a Venetian attack on Zara.[59] With no effect, Innocent scolded Emeric for his delays and his attacks on Christians while enjoying the benefits of a crusader.[60]

It did not take long for Emeric to learn of the new crusade forming at Venice. Unsurprisingly, he did not find the prospect of a Venetian fleet filled with more than thirty thousand troops sailing down the Adriatic particularly comforting.

He suspected that the Venetians would be unable to resist using the army to restore control over Zara. Immediately, even while the Franks and Venetians were
still negotiating, he sent a letter to Rome expressing his fears and reminding the
pope of the special privileges that he as a crusader enjoyed.[61] Although Innocent was displeased with Emeric's delays, he agreed that the protection of the
Church must be respected. After confirming the crusaders' treaty, therefore, Innocent gave the Venetian envoys a verbal message for their lord: Stay out of
Emeric's lands.[62] Since Venetian and Hungarian interests intersected only at Zara,
this was a clear warning that Dandolo must put any idea of recapturing the city
out of his head.

The pope's message could not have been either unexpected or very welcome.
Zara was a direct threat to Venetian security. The idea of sending most of Venice's
military might on crusade while this enemy remained at home was unthinkable;
no crusading lord would do such a thing. Ever since the First Crusade the common assumption had been that one who took the cross might have to wage war
against Christians to stabilize his domains before departure. Richard the Lionheart, for example, had waged rather brutal wars against fellow Christians and
even fellow crusaders before sailing to the Holy Land.[63] It would be remarkable,
therefore, if the matter of Zara did not arise in the ducal court while the crusade fleet was being readied. Like Innocent, Dandolo may have believed that the
king of Hungary would soon fulfill his own crusade vow and thus negate any
danger the rebellious town may have posed. But what if he did not? What if he
remained in Hungary with his full military strength, hiding behind his vow and
watching as Venice's warships sailed out of the Adriatic? Could Venice trust in
the goodwill and piety of Emeric? These were the questions that Dandolo and
his councilors had now to consider seriously.

More pressing at the moment was the fulfillment of the treaty. It was to be
the largest project ever undertaken by Venice or, for that matter, any maritime
power since Antiquity. Dandolo immediately ordered a complete suspension of
all overseas commerce for eighteen months so that private merchant vessels could
be drafted into service for the fleet.[64] These large sailing vessels were to carry the
passengers, provisions, and military gear. One was the great roundship *Paradise*,
owned by Tomaso Viadro and captained by Deodato Bianco. It left Venice in July
1201, conducted trade in the East, and returned by July 1202, when it took its
place in the crusade fleet.[65] But few ships were as large as the *Paradise*. It is not
clear how many of these transport vessels were assembled, but it was a sizable
number.[66] Between May 1201 and June 1202 the Venetians also prepared a fleet of
50 war galleys and some hundred fifty horse transport galleys.[67] Most of these

would have had to be constructed. In later centuries the doge could have ordered vessels from the famous Venetian Arsenal, but in 1201 shipbuilding was still largely a private enterprise practiced in small shipyards throughout the lagoon.[68] Beyond the vessels, Venice also had to secure the tons of provisions necessary to feed the army while at sea.[69]

Perhaps the most difficult obstacle for the commune was the manpower requirement. John H. Pryor has estimated that crews for 150 horse transport galleys and 50 war galleys would require around twenty-seven thousand men. In addition, another forty-five hundred men would be needed to man the transport vessels.[70] To raise so large a force, the communal government instituted a lottery at the parish level. Balls of wax were prepared, half of which had embedded within them a small slip of paper with something written on it. These were entrusted to priests, who blessed them and oversaw the drawing by all Venetian men. Those who ended up with the embedded script were required to join the crusade.[71] If we assume that Venice had a population of one hundred thousand in 1202, then virtually all the adult male population would have been needed for the enterprise. That seems excessive, particularly when the lottery was designed to draft one half of the men. The remainder must have come from levies in other cities that owed military service to Venice.[72] In any case, Enrico Dandolo did not stretch the truth when he told the envoys that their request was a weighty matter. Indeed, the enormity of the effort makes clear why the decision to crusade had to be collectively ratified by the arengo.

One would expect that in a commercial city like Venice, where notaries did a thriving business, there would be an abundance of documents describing the year-long preparation for the crusade. Unfortunately, that is not the case. It is a lesson in the extremely poor survival rate of state documents from this period— most consumed in later fires in the ducal palace—that almost nothing remains to describe the means by which Venetians fulfilled their part of the treaty. Nevertheless, all observers, even those hostile to Venice, agree that they did indeed fulfill their obligations to the letter.[73]

As the months passed and the Venetians prepared for the arrival of the Franks, Dandolo and his councilors kept close watch on events to the north.[74] The young and powerful Thibaut of Champagne died only weeks after Innocent had confirmed the treaty. The barons searched around for a leader and finally offered the position to Marquis Boniface of Montferrat. Unlike the French magnates, Boniface was a mature man in his fifties with a lifetime of practical experience and a family well-connected to the rulers of Byzantium and the crusader kingdom. He was, however, an ally of Genoa, which may have caused some concern in the ducal court.[75]

More troubling was the French crusaders' early disregard of the terms of the treaty. On behalf of their lords the envoys had sworn that payment for provisions and transportation would be made in four installments by April 1202. The first installment of 15,000 silver marks was due on August 1, 1201, the second payment of 10,000 on November 1, the third of the same amount on February 20, 1202, and the final installment of 50,000 marks by the end of April.[76] It appears that none of these payments was made. Indeed, by June 1202, when the first crusaders began to arrive in the lagoon and the fleet stood ready to sail, the French had apparently paid nothing save the small down payment they had borrowed more than a year earlier.[77] None of the crusader accounts mentions this problem, but it must have been a source of grave concern to Dandolo and the other Venetian leaders. The payment timetable was a crucial element in their attempt to manage the risk that the crusade posed. Had the payments been made as promised, the Venetian government would have used those funds to offset the enormous costs of the fleet and provisions. As it stood, by June 1202 the Venetians had been forced to absorb the entire cost and were thus utterly reliant on the arrival of the crusaders to save them from financial ruin. The stakes could not have been higher.

At first all seemed to be going reasonably well. Eager and enthusiastic crusaders began arriving in Venice in June and were housed in the many pilgrim hostels around the city. There was, of course, not enough room in Venice to accommodate almost thiry-four thousand warriors, let alone forty-five hundred horses, nor would it have been safe to do so. To protect his people and his city, Dandolo ordered the early arrivals to relocate to the island of San Nicolò (the modern Lido), where they could establish a military camp.[78] Subsequent crusaders were taken directly to the island. Over the course of the next few weeks the flow of arrivals began to taper off. On June 29, the Venetians had everything in readiness for the crusaders, just as they had covenanted. Hundreds of major vessels were anchored and prepared for departure, thousands of Venetian sailors and marines stood ready, and tons of provisions waited on the docks. The situation on San Nicolò, though, was quite different. Less than one-third of the projected number of crusaders had shown up. It was plain to everyone that the gap between the army and the fleet spelled trouble.[79]

The papal legate, Cardinal Peter Capuano, arrived in Venice on July 22, nearly a month after the scheduled date of departure.[80] His colleague, Cardinal

Soffredo, was already on his way to the Holy Land to prepare for the arrival of the crusade.[81] Peter's first act was to absolve the crusading vows of the poor, the sick, and the women and send them home.[82] Beyond that, however, there was little that he could do.[83]

By the end of July, Enrico Dandolo had a debacle on his hands. The fleet had stood idle for a month while the Frankish leaders requested additional delays in payment to allow more crusaders to arrive. Although various groups did trickle in throughout July and even August, many more decided to find transportation elsewhere. Crusaders were bound by their oath to God to make their way to the land of His Son. They were not bound by the oaths of the counts of Champagne, Blois, and Flanders. If they could find a better situation for themselves at another port, most crusaders felt no compunction about going there. Villehardouin blamed all the problems that confronted the Fourth Crusade on these men, yet that is hardly fair. Even had every one of them come to Venice the army would not have reached its projected size. The real blame lay with Villehardouin himself, as well as his colleagues on the embassy to Venice, for it was they who had contracted for a fleet far larger than the crusade army needed or could afford.[84]

With each passing day the situation became more desperate. Conditions on San Nicolò were not good; the summer sun baked the soldiers, who had nothing to do all day but stare across the water at rich Venice with its awe-inspiring fleet docked safely out of reach. As might be expected, the men grumbled against the Venetians for the delay. They were ready to depart, why could they not do so? Why must they wait day after day on this miserable sand bar? Although it is often claimed that the crusaders were virtual prisoners on the island, utterly reliant on Venice for sustenance, the numerous defectors from the host attest to the easy travel on and off the island.[85]

Matters could not remain as they were. For the first time in its history, Venice was playing host to a large foreign army—and that army was upset. So too were the Venetians, who were angry with the Franks for their repeated failure to meet their obligations. The people of Venice had undertaken enormous expense, not only in the building of the fleet, but also in lost revenues from overseas commerce. At the center of this maelstrom was Enrico Dandolo. It was he who stood between both groups, attempting to find a solution. For the Venetians, Dandolo was the architect and chief proponent of the treaty with the French, whereas for the French, Dandolo was the voice of Venice.[86] Both groups wanted something from the other and it would tax all the doge's skills to find a solution.

EIGHT

VENICE & the DIVERSION

t some point in late July or August, Enrico Dandolo traveled out to the island of San Nicolò and met with the Frankish leaders. He told them what they already knew: The Venetians had produced the fleet and acquired the provisions that the crusaders had ordered. It was time—past time—for payment. The barons agreed. The hope that more crusaders would arrive was no longer realistic, so they began collecting payment from the host.[1] In the end, they did not have enough to pay half what they owed to the Venetians. Dandolo was upset by the news. He reiterated that the crusaders must fulfill their promises and threatened to cut off food and water if they did not.[2] It was an idle threat; supplies continued to be delivered. Nevertheless, the situation was dire. The Venetians could not afford to finance the Franks' crusade, nor should they be expected to. The crusaders could not pay; the Venetians could not renounce payment.

In the doge's Small Council, where the pious enthusiasm of the Venetian people had been translated into a carefully constructed treaty, the possibility that the army would not meet the French projections was addressed. Since Venice would bear the cost of producing a fleet of the contracted size regardless of recruitment successes in the north, the crusade leaders had sworn to pay the entire covenanted sum even should the numbers of crusaders fall short.[3] In this way they had attempted to manage the risk of the operation. The barons were well aware of this. Sometime in mid- to late August they told their comrades that they must give all their wealth in order to reimburse the Venetians and begin the crusade.[4] The majority of crusaders refused, arguing that they had already individually paid their full passage; it was not their fault if others had failed to appear.[5] At last, the leading barons gave all they had and could borrow in an attempt to make up the deficit. When all was accounted for, they still lacked 34,000 marks of the 85,000 owed.[6]

Dandolo recognized that there was no sense in issuing additional threats. The hard fact was that the crusaders were out of money.[7] Camped on San Nicolò, they would never be able to pay for the fleet they had ordered—and the clock was ticking. Soon it would be winter, when travel in the Mediterranean was impossible. If a solution could not be found within the next four to six weeks, the fleet would be forced to remain in Venice until March 1203.

The Venetian people were disgusted and outraged at the turn of events. Were this an ordinary commercial contract in Venice, the failure of one party to meet his obligations would carry with it a strong penalty. Many of the citizens appear to have favored disbanding the fleet and keeping the 51,000 marks rendered as payment for ship construction and lost revenues. Although this may have satisfied popular anger, it would have caused more problems than it would have solved. Dandolo pointed out to his council that Venice's reputation in Christendom would suffer enormously if they pursued that course of action. Not everyone would agree that Venice had the right to keep the money already paid,[8] including, certainly, the crusading host, who were already in a foul mood and could well become violent if forced to leave Venice without their treasure. The Venetians were in a foul mood, too, but the cooler heads of the oligarchic councils were able to keep them in check. Thus, the governmental reforms of the twelfth century passed an important test, avoiding a popular response that could easily have resulted in a cataclysm for Venice far more destructive than the events of 1172.

As doge, Dandolo was specifically forbidden to spend or promise Venetian funds without the approval of the Great Council.[9] He therefore had no authority to cancel or suspend the remaining debt of 34,000 marks. Indeed, his authority was probably already shaky, given the current disaster. Nevertheless, he had to act. A meeting of the Great Council was called and Dandolo explained the situation. We can imagine that the old doge had to endure quite a few recriminations for putting Venice into this bind. The commune was out 34,000 marks—almost nine tons of pure silver.[10] Dandolo suggested to those assembled that they allow the crusade to sail without payment, provided that the French agree to make it up when they had captured some booty.[11] This plan had its own problems, though. As someone on the council may have pointed out, this put the commune in the position of risking 34,000 silver marks of its own money on the financial success of the mission. Crusades were not generally very lucrative enterprises. If the crusaders could capture Alexandria or Cairo there would, of course, be more than enough to make good on Venice's losses. But what if they could not?

To compensate the people of Venice for the additional delay in payment and the risk to their money, Dandolo suggested that the crusaders help to recapture Zara on their journey down the Adriatic. In this way, even if the Franks were never able to make good on their debt, at least the Venetians would receive something.[12] Despite papal admonishments, the king of Hungary continued to ignore his crusade vow, except when it suited him to acquire papal favors or protection.[13] The doge had already sent word to Venice's possessions along the Dalmatian coast to expect the crusade fleet to put into port to gather additional men and supplies.[14] It is impossible to believe that the Venetians planned to sail this armada placidly by rebellious and dangerous Zara with no attempt at all to restore it to obedience.[15] The king of Hungary certainly did not think it likely, which is why he so quickly wrote to the pope requesting protection. But there is a great difference between a show of force and an armed siege. The latter was a possibility only with the consent of the Franks. To suspend their debt, the Great Council decided, they would have to give that consent.

There remained, however, the problem of the pope. As we have seen, Innocent had already sent a verbal warning to Dandolo that the lands of Emeric were under papal protection, and he had specifically forbidden the doge to use the crusade to settle his score with Hungary. The pope's attitude seemed grossly unfair to Dandolo and his councilors. Zara was a Venetian possession that had treacherously rebelled and, with the Hungarians and Pisans, had done everything in its power to harm Venice. In an attempt to reconcile the recapture of Zara with the earlier papal directive, the doge concluded that the pope's prohibition must have expired. Back in 1201, when there was so much enthusiasm for the crusade and it seemed that Emeric might do his part for the faith, Innocent had been right to extend his protection to Hungary. But things were different now. After more than a year Emeric was not one step closer to fulfilling his vow. Instead, he had spent his time waging war against his Christian neighbors, all the while insisting that they respect his privileged status. Dandolo saw this as a perversion of the crusade indulgence—a cynical attempt to use the cross as a shield. The pope, he insisted, could not condone it.[16]

The reasoning was self-serving, of course. Although Emeric was far from the model crusader, Dandolo had no reason to believe that the pope had actually withdrawn the Church's protection over Hungarian lands. Still, he was right about Emeric's attitude toward his crusade vow.[17] In any event, there were simply no other options. Without the restoration of Zara it is unlikely that the doge could have persuaded the Great Council to suspend a debt of such enormity. Without the suspension of the debt the crusaders could not get under way, and they would all return to square one, with a broken treaty and an angry army and populace. Zara was a compromise between the crusaders' desire to depart immediately without fully paying for the fleet and the view popular among Venetians that owing to the crusaders' insolvency the army should be ejected, the fleet disbanded, and the money already paid retained against losses.[18] Like all compromises, the plan to go to Zara was imperfect, but it averted a greater evil and seemed justified—or at least justifiable.

With the support of the Great Council, Dandolo crossed over to meet with the crusade leaders. He brought to their attention the lateness of the year. Summer was already waning and soon the sailing season would come to an end. The crusaders needed a place to spend the winter—a place, that is, other than Venice. He reminded them that their predicament was their own fault, for the Venetians had been ready to sail on June 29, as promised. Why not make the best of a bad situation? The rebellious city of Zara was not far and had everything the army needed to pass a comfortable winter. If the Franks would agree to help recapture it, the Venetians would suspend the remaining debt until it could be made up in booty. Thus, by helping their allies to perform a righteous task, the crusaders could solve two pressing problems: the moribund crusade and the need for a place to spend the winter months.[19] After contentious deliberations the crusade leaders agreed to the Venetian plan.[20]

On a Sunday that was a great holiday, probably September 8, the Nativity of the Virgin, the church of San Marco was filled with Venetians and crusaders.[21] Before mass, Enrico Dandolo, in full ceremonial garb, mounted the pulpit to address his people. Villehardouin, who was present, recorded his words thus: "Sirs, you are joined with the most valiant men in the world in the greatest enterprise that anyone has ever undertaken. I am old and weak and in need of rest, and my health is failing. But I see that no one knows how to govern and direct you as I do, who am your lord. If you agree that I should take the sign of the cross to protect and lead you, and that my son should remain and guard the country, I will go to live or die with you and the pilgrims."[22] Dandolo and his Venetian audience saw in this emotional spectacle more than we do today. They heard in Dandolo's plea an echo of the plea delivered at the same podium by Doge Domenico Michiel when he donned the cross in 1121. Then it was a young Enrico Dandolo who watched as Michiel filled the church with zeal, causing thousands of Venetians to follow his example and join the crusade. Among them, as we have seen, were Enrico Dandolo's grandfather, father, and uncle.[23] Dandolo had already imitated his famous predecessor by suspending all overseas trade in preparation for the enterprise. Now he completed the picture by taking the cross, delivering a moving speech, and leaving his son in charge of Venetian affairs dur-

ing his absence—all just as Michiel had done. As in 1121, San Marco rang with
the cries of Venetians assenting to Dandolo's request and clamoring to take up
the burden themselves. Dandolo then descended from the pulpit and knelt in
tears before the high altar, where he received his cross, not in the customary fashion upon the shoulder, but upon his cloth crown, where it would be more prominent.[24] The French crusaders rejoiced at the doge's enlistment not only because
of the numbers he drew in his train but also because of their confidence in his
wisdom.[25]

Why did he do it? Those who view the doge in the darkest terms see his donning of the cross as a cynical ploy to seize control of the crusade. As Nicol
writes, Dandolo could now "lead them where he wished."[26] There is no deny-
ing that the doge planned to play an important role in the leadership of the crusade, just as the various Frankish barons did. He was, after all, the elected leader
of more than half the crusading force. It is also true that, by virtue of Venice's
latest agreement with the Franks, Dandolo would be the de facto leader of the
crusade until the conquest of Zara. But beyond that, the doge could not exercise control over the entire crusade. No one could—that was one of the problems that plagued all crusades.

Some have suggested that Dandolo's departure for the East was a clever attempt to subvert the communal government and lay the foundation for a dynasty
in Venice. With his emotional display, then, the old doge was able to bypass the
Great Council, securing the vice-dogeship for his son, Ranieri, by popular acclamation. Yet this view can only be accepted if one ignores previous Venetian
history. It was already a well-established custom in Venice for a doge to leave
his son or kinsman to exercise power while he was away. Domenico Michiel left
his son Leachim and his kinsman Domenico to act as vice-doge when he crusaded in 1122.[27] In March 1168, Vitale Michiel had his son-in-law, Giovanni Dandolo, act in his stead.[28] In the dynamics of the ducal court it was important that
families be represented. It was perfectly natural, then, for Venetians to accept a
member of the doge's family as a substitute while he was unavailable. Although
the vice-doge had the full authority of the doge, he had no place of privilege
when choosing a successor. Given the new, complex process of electing doges,
it is difficult to see how any one family could hope to dominate the process. Indeed, no family ever could.

The assent of the arengo did, however, change the nature of Dandolo's power
in one important way: It made him the leader of the Venetian crusaders. That
he was doge has tended to obscure this important fact. Although Dandolo retained his title, he ceased to function as doge the moment he departed on cru-

sade; that is, after all, why they selected a vice-doge. Acting with the councils, Ranieri Dandolo was as fully active as any doge; his father was not. Although Enrico Dandolo would make decisions, enter into agreements, and have dealings with foreign powers during the course of the crusade, he did nothing in the name of the commune. He took with him men to council him, yet they were not officials of state.[29] During the crusade, Dandolo in no way "behaved like a doge from an earlier age."[30] He behaved, instead, like a military commander, which is precisely what he became when he took his crusade vow.

Like most crusaders, Dandolo had something to gain by taking the cross. To start, he gained the respect and admiration of his people, who saw in him an echo of Venice's past glories. This was no small matter given the beating his reputation must have taken during recent events. Perhaps Dandolo also wanted to be present when Zara surrendered. Clearly, there was no love lost between him and the people of Zara. The Dandolo name had for decades been a symbol of humiliation and oppression for Zarans, who chafed under the ecclesiastical jurisdiction of Patriarch Dandolo and withstood the naval attacks of Doge Dandolo. Still, he could have accompanied the fleet to Zara without actually joining the crusade. When he spoke of his unique ability to lead the Venetians, he may have been thinking about his familiarity with Alexandria, which he acquired in the aftermath of the failed Norman attack in 1174.[31] All these factors may have figured into his decision to take up the cross. But, like most crusaders, Dandolo also took his vow with extraordinary emotion. Like his comrades-in-arms, he believed that he was giving up all to serve Christ. Now in his nineties, Enrico Dandolo could not help but be mindful of the next world. Surely he knew that his chances of returning to Venice were very poor. He left home not merely for material gain but also for the salvation of his soul. In that way, too, he was like most crusaders.

September 1202 was a busy month as the Venetians and Franks made final preparations for their long-delayed departure. Enthusiasm was high in most, but not all, quarters. The papal legate, Peter Capuano, was faced with a thorny problem. Aside from Dandolo and a few members of the councils, Peter was one of the few persons in the lagoon aware that the pope had forbidden the use of the crusade for an attack on Hungarian territory. Yet what could he do? If he publicly condemned the new agreement between the Frankish and Venetian leaders, the crusade would grind to a halt and inevitably disintegrate; none of the parties would accept the continued presence of the Franks in the lagoon for the entire winter. Faced with this dilemma the legate decided to volunteer no information not specifically requested, simply allowing the crusade to begin without reference to the deal that had set it in motion.[32] In other words, Peter took advantage of the leaders' decision to keep the matter of Zara to themselves. Since the rank-and-file crusaders knew nothing about the diversion, Peter saw no reason to inform them.[33] Like Enrico Dandolo, the cardinal was squeezed between two conflicting imperatives and forced to find a middle way.

Unfortunately, news of the plan to recapture Zara began to spread among various crusade leaders and perhaps even into some pockets of the rank and file.[34] The crusading bishop, Conrad of Halberstadt, heard about it and at once went to Capuano. Conrad had not been involved in the negotiations with the Venetians and was therefore eager to learn whether the capture of Zara had the approval of the pope. Capuano replied frankly, saying that it did not, but that Innocent would rather overlook it than have the army dissolve. He insisted that under no circumstances was the bishop to abandon the crusade. Rather, Conrad should travel to Zara with the host and, once there, act according to his conscience.[35] Capuano was clearer when the crusading abbot, Martin of Pairis, along with several other religious came to see him worried about the news of the diversion. Martin wanted nothing to do with an attack on a Christian city and begged the legate to absolve him of his crusade vow so that he could return to his monastery. Capuano flatly refused. He ordered Martin and his companions to remain with the host. He also enjoined them to do all that they could to stop an attack on Christians once the crusade was under way.[36] He gave similar counsel to others.[37]

Given his advice to Conrad and Martin, it appears that Peter Capuano saw the departure of the crusade and the reconquest of Zara as two separate matters. The first was good, the second bad. He was willing to assist with the good by keeping the crusaders together despite their doubts. He planned to deal with the bad later, when his actions would not jeopardize the crusade. Evidently he hoped that once the crusade had landed at Zara and the French were informed of the pope's prohibition they would refuse to take part in the siege.[38] Whether they did or not, however, Peter would at least have discharged his duty to the king of Hungary and kept the crusade moving forward as well.

Enrico Dandolo and his councilors, of course, would have seen things quite differently. The departure of the fleet and the attack on Zara were not separate matters for them, but two sides of the same bargain. The Venetians were taking a great financial risk, bailing the Franks out of their troubles, in return for their help at Zara. The departure of the crusade fleet was predicated on that help. From their point of view, then, Peter Capuano was a dangerous threat. He had the power publicly to condemn the plan to go to Zara at any time, yet he refrained from doing so while the Venetians loaded up the vessels and prepared for the fleet's departure. They suspected that he would deliver his condemnation at Zara.[39]

To remove that possibility the Venetians informed Capuano that he would not be allowed to travel with the crusade as papal legate. If the cardinal wished to come along as a preacher, that was all well and good, and he could speak out to his heart's content about the evils of the diversion to Zara. But Dandolo would not suffer Capuano to sail quietly out of Venice and only later forbid a siege of the city in the name of the pope.[40] The legate was, of course, upset by the doge's parry, yet there was little he could do about it. Dandolo, after all, controlled access to the fleet. Unable, therefore, to prohibit the attack on Zara at Zara, and unwilling to do so at Venice, Capuano returned to Rome.[41]

With that problem seemingly out of the way, Dandolo was free to concentrate on the final preparations of the fleet as well as his own departure. The transport and horse transport vessels were turned over to the various leaders. Food and other supplies were loaded on board. Petraries and mangonels, three hundred of them, were loaded on the vessels.[42] It is unfortunate that the documentary record in Venice is so poor in this early period, for it prevents us from getting a clear view of the activities and attitudes of the Venetian crusaders. There is, however, one small piece of evidence. A will made just before the fleet departed provides a rare glimpse into the human side of one of the thousands of Venetians who took the cross in 1202.[43] It was made in October 1202 by Walframe of Gemona, an "inhabitant," or non-native resident, of Venice dwelling in the parish of San Stae. Walframe was a man of some wealth and probably young. His father, Enrico, was still alive, and, although Walframe was married, he mentioned no children. In his opening remarks, Walframe resolutely affirmed that he was "prepared to go in the service of the Lord and his Holy Sepulcher." In his will, he returned to his wife, Palmera, her dowry of 70 lire and left her three houses, which he and his father had given to her as a morning gift after their wedding. He further left her 300 lire to be distributed for his soul if he was killed on crusade. Given the lateness of the will, it must have been drawn up just before the fleet sailed. It is interesting that a priest at San Marco penned the document, rather than one from Walframe's own parish. It may be that clergy at San Marco provided notarial services for Venetians preparing to board the crusade vessels near the church. It is not difficult to imagine hundreds of men gathering their goods, bidding farewell to their loved ones, and putting their final affairs in order in the great open space of the still unpaved Piazza San Marco.[44] What became of Walframe, whether he ever returned to Palmera in San Stae, we shall probably never know. But Walframe of Gemona is the only Venetian crusader, with the exception of Enrico Dandolo, whose name is known with certainty.[45]

Finally ready to sail, the crusade fleet was a magnificent spectacle, comprising approximately fifty large transports, one hundred horse transport galleys, and sixty war galleys, as well as numerous auxiliary craft.[46] Although not all of the vessels and sailors prepared for the crusade were needed, most were. Many of the sailing ships had been assigned to certain "high men," who would not willingly share with their peers. Although a particular lord might not have had as many men arrive as he had hoped for, he would nonetheless want his own vessel. It appears, then, that about half of the transports and one-third of the horse transports were unneeded, and therefore left behind. The total number of Venetians on the crusade, therefore, may have been as high as twenty-one thousand—almost double the number of non-Venetians.[47]

The Venetians had uniquely constructed their fleet for an attack on Egypt. Fifty or more galleys would be required to defeat the Ayyubid navy, which would attempt to contest an enemy landing and retain control of the Nile. The horse transports were designed to operate in shallow water and back up to wide sandy beaches—perfect for the Egyptian shore. Scholars who insist that the Venetians planned all along to attack Constantinople must explain why they constructed a fleet that was not only ill-suited to such a task but expertly crafted to assault Egypt.[48]

The ceremony-laden departure of the crusaders occurred during the first week of October 1202. The last to take ship was Enrico Dandolo. Adorned in his colorful robes of state and his cloth crown emblazoned with the crusader's cross, he boarded the doge's vermilion galley. Four silver trumpets used on solemn occasions blared before him and drums rattled to attract attention to the show.[49] The various colored banners were raised and the sides of the ships and the castles were girded with the shields of the crusade leaders, each painted brilliantly to distinguish its owner. The clergy mounted the castles or poops of the ships to chant the *Veni creator spiritus*. As Dandolo's galley began to move followed by the rest of the fleet, a hundred trumpets of silver and brass signaled the departure and countless drums and tabors beat excitedly. Soon they passed the familiar island of San Nicolò on the right and moved out of the lagoon into the Adriatic.[50] Enrico Dandolo could not see the beauty of Venice as he departed, but he could hear the pomp as the cheering Venetians took one last look at their aged leader.

Zara was not the fleet's first stop, only the most important. The armada put in at a number of ports along the Dalmatian coast to insure continued loyalty and support. Since these cities owed military service to Venice, the doge could fill out his complement of rowers and marines and put aboard additional supplies.[51] Part of the fleet under the doge's command sailed directly across the Gulf of Venice at the head of the Adriatic to Pirano, in western Istria, arriving on October 9. Trieste, the greatest of the Istrian ports, and Muggia, a smaller town about five miles down the coast, fearing the power the doge had assembled, hurriedly dispatched large embassies of prominent citizens to do him honor. Overlooking their wrongdoings, which both towns were forced to acknowledge in new treaties, Dandolo received them into his grace, sending the emissaries back to their cities to prepare his reception. Shortly thereafter the doge sailed up the coast to Trieste, where the citizens received him with great honor. The priests turned out in their finest vestments, innumerable candles were burned, and all the bells of the city rang noisily. In a solemn pact Trieste pledged its loyalty to Venice.[52] The ceremony was then repeated at Muggia. The pacts are almost identical.[53]

The crusaders arrived at Zara in two groups on November 10 and 11.[54] Although the Fourth Crusade did not reach its projected size, it remained an imposing force. Since departure for Egypt was out of the question until the following March, the crusaders also had plenty of time. The fall of Zara was a virtual certainty—something that did not escape the Zarans. Without their Pisan or Hungarian allies to relieve them, they had no choice but to offer terms. Two days after the fleet's arrival, a deputation of citizens came to the crimson pavilion of the doge. They offered the surrender of the city and its goods to his discretion with the sole condition that the lives of the inhabitants be spared.[55] This was a rich moment for Enrico Dandolo. After many decades of arrogant rebellion and attacks on Venetian interests, now, at last, Zara was at his mercy. The doge replied that he would have to confer with his allies before accepting the surrender.[56]

What did Dandolo feel he had to discuss? Surely, the French barons would not have opposed sparing Christian lives. It is not even clear that the doge was required to confer with the French at all; the siege of Zara was a Venetian initiative in which the French had agreed to participate in order to defer their debt. Perhaps there was an element of piling on in Dandolo's decision to leave the envoys waiting in his tent, wringing their hands over their own lives and those of their loved ones, while he conferred with the French. Whatever the reason, the decision was a bad one. Had he immediately accepted the Zaran surrender much of the trouble that followed could have been avoided.

Shortly after Dandolo left his tent a group of knights and clergy entered. They represented a dissident faction of crusaders opposed to the capture of

Zara. They were led by Simon de Montfort, a zealous man who would a few years later turn his sword against heretics as the leader of the Albigensian Crusade. There is reason to believe that several members of this faction had a close relationship with Peter Capuano and were dismayed when the Venetians blocked him from accompanying the crusade.[57] Since then, the papal legate had made good time back to Rome, where he informed Innocent of the situation. At once, the pope fired off a stern letter forbidding the crusaders to attack Zara. It eventually came into the hands of one of Simon's partisans, Abbot Guy of Vaux-de-Cernay. Simon informed the frightened Zarans that the Franks would not help the Venetians capture a city under the protection of the Church. Enormously relieved, they thanked Simon for his honesty and returned to the city.[58]

Meanwhile, Dandolo had related the happy news of the bloodless surrender of Zara to the barons, who immediately voted to accept it. The leaders accompanied the doge back to his tent to seal the agreement. Of course, when they arrived there were no Zarans to agree to anything—only the defiant members of Simon's faction. They made no secret of their actions, explaining calmly how they had scuttled the surrender. Before much more could be said, Guy of Vaux-de-Cernay stepped forward, probably with the papal letter in hand, and exclaimed, "I forbid you, on behalf of the Pope of Rome, to attack this city, for those within are Christians and you are crusaders!" To ignore this prohibition, he continued, would mean instant excommunication.[59]

It appeared that Enrico Dandolo was checkmated. He had refused to allow Peter Capuano to accompany the crusade to avoid just such a papal prohibition delivered at the eleventh hour, after the Venetians had made good on their part of the bargain. The speedy arrival of Innocent's letter meant that Dandolo had alienated a papal legate with nothing to show for it. Indeed, the legate could at least have been reasoned with, unlike the harsh and intractable words of the pope's missive. With hindsight it appears that the old doge had made another poor decision. Reacting to a catastrophe that was in part his own making, filled with self-righteousness for his cause at Zara, Enrico Dandolo by his own actions was now poisoning the previously robust relationship between Venice and the papacy. But the doge's options had been and remained extremely limited. Innocent may not have liked Dandolo's methods, but they did save his cherished crusade.

Dandolo and his countrymen were plainly upset. According to one report, some of the Venetians tried to kill Guy of Vaux-de-Cernay after he delivered his fiery denunciation. They were stopped by the ready swords of Simon de Montfort and his companions.[60] Dandolo then turned to the barons, saying, "Lords, I had this city at my mercy, and your people have deprived me of it; you have promised to assist me to conquer it, and I summon you to do so."[61] The majority agreed that they must honor their word. Only a few joined Simon de Montfort, who pitched his tent away from the city so as to have nothing to do with the sinful act.[62] After a five-day siege, on November 24 the city was occupied and put to sack.[63] The men of Zara fled into the mountains, where they organized themselves into guerrilla bands.[64]

As Dandolo had told the French, Zara was a pleasant place to spend the winter. The Franks were quartered in the city center, and the Venetians moved into houses near the port, where they could tend to their ships and communicate with home. Still, many among the Frankish rank and file were not at all pleased by the situation. Their leaders had taken the best dwellings and left them with hovels. They were still impoverished, because the wealth of Zara belonged to Venice, not the crusade, and was therefore not subject to the equal division agreed to in 1201. They had waited for months at Venice and were now told to wait additional months at Zara. They had risked their lives to capture a city and received virtually nothing in exchange. It galled them to have the Venetians warn them off further theft or destruction in the newly won city. No longer willing to take orders from these sailors, some of the common soldiers lashed out against them. Three days after the conquest, near the time of vespers, bloody street fights began to erupt between the rank-and-file Franks and Venetians. The crusade leaders donned their armor and rushed into the midst of the melee to separate the combatants. No sooner had they quelled the fighting in one district than it would erupt in another. It took all night to restore peace. By sunrise about a hundred men lay dead and many more wounded. The doge and the leaders of the crusade spent the rest of the week soothing bitter feelings.[65] If proof were needed, the terrible night of blood and riot showed the wisdom of Dandolo's decision to quarter the crusaders on the Lido during their stay at Venice.

There was another matter troubling the conquerors of Zara: the state of their souls. By virtue of the pope's letter the attack on Zara had triggered an automatic excommunication of those involved.[66] This was a serious matter. Crusaders took the cross to earn eternal life, not perpetual damnation. It was the unkindest cut of all for the Frankish rank and file, who, after months of delays and hardships and with little or no material gains, had now succeeded only in winning an excommunication. For this, too, they blamed the Venetians—and with some cause. To calm the fears of the host, the majority of the crusading bishops administered a general absolution and lifted the ban.[67] Of course, the bishops had no authority to do any such thing; but the average crusader did not know that and he slept more soundly for his ignorance. Perhaps this, more than anything else, helped to bring permanent peace between the Franks and Venetians.

The Frankish barons immediately sent a delegation to Rome to plead their case to the pope and to request a canonical absolution.[68] The Venetians did not. Dandolo's refusal to beg forgiveness for the attack on Zara infuriated Innocent III, confirming for him the Venetians' evil intentions.[69] Modern scholars have tended to see it the same way. Yet, the situation is rather more complex. As leader of the Venetian crusaders, Dandolo was in no position to send envoys to Rome at that time. King Emeric of Hungary had already contacted the pope demanding the return of Zara and full restitution.[70] The restoration of the *status quo ante*, therefore, would be the pope's rock bottom price for absolution. It was easy enough for the barons to swear to such a thing, which they did.[71] Zara did not belong to them and, in any event, they had no intention of paying one penny to the king. For the Franks, therefore, a papal absolution was essentially free.[72] Dandolo, on the other hand, had no authority, either as doge or as crusade leader, to give away Venetian property; that would require a decision of the Great Council in Venice. Sending envoys to the pope, therefore, would not have brought the Venetians any closer to absolution. Indeed, it would allow Innocent to formalize demands for restitution that the Venetians could not at that time fulfill.

In practical terms, Dandolo's failure to send representatives to the pope had no immediate effect. All rank-and-file crusaders, French and Venetian alike, presumed that their bishops had absolved them. When the Frankish envoys to the pope returned to Zara in the early weeks of 1203, they brought with them an angry letter invalidating those absolutions. Innocent demanded that the barons ask pardon of the king of Hungary, return to him all that had been taken at Zara, inform the rank and file that they were never again to attack Christians without prior papal approval, and forward sealed oaths to Rome swearing that they and their heirs would render full satisfaction for their crimes. Only when these things had been accomplished would Innocent authorize his legate or nuncio to absolve them.[73] The French barons were willing to send off sealed oaths, which cost little, although they apparently balked at the requirement to bind their heirs.[74] They made no attempt, however, to meet Innocent's other requirements. Instead, they simply suppressed the papal letter. At the leaders' behest, the crusade bishops preached to the host that the pope had willingly absolved everyone.[75] Dandolo and his advisors, of course, knew the truth. But for them, timing was everything. They were willing enough to ask the pope for forgiveness and absolution, but not just yet.

About mid-December 1202, the titular leader of the crusade, Boniface of Montferrat, arrived at Zara.[76] He had not accompanied the fleet on its journey, but was instead detained by other business, which probably included a visit to Rome. In any case, as a partisan of Genoa, Boniface had no desire to assist Venice in wars against her neighbors.[77] Only one or two weeks after his arrival, envoys from the court of Philip of Swabia, one of the contenders for the German throne, sailed into Zara's port. They brought with them a story of treachery and intrigue—one that would change not only the course of the crusade but the history of Venice as well. Enrico Dandolo and a small group of the leading French barons gathered in the doge's residence to hear what the envoys had to say.[78]

The Germans' arrival was no surprise to several of the barons assembled that day. Boniface of Montferrat, for one, was familiar with their mission. Speaking for Philip of Swabia, the envoys asked the crusaders to have mercy on a young man of about seventeen years of age, one Alexius Angelus. Alexius was the brother-in-law of Philip of Swabia, the brother of the German ruler's wife, the Byzantine Princess Irene. The young man's father was the former Byzantine Emperor Isaac II, who had been treacherously overthrown and blinded by his own brother, also named Alexius, in April 1195. Since then, Isaac had been kept in comfortable confinement in Constantinople, while Alexius III's nephew, the young Alexius, was watched—though not too closely. In 1201, the young man escaped his uncle's agents, took a Pisan merchant vessel to Ancona, and ultimately made it to Germany and the court of his brother-in-law.[79] Like any Venetian doge, Enrico Dandolo was well acquainted with Byzantium's various imperial coups. He may or may not have known about the escape of young Alexius, which at the time was a minor matter. The young man had been born before his father became emperor in 1185, so it was generally thought that he had no legitimate claim to the throne.[80]

Shortly after becoming leader of the crusade, Boniface of Montferrat had traveled to Hagenau, where he spent Christmas with his lord, Philip of Swabia. It was there that he came upon the young Alexius Angelus. During the long winter nights, Boniface had the opportunity to discuss many matters with his hosts. Alexius and Irene were understandably upset about the treachery of their uncle. By rights, they insisted, young Alexius should be the emperor of Byzantium. Boniface was naturally sympathetic to them; his own family had suffered as a result of palace intrigue in Constantinople. It could have escaped no one's attention that Boniface was the new leader of a powerful army bound for the East, so they discussed using the crusade to topple Alexius III in favor of the young prince. Boniface promised to do all that he could to move the crusade in that direction.[81] In the spring of 1202 both Alexius Angelus and Boniface of Mont-ferrat made unsuccessful attempts to win the pope over to the young man's cause.[82] That summer, while crusaders were still converging on Venice, Alexius sent envoys to the crusade barons asking for their assistance and promising rich rewards in return.[83] The barons were intrigued, particularly given their difficult financial situation. They sent an envoy with the young man to the court of Philip of Swabia to discuss the matter further. If the German king would endorse the plan, the barons agreed to assist Alexius to his throne if he, in turn, would help them in Egypt.[84] Of course, all of this was kept confidential, restricted to the few barons involved. Enrico Dandolo, who had only recently taken the crusader's cross, was not included.[85]

And so it was that in a Zaran palace in January 1203 the envoys of Philip of Swabia addressed Dandolo and the other barons. They affirmed their lord's de-sire to send his brother-in-law to the host and stressed the responsibility of all crusaders to aid the downtrodden.[86] In return for their assistance, Alexius prom-ised richly to reward the crusaders once he had obtained his throne. First, he would place the Byzantine church under obedience to Rome. Next, he would provide supplies for the crusading army and, more importantly, pay them 200,000 silver marks. He also committed to raising an army of 10,000 men to join the crusade for one year and to maintain 500 knights in the Holy Land for the rest of his life.[87] The German envoys assured the crusaders that the majority of the citizens of Constantinople desired the overthrow of the usurper who occupied the throne.[88]

Historians have wrongly tended to see Enrico Dandolo as the main propo-nent of the German proposal.[89] From the beginning, this was the project of Boniface of Montferrat and a few French leaders.[90] It is possible that Dandolo knew something of the secret negotiations between the barons and the German court, although there is no evidence for it.[91] It is equally likely that the barons decided to keep the matter to themselves, just as they had kept it from their own people. The doge likely heard something about the Byzantine prince's plans be-fore the German envoys arrived at Zara. In Constantinople, Alexius III was fully informed of his nephew's intentions by mid-1202, when he wrote to the pope to dissuade him from supporting the scheme.[92] The emperor would surely have mentioned this to ambassadors shuttling between Venice and Constantinople at the time. It would not be surprising if he dispatched a special mission to Venice, similar to the one sent to the pope, attempting to dissuade the Venetians from supporting the Byzantine prince's claims.

Unfortunately, we know nothing with certainty about Dandolo's deliberations on Alexius's offer. There was, of course, much to commend it. The crusaders would have a fair chance of success at Constantinople, where armed rebellions had become commonplace. There was nothing new about an imperial hopeful purchasing foreign troops to support a bid for the throne; Alexius I Comnenus had come to power in precisely that way. If the crusaders could inconvenience the citizens of Constantinople sufficiently and if there was a viable rival faction in the palace or along the walls, then it was certainly possible that the young Alexius could be the next emperor.[93] In that case, the Venetians would stand to receive 100,000 marks, while the crusaders' reward would allow them to pay off their outstanding debt and put the enterprise firmly on its feet.[94] The professed obedience of the patriarch of Constantinople to the pope would also go a long way toward smoothing over relations between Venice and the papacy. It was also true that Alexius III had in turn favored the Pisans and the Genoese, something that had hurt Venetian business in the empire.[95] The installation of a new emperor who owed his position to Venice would undeniably be a boon to the merchants of the lagoon and a blow to their rivals.[96]

Dandolo and his advisors also had to consider the downside of the German proposal. There was the obvious possibility that Alexius III might weather the attempted coup. Most armed attacks on Constantinople to remove an emperor did, after all, fail. If Alexius III could hold on to power within the palace, then the game would be over. Dandolo knew, as anyone with knowledge of Constantinople knew, that a force of their size could never take Constantinople by storm; the emperor had troops in the city several times their number, and the mammoth walls, numerous towers, and deep moats had deflected armies ten times larger. Armed coups at Constantinople had succeeded only when they provided support for rebellion within the city itself.[97] The young prince insisted that he had sufficient backing in the capital to overthrow his uncle, but Dandolo had to consider that he might be wrong. Coups are never sure things—particularly in the treacherous world of Byzantium. If the crusade failed at Constantinople, Venice would be sorely harmed. Although Alexius III was less than scrupulous in meeting his obligations to Venetians, he nevertheless let them go about their business. And that business was very profitable. The lion's share of Venice's overseas trade went through Byzantium.[98] The Venetian Quarter in Constantinople was a thriving commercial center. Dandolo himself had painstakingly negotiated a new and very favorable trade agreement with Alexius III in 1198. Relations between Byzantium and Venice had been better, but overall they were normal.[99] Even the reparation payments for the seizure of Venetian goods in 1171 were no longer a serious matter. By 1203, Venetians had recouped more than 85 percent of their estimated losses.[100] There was, in short, much to lose if Venice took part in an unsuccessful challenge to Alexius III. The Fourth Crusade had already cost the Venetians dearly; a diversion to Constantinople could cost them even more.

Dandolo's dilemma was real. In return for the possibility of a more profitable position in Byzantium, he would have to risk Venice's already profitable position, as well as the property and perhaps lives of thousands of Venetian residents there. In return for the possibility of a friendlier emperor, Dandolo would have to chance wiping away two decades of work—much of it his own—to foster a peaceful and stable relationship between Venice and Byzantium. It was, by any reckoning, a big gamble.

In the end, the doge took the gamble. On the face of it the decision seems imprudent or even foolhardy, traits not associated with Dandolo by those who knew him. Yet, there likely were considerations of which we are ignorant. Perhaps the doge had intelligence from Constantinople that confirmed Alexius III's weak position. He may have judged that the crusaders had a greater chance of acquiring the funds to pay their debt in Constantinople than in Egypt. Dwindling provisions also appear to have played a role in his decision.[101] Although all or none of this may have been true, there was one factor that Dandolo could not ignore: The leading barons, including the commander-in-chief of the crusade, had already committed themselves to sailing to Constantinople. Their decision put enormous pressure on the Venetians to agree as well. If they did not, it is difficult to see how the crusade could have been preserved. In the end, therefore, the Venetians cast their lot with their allies.

The merits of the German proposal were discussed throughout the host. Most of the Franks were opposed to the idea. Undaunted, the leading barons, Boniface of Montferrat, Baldwin of Flanders, Louis of Blois, and Hugh of Saint Pol, as well as eight of their followers met once more with the German envoys in the doge's palace and accepted the offer. They would be shamed, they said, if they refused it. The conventions were drawn up, sanctioned by oaths, and sealed.[102] The German envoys, accompanied by two crusaders, returned to their king. They promised that young Alexius would join the host at Zara before April 20, 1203.[103]

Throughout February and March the Venetians prepared for the departure of the fleet. As the weather improved, Zaran fighters began harassing the city. The Frankish forces were depleted by desertions, led by those who no longer had faith in their leaders.[104] At last, April arrived and the crusaders were once again ready to sail. The plan, of course, was to remain until April 20, when the prince would arrive. However, on April 7, the entire army evacuated Zara and made camp near the harbor. For the next two weeks the Venetians tore down the rebellious city brick by brick. When they had finished, nothing was left standing save churches and bell towers.[105]

The decision to destroy Zara must have come from Venice itself, since only the Great Council had the authority to dispense with a Venetian possession. An interesting decision, it sheds light on the unique circumstances of the city's capture. The usual Venetian practice would have been to administer oaths of loyalty to the people, garrison the rebellious town, and appoint a Venetian official to administer it. Zara was a strategic and profitable port. Why then did the Venetians choose to destroy it?

As is often the case when a conqueror destroys a hard-won prize, the simple answer is that he cannot hold it. The members of the councils knew well that they lacked the manpower to defend Zara. It remained in Venetian hands during the winter of 1202–3 only because a large army was garrisoned within. Just outside awaited an alliance of Zaran and Hungarian forces determined to retake the city when the time was ripe.[106] When the crusade sailed away with most of Venice's military might, it is highly unlikely that those who remained could have resisted the coming attack. Faced with this likelihood, the Venetians judged it better to destroy Zara and leave the ruins to their enemies.

The destruction of Zara also served the needs of the Venetian crusaders. Pope Innocent had already made clear that he wanted the city returned to the king of Hungary before he would lift their ban of excommunication.[107] This was a crucial consideration for the Venetian crusaders, and had been for many months. Enrico Dandolo and his advisors were naturally eager to obtain absolution.[108] At the time, there was no reason to believe that they could not do so. Despite what the rank and file believed, *all* crusaders—both Franks and Venetians—remained excommunicated throughout their winter stay at Zara.[109] The destruction of Zara made it possible at last for the Venetians to request their own absolution. The papal requirement that the city be returned to Emeric of Hungary was moot. The ruins were there—he could take them if he wished.

So it was that in April 1203 Enrico Dandolo dispatched envoys representing the Venetian crusaders to the papal legate, Peter Capuano, who was watching events from across the Adriatic in Benevento.[110] The exact charge of the envoys is not known with certainty, but it at least included discussing terms for the Venetians' absolution.[111] They would also have had to address the willingness of the Venetians to accept the cardinal as papal legate.[112] Capuano was not pleased to see them. For the past month he had been receiving reports about the planned expedition to Constantinople. Sometime in late February or March he had written a letter to Innocent III requesting guidance on several questions, including whether he should rejoin the crusade. He was also unsure what to do about the Venetians. What if they refused to obtain absolution or to accept him as legate?[113] Capuano waited patiently for a response from Innocent, but it was not forthcoming. Rome was convulsing under factional warfare in early 1203, so the pope's attention was elsewhere.[114] At last Peter Capuano decided to act on his own. Although the Franks had not completed the pope's requirements for absolution, they had shown contrition. Taking what he could get, the legate sent a nuncio to Zara to lift the excommunication of the Franks.[115] The Venetians were another matter. They had refused to recognize his authority, failed to show contrition for their sins, and were now supporting the plan to sail to Constantinople. The legate, therefore, sent to Zara a formal bull excommunicating the Venetians.[116] The Venetian envoys and papal nuncio appear to have crossed the Adriatic at the same time, traveling in different directions. When the Venetian envoys arrived to meet with the papal legate, he refused to receive them, saying that he would have nothing to do with excommunicates.[117] Not surprisingly, the envoys were upset by the legate's attitude and returned to the doge to report on the situation.[118]

Back in Zara the crusade barons were pleased that they had been absolved, but thunderstruck by the papal legate's decision to excommunicate the Venetians. If Dandolo had not yet heard of Capuano's decision from his envoys, he probably learned of it now from Boniface of Montferrat.[119] Dandolo and his councilors informed the marquis that they had already dispatched an envoy to Rome to speak with the pope about the attack on Zara.[120] This may have been a result of Peter Capuano's refusal to treat with the Venetians. Boniface also learned, probably from Dandolo, that if the excommunication of the Venetians was made public, the fleet would dissolve.[121] Venetians like Walframe of Gemona had taken the cross to save their souls, not to lose them. If they knew that a formal bull of excommunication had been promulgated against them, most, if not all, would refuse to go anywhere until they had obtained absolution.[122] Without a fleet, the crusade would be over. To hold the fragmented enterprise together, Boniface suppressed the bull. He then wrote to the pope urging him to reconsider.[123] In an accompanying letter, Baldwin of Flanders, Louis of Blois, and Hugh of St. Pol also pleaded with Innocent not to require the publication of the bull lest the Venetians abandon the crusade. In addition, they asked the pope not to punish Boniface for suppressing the excommunication.[124]

A few historians have accused Boniface and the other barons of misrepresenting the situation to Innocent. The leaders, it is argued, knew very well that the Venetians would not abandon the enterprise if told the truth about their excommunication. Rather, they feared that the publication of the bull would lead to more desertions among the Franks, who would refuse to associate with the excommunicated sailors. Knowledge of the state of Venetians' souls might also lead to a stronger resolve among the rank and file not to travel to Constantinople lest they again incur the pope's wrath.[125] The barons certainly feared that the bull would lead to the dissolution of the Frankish army, and they said as much in their letters to the pope. John of Noyen, one of the Frankish envoys to Rome, had told Innocent the same thing months earlier.[126] But that in no way suggests that their fears concerning the breakup of the Venetian fleet were contrived or insincere. Given that the collapse of the army would spell the end of the crusade, adding the assertion that the fleet would also dissolve if the excommunication was made public adds nothing to the seriousness of the problem. Why, then, lie to the pope? In fact, the only evidence that the barons were untruthful in their letters is the usual stereotype of Venetians as cynical merchants who cared only for the things of this world. As we have seen throughout this study, however, medieval Venetians, like most medieval people, cared deeply about their faith and worried over the state of their souls. Just as Venetians did not want to risk hell by trading with infidels, they would not knowingly risk it to carry these Franks to Constantinople.

At about the same time that Dandolo was dispatching envoys to Innocent III and his legate, two ambassadors from Venice were sent to meet with Alexius III in Constantinople.[127] This embassy, overlooked by virtually all scholarship on the crusade, presents an intriguing problem. What was its purpose? The mere existence of the mission suggests that Ranieri Dandolo and the Great Council wanted to inform the emperor of events ahead of the arrival of the crusade. The two ambassadors were officers of the Venetian government, not envoys from the crusade;[128] neither they nor Venice had any authority to make deals or demands on behalf of the Frankish leaders. Making this clear may have been another purpose of the embassy. As it happened, the ambassadors never made it to Byzantium but were captured by Zaran corsairs on their way down the Adriatic. Perhaps another embassy was sent.

Back in Zara the crusade leaders at last turned their attention to their departure. Horses, tents, siege machinery, and provisions were loaded aboard the Venetian vessels. On April 20, 1203, all was in readiness, although the Byzantine prince was running late. The fleet set sail for Corfu, leaving Dandolo and Boniface behind to wait for him.[129] The Byzantine prince finally arrived on April 25, the feast of St. Mark.[130]

Before leaving Zara, Enrico Dandolo conceded the castle of Chessa on the nearby island of Pago to Roger Morosini, the count of Arbe. A kinsman, Marco Dandolo, witnessed the concession.[131] Although the doge could not stop the Zarans and their Hungarian allies from returning to the ruined city, the next best thing was to maintain strongholds on strategic islands nearby. Another kinsman, Vitale Dandolo, was made commander of what was left of Venetian forces in the Adriatic.[132] Nevertheless, no sooner had the crusade departed than the Zarans, with the help of Prince Andrew of Bosnia, captured Chessa and destroyed it.[133] With Hungarian help, the Zarans also began preying on Venetian ships, capturing among other things the Venetian embassy to Constantinople. The ambassadors, Roger Permarino and Pietro Michiel, were eventually released, although their losses were severe—totaling some 900 Venetian lire. Vice-Doge Ranieri Dandolo hit upon a scheme to repay the ambassadors at Zaran expense. In July 1203 he gave the two men authority to seize Zaran-held property on Venetian-controlled islands under the jurisdiction of the count of Arbe and use the income from those properties to make good their losses.[134]

By the end of 1203 many Zarans had returned to their city and begun the process of rebuilding. With insufficient forces to contest their return, Ranieri Dandolo ordered the construction of a small fortress on the island of Ugliano (modern Ugljan), which the Venetians called Malconsiglio (bad advice). The island lay directly across from Zara, separated from the city by only a few miles of water. From there a Venetian force kept watch on the Zarans and impeded vessels attempting to enter or leave the harbor.[135] Matters remained tense for the next year. Sometime in 1204, the archbishop of Zara, who was also the city's temporal leader, hired ten galleys from Gaeta that were docked in Split to sail to Zara and attack the Venetians. Interestingly, he used royal funds that had been earmarked for crusading purposes to pay the mercenaries. The marines of Gaeta sailed directly to Malconsiglio, destroyed the fortress, and put the entire garrison to the sword. In retribution, Ranieri Dandolo sent a squadron of Venetian galleys to devastate the archbishop's own island fortress at Vragnizza.[136]

In spring 1205, after the Venetian crusade fleet had returned home, Ranieri Dandolo sent a sizable war fleet under the command of Vitale Dandolo to punish Zara.[137] Although the Zarans had worked hard to rebuild their city, they still lacked the fortifications necessary to defend against the fleet. To avoid further destruction of their city, the Zarans sent envoys to Vitale Dandolo to negotiate a permanent peace. The resulting agreement represented a complete victory for Venice. The Zarans agreed to swear loyalty to the commune and to accept a Venetian count as their ruler; Vitale Dandolo took that job. Equally important, the Zarans accepted a new archbishop to be chosen by Venice. He was Leonardo, the abbot of the Venetian monastery of Santa Felice. Archbishop Leonardo, of course, was quite willing to accept submission to the patriarch of Grado, thus eliminating one of the major causes of strife between the two cities.[138] So began a long period of peace for Zara, now firmly under Venetian control.[139]

The Fourth Crusade's diversion to Zara did not end Venice's problems with the city, but it did lead in that direction. More importantly, the crusade's destruction of the rebel port insured that the Zarans would be unable to do much damage to Venetian interests while the bulk of the commune's forces were crusading. Although the pope was understandably angry about the attack, he recognized that for the Franks, at least, it was excused by necessity. Unfortunately, he did not view the Venetians' predicament with equal charity. Instead, Innocent became convinced that Enrico Dandolo had hijacked the crusade for his own purposes—which, in truth, he had. Still, the diversion to Zara preserved the crusade in which Innocent put so much of his hope for the Holy Land. An imperfect compromise, to be sure, it nevertheless allowed Dandolo to finance an enormous loan from the people of Venice to an army with a very poor credit history. Given the record of booty acquisition on previous crusades, it must have seemed unlikely that the Venetians would ever be repaid. The destruction of Zara gave them something, at least—but it also brought them the enmity of the Holy See, which would endure long after the Fourth Crusade had come to a close.

NINE

THE CONQUEST of CONSTANTINOPLE

hile Ranieri Dandolo tried to manage affairs in the Adriatic with a skeleton force, the attention of all Venetians was largely taken up by the events of the crusade. With more than half of Venice's men and most of her sea power committed to the enterprise it could hardly be otherwise. For those at home as well as those on crusade the stakes were high. An enormous amount of money remained unpaid and the prospects of collection were not improving. And now the crusade was headed to Constantinople, a source of great profit for the Venetians and home to thousands of their countrymen. For those left behind it was a time of watching, waiting, and prayer.

Throughout the Fourth Crusade's extended stay at Venice and its subsequent mission to Zara, the enterprise had largely been under the control of the Venetians. Unable to meet their commitments, the Frankish leaders agreed to serve the interests of the commune for a time. With the fall of Zara, that interim obligation was met, thus allowing the leaders to choose freely the direction of the fleet. This shift in command is most evident in the sudden arrival of Boniface of Montferrat in December 1202, followed a few weeks later by the envoys of Philip of Swabia. The function and motivation of the crusade was changing. No longer could Enrico Dandolo direct the crusaders according to his will, as he did outside the walls of Zara. Instead, the doge took his place among a group of leaders, who would henceforth decide the course of the crusade. Their decision to take up the cause of young Alexius Angelus had the ancillary effect of transferring the primary mantle of leadership from Dandolo to Boniface. Although the doge supported the diversion, it was the marquis who had championed it from Rome to Venice to Corfu. As long as the wayward Byzantine prince remained with the crusade, he would stay firmly within the circle of Boniface of Montferrat.[1]

This is not to say that Dandolo and the Venetians became mere hired contractors. They were crusaders, like the Franks, and made up a large portion of the fighting force. They also managed the fleet, without which the crusade was impossible.[2] For these reasons, Dandolo remained an important, although by no means privileged, voice in the councils of the barons. He expressed his opinion along with the others, and his advice was usually, although not always, heeded. In all matters it was the council that made the final decisions—an arrangement not unfamiliar to a Venetian doge.

Dandolo, Boniface, and Alexius sailed along the Dalmatian coast accompanied by a squadron of Venetian galleys. Taking their time, they stopped at several Byzantine ports, including Durazzo, to introduce the prince to the citizens and demand their allegiance. Since it cost little, the citizens were willing to comply.[3] In late May 1203 the three joined the main body of the crusade at Corfu. Amid great excitement, the crusaders welcomed Alexius.[4] As for the Venetians, they are absent from contemporary accounts of the crusade's three-week stay on the island. Undoubtedly they lodged near the main port, where they kept busy maintaining and defending the fleet. The Franks were camped outside of town. It was here that the soldiers learned that their leaders had committed them to sailing to Constantinople, and the ensuing dissension in the ranks was so great that the crusade nearly collapsed. In the end, however, the rank and file agreed to perform the task if it was done speedily and if they were assured of quick transport to the Holy Land afterward.[5]

The sailors of Venice were, of course, no strangers to Corfu. Standing at the mouth of the Adriatic, it had long been a place of importance to them. A century earlier, thousands of Venetians had died defending the island for the Byzantine Empire. The Crusade of 1122 had wintered at Corfu and unsuccessfully besieged the citadel in retaliation for the emperor's refusal to renew Venetian trade privileges. After peace had been made with Byzantium, Venetian merchants occasionally did business in Corfu's markets.[6] Despite the circumstances of their stay in 1203, there does not appear to have been any discord between the Venetians and the people of Corfu at this time.[7]

On May 24, 1203, the crusade fleet unfurled its sails and left the pleasant island. Rounding Cape Malea, the vessels followed the usual route to Constantinople: hugging the Greek coast before entering the Gulf of Euboea, then crossing the Aegean to pass through the Dardanelles and into the Sea of Marmara. Along the way, they stopped at additional Byzantine ports to demand allegiance to the prince and to take on supplies. Finally, on June 23, they cast anchor before the abbey of St. Stephen, about seven miles southwest of Constantinople.[8] Here they were in full view of the great city. For Enrico Dandolo and the Venetians it was a familiar sight. Not so for the Franks. Very few of them had ever been to Constantinople—indeed, few knew that so large a city existed in the world. They had never beheld so many and such magnificent palaces, and the many domes of Orthodox churches were also a strange and marvelous sight.[9] Constantinople was simply outside the ken of the northerners; the ten largest cities in western Europe would have fit comfortably within its walls.[10]

Before going any farther the leaders held a council at the abbey to discuss strategy. Many opinions were heard and argued, although few were based on any real knowledge of the area. More than one brave knight counseled a general march to the southern land walls of the capital, where they could prepare for an attack.[11] Perhaps only the Venetians knew the foolhardiness of such a plan. The mammoth fortifications of Constantinople were legendary, having deflected armies many times the size of the Fourth Crusade. Within the walls, Emperor Alexius III commanded a garrison that outnumbered the crusaders three to one.[12] Nevertheless, the aged Dandolo remained silent at the meeting until all had had their say. Then, according to Villehardouin, the doge rose and spoke:

> Lords, I know the conditions of this land better than you because I have been here before. You have undertaken the greatest and most perilous enterprise that anyone has ever undertaken. It would therefore be appropriate if you acted prudently. Know this, if we go overland, the country is large and broad, and our people are poor and short of food. Therefore, they will disperse across the land to acquire food, and there are a great many people in this country. We will, therefore, not be able to keep so good a watch that some of ours would not be lost; and we cannot afford any losses, for we have very few people for that which we wish to do.
>
> There are islands nearby, which you can see from here, that are inhabited and can furnish grains and victuals and other resources. Let us take port there and take the grain and the provisions of the land. And when we have loaded aboard the provisions, let us go before the city and do that which Our Lord has prepared. For he who has food wages war more securely than he who does not.[13]

In this council as in others, Dandolo's was the voice of experience and wisdom tempering the youthful daring of the French leaders. In this case, he stood in opposition to the knights' natural desire to see an objective and attack it forthwith. Rather than bravado, Dandolo stressed logistics and common sense. The

army needed food and Constantinople was much larger than the Franks realized—these were the two points the doge needed to get across. He succeeded.
The barons agreed to board the Venetian vessels on the morrow.[14]

When the fleet sailed north it went directly past the great city. Crowds of
Greeks perched on the sea walls of Constantinople to get a look. Because of
the high hills in the city many others could see the impressive armada from
rooftops or even from grassy knolls in the old acropolis (modern Seraglio Point).
In a city saturated with spectacle, where the unusual was commonplace, the large
and colorful crusader fleet was still a sight to behold.[15]

The crusaders made landfall at Chalcedon, a beautifully rich city across the
Bosporus strait from Constantinople, where they disembarked and foraged for
food. Three days later, on June 26, Dandolo moved the fleet about a mile north,
to Scutari, where it would be easier to cross over to Constantinople at the appropriate time. The Franks followed overland and took residence there. One of the
emperor's summer palaces became the new headquarters for the crusade leaders.[16]

Then came the time of waiting. Young Alexius had assured the barons that his
mere presence at the head of an army would cause the people of Constantinople
to rise up and overthrow the tyrant. Well acquainted with Byzantine politics, Dandolo knew that coups were not uncommon in Constantinople, although his advice
at St. Stephens and his decision to move the fleet make plain his belief that a show
of force would be necessary to bring events to a head. Given the history of similar imperial contests in the previous few centuries, that was a reasonable judgment.
Yet there was a strong unwillingness among the barons, fueled by an under-
standable reluctance to attack so large and powerful a city unless absolutely necessary, to acknowledge that the pretender may have been wrong about his support
among the people. And so for nine long days they waited and watched, always expecting the promised revolt or at least some news of conditions in the city from
young Alexius's friends. Nothing happened; the city seemed to ignore them.[17]

By this time Enrico Dandolo must have had a fairly good idea of the situation in the city, given that there were approximately ten thousand Venetian residents there.[18] Constantinople was, after all, not under siege. Even if the city
gates were closed (although there is no reason to believe that they were), one half
of the Venetian Quarter lay outside the sea walls along the Golden Horn, making travel to Scutari easy enough.[19] Dandolo, therefore, likely knew about Alexius III's agents, who were spreading word among the people that the young prince
had promised to lay the Orthodox Church prostrate before Rome.[20] The doge
needed no one to tell him that the Pisan residents of Constantinople would vigorously defend Alexius III's reign against the challenge of a Venetian candidate.

The crusade leaders met to discuss the situation. The French were anxious to inform the people that they were not enemies, but friends who had come to deliver Byzantium's beloved, rightful lord.[21] They could not understand that for most Greeks a rightful lord was whoever could seize and hold power in the capital. Dandolo, who knew this fact of Byzantine life well, no doubt tried to explain matters to his allies. His case was not helped by the arrival of an imperial envoy expressing bewilderment at the crusaders' presence at Constantinople and offering supplies to help them on their way to the Holy Land. This bit of diplomatic subterfuge left the false impression with the French that even Alexius III did not know the reason for the crusaders' journey to Byzantium.[22]

On several occasions the barons dispatched vessels to the sea walls or messengers to the city gates to explain their mission. Each time they received the same answer—a flurry of missiles.[23] At last they decided to concentrate their efforts on one final, high-profile attempt to communicate with the people. On July 3 all sixty of the Venetian war galleys rowed out across the Bosporus, taking up a position very close to the capital's sea walls. Enrico Dandolo, Boniface of Montferrat, and the young Alexius were aboard one of the galleys, probably the sumptuous vessel of the doge. As expected, the galleys drew a large crowd of onlookers. The crusaders displayed the prince while shouting, "Behold your natural lord!" They cried out the crimes of Alexius III and stressed that they had not come to do harm to the people but rather to defend and assist them. They urged the Greeks to take action against the usurper, but if they refused, the crusaders promised to do as much damage to the city as they were able.[24] Their words were well chosen. As with any armed coup in Byzantium, it was essential to make the citizens understand both the goodwill of the army if their claimant was accepted as well as their intention to become a destructive force if he was not.

This fanfare at the sea walls was not Enrico Dandolo's idea, although Robert of Clari later credited him with it.[25] Instead, it was the final act in an ongoing French attempt to communicate with the Greeks. Since he took part in it, we may assume that the doge was not strongly opposed to the demonstration, but he must have held little hope that it would work. Perhaps the dramatic display of the young Alexius was a compromise of sorts, the result of an agreement to try it the barons' way one last time. Despite the effort, however, the people of the city responded as they had before, with insults and missiles. With heavy hearts the crusaders returned to Scutari and prepared for war.[26]

On the morning of July 5 the Venetian galleys began crossing the Bosporus, each towing behind it a barge packed with archers and crossbowmen.[27] The plan was to attack the northern suburb of Galata, the key to the secure harbor of the Golden Horn. Alexius III arrayed a large force along the shoreline to contest the landing, but they fled when fired upon by the Venetian advance force. With the way clear the mounted knights poured out of the horse transports, which backed up to the shore. Anxious to get the fleet out of unsheltered straits, Dandolo urged the barons to focus their efforts on the Tower of Galata, to which was fastened one end of a great floating chain barring the mouth of the harbor. The doge suggested that he prepare stone-throwing siege engines on his vessels, which he would then line up along the chain and bombard the tower. The Franks could do the same from the land, thus besieging it from all sides.[28] This they did the following day. Within a few hours they had captured the tower and lowered the chain. The Venetian fleet swarmed into the harbor, falling upon the few dilapidated Byzantine galleys, barges, and light craft within.[29] The Venetian fleet now covered the Golden Horn, safely protected from the elements.

Once again a council of the leaders was held. Dandolo and his fellow Venetians pointed out that the fortifications along the Golden Horn were the city's weakest defenses and urged an attack there. They described their plan to outfit the vessels with flying bridges attached to the masts to allow soldiers to be lifted above the walls, where they could more easily fight against the defenders. The idea of clinging to scaffolding some hundred feet in the air, attached to a rocking boat amid the chaos of war, did not appeal to the Frankish soldiers. The knights wanted their horses, weapons, and armor—and solid ground on which to use them. Neither side was willing to budge, so they settled on a compromise: The Franks would attack the land walls near the Blachernae Palace at the northern apex of the triangle of Constantinople; the Venetians in their ships would assault the nearby harbor walls.[30]

On the morning of July 17 the attack on Constantinople began. Dandolo had drawn up his ships in battle formation along the shore. The transport vessels began their approach, followed by the smaller and more vulnerable galleys. As the transports came within range, the artillery mounted on the towers began to shower down stones, although miraculously none damaged the vessels. Crossbowmen and archers from both sides fired away, filling the air with bolts and arrows. The ferocity of the defenders' missile fire kept the captains of the transports from pressing too closely to the shore. A few vessels were able to graze the walls with their bridges, but they quickly retreated to avoid the deadly shower of stones. After additional failures, the Venetian assault stalled.[31]

At this point Enrico Dandolo did an amazing thing. Standing on the prow of his galley, fully armed, and with the banner of St. Mark waving in the wind before him, the blind old doge had been listening intently to the sounds of battle and the description of events from his men. When the advance of the transport vessels halted, he ordered his own galley to advance to the shoreline and run aground beneath the walls. Not surprisingly, his men questioned the wisdom of this tactic. Dandolo erupted in fury, promising to do bodily harm to them if they did not put his vessel on shore. And so the rowers put their backs into it, and the vermilion galley moved swiftly forward. All along the line Venetian sailors watched in surprise as the doge's vessel came out from behind the transports and sped toward shore. Amid the torrents of missiles they could see the winged lion of St. Mark and behind it the figure of their doge, still standing bravely on the prow. As soon as the galley made a landing, several men grabbed the standard and planted it on shore. This incredible display of courage gave heart to the Venetians. At once the roundships moved forward and the marines rushed to the flying bridges. Some managed to gain a foothold on the walls while others came ashore and scrambled up ladders. The Greek defenders fled, allowing the Venetians to move quickly across the fortifications, ultimately capturing twenty-five towers.[32]

There can be no doubt that Dandolo's heroism was startling and decisive. The picture of the old doge, face in the wind, crashing against the shore of Constantinople is deservedly one of the most enduring in the history of Venice or, for that matter, the Middle Ages. Perhaps that is why it is sometimes exaggerated. From the canvas of Tintoretto in the Chamber of the Great Council to the pages of Edward Gibbon's *Decline and Fall of the Roman Empire*, Dandolo has been depicted as the first warrior on shore, leading his countrymen into battle against the Greeks.[33] In modern historical works it is still possible to hear about the old doge waving the banner of St. Mark, shouting to his forces, and jumping ashore with the army.[34] Even in the pages of the *New York Times* one can read that Dandolo "led the way, shouting, through the breach."[35] It is this exaggerated scene that has led some to conclude that the doge could not have been as old or as blind as eyewitnesses record. In truth, though, Dandolo never physically moved during the entire episode. He did not grasp or wave the banner, nor did he shout orders to the other ships (which would have been impossible in any case). He did not even get out of his galley.[36] Dandolo was able to carry the load of his armor and maintain his footing on a moving vessel—but as anyone who has watched elderly women crossing the Grand Canal on *traghetti* weighed down by their shopping bags can attest, this is quite normal for Venetians. In short, Dandolo's dramatic act was well within the abilities of a vigorous man with no sight and abundant age.

With control of a large segment of the harbor walls, the Venetians opened the gates and began to flood into the Petrion and Blachernae districts, capturing plenty of horses and booty. Once they had passed into the city, however, the sailors were out of their element. Alexius III dispatched reinforcements to the region, probably including the elite Varangian Guard. After taking casualties, the Venetians fell back to the wall, setting fires to cover their retreat.[37] A strong wind fanned the fires into a massive and uncontrollable inferno, which quickly reduced a wide area of the northern city to smoldering rubble.[38] Dandolo sent word of his success to the Franks, who had thus far failed to make a dent in Constantinople's land defenses. They were understandably pleased by the news, particularly when several hundred captured horses accompanied it.[39]

The damage to the city and popular discontent with Alexius III's ability to prevent it was dangerous for an emperor with a challenger outside. Late that night Alexius III fled Constantinople with a thousand pounds of gold and as many precious stones and pearls as he could carry. Planning to use the money to raise additional forces, the emperor left his wife and heir behind to manage things in his absence. Given the poor quality of native troops, he probably planned to return with a mercenary army. But the Byzantine aristocracy was unwilling to endure the current danger any longer. With Alexius III gone, they restored the crown to his blind brother, Isaac II. At once messengers were sent to the crusader camp with the news that the father of the young prince was again in power. The gates of the city were flung open and the crusaders were welcomed as heroes.[40]

For the thousands of Venetian residents of Constantinople this must have been a joyous occasion. Most of them lived within the city's Venetian Quarter, a district that lay along the southern edge of the Golden Horn from Perama to the Phanar district—about one-third mile in length. Today this is about half the area along the Golden Horn between the two bridges. Half of the Venetian Quarter in 1203 was outside the city's sea walls, where residences and shops fronted a central road, and farther toward the shore stood landing stages for merchant vessels.[41] A gate, the Porta Drungarii, provided access to the other half of the district within the walls. Here a portico street (*embolum*) ran the length of the Venetian Quarter, with houses and shops on both sides. The name of this street was also commonly used to refer to the entire quarter. Aside from residences and shops, the Venetians also had a central warehouse for the storage and sale of commercial goods. There were several religious institutions in the quarter, including a church of San Marco and a monastery of San Giorgio, both affiliated with their namesakes in Venice. The largest and most important church was San Acydinus, owned by the Patriarchate of Grado since 1107 and a major source of income for the see. San Acydinus had its own bakery and shops and owned other rental properties in the quarter. In addition, the church held the official weights and measures for all Venetian business conducted in Constantinople. These, too, were leased to agents. The Patriarchate of Grado owned most or all of the eastern portion of the enclave.[42] Outside the Venetian Quarter one could still find a large number of Venetian residents, primarily those not directly involved in commercial shipping.[43]

For several days the crusaders had free run of the city. Shortly thereafter Isaac II requested that they take up residence across the harbor, in Galata and Estanor, where they could await their reward. They obliged, although they continued to enjoy free access to Constantinople.[44]

On August 1, 1203, the young prince was crowned coemperor Alexius IV.[45] With the transfer of power now complete, Dandolo's immediate concern was the payment of the Franks' outstanding debt to Venice. Shortly after his coronation, Alexius had paid 100,000 silver marks to the crusaders, which was divided evenly between the Franks and Venetians as they had covenanted. This allowed the Franks to pay their debt of 34,000 marks, finally closing the books on the troubled Treaty of Venice.[46] In that respect, Dandolo's gamble had paid off, at least for the moment.

But all was not well in Constantinople. Alexius was having a difficult time coming up with the money to pay the crusaders, so he proposed that the crusading host remain in his service until the beginning of the next sailing season, in March 1204. At his own expense he would renew the lease on the Venetian fleet for an additional year, to June 29, 1204.[47] Dandolo would naturally have preferred the immediate payment of the emperor's debt, but he also had to consider the ramifications for Venice if the crusade left Alexius IV to fend for himself. Alexius III still held sway over parts of the empire,[48] and if he managed to recapture the capital while the crusaders sailed to Egypt, the Venetians of Constantinople would be the first to suffer. Dandolo, therefore, strongly favored Alexius IV's proposal as did the other barons, though they knew that it would be a hard sell with the rank and file.[49] Dandolo's support for Alexius's plan, therefore, meant little without the agreement of the host. Because of their agreements and oaths, the barons would be forced to leave for Palestine if the army demanded it.[50]

With much debate, rancor, and cajoling from their leaders, the crusaders agreed to remain at Constantinople until March 1204.[51] All that was left was for Dandolo to draw up the contract with Alexius IV to extend the Treaty of Venice for one year. The treaty itself does not survive, although it presumably resembled the original. Based on a subsequent treaty, it appears that Dandolo charged the emperor 100,000 marks for the services of the fleet.

With that settled, Alexius and Boniface of Montferrat led a contingent of crusaders into Thrace in an attempt to capture the deposed usurper and restore control over the region. In their absence the seething anger of the Byzantine people began to boil over in Constantinople. Around or probably on August 18, a Greek mob attacked the Latin Quarters.[52] They made no distinction between friend and foe, torching the homes of Venetians, Pisans, Genoese, and Amalfitans. Hundreds of residents boarded vessels and crossed over to Galata and the safety of the crusader camp.[53] This effected the otherwise impossible: reconciling Pisans with Venetians.[54] The former enemies were now united in their desire for revenge. It would be surprising if some of the displaced Venetians did not petition their doge to retaliate against the Greeks or forcibly restore them to their quarter. Yet Dandolo, like the Frankish barons, had no desire to provoke a war with Constantinople, particularly when the crusade had been contracted to serve the emperor. Unable to get help from their leaders, a small number of Venetian and Pisan residents began rounding up support among the rank and file.[55]

On August 19, a group of armed Flemings, Pisans, and Venetians crossed the Golden Horn on fishing boats, entered the city, and began setting fires. Before they were finished, one of history's most destructive blazes had been set.[56] For three days it raged across Constantinople's mid-section—the most populous and opulent region of the city. An estimated hundred thousand Byzantines lost their homes; the material costs of the fire were astronomical.[57] In the wake of such destruction, it was no longer safe for a Latin of any stripe to live in Constantinople. Fifteen thousand of them took what they could and fled across the harbor to the protection of the crusaders.[58]

Because of the actions of a few Venetian and Pisan hotheads, their countrymen in Constantinople had been sorely injured and the city itself dealt a terrible blow. The great fire probably left the Venetian Quarter unscathed, but it was now abandoned and no one knew when it would be possible for the residents to return. The Pisans were not so lucky, for their entire quarter had been consumed by the inferno.[59] More importantly, the fire had physically separated the Greeks and Latins, something that boded ill for the future.

On November 11 Alexius IV and Boniface of Montferrat returned from their expedition, which had not been as profitable as expected. The young emperor, surrounded by a strong anti-Latin faction in the palace, reluctantly concluded that he would never be able to pay the crusaders what he owed, let alone honor his contract with Dandolo.[60] So he tried to ignore them. The emperor's tactic was a source of grave concern to all the leaders, but none more so than Dandolo. The original Treaty of Venice having expired, the Venetian fleet was apparently once again employed by someone who did not pay his bills. At least in the crusaders' case they had accepted their responsibilities and done all that they could to discharge them. The same could not be said of Alexius. Like the Frankish barons, Dandolo knew that in March 1204 the host would demand to be transported to the Holy Land to fulfill their long-delayed vows. That would probably be impossible unless the emperor made good on his contract. A doge in Venice, with the support of the Great Council, could command private vessels to take part in a crusade or other military operation, but Dandolo probably lacked that kind of power at Constantinople. Furthermore, he and the other Venetians would be reluctant to leave Byzantium without their promised payment. Something had to be done to insure that the emperor's accounts were settled, and soon.

Dandolo met in council with the barons. Everyone felt strongly that Alexius had no intention of honoring his word. The doge likely drew their attention to the problem of the fleet's payment and the necessity that additional funds be found. At last the council decided to send an embassy of three Franks and three Venetians to the emperor to deliver an ultimatum: If Alexius would not keep his promises, the crusaders would extract their payment from his lands. Geoffrey of Villehardouin was one of the Frankish representatives; as usual, he did not record the names of the Venetians, saying only that Dandolo selected "three high men of his council."[61]

In the imperial palace the envoys delivered their ultimatum. The members of the Byzantine court exploded in rage at this barbaric insult to the majesty of Rome. Alexius, now captive to the anti-Latin faction, said nothing. Fearing for their lives, the envoys made a quick retreat. When the crusade leaders heard what had happened, they prepared to wage war against the Byzantines to acquire their due. The Frankish knights excoriated the Greeks for their lack of honor. While honor was important to medieval Venetians, they would also have been outraged by the emperor's refusal to fulfill the terms of his sworn, written contracts. In this case, then, the chivalric and bourgeois ethics of the host coincided perfectly, more than justifying a war of plunder.[62]

Throughout the remainder of the winter, while the Franks energetically pillaged the nearby towns and countryside, the Venetian fleet made almost daily raids along the Bosporus.[63] Alexius IV's popularity in the city plummeted to new lows, sparking a successful coup, which landed his *protovestiarius*, Alexius Ducas Mourtzouphlus, on the imperial throne.[64] With great energy, Alexius V oversaw every aspect of defensive operations on the city's harbor walls. He did all that he could to put a stop to the crusaders' raids on the countryside, but his efforts were hamstrung by the poor quality of the imperial troops. Faced with this situation, Mourtzouphlus decided to try negotiations.[65]

The new emperor considered Boniface of Montferrat, who had been the liaison between the crusaders and the imperial court since the elevation of Alexius IV, too partisan to strike a deal, so he requested a meeting with Enrico Dandolo. On February 7, the doge boarded his galley and was rowed up the Golden Horn to a point near the monastery of SS. Cosmas and Damian.[66] Dandolo remained aboard ship while Mourtzouphlus was mounted on the shore. Since he had asked for the meeting, Mourtzouphlus must have had something to offer. Perhaps he promised to restore Venice's favored commercial position in the empire after matters had cooled down, or to provide the Latins with provisions and a distant campsite if they would leave Constantinople. Unfortunately, there is no record of what he put on the table. Dandolo's position, however, is clear. The doge promised that the crusaders would use their influence with Alexius IV to reduce Mourtzouphlus's punishment if he would release the imprisoned emperor and beg his forgiveness. He also insisted on the immediate payment of 5,000 pounds of gold, the equivalent of 100,000 silver marks. It is not clear whether this sum was meant to pay off Alexius IV's outstanding debt to the crusaders or his contract with the Venetians, both of which roughly totaled that amount. Finally, Dandolo demanded that the Greek church be immediately restored to Roman obedience and a Byzantine force prepared to sail with the crusaders when they departed in March.[67]

Dandolo did not expect Mourtzouphlus to accept these terms. Indeed, the doge was not negotiating in good faith at all. Unbeknownst to the emperor, while he exchanged words with Dandolo a Latin cavalry force was preparing to capture him. The knights charged into the area at full speed. Sensing treachery, Mourtzouphlus turned his horse and galloped through the city gates.[68] From Dandolo's perspective Mourtzouphlus had nothing with which to bargain. The crusaders' covenants were with Alexius IV, not him. In any event, Mourtzouphlus was in no better position to pay the Latins their due than was his predecessor. To do so would have made him as unpopular as Alexius, and for the same reason. Although Dandolo was naturally concerned about Venice's position in Constantinople, the restoration of Alexius IV would be a surer basis for that. Even if Alexius were never restored, recent Byzantine attacks on all Italian residents meant that Venice would have an equal chance of recouping its losses when the time came.[69]

For his part, Mourtzouphlus came away from the meeting with a clear understanding of Alexius IV's importance to the crusaders' position at Constantinople. It was he who had committed so much of Byzantium's wealth to these Latins. Dandolo's refusal to recognize Mourtzouphlus as emperor was especially galling. Therefore, on the night of February 8–9, he had Alexius IV strangled. The emperor attempted to pass it off as a natural death, giving the young man a full state burial and weeping tears over his grave. In this way he hoped to wipe the crusaders' contractual slate clean and pave the way for a negotiated settlement. But the Latins were not fooled.[70]

The death of Alexius IV presented another problem for the leaders, particularly Enrico Dandolo. It brought the entire contractual house of cards crashing to their feet. The Treaty of Zara was now void. The extension of the Treaty of Venice, undertaken by Alexius IV to keep the crusaders at Constantinople until March, was also defunct. Since the original Treaty of Venice had already expired, the Venetian fleet no longer had an employer. The only sworn commitments that still survived were the vows that the leaders had made to the host to take them to Palestine in March no matter the situation in Constantinople, and the vow each crusader had made to God to deliver the land of His Son.[71]

The crusade clergy salvaged the situation, although they had to act in defiance of the pope's orders to do so. After consulting together, the bishops and abbots proclaimed Mourtzouphlus a murderer, his people abettors of murder, and the Greek church again in schism with Rome. For those reasons, they extended the crusade indulgence to all soldiers who waged war against Constantinople with right intention. As a result, the rank and file no longer had a reason or a right to demand transport to the Holy Land in March, since the work of God was now on the Bosporus. Or so they thought. In fact, Innocent III had already unambiguously forbidden any attack on the Byzantines. The rank and file, however, were as ignorant of this as they were of the continued excommunication of the Venetian crusaders.[72]

The cleansing of Venetian souls had, in fact, remained a priority for Dandolo since April 1203, when he had unsuccessfully attempted to secure absolution from the pope and his legate. The excommunication remained a closely guarded secret of the crusade leaders. Aside from Dandolo and a few of his advisors, the Venetians all believed that they had been absolved along with their Frankish allies almost one year earlier.[73] It was Dandolo's task to make certain that this perception became a reality—and soon, lest the truth come out and cause the collapse of the enterprise. Back in August 1203, shortly after the coronation of Alexius IV, Dandolo had written to the pope again requesting absolution, this time stressing all the good that had come from the diversion to Constantinople.[74] On February 25, 1204, Innocent responded to the doge. In a sternly worded letter, he blamed Dandolo bitterly for the destruction of Zara, a city that he knew full well was under the protection of Rome. He scolded him for his rejection of Peter Capuano as well as his support for attacks on Christians in the East. Finally, he warned the doge not to rest smugly in his victory, for although matters had turned out well, it would have been far better if the crusade had made its way directly to the Holy Land. Nevertheless, after cataloging these crimes, Innocent shifted his tone, professing that "we refer to these matters for your correction in a spirit of genuine affection because the father corrects the son whom he loves." He commanded Dandolo and his countrymen "to atone for the blemishes of your sins with tears of repentance," once they had received absolution. He continued, "Thus having sought absolution in humility and having received it with devotion, you might press on with full strength toward the recovery of the Holy Land."[75]

Aside from the harsh admonishment, Innocent's letter contained almost everything that Dandolo could have wanted. It paved the way for, and indeed anticipated, the absolution of the Venetians. Although the papal legate could impose his own conditions, the pope's letter referred only to "tears of repentance." As Dandolo had foreseen, now that Zara (or what was left of it) was again in Hungarian hands, it no longer stood as an impediment to absolution. The pope's reply probably reached Constantinople in late March. At once Dandolo sent envoys to Peter Capuano in Syria to again request absolution, a request now strengthened by the pope's own words. Although the Venetians remained excommunicated on the eve of the attack on Constantinople, Enrico Dandolo had every reason to believe that they would be restored very soon.[76]

Throughout the month of March 1204, people on both sides of the Golden Horn worked diligently to prepare for the impending war. The Franks' dismal failure in their attack on Constantinople's land walls the previous July led them now to accept the wisdom of Dandolo's advice, which they had previously rejected. All forces, Frankish and Venetian, would be concentrated on a seaborne assault of the harbor walls. In response, Mourtzouphlus strengthened the fortifications there, adding new wooden towers to the walls and increasing the height of the existing towers in an attempt to counteract the effect of the Venetian flying bridges. Dandolo, therefore, ordered the flying bridges to be raised even higher. He also oversaw the installation of stone-throwing machines on vessels and the covering of the fleet with timbers, vines, and hides to ward off projectiles and fire. A hero to his men—particularly after his performance in the first assault of the city—Dandolo moved among them, bolstering their spirits.[77]

Although the preparations went well, two problems remained for the doge. The first and most immediate was the matter of the fleet's pay. The original contract with the Frankish crusaders had expired; apparently no payment was ever made on Alexius IV's extension of the contract. The Venetians naturally wanted their money. They alone bore the expense of the repair and upkeep of the fleet, as well as continued lost commercial revenues. If the army were to capture booty in Constantinople, the Venetians believed that it would only be fair for Alexius IV's debts to be settled before any general treasure division.[78] One way or the other, the vessels would have to be paid for. If the spoils were evenly divided, the Venetian share would have to go first to the fleet, and only the remainder to individual Venetian crusaders. Understandably, the Venetian rank and file would not support the idea that they alone should pay Alexius IV's bills.

Dandolo's second problem was more delicate and potentially more serious. If the crusaders were successful in capturing Constantinople, it was not at all clear who would be the new emperor or how his empire would be organized. From Venetian residents who fled Constantinople in August, or Latins expelled at the beginning of March, or from his own experience with Byzantine culture, Dandolo probably realized that the people of Byzantium saw Boniface of Montferrat as an imperial contender.[79] If the crusaders gained entry into the city and put Mourtzouphlus to flight, the people would presumably welcome the new emperor according to their time-honored rituals and with all haste crown him in Hagia Sophia.[80] As a partisan of Genoa, Emperor Boniface's reign might be problematic for Venice. More importantly, though, Boniface's assumption of the throne could cause strife among the Latin lords, particularly among those who wanted the throne for themselves or who believed that they had not been sufficiently rewarded in wealth or land. In short, unless there was an articulated procedure for selecting an emperor and distributing offices and land, the potential for instability in a new empire would be considerable. Like all Venetians, Dandolo strongly and consistently favored stability in Byzantium.[81]

The doge addressed both of these problems in March during a general assembly of the host. After a wide-ranging discussion, about which we are told nothing, the crusaders finally settled on a plan. The written form of the agreement, known as the Pact of March, laid out in detail the ground rules for the conquest of Constantinople. It was sworn to by Enrico Dandolo, on one side, and Boniface of Montferrat, Baldwin of Flanders, Louis of Blois, and Hugh of Saint Pol, on the other.[82] The treaty begins by committing all parties to undertaking a vigorous attack on the capital. If, with God's help, they should gain entry into the city, all booty would be brought together into one place for an equitable division. First and foremost the unpaid debts of Alexius IV should be settled.[83] When Alexius died he owed the crusaders as a whole approximately 100,000 silver marks on the Treaty of Zara. He also owed the Venetians an additional 100,000 silver marks for the extension of the Treaty of Venice. Therefore, the Venetians were owed 150,000 marks when Alexius was murdered and the Frankish crusaders 50,000 marks.[84] The pact stipulated, therefore, that when the booty was divided the Venetians would receive three portions for each single portion that went to non-Venetians. All foodstuffs should be divided equally from the start. If they were able to lay hands on less than the amount owed, both sides would simply have to live with their losses. If, on the other hand, the booty exceeded that total, all excess funds would be divided equally between the Franks and the Venetians in accordance with the Treaty of Venice. In this way the expense of the fleet would not have to be shouldered by the Venetian crusaders alone.

It was further decided that if the city itself should fall, six Franks and six Venetians would be chosen to elect an emperor. The new emperor would receive one-quarter of the city and empire as well as the Great Palace and Blachernae Palace in Constantinople. The remaining three-quarters would be divided equally between the Franks and the Venetians. If the emperor should be selected from among the Franks, the Venetians would have the right to Hagia Sophia and the patriarchate, and vice-versa. Twelve Franks and twelve Venetians would then be elected from among the wisest men to allocate fiefs and offices among the leaders and to establish the services that the recipients would owe to the emperor in return. All crusaders swore to remain by the emperor's side until the end of March 1205, at which time they would be free to go where they pleased.[85] They also agreed that no citizens of a state at war with Venice should be admitted into the empire. Although this last provision may have meant little to the Franks, it was a potential bonanza for Venice. No longer reliant on the promises of unreliable emperors, Venetians in this hypothetical empire would have their position guaranteed by its founding charter. Moreover, the position of Venice's rivals in the empire would depend solely on the goodwill of the Venetian people.[86]

The last clause in the pact returns to the question of feudal service. Its odd placement in the document suggests that it was an amendment or a late compromise between Dandolo and the barons. The clause addresses the matter of Byzantine territories allocated to the Venetians. Should those landholders owe fealty and service to the emperor in Constantinople or to the doge in Venice?

In other words, should the Venetian share of the conquests remain within the empire or should it become part of the commune's overseas holdings? This was an important question, for it bore directly on the Venetian state's relationship to the actions of the crusade. Dandolo had no authority to commit Venice to overseas territorial acquisitions, nor would it have been wise to do so. Instead, he and his councilors appear to have built on the model of other Venetian overseas colonies in Palestine, particularly at Tyre.[87] There the Venetians constituted a colony within a foreign state. Venetian citizens in Tyre owned and governed one-third of the city, which they had received after the Crusade of 1122. Nevertheless, they remained within the political framework of the Kingdom of Jerusalem. The communal government in Venice naturally took an interest in Tyre, but it had no obligation to defend or support it as Venetian territory. Enrico Dandolo, therefore, agreed in the Pact of March that Venetians who acquired lands or offices as a result of the conquest of Constantinople would swear fealty for them to the emperor and the empire. He insisted, however, on an exemption for himself. As the leader of the Venetian crusaders he was within his rights to make treaties and agreements that affected the expedition and its outcome. As doge of Venice, though, he had no power to bind himself, his successors, or the commune to a foreign ruler. For that reason, although Dandolo was not required to swear fealty for any land, office, or honor he might receive, anyone to whom he delegated authority over those things would do so. This narrow exemption brought the Pact of March into conformity with Venetian law—a necessity if the doge was to accept it.[88]

The long-anticipated attack came on Friday, April 9. In a line the Venetian vessels made their way amid fierce missile fire toward the walls of Constantinople.[89] The fighting raged most of the day, but the crusaders were unable to breach the city's defenses. An unusual south wind hampered operations, driving the transport ships back from the walls, enabling only five of them to draw close enough to the towers to exchange blows with the Greeks.[90] None could affix its assault bridge.[91] After suffering heavy casualties, the crusaders retreated to the opposite shore of the Golden Horn.[92] Suddenly the Pact of March looked hopelessly idealistic.

This was the first major defeat of the crusaders since their arrival at Constantinople, and it did not go down well. Convinced that God himself opposed their actions, the common soldiers and many of the leaders wanted to abandon the whole project. That evening at about six o'clock another general assembly of the host convened. The meeting was contentious. Many wanted to withdraw, board the Venetian vessels, and head east. Others argued that the tactics of the assault were deficient. Why attack the walls that Mourtzouphlus had so strongly reinforced? Why not bring the fleet out of the Golden Horn and attack the sea walls along the Bosporus or the Sea of Marmara? Dandolo objected to this plan, pointing out that the strong current running down the strait would make a naval assault there impossible—the fleet would be swept away.[93]

The Venetian position at the assembly, although not explicitly recorded, is not difficult to surmise. Sailing away to the Holy Land may have been a popular idea among the common soldiers, but it was probably impossible. The Venetian fleet, consisting mostly of privately owned vessels, had not been reimbursed for its services and no longer had any contractual obligation to the Franks. Unless the funds could be found to make good on the promises of Alexius IV it is difficult to see how anyone, Venetians or Franks, could afford to wage war in the East. That left two options: either negotiate with Mourtzouphlus or have another go at the walls. Since the fleet was still in good condition, Dandolo and his countrymen probably favored the latter option. After a long and emotional meeting, the crusaders decided to attack the city once more. They agreed to spend the next two days resting, refitting the ships, and repairing the equipment before assaulting the same walls on Monday, April 12. They also decided to improve their chances by binding the transports together two by two, so that a greater force could be brought to bear against each tower.[94]

On the appointed day the Venetian fleet again began its run toward the fortifications of Constantinople. Once again the fighting was fierce all along the walls, both at their foundations and at the highest reaches of the towers.[95] At about noon a north wind arose, blowing the transport ships toward shore. Two of the largest vessels, the *Paradise* and the *Pilgrim*, bound fast together, were able to position a flying bridge directly on a reinforced tower.[96] An unnamed Venetian scrambled onto the tower, but was cut to pieces by the defenders. A French knight named André d'Ureboise was more successful. After climbing onto the tower from the assault bridge he single-handedly put to flight the Byzantine troops stationed there. Soon another tower was captured in the same way.[97]

Yet, despite these victories, it was not Venetian maritime skill that won the day. Instead, the city was captured because of the efforts of one warrior-priest, Aleaumes of Clari, who, on the shore, wriggled through a hole in the wall and, with a good measure of fearlessness and ferocity, sparked a panic among the defenders. He and his companions then opened a gate allowing the mounted warriors to rush into the city.[98] The Byzantine forces, still greatly outnumbering the crusaders, could not retreat fast enough. For all practical purposes, Constantinople had fallen.[99]

TEN

THE VENETIANS in the
LATIN EMPIRE, 1204–1205

he sack of Constantinople was the most profitable and shameful in medieval European history. Oaths sworn on relics to leave the city's churches, monasteries, and women unmolested were routinely ignored. The loss of life and the destruction of the physical city were great. Wealthy, opulent, and beautiful, the Queen of Cities was quickly reduced to a dilapidated, depopulated, and burnt-out shell.[1] Little is known about the conduct of Venetians during the sack; presumably they enriched themselves as vigorously as their Frankish allies. However, in Nicetas Choniates' account of his own circumstances Venetians are described quite favorably. It was Domenico, a Venetian wine merchant, who protected Choniates and his family from the looting and rape of the French soldiers. Interestingly, although Nicetas Choniates had nothing but scorn and condescension for Venetians generally, he was clearly grateful for the human kindness he received from Domenico and his compatriots.[2]

Venetians were probably involved in their share of theft and destruction during the sack, but they were also more inclined to preserve Byzantine art than to destroy it. Exquisite reliquaries, chalices, and other precious objects were returned to Venice, where they ended up in the treasury of San Marco.[3] The doge's church was likewise adorned by numerous precious marbles and sculptures. Among the latter were the dark tetrarchs taken from Constantinople's Philadelphion and affixed to a corner of the church of San Marco.[4] Enrico Dandolo's most famous war trophy, however, was a quadriga of bronze horses, originally part of a charioteer group at the Hippodrome. Apart from their beauty, there seems to have been no special reason to single these statues out for preservation when almost every other bronze in the Hippodrome was melted down for coin.[5] When the horses arrived at Venice, they were mounted above the main entrance of the church of San Marco. Ironically, in a city of no horses these gilded steeds became for centuries a symbol of the Most Serene Republic.[6]

It is interesting that Dandolo chose to send so many of the spoils as gifts to the Commune of Venice. These artistic treasures dramatically enriched the civic spaces of the ducal chapel and the Piazza San Marco. The doge also sent relics to various churches and monasteries in Venice.[7] In the fifteenth century Venetian chroniclers began to report that Dandolo had sent rich marbles back to his son, Ranieri, to be used in the building of the family palazzo on the Grand Canal.[8] The story remains popular today, despite the lack of any evidence for it.[9] It probably originated with a garbling of earlier chroniclers' reports of Dandolo sending marbles back for San Marco, combined with patrician puffery and patriotic breast-beating typical of early modern writing.[10] Like so many other Renaissance legends of Enrico Dandolo, the story of the palazzo marbles is probably untrue.

After reestablishing some measure of order in Constantinople, the Latins prepared for the solemnities of Holy Week amid their newly acquired wealth and luxury.[11] It must have been particularly poignant for the Venetians that the feast of St. Mark coincided with Easter Sunday. Enrico Dandolo took residence in a splendid dwelling, probably the patriarchal palace near Hagia Sophia.[12] Boniface of Montferrat had already moved into the Great Palace, while Baldwin of Flanders contented himself with Blachernae Palace.[13]

Shortly after the holy days, Dandolo and the barons began to implement the provisions of the Pact of March. They issued a joint order for all booty to be brought to one of three churches, each guarded by an equal number of Frankish and Venetian soldiers.[14] The mountains of treasure collected represented only a fraction of the real take; the rest was held back by those who had no desire to share the wealth with their comrades.[15] The assessment of the rendered treasures was undoubtedly a laborious procedure. Precious stones and cloths would have to be converted into silver or gold for distribution.[16] And, of course, there was the counting and recounting necessary to make certain that all parties were satisfied with the accuracy of the assessment. In the end, the hoard was valued at 300,000 silver marks.[17] There appears to have been some initial confusion over the division mechanism. According to the Pact of March, the Venetians were to receive a 3:1 ratio until Alexius's debts had been paid off. In practice, that meant that of the first 200,000 marks, the Venetians should have received 150,000. Instead, the entire treasure was divided equally, with 150,000 marks going to each party. This was precisely what Dandolo had hoped to avoid, since it meant that the entire Venetian share would be consumed by Alexius's debts, leaving nothing for the Venetian rank and file. Later, perhaps after Dandolo had protested, the Frankish leaders paid 50,000 marks to the Venetians to bring the treasure division in line with the Pact of March.[18] After paying for the fleet, therefore, the Venetians had 100,000 marks to distribute among themselves—the same amount the Franks ended up with. The northerners divided their booty according to rank, with twenty marks going to each knight, ten marks to each sergeant or cleric, and five marks to each foot soldier.[19] It is unlikely that the Venetian maritime force made up of citizens of a commune would follow this example. They probably divided the booty equally among themselves, thus rendering about ten marks, or five pounds of silver, to each Venetian crusader.[20]

The next order of business was the election of an emperor. As agreed to in the Pact of March, the Venetians and Franks set about choosing their respective six electors. At the Great Palace the barons held a parliament, but it was so contentious that it adjourned without resolving anything. At issue was the desire of the greater men to secure positions for their partisans among the Frankish electors. After a day or more of wrangling, most of the barons abandoned their imperial hopes and fell in line with one of two top contenders: Boniface of Montferrat and Baldwin of Flanders.[21] Boniface had previously been considered the clear favorite. He was the titular leader of the crusade, linked by marriage to the Angeli, and already thought to be the emperor by most Greeks.[22] He had possession of the Great Palace and was either married or engaged to marry Margaret, the widow of Emperor Isaac II.[23] For his part, Baldwin of Flanders lacked Byzantine connections, but he was a powerful and wealthy lord, much loved by the men, and already in control of Blachernae Palace.[24] Neither man would consent to the other's slate of electors. The contest became so intense that many feared that the loser would abandon the host, thus greatly weakening the fledgling empire. To avoid that, it was agreed that whoever failed to win the crown would immediately receive as a consolation prize all Byzantine lands east of Constantinople as well as the Morea (Peloponnese).[25] As some have suggested, Enrico Dandolo may well have devised this solution.[26] Whether he did or not, parceling out property before the formal partition would have required an amendment to the Pact of March, which in turn needed the approval of the doge and his councilors. After additional maneuvering, the Franks finally settled on six members of the clergy to serve as electors.[27]

Dandolo and his fellow Venetians had much less trouble settling on their six. Being quite familiar with the business of naming electors, they devised a nomination method clearly based on the selection of ducal electors in Venice. Enrico Dandolo appointed four men, who then swore on relics to choose the six men who, they believed, were best qualified to act as imperial electors. When the names were announced, each of the six was forbidden to speak or listen to anyone lest he be influenced or corrupted. Before the election, they attended a Mass of the Holy Spirit and prayed for guidance.[28]

Beginning in the sixteenth century Venetian chroniclers started providing a standard list of the six electors: Doge Enrico Dandolo, Vitale Dandolo, Ottavio (or Ottone) Querini, Bertuccio Contarini, Nicolò Navigaioso, and Pantaleone Barbo.[29] It is hard to put much faith in these names when they are always followed by a completely erroneous list of Frankish electors. There is certainly no contemporary evidence that the doge himself served as an elector. On the contrary, Villehardouin makes clear that Dandolo was with the rest of the nobles when the electors announced their decision.[30] In the seventeenth century Paolo Ramusio dropped Enrico Dandolo from the list, noting that the sixth elector was variously named in his sources as either Giovanni Baseggio or Giovanni Michiel.[31] Vitale Dandolo probably appeared on the list because of the mistaken belief that he was the admiral of the crusade fleet, when in fact he was the commander of Venetian forces in the Adriatic while the crusade was away.[32] A Pantaleone Barbo was alive in May 1187, but there is no evidence that he traveled with the crusade.[33] The name of Ottavio Querini, however, does ring true. In 1198 he served Enrico Dandolo as an ambassador to Alexius III. Three years after the imperial election Querini was made Venetian podestà of Constantinople.[34] Of course, all six names may be early modern inventions.

At some point before the election, Enrico Dandolo suggested that Boniface of Montferrat and Baldwin of Flanders evacuate their palaces. The Pact of March was clear that the two palaces were to belong solely to the new emperor, so it was only right that neither should be occupied during the election. More importantly, both palaces were well fortified, and Dandolo probably wanted to insure that the loser of the election not be tempted to disregard the results.[35] Here again his overriding motive was to insure political stability.

With Venetians making up half of the electoral committee Enrico Dandolo was theoretically in a much better position to obtain the imperial throne for himself than either of the two Frankish contenders. It is clear, though, that early on the doge removed himself from consideration. The tug-of-war over the Frankish electors would have been senseless if Dandolo was a candidate; the stakes were high precisely because both sides believed that the Venetian electors were up for grabs. Furthermore, the agreement to provide lands to the loser of the election presumed a two-way race, because it provided for the defeat of only one man. Since the Venetians signed on to that agreement, they must have seen things the same way.

It is not difficult to see why Dandolo was not a candidate for the throne. Although he had earned the respect of the crusaders, at some ninety-seven years of age he clearly would not be with them much longer. Nicetas Choniates reported that Dandolo was disqualified because of blindness, but that seems unlikely.[36] The Latin electors were not bound by Byzantine custom, and in any case they had watched the elevation of blind Isaac II only a year earlier. The chief reason that Dandolo declined the imperial honor was that it stood in opposition to his goal of forming a sustainable and stable government at Constantinople. The Venetians were willing to alienate a great deal of property to insure that when either Boniface or Baldwin lost the election, he did not abandon the empire. Would they risk alienating both men by electing their doge? The earliest Venetian sources and virtually all later ones agree that the Venetians declined to elect Dandolo because they feared an exodus of angry Franks.[37]

In any case, Dandolo had no authority to saddle the dogeship of Venice with the diadem of Constantinople. That would require the consent not only of the Great Council but probably also of the arengo. Theoretically, he could resign the dogeship to become the founding member of a new imperial dynasty, yet in practice that would alienate both the Franks and the Venetians, leaving him bereft of support.[38] In short, the idea of Enrico Dandolo becoming the next Roman emperor was, from everyone's perspective, a bad one.

At long last the twelve electors met, on May 9, 1204, in a chapel of the doge's palace. Dandolo and the barons remained elsewhere in the building while throngs of others waited outside.[39] Over subsequent centuries, Venetian authors provided increasingly detailed descriptions of the electoral committee's deliberations.[40] The truth, though, is that no one knows precisely what happened behind the closed doors of the chapel. Perhaps, as the Venetian sources maintain, Enrico Dandolo did receive some votes on the first ballot. If so, these would have represented only a courtesy on the part of the Franks or a point of honor for the Venetians. In the end, though, the Venetians supported Baldwin of Flanders. He was an honorable man who had kept his commitments to Venice. He was not saddled with the baggage of Byzantine aristocracy as was his opponent, Boniface of Montferrat.[41] Instead, Baldwin promised a fresh start, free from the poisonous intrigues of the past. The young Baldwin also looked to Enrico Dandolo as to a father—something that the mature Boniface did not do.[42] There was, of course, the matter of Boniface's ties with Genoa, which made him less trustworthy from the Venetian perspective.[43]

At about midnight Bishop Nivelon of Soissons announced the election of Baldwin of Flanders. The crusading host erupted with joy. Although some of Boniface's supporters mumbled in disgust, the marquis himself was gracious in defeat.[44] On May 16, in a splendid ceremony in Hagia Sophia, Baldwin was crowned emperor.[45]

With that settled, Dandolo again took up the problem of the pope in Rome. Sometime between April and June 1204, the Venetian envoys to the papal legate returned to Constantinople.[46] Accompanying or following them was the treas- urer of Nicosia in Cyprus, whom Peter Capuano had charged with lifting the excommunication of Enrico Dandolo and the Venetians. The doge was required to swear an oath to something, but just what is not clear.[47] It did not include the return of Zara, which was already in Hungarian hands. Nor, it seems, did it re- quire compensation to the king of Hungary. As it happened, the king had re- cently written to Innocent inquiring as to when the Venetians would make good his losses. On September 15, 1204, the pope replied that he did not know, as the Venetians had apparently not yet requested absolution. Until they did so, Inno- cent continued, he would refuse to ratify the election of the patriarch of Grado.[48] Clearly, then, the pope considered reparations for the conquest of Zara to be a requirement for absolution.

Shortly after receiving absolution, Dandolo wrote a letter to Innocent, in- forming him of it and launching into a justification for the attack on Zara.[49] The tone of this portion of the letter is rather matter-of-fact, suggesting that the doge was trying to have the last word on a closed subject. He was certainly not apolo- getic, nor did he refer to any kind of restitution. Instead, Dandolo plainly asserted that the Venetians had been within their rights to recapture a rebel stronghold. He admitted to hearing that Zara was under papal protection but insisted that he did not believe that either Innocent or his predecessors were in the habit of extending crusader privileges to those "who only assume the Cross in order to wear it, not even to complete the journey for which pilgrims normally assume the Cross but to acquire the possessions of another and to criminally hold them."[50] The obvious implication was that it was not the conquest of Zara that was unjust, but the excommunication of the Venetians. Dandolo coyly pressed this point further: "Your Holiness saw fit to issue a sentence of excommunica- tion against me and the Venetians. We patiently and humbly endured it."[51]

Innocent wrote a short reply to Dandolo, acknowledging the report of ab- solution, yet clearly cautious about the details[52]—and for good reason. During the summer of 1205, the pope learned that Peter Capuano had authorized the lifting of the excommunication without requiring the Venetians to make any compensation whatsoever to Emeric of Hungary.[53] In an angry letter, Innocent rebuked his legate for the absolution, "which was wrongly essayed contrary to ecclesiastical form."[54] In truth, though, the fault was at least partially Innocent's, for it had been his letter of February 25, 1204, that appeared to set the price for absolution merely at "tears of repentance." It is not difficult to see how Peter Capuano could have read that letter as a mandate to reduce the requirements for lifting the excommunication so that, with its diversions behind it, the crusade could sail quickly to the East.[55] The Venetians would certainly have made that case.

Along with the letter, Enrico Dandolo also sent two envoys to the pope. They were Andrea da Molin and the doge's nephew, Leonardo Navigaioso.[56] Dandolo gave them two charges.[57] First, they were to seek Innocent's confirmation of the Pact of March. This was crucial for the Venetians, since by virtue of the pact they had become the heirs of the patriarchate of Constantinople. It was likewise important because the agreement proposed excommunication for those violating its provisions. Second, the envoys were to address the matter of Enrico Dandolo's crusading vow. Because of the growing feebleness of advanced age, the doge wanted the pope to relieve him of the cross. In return, Dandolo promised to see to it that a fleet was made available to transport the crusaders to the Holy Land. Innocent's reply to the doge was rich with irony and not a little sarcasm. He refused to ratify the Pact of March because it treated ecclesiastical property like plunder and because its provision for amendment gave laymen the right to invoke excommunication at will. "Moreover," Innocent remarked, "since these agreements were entered into for the honor of the Roman Church (and it is stated in almost each section that everything redounds to its honor), we ought not and cannot confirm what . . . diminishes the honor of the Apostolic See."[58] As for Dandolo's crusading vow,

we are mindful that your honest circumspection, the acuteness of your lively innate character, and the maturity of your quite sound advice would be beneficial to the Christian army far into the future. Inasmuch as the aforesaid emperor and the crusaders ardently praise your zeal and solicitude and, among [all] people, they trust particularly in your discretion, we have not considered approving this petition for the present time, lest either we be blamed by someone or other should the army that has been prepared to aid the Holy Land break up on this account, or someone or other could fault you, claiming that you took up the sign of the Cross not out of homage to Him Crucified, if, having now avenged the injury done you and yours, you do not avenge the dishonor done Jesus Christ, and having vanquished your enemies, you neglect to vanquish the enemies of the faith.[59]

Innocent, nevertheless, was willing to consider the request at a later time, but for now he saw no reason to let Dandolo off the hook.[60]

The doge's envoys also had the difficult task of obtaining the pope's confirmation of the newly elected patriarch of Constantinople. Shortly after Baldwin's coronation, Enrico Dandolo appointed Venetian canons to Hagia Sophia. In Venice, as we have seen, ecclesiastical elections were to be free of secular influence. In Constantinople, given the stipulations of the Pact of March, the doge and his council felt justified in safeguarding the election of a Venetian. All canons were required to swear an oath that they would do just that. They chose Thomas Morosini, a man born of an illustrious Venetian family but currently a subdeacon living in a monastery near Ravenna.[61] Morosini had earlier spent an extended period of time in Rome and was well known to Innocent III and the Curia as a man of nobility, wisdom, and learning.[62] His Roman connection must have figured prominently among the canons, who of course hoped to obtain the pope's confirmation. Given Innocent's attitude toward the Venetians of the crusade, it is not surprising that the canons turned to one whose hands were unsoiled by the enterprise, withdrawn from the world and, indeed, from Venice itself.

The canons sent their own envoys to Rome to inform Innocent of the election and to request his confirmation. They probably traveled with the doge's envoys, who brought with them the same request. Yet the two sets of messengers approached their mission quite differently, as was apparent to the pope at once.[63] The doge's ambassadors naturally viewed matters from a secular perspective. The crusaders had made a solemn agreement. The Venetians had made good on their part of the bargain, helping to conquer Constantinople and leaving the imperial throne to the French. It was now up to the French to deliver the patriarchate. The envoys were no doubt unhappy to discover that French clerics at Constantinople had actually lodged a protest with the pope, appealing the outcome of the patriarchal election.[64] The doge's men would naturally view this as plain treachery. They insisted that the pope respect the sworn oaths of the crusade leaders and confirm the election of Morosini.[65]

For their part, the envoys of the Venetian canons insisted on nothing. As churchmen they knew full well that, no matter how many leaders had sworn to it, the Pact of March simply could not dispose of a cathedral and patriarchate as if they were spoils of war. The French clergy knew this, too, which is why they contested the election. The envoys of the Venetian canons, therefore, humbly requested papal confirmation not as a right, but as a favor.[66]

From the letters he was receiving from others at Constantinople, Innocent feared that depriving Venice of the patriarchate could harm the fledgling empire and the crusade. Although the French clergy may have wanted him to rebuff the Venetians, the crusader barons clearly did not.[67] The challenge and appeal were withdrawn, probably at the request of the pope.[68] Nevertheless, Innocent could not condone the patriarchal election itself. Authority to appoint canons to a new cathedral rested with the pope and his legates, not with a secular prince like Enrico Dandolo. Innocent, therefore, declared the election void and then appointed Thomas Morosini to the patriarchate of Constantinople himself. In this way, he hoped to preserve the rights of the Church as well as the viability of the crusade.[69]

Morosini arrived in Rome in March 1205. Since he was only a subdeacon, the pope ordained him deacon on March 5, a priest on March 26, a bishop on March 27, and finally bestowed on him the pallium on March 30. In addition, Innocent gave him numerous privileges and properties in Constantinople.[70] The pope made clear to the new patriarch, and later to the vice-doge in Venice, that the papal appointment of a patriarch was an exception, not a rule. In the future, he maintained, the cathedral chapter of Hagia Sophia could freely elect Morosini's successors in accordance with canon law. Since Innocent did not recognize the validity of the current chapter, Patriarch Morosini was to appoint new canons from all nationalities.[71]

With that settled, the patriarch traveled to Venice, where he planned to ordain new canons from the local clergy and take ship for Constantinople. He did not receive as warm a homecoming as he might have anticipated. The conservative oligarchy that had successfully salvaged the troubled crusade back in 1202 was clearly troubled by the drastic outcome of the enterprise. Modern scholars have tended to cast the Venetians in the wake of 1204 as avaricious merchants licking their chops over the fat morsel of Byzantium. In truth, Venice's leaders were cautious men who had built a cautious government. They thought carefully about risk and return, especially when it came to the well-being of the commune. All their actions demonstrate that they were determined that the new chaos sweeping the Aegean would not harm Venetian interests. From their perspective the fall of Constantinople posed an enormously dangerous risk, one that would need to be managed as effectively as the crusade that had spawned it.

Although Enrico Dandolo simply wanted the pope to confirm Morosini as patriarch of Constantinople, those in Venice were more worried about the specifics. Innocent had bestowed on Morosini and his successors all ecclesiastical properties in Constantinople,[72] which posed a problem for the mother church of Venice, the patriarchate of Grado. As we have seen, Grado relied heavily on the income from its properties in Constantinople's Venetian Quarter. The churches of San Acydinus, San Marco, Santa Maria, and San Nicolò in Constantinople, as well as other Venetian churches elsewhere in the empire, had long been exempt from the Orthodox patriarchate.[73] It was not right, the Venetian leaders contended, that these privileges should be stripped from Grado simply because Hagia Sophia was under Latin control. They insisted that Morosini at once exempt Grado's properties from any exactions.[74]

The Venetian leaders were also worried that subsequent Latin patriarchs of Constantinople might use their position to prey on the Venetian church in Byzantium. A Venetian patriarch was, after all, something quite different than a Venetian patriarchate. To insure that the Venetians remained in the see, they requested that newly ordained canons swear an oath to elect and accept only Venetians or Venetian residents of at least ten years into the clergy of Hagia Sophia.[75] Morosini was asked to take the same oath.[76]

Morosini denied all of the requests; Ranieri Dandolo, therefore, denied him transport out of Venice. The standoff continued through April. Not expecting an extended stay on the Rialto, Morosini began to run short of funds and soon got into trouble with creditors.[77] Finally, in May 1205, the patriarch and his canons took the oaths.[78] Morosini added to the oral version of his, "reserving the rights of the Apostolic See." The plight of Thomas Morosini is one more example of the independence of the medieval Venetian clergy. Like Patriarch Enrico Dandolo of Grado, Morosini was neither a pawn of the commune nor a factional leader but a man committed to the rights of the Church—even when those rights stood in opposition to the interests of Venice. By the same token, the communal government was determined to defend the income that supported the patriarchate of Grado and the right of Venetian churches in Byzantium to be free from Constantinople's authority. In other words, they sought above all to minimize the effects of the fall of Byzantium on Venice. This would remain their policy for many years.

As it happened, Innocent thought better of his promise to leave the election of Constantinople's patriarchs to the cathedral chapter. In May 1205, even as Morosini was taking his oath in Venice, Innocent changed the rules. He decreed that Morosini's successors should be elected not only by the members of the cathedral chapter but also by the prelates of all thirty conventual churches in Constantinople, most of which would be under the control of the Franks. His clear purpose was to parry the Venetian attempt to monopolize the patriarchy by diluting their power over succession.[79] He also wrote to Benedict, cardinal-priest of St. Susanna and papal legate to Constantinople, that the patriarch must appoint suitable candidates to the cathedral chapter, men who were literate, honest, and of all nationalities. If he failed to do so, Innocent instructed Benedict to name the canons himself.[80]

Thomas Morosini has been characterized by Robert Lee Wolff as an "exceedingly passionate and quarrelsome" man because he was at one time or another at odds with just about everyone.[81] That may be true. And yet a grasping patriot who sought only the good of Venice would have clashed only with the pope and his legates, not with the vice-doge in Venice and the Venetian podestà in Constantinople, as Morosini would do. The new patriarch was a man removed from the tranquility of monastic life and thrust into a power struggle between Venice, the papacy, and the clergy of the Latin Empire. At the same time, he diligently defended the rights of his new see. It is not surprising, then, that he was unable to get along with everyone at all times. From its very beginning, the Latin patriarchate of Constantinople was wracked with controversy, and so it would remain throughout its five troubled decades of existence.

Back in Constantinople, Enrico Dandolo had more immediate matters of concern. Shortly after the coronation of Baldwin of Flanders, Boniface of Montferrat requested Asia Minor and the Morea, which had been pledged to the loser of the imperial election. Baldwin willingly gave them to him. But the marquis was not really interested in Asia; instead, he dreamed of claiming the crown of Thessalonica, which Manuel I Comnenus had promised to his brother Renier many years earlier.[82] Boniface, therefore, offered to make a trade: Byzantine Asia Minor for the kingdom of Thessalonica. Baldwin refused, saying that until the partition of lands it was not his to give. This did not sit well with Boniface. In fact, when Baldwin later marched into Thessalonica, Boniface rebelled, capturing Demotica and besieging Adrianople.

When the barons in Constantinople heard of the rebellion they dispatched Villehardouin to Adrianople. The marshal of Champagne, a constant defender of unity in the crusading force, was on good terms with the marquis. Nevertheless, he had harsh words for him. After much discussion, Boniface agreed to put the argument between himself and the emperor before a council consisting of Count Louis of Blois, Conon of Béthune, Doge Enrico Dandolo, and Geoffrey of Villehardouin himself. It was not clear whether Emperor Baldwin would be willing to accept this arbitration, but Villehardouin promised that the barons would do everything in their power to persuade him.[83]

The decision to put the quarrel before a committee in Constantinople averted a war between the crusaders. At first glance it is difficult to see why Boniface agreed to it, but the answer can be discovered in the direct and rather ingenious intervention of Enrico Dandolo.

Villehardouin was accompanied on his trip to Adrianople by two Venetian ambassadors: Marco Sanudo, who was a nephew of Doge Dandolo, and Ravano delle Carceri of Verona.[84] It had come to the attention of the Venetians in Constantinople that Boniface was willing to sell his title to the island of Crete, which he had received from Alexius IV. He had already offered it to the Genoese but had as of yet received no answer.[85] Dandolo was naturally eager to keep this strategic island out of Genoese hands and equally keen to see it developed as a Venetian possession. He therefore sent his men to Boniface with a proposal to purchase the rights to the island for 1,000 silver marks. Of course, the actual conquest of the island would cost much more—indeed, it would one day cost the life of Enrico Dandolo's son.

The sale of Crete is usually considered in relative isolation, as a business deal and nothing more. This, however, distorts its fundamental purpose. Many have cast Dandolo as a vulture of sorts, swooping in to seize Crete while Boniface was wounded and in danger. Although the marquis would have preferred to sell to his Genoese friends, the Venetians, it is argued, had cash on hand, which Boniface sorely needed if he was to prosecute a war.[86]

Fortunately, the treaty survives.[87] Viewed within its historical context, it quickly becomes clear that Dandolo and Boniface concluded much more than a real estate deal. According to the agreement, signed on August 12, 1204, Boniface gave to Dandolo and the Venetians the island of Crete, a 100,000 gold hyperper debt owed to him by Alexius IV, a fief that Manuel I had given to Boniface's father, the city of Thessalonica and its surrounding areas, and all lands that he had or would have in the Byzantine Empire both east and west of the Bosporus. In return, Dandolo gave to Boniface 1,000 silver marks and a promise of unspecified lands in the western part of the empire with an annual income of 10,000 gold hyperpers, to be assessed by a friend of Boniface and a friend of the Venetians after the partition of the empire. Boniface would hold these lands through the doge, but he would also have complete control over them, as well as the right of inheritance. Service for the lands would be due to the emperor, not the doge. In addition, the Venetians and Boniface agreed to defend each other's lands in the Latin Empire. If at any time Boniface were to break the treaty, he would be required to return the property and the 1,000 silver marks to the doge.[88]

Crete, therefore, was not sold for 1,000 marks. It was part of a much larger deal. This is made doubly clear by the provision that Boniface must return the

1,000 marks if he broke the covenant, whereas the Venetians need not return Crete for any reason. In this treaty Boniface gave the Venetians everything he had in Byzantium and many things he did not have. He gave a piece of paper saying that he owned Crete; a bad debt note valuable only by virtue of its gold seal; a fief that did not belong to him; an assignment of lands in Asia Minor that he did not want; the Morea, which he probably did want but was in no position to acquire; and a highly dubious claim to Thessalonica. In effect, Baldwin gave away everything because he had nothing. In return he received some ready cash, but, more importantly, a guarantee from Dandolo that one way or the other he would receive either Thessalonica and the Morea or lands of equal value in Greece.

From Boniface's point of view there were only a few possible outcomes of his decision to put the quarrel before the council—and all of them were provided for by his agreement with Dandolo. If the council met and ruled in his favor, then Thessalonica would, by virtue of the treaty, go directly to the Venetians, and the doge could then render it to Boniface. If the council met and ruled against Boniface, then he would have nothing, but once the division of lands was completed, Dandolo would bestow on him the promised territory. If Venice received Thessalonica in the partition, so much the better. If not, lands of comparable worth would go to the marquis. If the council met and ruled in Boniface's favor but Baldwin refused to accept the ruling, or if the council never met because Baldwin refused to put the dispute before it, the result would still be the same. In all cases, whatever the council decided, Boniface would receive his Greek lands from the doge, not from the partition of the empire.[89]

Like the Pact of March, the treaty with Boniface carefully avoids obligating the commune of Venice in any way. As the leader of the Venetian crusaders, Dandolo was within his rights to negotiate the spoils of the campaign. He had no authority, though, to treat with foreign powers in the name of Venice or to commit the state to anything without the approval of the Great Council. Boniface was to hold his properties as a vassal of the doge, his successors, and the Venetians. The doge and the Venetians were crusaders with a legitimate right to bargain with their rewards. In hindsight, the naming of Dandolo's successors appears to implicate future doges in the arrangement, but it did not. This was instead a reference to the successors of Dandolo's role in the Latin Empire. In other words, it referred to the next "lord of three-eighths of the Roman Empire," not to the next doge of Venice; the two were not necessarily one.[90]

It would be instructive to know more about the subsequent negotiations with Baldwin. Villehardouin records that messengers were sent to the emperor warning him with a thinly veiled threat against an attack on Boniface at Adrianople.[91]

Not wishing to lose the friendship of Dandolo and the barons, Baldwin returned to Constantinople. For four days, however, he refused to put the quarrel before the council.[92] Villehardouin steadfastly refused to provide the reasons for Baldwin's reluctance or the arguments that finally swayed him. They are, however, not hard to guess. It could not have escaped the emperor's notice that the council was willing to buy peace with Boniface. Based on Robert of Clari's report of the emperor's mindset at the time, it is safe to assume that he would not willingly allow Boniface to be rewarded for treason and treachery.[93] Here the treaty between Venice and Boniface may also have played a role in bringing the emperor to arbitration. When the Flemish knight stood staunchly on his chivalric principles that treason deserved death, not a kingdom, Dandolo, whom Baldwin greatly admired, could point out that Boniface had already given to the doge and his people all rights to Byzantine lands—Thessalonica included. To agree to the council's arbitration, therefore, was merely to allow Thessalonica to be handed over to the emperor's Venetian allies. Of course, Venice would instantly give those lands to Boniface, but that would not be the emperor's doing. In effect, then, Dandolo's treaty with Boniface may have acted as a fig leaf for Baldwin, allowing him to hold on to his principles while letting go of Thessalonica.

The treaty between Venice and Boniface is now commonly remembered only for the sale of Crete because, in the end, that is all that Venice came away with.[94] Yet in August 1204 Crete was a lesser consideration. More important then was Dandolo's continued desire to form a unified and stable Latin Empire.[95] The treaty with Boniface was a means of brokering peace among the crusaders by making the Venetians liable for any penalties exacted of Boniface of Montferrat. It also cleared away the underbrush of Montferrat claims on previous emperors—claims that could poison future relations between the marquis and Baldwin. In one short document, without ever openly proclaiming its purpose, the treaty wiped away all tangible reasons for disputes and quarrels between the two leaders; that it did all this while gaining Crete for Venice is further evidence of Dandolo's political acumen.

When Boniface returned to Constantinople, the doge and Louis of Blois rode out to meet him and escort him safely into the city.[96] The Council of Four convened at once to examine the question. Since Venice would have to make good Boniface's losses if he did not receive Thessalonica, Dandolo certainly favored giving it to him. At least two of the others did, too, because the committee quickly ruled in Boniface's favor.[97] The marquis's original offer to the emperor, therefore, was accepted. Baldwin received Byzantine Asia Minor while Thessalonica went to Boniface.[98] By virtue of the August treaty, Boniface's territories, including the Morea, immediately became Venetian property. Dandolo rendered Thessalonica and its lands to the marquis at once. The Morea, it appears, was another matter. The treaty made clear that Dandolo was required to give Boniface lands with an income of 10,000 gold hyperpers. The kingdom of Thessalonica took care of a large portion of that, but the rest would have to be assessed by both parties, as provided for in the treaty.[99] Nothing, of course, could be done until the final partition was complete.

Dandolo's purchase of Crete did not sit well with the Genoese, who were outraged that the old doge had plucked the prize from their hands. The result was an unofficial war between Venice and Genoa.[100] In September 1204, only one month after the deal, six Genoese galleys raided the port of Modon and captured a Venetian vessel.[101] Aboard was Brother Barozzi, the Venetian Master of the Temple in Lombardy, who had been entrusted with a large number of precious relics, jewelry, cloths, and other ecclesiastical items to be given as gifts to Innocent III and the Templars. The pope was furious at the theft and threatened Genoa with interdict if restitution was not forthcoming.[102] It was probably also at this time that Enrico Dandolo ordered most of the Venetian fleet at Constantinople to return home.[103] In part this was owing to the increased threat at home, both from the Genoese and the Zarans, but it also coincided with the end of the fleet's contract.

Before the war vessels departed, Dandolo's nephew Marco Sanudo requested the use of eight unmanned galleys for a retaliatory strike against the Genoese pirates. The doge granted the request. At his own expense, Sanudo armed and manned the galleys and then sailed to the island of Naxos, where the Genoese held a castle. A long siege began, stretching into the winter. It is said that Sanudo destroyed his own vessels, thus removing any possibility of retreat. At last the castle and then the island surrendered to him. Although Naxos was later assigned to the Franks, neither they nor the Venetians ever laid claim to Sanudo's conquest. After subsequent island conquests, he was later invested with the title Duke of the Archipelago by the emperor.[104]

By September 1204 the time for the final partition of the Byzantine Empire was drawing near. The land commission, made up of twelve Venetians and twelve Franks, had probably begun its work back in May. In order to come to a division that all sides would consider equitable, the commission carefully assessed the relative values of the regions and cities. It probably relied on tax records from 1203 or other recent years.[105] According to Nicetas Choniates, it also dispatched assessors to various regions.[106] Then came the long process of negotiations in which the inherent value of properties was weighed against personal preferences and the natural desire to form contiguous blocks of land.[107] It is likely that the commissioners first completed their work in mid-August, when the city of Constantinople was divided between the emperor, the Franks, and the Venetians.[108] Yet, the rebellion of Boniface of Montferrat and the impending decision of the Council of Four obviously delayed the final disposition.

With peace restored, the empire was divided, probably on October 1, 1204.[109] The divisions were made in three stages (see fig. 9). First was the division of property in the capital, which, as mentioned, had been completed a few weeks earlier. Second came the division of lands near the capital. The emperor received, naturally enough, Constantinople and the territories adjoining it in Thrace. The Venetians received the Sea of Marmara shoreline from Heraclea, which was the emperor's westernmost port, almost to the end of the Gallipoli peninsula. In addition, they received the inland city of Adrianople and a swath of territory connecting it to the sea. The Franks received the rest of Thrace, including lands on both sides of the Venetian territory and running west to Baldwin's kingdom of Thessalonica. The third stage was the division of the remainder of the empire. The emperor received Asia Minor, which was his by virtue of the exchange with Boniface. He also received most of the major islands of the Aegean. The Venetians received all of the lands on the mainland west of the Pindos Mountains, the Gulf of Corinth, and the Morea. They also had the islands of Salamis, Aegina, Andros, and both ends of Negroponte (Euboea). Crete, which Dandolo had purchased from Boniface, does not appear in the Treaty of Partition. This is logical, since the island had been granted to Boniface before the conquest and was, therefore, not part of the spoils. The Franks received Macedonia, Thessaly, and Attica.[110] It was probably at this time that Enrico Dandolo assumed the title "lord of three-eighths of the Roman Empire," a personal honor not yet related to the office of the doge.[111] He may also have received the Byzantine title of Despot.[112]

Boniface of Montferrat's share in the final division has caused some scholarly consternation, partly because his territories were omitted from the Treaty of Partition. Problems of interpretation invariably arise when the specifics of Boniface's treaty with the Venetians are ignored or the marquis's subsequent actions are viewed in isolation.[113] In order to understand the mechanisms of Boniface's distribution we must first recall that it was a Venetian operation. According to the agreement of August 1204, all of Boniface's territorial claims, past or future, were transferred to Dandolo and the Venetians. They in turn were responsible for providing the marquis with lands with an annual income of 10,000 gold

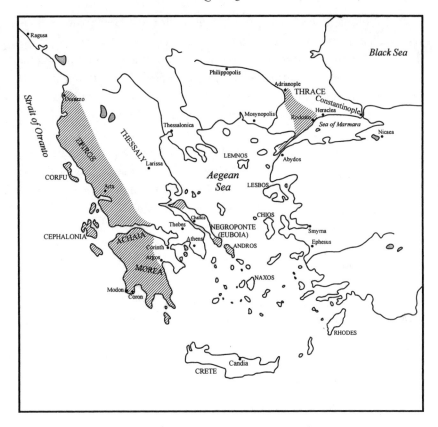

Figure 9. Lands assigned to the Venetians in the Treaty of Partition, October 1204.

hyperpers. Some portion of that had already been rendered when Boniface was awarded Thessalonica.

Shortly after the partition, in November 1204, Boniface of Montferrat marched south and took possession of Beoetia, Corinthia, the eastern part of the Morea, and the central portion of Euboea. Since these important regions had been omitted from the Treaty of Partition when it was published one month earlier, we can be reasonably certain that they, like Thessalonica (which was also omitted), were set aside for Boniface.[114] The Morea, which had belonged to Boniface, was transferred to Venice by virtue of the August treaty. The same treaty, however, made Venice liable for handing over additional lands to the marquis. It is likely, then, that the omitted territories were originally allotted to Venice and then removed from its column before the partition document was drafted. A glance at the map appears to confirm this. Boniface's territories look very much as if they were carved out of a contiguous Venetian whole. Indeed, it is difficult to understand the allotment of Salamis, Aegina, Andros, and the tips of Euboea to the Venetians unless they had originally been clustered around other Venetian allocations.

The precision of the Treaty of Partition was soon forced to make way for realities on the ground. During his campaign, Boniface of Montferrat captured nearby Athens, which had been apportioned to the Frankish crusaders. No complaint was lodged.[115] As we have seen, Marco Sanudo captured Naxos, which belonged to the emperor. The Duke of the Archipelago simply did homage to the emperor for the island and for the remainder of his Aegean conquests. In much the same way, Geoffrey of Villehardouin (the nephew of the chronicler) and William of Champlitte conquered the greater portion of the Morea, which was supposed to be a Venetian possession. Only in 1209 did the Venetians succeed in getting the prince (now Villehardouin) to acknowledge that he held the Morea as a Venetian fief. Similarly, when Ravano dalle Carceri became lord of all Euboea by force of arms, he did homage both to the commune of Venice and to Boniface of Montferrat for the island.[116]

Many more were just as eager for land. After the Treaty of Partition had been ratified the Frankish knights apportioned fiefs and prepared to conquer them. They sallied forth in such great numbers that few remained in Constantinople— of the leaders, only Emperor Baldwin, Louis of Blois, Hugh of St. Pol, and Enrico Dandolo.[117] At first things seemed to be going well for the Latins; not only were their conquests impressive, but they managed to capture Alexius V Mourtzouphlus, who had been blinded by Alexius III shortly after the fall of Constantinople.[118] Mourtzouphlus was sent back to the capital, arriving in early November 1204.[119] He was given a speedy, although hardly impartial trial on the charge of murdering his lord, Alexius IV. The former emperor defiantly stated that he had killed a traitor to the empire and would do the same to any others guilty of such crimes. Unimpressed, the court found him guilty and sentenced him to death. He was taken to the Forum Tauri, where he was forced to leap from the top of the Column of Theodosius.[120] Robert of Clari reported that it was Enrico Dandolo who devised the punishment, remarking, "For a high man, high justice!"[121] The quip certainly became popular at the time, for it is also mentioned by Geoffrey of Villehardouin and Gunther of Pairis.[122] However, since Clari is the only one to attribute it to Dandolo, it may not have been of the doge's devising.

For the next few months, Dandolo's attention was probably focused on the Venetian community in Constantinople. As he had done in 1184, Dandolo probably presided over property disputes and other judicial matters. The question of Venetian government in Constantinople and its relationship to the Venetian commune back home also needed to be ironed out. Perhaps Dandolo supported the later plan to elect a strong Venetian leader, a podestà answerable to the doge in Venice. There is no evidence, however, for the modern assertion that he envisioned a "new Venice" on the Bosporus, independent and perhaps even superior to the communal government on the Rialto.[123] As crusade leaders, Dandolo and his advisors played important roles in the formation and management of the Latin Empire, roles that were inherently different than those of a doge and his councilors in Venice. They had become de facto a part of the imperial government, a situation that would be confirmed and regularized in October 1205.[124] Nevertheless, Dandolo was at all times extremely careful to avoid usurping the authority of the commune. When necessary, as it had been when crafting the Pact of March, he secured exemptions for the government of Venice. He had acquired a great deal in Byzantium. Nevertheless, he preserved the commune's right to decide for itself how fully it wished to share in the fruits and the responsibilities of the conquest.

Like many of his fellow crusaders, Dandolo also thought about returning home.[125] The Pact of March had committed everyone to remain in Byzantium until March 1205. As that date approached, thousands of crusaders prepared to sail home.[126] In an effort to stop them, the papal legate agreed to absolve the crusade vows of any man who would remain until March 1206,[127] but that was only offering what most believed they already had. In March 1204, the crusade bishops had led the crusaders to believe that their vows would be fulfilled if they attacked Constantinople and remained for one year.[128] This they had done, and they were ready to go home. So too, apparently, was the ancient doge of Venice, but under the watchful eye of the pope and his legate, Dandolo had no option but to remain in Byzantium for at least an additional year.

It was around February 1205 that events turned against the crusaders. Ioannitsa, king of the Vlachs and Bulgarians, struck up an alliance with Byzantine lords in Thrace aimed at overthrowing the Latins. Demotica was the first to rebel, followed soon after by Venetian-controlled Adrianople. Emperor Baldwin, Louis of Blois, and Enrico Dandolo met at the palace to consider the situation, which potentially threatened Constantinople itself. Most of the Latin forces were scattered across the empire, leaving only a skeleton force in the capital. The three leaders decided to send messengers to the emperor's brother, Henry of Flanders, ordering him to abandon his conquests and return at once to Constantinople. Similar orders were sent to knights in other parts of the empire.[129]

In March, Baldwin and Louis of Blois led a smallish force of one hundred forty knights out of Constantinople. After meeting up with an advance guard under the command of Geoffrey of Villehardouin, the Franks rode to Adrianople, arriving on March 29. Their subsequent assault on two gates of the city failed owing to their small numbers.[130]

Hugh of St. Pol had died of gout some months earlier, making Enrico Dandolo the only member of the senior leadership in Constantinople.[131] He collected an army about the same size as that led by the emperor and sallied forth in the first week of April. It is astonishing that the aged and blind doge took it upon himself to lead this army personally. It was to be a fateful decision, both for the crusaders and for Dandolo himself. When they arrived, the doge and his men camped before another of Adrianople's gates.[132]

Sometime around Easter (April 10) Ioannitsa arrived with his troops. On Easter Wednesday, the two forces clashed. With his Cuman light cavalry, Ioannitsa goaded the knights into an unwise charge, surrounding them and inflicting heavy casualties. The crusaders agreed not to be fooled again, but the very next day a similar tactic allowed Ioannitsa to completely surround them. Louis of Blois was twice injured, but he refused to leave the emperor. Baldwin refused to retreat. The result was a smashing defeat for the crusaders. Most were killed, including Louis of Blois. The emperor was captured and feared dead. The rest fled for their lives. Villehardouin and his men, who guarded the camp, were able to deflect the Cuman advance for the moment, but there was no doubt that Ioannitsa had sufficient forces to crush them when he wished.[133]

Villehardouin called Enrico Dandolo to the defensive line. In a private conversation, the marshal of Champagne related the disastrous results of the battle and his fear that none of them would escape. The doge devised a plan. Villehardouin and his men would remain in full battle array, holding the field until nightfall. Dandolo would go to the tents of the survivors and do all he could to restore their courage. The able-bodied would be armed, the wounded prepared for transport. After dark, Dandolo would lead them on a march to the sea, with Villehardouin and his men bringing up the rear. The plan worked flawlessly.[134] Dandolo cleverly ordered the lighting of torches and fires in the crusader camp to give Ioannitsa the impression that it was still occupied.[135]

For the next three nights the crusaders were on the move, always just ahead of Ioannitsa's pursuing army. Their numbers were increased when they met a contingent of Louis of Blois's men on their way to Adrianople. Finally, on April 16, they reached the city of Rodosto, which had been assigned to the Venetians in the division. The Greeks there surrendered peacefully. After securing the city, the Latins held a council to discuss their options. Concluding that the gravest danger was at Constantinople, they sent messengers by sea to inform those in the capital that there were survivors from Adrianople who would come as soon as possible.[136]

That was welcome news, but the defenders of Constantinople had greater problems still. With the expiration of the year of service approximately seven thousand crusaders boarded Venetian vessels and headed home. Peter Capuano and others begged them to stay, but to no avail. One day after Dandolo and the others had arrived at Rodosto, they spied five of the vessels sailing south. They, too, urged the men not to abandon the empire. The crusaders on board promised to sleep on it, but before dawn they hoisted their sails and disappeared over the horizon.[137] Villehardouin bitterly blamed these men, but they had kept their word in every respect.[138] As the leaders of the First Crusade had learned a century earlier, there is never a good time for a conquering army to return home.

During the next few days various Latin leaders and their contingents arrived at Rodosto. Among them was Henry of Flanders, who, along with the others, shed many tears over the disaster at Adrianople. After a few days of discussion, the leaders agreed to accept Henry as regent of the empire[139]—although it was not clear that there would be an empire for very much longer. Ioannitsa and his armies had captured most of Thrace, almost to the walls of Constantinople. It was essential that the forces at Rodosto get to the capital as soon as possible; with no fleet, they would have to travel overland. Dandolo left a force of Venetians and Greek vassals to defend Rodosto and joined the other leaders on their trek.[140] It was a difficult three-day journey, but at last they rode through the gates of the great city, probably in early May 1205. The situation was desperate. Their numbers were few and their capital was trapped between Ioannitsa to the west and Theodore Lascaris to the east. They sent messengers to Europe seeking additional aid and then hunkered down behind the walls of the city.[141]

Enrico Dandolo was not well upon his return to Constantinople. The long days of riding to Adrianople, then to Rodosto, and back again to Constantinople had taken their toll on his aged body; indeed, such rigors would have been taxing for a young man, particularly one with limited experience on horseback. At some point during the journey, the riding caused or exacerbated an inguinal hernia in the doge's body.[142] This condition, in which a portion of the small intestine slips through a weakness in the abdominal muscles near the groin, is today easily repaired by surgery. However, if left untreated in men, the intestines can slip all the way into the scrotal sac. That is what happened to Enrico Dandolo.[143] The hernia can cause a complete blockage of the intestines or gangrene in the strangulated section, and, as one might imagine, it is excruciatingly painful. In either case, the condition is fatal. Sometime in May 1205, Doge Enrico Dandolo received last rites and died, far from home, like his father, in the city of the Caesars.[144]

The old doge was greatly mourned by Venetians and Franks alike. He had been a source of wisdom for the leadership and an inspiration to the rank and file. His death was one more blow to an empire already reeling. Despite his best efforts, Dandolo failed in his attempt to lay the foundation of a strong and stable Byzantine state. The Latin Empire of Constantinople would survive for five decades, always teetering on the edge of destruction.

With full honors, Dandolo's body was taken to Hagia Sophia and placed in a tomb, probably in the gallery. He was the first and only person to be buried in Justinian's great church. There his body rested for more than two centuries, until the world changed again and Constantinople was Christian no more.[145]

EPILOGUE:

BIRTH of a MARITIME EMPIRE

he Venetian people received much more than they bargained for, indeed much more than they wanted, from the Fourth Crusade. What was supposed to be a glorious return to Egyptian waters turned into the destruction of the Byzantine Empire, leaving chaos and uncertainty in its wake. It is often said that the Venetians sought the conquest of Byzantium because they both loathed and feared the instability of the Byzantine government. Yet, even at its worst, the situation in the empire was more stable before its collapse and dismemberment than afterward. Consumed by swarms of conquerors and privateers, the bloated corpse of Byzantium was a wretched and dangerous thing. Although the fall of Constantinople would one day be a boon to Venice, in the short term it posed considerable problems. As we have seen in the matter of the patriarch of Constantinople, the communal government in Venice approached the entire matter with great trepidation. The new Venetian political order, naturally conservative and risk averse, had managed to salvage the debacle of the Fourth Crusade while it foundered at Venice. The ruinous aftermath of the crusade presented yet another, more dangerous, challenge.

Enrico Dandolo had understood this. Throughout the Fourth Crusade and the foundation of the Latin Empire he was careful to commit Venice itself to nothing. Venetians were an active, indeed integral part of the new empire, yet their status vis-à-vis Venice was not unlike that of their countrymen in Tyre, albeit on a much larger scale. They constituted a colony within a foreign state, responsible for the government in their areas and the defense of the greater whole, while remaining Venetian citizens obedient to the Republic.[1] At the same time, Dandolo left the door open for Venice to take control over as much or as little of the war spoils as it wished.

Because the Venetians were built into the constitution of the Latin Empire, Enrico Dandolo had to be replaced right away. Very shortly after his death they assembled to consider the matter. Given the gravity of the circumstances, the leaders decided not to wait for word from Venice; instead, they provisionally elected Marino Zeno as their podestà until such time as the communal government could confirm him or appoint someone else. Zeno, therefore, was Enrico Dandolo's successor in his role as leader of the Venetians in the Latin Empire. Not surprisingly, he also took Dandolo's title "ruler of three-eighths of the Roman Empire" and surrounded himself with judges and other court functionaries similar to those of a doge.[2]

Zeno's election is usually interpreted as a power grab, an attempt to usurp the authority of the mother country or to form a separate state.[3] Some have even claimed that a plan was hatched to make Constantinople the capital of a new Venetian empire. Yet there is no good evidence to support these assertions. The alleged plan to move the capital appears in no contemporary documents, nor is it mentioned in any chronicles or histories until the sixteenth century. It was first recorded by Daniele Barbaro, an official historian of the Republic writing between 1512 and 1515. Beginning with Robert Lee Wolff and Freddy Thiriet, scholars have tended to accept Barbaro's testimony, suggesting that the proposal was an attempt to rein in a recalcitrant and overly powerful colony.[4] Despite Thiriet's rather strained arguments for Barbaro's veracity on this point, it is difficult to see how so momentous a debate could have been ignored by Andrea Dandolo and every other Venetian writer before the sixteenth century. Furthermore, it makes very little sense. Moving the capital to a troublesome colony is not a victory for the mother country, but rather its complete demise. I know of no colonial power in human history to have contemplated, let alone gone through with, such a plan. Another complication is the fact that Constantinople was already the seat of an empire. Even if the Venetians could have removed the Frankish rulers from the city (not an easy prospect), it would have meant war with just about everyone. The Franks would naturally take it badly, but so would the pope; a crusade against Venice would not be out of the question. In return for all this strife, Venice would acquire a dilapidated capital surrounded by enemies while leaving behind the impregnable and prosperous city of the lagoon. No one, especially a patriotic Venetian, would seriously consider so foolish a proposal.

The truth is that the Venetians at Constantinople acted cautiously, prudently, and above all respectfully to the authority of the communal government back home.[5] In short, they did just as Enrico Dandolo had done. Immediately after the election of the podestà they sent to Venice messengers, who arrived in July

1205.[6] They informed Vice-Doge Ranieri Dandolo of the sad, yet hardly unexpected news of his father's death. They then related the manner and outcome of the election of the podestà, stressing that they had in no way wished to infringe on the authority of the Venetian government but had merely taken action as an interim solution to the problem. If the new doge wished to appoint a different podestà, they would gladly accept him.[7] These are hardly the words of a defiant or rebellious colony; rather, they were carefully chosen in a time of great uncertainty. The identity of the next doge and his attitude toward the outcome of the Fourth Crusade were unknown to everyone. The Venetians at Constantinople were therefore at pains to reassure Ranieri Dandolo that they would in every way follow the will of the home government.

Now a lame duck, Ranieri Dandolo thought it best to leave the matter to his successor. He sent the messengers back to Constantinople with orders to get everything in writing from the podestà.[8] He then initiated the now-settled process of choosing a doge. The forty electors chose Pietro Ziani, the son of Doge Sebastiano Ziani.[9] With that last duty discharged, Ranieri Dandolo, after almost three years on the throne of St. Mark, graciously and honorably returned to private life.[10]

As ordered, on September 29, 1205, Marino Zeno sent back to Venice a written report of the situation in Constantinople.[11] After studying the matter, Doge Ziani allowed the election of the podestà to stand, which suggests rather strongly that he did not view it as a threat to his own authority. Indeed, it is clear that Ziani and his court wanted to involve Venice as little as possible in the fledgling Latin Empire. Back in May 1205 a Venetian fleet escorting Patriarch Morosini to Constantinople had conquered Durazzo and Corfu.[12] These were strategically vital areas on the Strait of Otranto guarding the mouth of the Adriatic Sea, so it may well have been on Ranieri Dandolo's orders that they were captured. Doge Ziani, therefore, claimed these and the coastal areas adjoining them for the commune of Venice. Everything else that Enrico Dandolo had won in the Treaty of Partition Ziani left to the jurisdiction of the Venetian podestà in Constantinople.[13] In other words, except for a small, strategically important area, largely already conquered, Venice simply did not want the Venetian share of the Treaty of Partition.

Ziani declared that the Venetian podestà of Constantinople, as "ruler of three-eights of the Roman Empire," would have to be self-sufficient, receiving nothing from the Venetian government. Nevertheless, despite this aloof stance, the doge was willing to allow individual Venetians to take part in the dismemberment of the Byzantine Empire for their own profit and at their own expense.

He gave a general license to all Venetians and their allies to conquer what they wished in Greece, provided that whatever they captured was sold or bequeathed only to Venetians. These territories would remain part of the Latin Empire, with no legal attachment to the Republic of Venice.[14]

Several underlying trends seem evident in the response of the Venetian government to the conquest of Constantinople and the partition of the empire. First, there appears to have been a strong aversion to Venice becoming a maritime empire. It is telling that Ziani did not take the imperial title "ruler of three-eighths of the Roman Empire," leaving it instead to the podestà of Constantinople.[15] Medieval Venetians viewed the boundaries of their world as the shores of the Adriatic Sea. Although they lived and worked in cities across the eastern Mediterranean, the Adriatic, they believed, belonged to them—it was their home, the right and proper place for Venetians. Ziani's decision retained that approach, securing the territories of the Adriatic for the state while leaving those outside for private initiative. Because this simple formula had served Venice well for centuries, there was an obvious reluctance to abandon it. There was also the consideration of cost. Empires are expensive and troublesome, requiring large investments of manpower and, in the case of Venice, war fleets. The seafaring merchants of the Republic would naturally look upon these expenditures and the accompanying disruption of trade with great skepticism.

It was Crete that shattered the Venetian dream of relative isolation in the cradle of the Adriatic. Ziani and his councilors appear at first to have had no idea what to do with the island. It was not part of the partition of the empire because Alexius IV had earlier given it to Boniface of Montferrat, who then sold it to Enrico Dandolo and the Venetians. Since Ziani made no immediate move to capture it, he may have considered the island to be within the podestà's jurisdiction; Crete was not on the short list of properties that the podestà was required to relinquish to the Venetian state.[16] In any case, the Genoese, still upset by Enrico Dandolo's lightning-fast purchase of the island after it had first been offered to them, prepared to step into the vacuum. In 1206 Enrico Pescatore, the Genoese count of Malta, led a sizable expedition against Crete, quickly capturing and fortifying virtually the entire island. At about the same time the Genoese pirate Leone Vetrano supported a rebellion in Corfu that freed it from Venetian control.[17]

These events forced the Venetians to a crossroads they had hoped to avoid. There was no question about recapturing Corfu, a Venetian possession that was simply too important to allow an enemy to hold. But what of Crete? The sources for subsequent Venetian expeditions to Crete are often confused and contradictory.[18] Nevertheless, they give the impression that at this stage the government was still trying to maintain the policy of restricting state operations to the Adriatic Sea and the Strait of Otranto. A fleet of some thirty galleys was dispatched under the command of Ranieri Dandolo and Roger Permarino. Its mission is not clear, but it at least included the reconquest of Corfu and the neutralization of Leone Vetrano and his band of privateers. It does not appear that Crete was one of its initial objectives.[19]

The fleet quickly made its way to Corfu and by force of arms reestablished Venetian control. Dandolo and Permarino then sailed into the Ionian Sea in search of Vetrano. They caught up with him at Modon on the tip of the westernmost peninsula of the Morea, an area infested with pirates. The Venetians captured the cities of Modon and Coron, arrested Vetrano and a number of his supporters, and hung them at Corfu.[20] According to Martino Da Canal, who is hardly a reliable source, Dandolo and Permarino then sailed to Crete, where they captured some Genoese galleys but were too few to invade the island.[21] This may be a confused reference to Dandolo's later expedition to Crete, or it may have happened but was simply an extension of the fleet's efforts to root out Genoese pirates.[22]

Dandolo and Permarino returned home victorious.[23] Yet their success also posed a problem. With the conquest of Coron and Modon, Venetian state interests were extended deep into the Ionian Sea. Given the war with Genoa and the high level of privateering in Greek waters, it was probably inevitable that Venetian force would have to be projected beyond the Adriatic. Yet with each new possession came new dangers. Crete was within easy striking distance of Coron and Modon. It was also a threat to Venetian shipping, a threat that would only escalate as the Genoese secured control of the island. Later Venetian chroniclers claimed that Enrico Pescatore petitioned the pope to crown him king of Crete.[24] Whether this is true or not, it was a danger. Crete was not part of the Latin Empire and therefore not subject to Henry of Flanders. The question of whether Ziani had left it to the podestà of Constantinople or retained it for Venice would be irrelevant if Genoa succeeded in legitimizing its possession of the island. If the Venetian state wanted what Enrico Dandolo had purchased, bold and immediate action would have to be taken.

It was in the late summer or autumn of 1206, perhaps just after the return of Dandolo and Permarino, that Venice began its transformation into a maritime empire. Nothing is known about the particulars, but the outcome is clear. Ranieri Dandolo was given command of a more powerful fleet, an army, and explicit orders to conquer the island of Crete.[25] Equally revealing, in Constantinople

Marino Zeno was informed that he was no longer to refer to himself as "lord of three-eighths of the Roman Empire."[26] Henceforth, that title would belong solely to the doge of Venice.[27]

The fleet set sail in late summer 1207.[28] Shortly before leaving, Ranieri Dandolo borrowed 70 lire from his kinsman, Marino Dandolo—perhaps for expenses on the voyage.[29] It was a debt he would never repay. The armada hoisted its sails and went directly to Crete. Against vigorous Genoese opposition, it captured the city of Candia. From there the Venetians spread across the countryside while the Genoese holed up behind their fortifications. Pescatore sent to Genoa for reinforcements, which probably arrived in the summer of 1208.[30] This was bad news for the Venetians, but more was still to come. During a fierce battle Ranieri Dandolo was wounded by an arrow and captured. He died in prison a few days later.[31]

There can be no doubt that Ranieri Dandolo was highly revered by the Venetian people, who, when they learned of his death, immediately sought to avenge it. A new fleet was outfitted and dispatched to Crete. In honor of his sacrifice— and presumably the deeds of his father, as well—Ranieri Dandolo's male offspring were exempted from taxation in perpetuity.[32] In remembrance of his efforts the Venetians redoubled their own to capture Crete. By 1211 it was theirs and would remain so for more than four centuries.

Venice's maritime empire had been born.

Appendix

DANDOLO GENEALOGY

Given the wealth and status consciousness of the early modern Venetian patriciate, it should come as no surprise that it produced an abundance of family histories and genealogies. Although these works can be quite useful for their own periods, they are wretchedly confused when it comes to anything before the thirteenth century. Family lore, legend, or just wishful thinking were often the sole bases for including people in the medieval portion of genealogies. The best of the genre is Marco Barbaro's *Famiglie nobili venete,* in the Österreichische Nationalbibliothek in Vienna; even that, however, contains numerous errors. The Tasca continuation of Barbaro's work, which is widely consulted in Venice, is even less reliable. The genealogy presented here is based as much as possible on contemporary archival documents. In a few cases it also makes use of chroniclers. The citations below reference specific relationships that allow each individual to be placed within the larger matrix. For some individuals there are additional references, but those listed here are sufficient to confirm their placement. Where no reference is listed, the source is Barbaro.

Andrea, f. Vitale: ASV, Mensa patriarcale, b. 93, no. 305; *Documenti,* 1: 251–3, nos. 256–57; Dandolo, 244; Schulz, "Houses of the Dandolo," 410, sack 1, no. 1.
Bonifacio, f. Marco: Schulz, "Houses of the Dandolo," 410, sack 1, no. 7.
Bono, f. Domenico, f. Bono: ASP, Archivi privati diversi, Pergamene diverse, b. 103.
Cecilia, wife of Tomà: ASV, Procuratori di S. Marco, Misti, b. 166.
Contessa (Minotto?), wife of Enrico: *Documenti,* 1: 338–39, no. 342; see Chap. 4, above.
Domenico: Dandolo, 205.
Domenico, f. Bono: ASP, Archivi privati diversi, Pergamene diverse, b. 103; Dandolo, 238, n.
Enrico (Doge), f. Vitale: ASV, Mensa patriarcale, b. 93, no. 305; *Documenti,* 1: 251–3, nos. 256–57; Schulz, "Houses of the Dandolo," 410, sack 1, no. 1.
Enrico (Patriarch of Grado), f. Domenico: Dandolo, 238, n., 244; *Documenti,* 1: 340–41, no. 344; ASV, Mensa Patriarcale, B. 9, nos. 6–10.

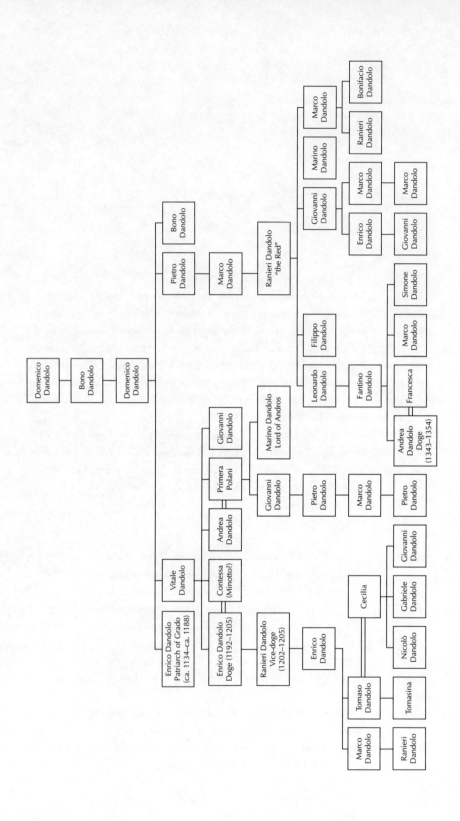

Enrico, f. Ranieri: ASP, Archivi Privati Diversi, Pergamene diverse, b. 103.

Francesca (Dogaressa): Schulz, "Houses of the Dandolo," 410, sack 1, nos. 14, 16, 18.

Giovanni, f. Ranieri "the Red": *Documenti,* 2: 390, no. 863.

Giovanni, f. Tomaso: Da Canal, *Estoires,* 264.

Giovanni, f. Vitale: ASV, Mensa patriarcale, B. 9, nos. 6–10; *Documenti,* 1: 340–41, no. 344;
    Schulz, "Houses of the Dandolo," 410, sack 1, no. 1.

Marco, f. Enrico: ASP, Archivi privati diversi, Pergamene diverse, b. 103.

Marco, f. Giovanni: Schulz, "Houses of the Dandolo," 410, sack 1, no. 6.

Marco, f. Pietro, f. Domenico: *Famiglia Zusto,* 52–56, nos. 23–24.

Nicolò, f. Tomà: ASV, Procuratori di S. Marco, Misti, b. 166.

Marino, f. Andrea: see Chap. 5, n. 7, above.

Pietro, f. Domenico: *Famiglia Zusto,* 52–56, nos. 23–24.

Pietro, f. Giovanni: Schulz, "Houses of the Dandolo," 410, sack 1, nos. 3, 4.

Primera Polani, wife of Andrea: ASV, Mensa patriarcale, b. 93, nos. 305, 315–17. See also
    Chap. 2, n. 117, above.

Ranieri, f. Enrico (vice-doge): Villehardouin, 1: 66–68, sec. 65; TTh., 1: 538–39, no. 135.

Ranieri, f. Marco: Schulz, "Houses of the Dandolo," 410, sack 1, no. 7.

Thomasina, illegitimate daughter of Tomà: ASV, Procuratori di S. Marco, Misti, b. 166.

Tomaso, f. Enrico: ASP, Archivi privati diversi, Pergamene diverse, b. 103.

Vitale, f. Domenico: ASV, Mensa patriarcale, b. 93, no. 305; b. 86; *Famiglia Zusto,* 52–56,
    nos. 23–24; Schulz, "Houses of the Dandolo," 410, sack 1, no. 1.

Abbreviations

ASP	Archivio di Stato, Padua
ASV	Archivio di Stato, Venice
Atti	Pozza, ed., *Gli atti originale della cancelleria veneziana*
BNMV	Biblioteca Nazionale Marciana, Venice
CDRC	*Codex diplomaticus regni Croatiae, Dalmatiae, et Slavoniae*
Cessi, PER	Cessi, "Politica, economia, religione"
Dandolo	Dandolo, *Chronica per extensum descripta*
Deliberazioni	Cessi, ed., *Deliberazioni del Maggior Consiglio di Venezia*
Documenti	Morozza dell Rocca and Lombardo, eds., *Documenti del commercio veneziano nei secoli XI–XIII*
FC	Queller and Madden, *The Fourth Crusade*, 2d ed.
IP	*Italia pontificia*
MGH, SS	*Monumenta Germaniae historica, Scriptores*
PL	Migne, *Patrologia Latina*
Reg.	Innocent III, *Die Register Innocenz' III*
RHC, Occ.	*Recueil des historiens des croisades: Historiens occidentaux*
RIS	*Rerum Italicarum scriptores*
Sanudo	Sanudo, *Le vite dei dogi*
TTh.	Tafel and Thomas, *Urkunden zur älteren Handels- und Staatsgeschichte der Republik Venedig*
Villehardouin	Geoffrey of Villehardouin, *La conquête de Constantinople*

Notes

CHAPTER I. RISE OF THE NEW FAMILIES

1. Dorigo, *Venezia origini*, 2: 514.

2. Ibid., 524; Castagnetti, "Insediementi e 'populi,'" 583–84.

3. Cessi and Alberti, *Rialto*, 9–17.

4. Muratori, *Studi*, 29–30.

5. Both buildings were later destroyed by fire and rebuilt.

6. Schulz, "Urbanism in Medieval Venice," 432–33; idem, "La piazza medievale di San Marco," 134–35.

7. Loredan, *I Dandolo*, 42–43. Cappelleri-Vivaro, *Famiglie venete*, 2: 25–28; BNMV, Cod. Marc. It. VII 37, fo. 1a; Sansovino, *Venetia città nobilissima et singolare*, 245–46.

8. Dorigo, *Venezia origini*, 222.

9. John the Deacon wrote in ca. 1018. *Cronaca*, 57–171. The early portions of the *Origo* were written in the mid-eleventh century. The first mention of a Dandolo in the later portions is Patriarch Enrico Dandolo; *Origo*, 127.

10. *Venetiarum historia*, 259, 274–76. Most later authors accepted this origin of the family. See e.g. Sanudo, 22; Barbaro, *Famiglie nobili venete*, 134v.

11. Barbaro, *Famiglie nobili venete*, 134v.

12. Demus, *The Church of San Marco in Venice*, 52–54; Mueller, "The Procurators of San Marco," 108.

13. Castagnetti, "Famiglie e affermazione politica," 623–26.

14. Editions of the document can be found in *Bilanci generali*, vol. 1, t. 1, 4–5; *Documenti relativi alla storia di Venezia anteriori al mille*, 2: 109, no. 58. Romanin also published the document, but he read "Vitus" instead of "Ursus." *Storia documentata*, 1: 217, no. 11.

15. Hodgson, *Early History of Venice*, 140–41.

16. Maranini, *La costituzione di Venezia*, 94; Cessi, *Le origini del ducato veneziano*, 326–27; Zordan, *Le persone nella storia del diritto veneziano prestatutario*, 156–57.

17. Kretschmayr, *Geschichte von Venedig*, 1: 120; Spinelli, "I primi insediamenti monastici lagunari," 162. On the relationship with the abbot, see *S. Giorgio Maggiore*, 2: 20, no. 1.

18. *S. Giorgio Maggiore* 2: 15–26, no. 1. This is the best edition, but the document can also be found in Ughelli, *Italia sacra*, vol. 5, coll. 1200–1203; Cicogna, *Inscrizione*, 4: 115–22; *Venetiarum historia*, 60–65.

19. Roberti, *Le magistrature giudiziare veneziane*, 1: 65; Cracco, *Società e stato*, 10; Zordan, *Le persone nella storia del diritto veneziano prestatutario*, 153–55, n. 20.

20. Cf. Castagnetti, "Famiglie e affermazione politica," 627; Ortalli, "Venezia dalle origini a Pietro II Orseolo," 417.

21. Dandolo, 200; Uhlirz, "Venezia nella politica di Ottone III," 32, 38–40.

22. *I trattati con Bisanzio*, 21–25; Pertusi, "Venezia e Bisanzio nel secolo XI," 155–60.

23. For further discussion of the chrysobull and its expression of Venetian independence, see Nicol, *Byzantium and Venice*, 40–42; Tûma, "Some Notes on the Significance of the Imperial Chrysobull to the Venetians of 992," 358–66; Lilie, *Handel und Politik*, 326–27.

24. John the Deacon, *Cronaca*, 155–60; Dandolo, 196–99; Kretschmayr, *Geschichte von Venedig*, 1: 135–41.

25. Nicol, *Byzantium and Venice*, 43.

26. John the Deacon, *Cronaca*, 167; Dandolo, 202.

27. Barbaro, *Familie nobili venete*, 134 r.; followed by Cappellari-Vivaro, *Famiglie venete*, 2: 30. In all cases the reports of Marco Barbaro should be used cautiously, but particularly for these early dates. Where it is possible to check his accuracy, it is often found to be flawed.

28. Castagnetti, "Famiglie e affermazione politica," 627–28.

29. Domenico Dandolo is referred to in all later sources as the foundation of the Dandolo clan. Dandolo, 205; Barbaro, *Famiglie nobili venete*, 134 v.; Da Mosto, *I dogi di Venezia*, 75.

30. Dandolo, 204.

31. See Geary, *Furta Sacra*.

32. Dandolo, 205.

33. Ibid.; *Venetiarum historia*, 73. The body was venerated by all two hundred nuns of the convent before it was enclosed in an altar. The altar inscription read "SANCTI THARASII EREMITAE CORPVS." Cicogna, *Inscrizione*, 2: 143. St. Tarasius, however, was neither a hermit nor a monk. After a secular career, he became patriarch of Constantinople in 784 and remained so until his death in 806.

34. Barbaro, *Famiglie nobili venete*, 134 v.

35. Dandolo, 212; *Venetiarum historia*, 78. Sanudo, 152 misplaces this to 1164. The treaty does not survive, but it is referred to in a later pact with Henry IV. See Rösch, *Venedig und das Reich*, 17, n. 40.

36. Bellavitis and Romanelli, *Venezia*, 36; Hodgson, *Early History of Venice*, 30.

37. The parish they founded, San Luca, was believed to have branched off from the older San Paternian. Muratori, *Studi*, 103. The location of the family's largest dwelling was apparently also quite close to San Paternian. See Chap. 3, text at n. 6.

38. On the growth of the Rialto region and the concentration of wealthy families there, see Bellavitis and Romanelli, *Venezia*, 28.

39. Corner, *Ecclesiae venetae*, 12: 259–60.

40. Ibid., 12: 252; Muratori, *Studi*, 101–3. According to Barbaro, the Dandolo founded San Luca with the Pizzamano, Corner, Cornarello, and Muazzo. *Famiglie nobili venete*, 134 r., 327 v. Cappellari-Vivaro, *Famiglie venete*, 2: 32, states that the church was built only by the Dandolo and Pizzamano families.

41. Corner, *Ecclesiae venetae*, 12: 252.

42. Aside from citations above, see also Tassini, *Curiosità veneziane*, 352; Piva, *Il patriarcato di Venezia*, 2: 112.

43. Schulz accepts that San Luca was established before 1072, but believes that the Dandolo clan did not live in the parish before the late eleventh or early twelfth century. "Houses of the Dandolo," 393, n. 11. It is possible, yet I am reluctant to separate the Dandolo family from the foundation of San Luca, given the wide range of sources, albeit late, that place them together.

44. This property was owned by Domenico Dandolo. See Chap. 3, text at n. 4. Given its proximity to San Paternian and its use as a site for a large house, it is reasonable to conclude that this was the original family domicile. This house was for a very long time the only large structure in the area; even in the late fifteenth century, the Barbaro woodcut shows no other large building near it. On the location and orientation of the building, see Schulz, "Houses of the Dandolo," 394–95.

45. On the original canals in this area, see Muratori, *Studi*, facing 100.

46. Maretto, *L'edilizia gotica*, 37.

47. The area on which the Ca' Farsetti now stands was still vacant before 1200. Schulz, "Houses of the Dandolo," 396. See also Chap. 5, text at n. 53.

48. Muratori, *Studi*, 30; Lilie, *Handel und Politik*, 30.

49. Maretti, *L'edilizia gotica*, 37. Despite the growth, agricultural land, stagnant pools, and marshes remained common features in medieval Venice. Land reclamation and filling continued into the fourteenth century. Schulz, "Urbanism in Medieval Venice," 422.

50. Maretti, *L'edilizia gotica*, 38; Muratori, *Studi*, 30–32; Crouzet-Pavan, "*Sopra le acque salse*," 32.

51. Nicol, *Byzantium and Venice*, 156–57.

52. Cessi, *Venezia ducale*, vol. 2, pt. 1, 79–85; Nicol, *Byzantium and Venice*, 55–56.

53. According to Anna Comnena, the siege began on June 17, 1081. *Alexiade*, 1: 143, (IV, 1). This is in agreement with Anonymous of Bari, *Ignoti civis Barensis*, 153, and Orderic Vitalis, *Historiae ecclesiasticae*, col. 520. Lupus Protospatharius, *Annales*, 60–61, and Romuald of Salerno, *Chronicon*, 192 place it in July. Chalandon, *Essai sur le règne d'Alexis Ier Comnène*, 74 n. 1, argues convincingly for June.

54. Anna Comnena, *Alexiade*, 1: 146, (IV, 2); William of Apulia, *La geste de Robert Guiscard*, 214–20.

55. *Annales venetici breves*, 70.

56. For a full relation of the war with references, see Madden, "The Chrysobull of Alexius I Comnenus," 24–27.

57. The document itself does not survive. The most recent editions, based on copies in later chrysobulls, can be found in *I trattati con Bisanzio*, 35–45; Borsari, "Il crisobullo di Alessio I," 124–31.

58. Dandolo, 217. Great scholarly controversy has accompanied the dating of the chryso-bull of Alexius I. Domenico Dandolo's mission has, unfortunately, become engulfed in the morass. For a complete discussion of the problem, see Madden, "The Chrysobull of Alex-ius I Comnenus," 33–36.

59. See e.g. the characterizations of Venetians by Cinnamus, *Epitome*, 280–82; Choniates, *Historia*, 171.

60. See e.g. *Documenti*, 1: 20–23, 27–29, nos. 17–20, 24–26.

61. Castagnetti, "Famiglie e affermazione politica," 631–32.

62. Dandolo, 220 n.; Sanudo, 156, n. 9.

63. In 1455 an engineer from Bologna, one Aristotle, was hired to straighten the campanile. Rather than saving it, the engineer completed the work of the earthquake four centuries earlier. The tower crashed to the ground, crushing a portion of the monastery of San Ste-fano and killing some inside. It was rebuilt in 1460. Sanudo, 157, n. 9.

64. After Vitale Falier's death in 1096, some Venetians threw bread at his tomb, saying, "Fill up on this, you who in life would not provide food for the poor!" Sanudo, 160, and n. 3.

65. *S. Giorgio Maggiore*, 2: 169–74, no. 69; *Atti*, 1: 31–36, no. 1. It is possible that Domenico Dan-dolo was in Constantinople when the donation was made. It is odd, nevertheless, that no other Dandolo was present to represent the family.

66. October 1094 (58 signers): *Venetiarum historia*, 84–85; Romanin, *Storia documentata*, 1: 283, no, 19; March 1098 (26 signers): Lazzarini, "Originali antichissimi," 224–25.

67. Prawer, *The Crusaders' Kingdom*, 485.

68. *Annales pisani*, 239.

69. E.g. Runciman, *History of the Crusades*, 2: 16; Kretschmayr, *Geschichte von Venedig*, 1: 213–15; Lewis, *Naval Power and Trade in the Mediterranean*, 241.

70. Monk of the Lido, 257.

71. Dandolo, 220; *Venetiarum historia*, 86.

72. Dandolo, 221.

73. Monk of the Lido, 255; Dandolo, 221; Sanudo, 161.

74. Dandolo, 221; Monk of the Lido, 255.

75. On the number of crusaders, see Queller and Katele, "Venice and the Conquest of the Latin Kingdom," 24–25.

76. Monk of the Lido, 257.

77. According to ibid., 258, the Venetians sent only thirty vessels against the Pisans' fifty. Cf. Dandolo, 221, Sanudo, 164. See Queller and Katele, "Venice and the Conquest of the Latin Kingdom," 21, n. 23.

78. Monk of the Lido, 259–64; Dandolo, 222; *Annales venetici breves*, 70; Queller and Katele, "Venice and the Conquest of the Latin Kingdom," 22; Pertusi, "La contesa per le reliquie di S. Nicola," 48–54.

79. Albert of Aachen, *Historia*, 517, 519; Fulcher of Chartres, *Historia*, 389; Queller and Katele, "Venice and the Conquest of the Latin Kingdom," 23–25.

80. Monk of the Lido, 275–78; Albert of Aachen, *Historia*, 521–23; Dandolo, 223; Sanudo, 164–65; Prawer, *Histoire du royaume latin de Jérusalem*, 1: 258–59.

81. See Appendix.

82. *S. Giorgio Maggiore*, 2: 211–14, no. 90; 2: 224–27, no. 97.

83. TTh., 1: 67–74, no. 32.

84. ASV, *Codice diplomatico veneziano*, no. 475.

85. Ibid., nos. 483, 485.

86. Late in life Vitale Dandolo was active in diplomacy abroad. See Chap. 3, below.

87. On the date of Enrico Dandolo's birth, see Chap. 3, text at n. 104.

88. Dandolo, 227.

89. According to ibid. the nobles did not know that St. Stephen was on board. When a storm blew up near Cape Malea, a heavenly voice announced the presence of the saint and the winds and sea were immediately calm. Leaving aside the miraculous salvation of the vessel, it is not credible that a single vessel would be carrying seventy-two members of Venice's leading families simply on a voyage of transportation. These families owned their own vessels, which they sailed frequently between Constantinople and Venice, so there was no need for them to crowd onto one.

90. *S. Giorgio Maggiore*, 3: 504, n. CXLIV.

91. Ibid. There are no extant documents that prove Orio Dandolo's paternity.

92. Ibid.

93. Sources disagree on the year of the translation. Dandolo, 227, n. 1; *S. Giorgio Maggiore*, 3: 504, n. CXLIV. Nicol suggests that the Venetians took the body of St. Stephen because of their anger over Alexius I's chrysobull of privileges given to the Pisans. *Byzantium and Venice*, 76. That seems unlikely since the relic arrived in the lagoon on June 7, 1110, at the latest, and it had been stolen much earlier. The chrysobull to Pisa was issued in October 1111. Lilie, *Handel und Politik*, 69–76.

94. Dandolo, 227.

95. See Hodgson, *Early History of Venice*, 246–47; Borsari, *Venezia e Bisanzio*, 65–66.

96. *Atti*, 1: 46, no. 5.

97. Dandolo, 228.

98. Romanin, *Storia documentata*, 2: 29; cf. Darù, *Histoire de Venise*, 1: 52–53; *Historia ducum veneticorum*, 73; Da Canal, *Les Estoires de Venise*, 32; Dandolo, 232. See also Hodgson, *Early History of Venice*, 252–53; Riley-Smith, "The Venetian Crusade of 1122–1124," 340–41.

99. On the identity of the vice-doges, see *S. Giorgio Maggiore*, 2: 319, no. 145; *Atti*, 1: 52–53, no. 7; Monticolo, "Due documenti veneziani del secolo dodicesimo," 72–73.

100. *Famiglia Zusto*, 26–27, no. 8. This document is a penalty imposed on Enrico Zusto for failing to cease conducting commerce and return to Venice. The ducal decree itself has not survived.

101. See Queller and Katele, "Venice and the Conquest of the Latin Kingdom," 30–31; Favreau-Lilie, *Die Italiener im Heiligen Land*, 140, n. 331.

102. Cinnamus, *Epitome*, 280–82.

103. Nicol, *Byzantium and Venice*, 77–78; Lilie, *Handel und Politik*, 367–68; Chalandon, *Jean II Comnène*, 1: 156.

104. *Historia ducum veneticorum*, 73; Dandolo, 233.

105. A twelfth-century copy, the earliest available, is in the archive of S. Nicolò of Bari. The best edition is by Giovanni Monticolo in Sanudo, 195–96, 200–216. There is a sixteenth-century and a seventeenth-century copy in Venice; BNMV, Cod. Marc. It. VII, 516 (=7882); Cod. Marc. It. VII, 551 (=7281). A fourth recension can be found in Sanudo, 195–97 (incorrectly dated May 1125). In the margin of the sixteenth- and seventeenth-century copies, next to the name of Vitale Dandolo, is the notation "padre di Rigo doxe." This may have been derived from the testimony of Barbaro, *Famiglie nobili venete*, 134 v. See also Monticolo, "Il testo del patto giurato dal doge Domenico Michiel," 116.

106. This seems a minimum age, given that he had at this time grown sons and at least one grandson.

107. When Enrico Dandolo became Patriarch of Grado in ca. 1134 he was described as young. He did not die until ca. 1188. Dandolo, 238, n.; 270.

108. William of Tyre, *Historia*, 546–49; Fulcher of Chartres, *Historia*, 452–53; Queller and Katele, "Venice and the Conquest of the Latin Kingdom," 31–33.

109. The best account of the siege, with full references, is Queller and Katele, "Venice and the Conquest of the Latin Kingdom," 36–39.

110. The concessions, contained in the so-called *pactum Warmundi*, are published in TTh., 1: 79–81, no. 40.

111. Advocates could be retained by any party in a dispute for the ducal court. They were not selected for their legal training, which was nonexistent at this time, but rather their eloquence and standing with the court. For this reason, advocates were always selected from among Venice's powerful families. Cessi, PER, 295.

112. *S. Giorgio Maggiore*, 320–22, no. 146.

113. The first document in which Vitale appears in Venice was executed in February 1127. He witnessed the confirmation of a transmission of four saltworks left to S. Giorgio Maggiore in the will of Stefano Foscari of S. Fantin. *S. Giorgio Maggiore*, 2: 328–29, no. 150.

114. Dandolo, 233–36; *Historia ducum veneticorum*, 74; *Translatio Isidori*, 321–24; William of Tyre, *Historia*, 545–76; Chalandon, *Jean II Comnène*, 1: 157–58; Lilie, *Handel und Politik*, 372–73; Nicol, *Byzantium and Venice*, 79–80.

115. *S. Giorgio Maggiore*, 2: 329–30, no. 151.

116. ASP, Archivi privati diversi, Pergamene diverse, b. 103.

117. Dandolo, 238 n.

118. ASP, Archivi privati diversi, Pergamene diverse, b. 103. Bono Dandolo was not a judge. Cf. Schulz, "Houses of the Dandolo," 393, n. 11.

119. This is also the conclusion of Castagnetti, *La societá veneziana*, 1: 119.

CHAPTER 2. PATRIARCH ENRICO DANDOLO AND THE REFORM OF
THE VENETIAN CHURCH

1. Sanudo, 194–95. Manuel Comnenus did not become the Byzantine emperor until thirteen years after Michiel's death. The inscription, probably added during Manuel's reign, refers to an alleged fear that the emperor felt at the memory of the famous doge. The medieval tomb was replaced by a larger and more ornate version in the sixteenth century.

2. Ibid., 38; Castagnetti, *La società veneziana*, 1: 109–10. Like the Dandolo, the Polani were later placed among the city's founders and credited with glorious exploits. See *Venetiarum historia*, 256, 274.

3. The document was Doge Domenico Silvio's confirmation of revenues for the patriarchate of Grado. *S. Giorgio Maggiore*, 2: 93–99, no. 31.

4. Pietro Polani witnessed a ducal donation to the monastery of S. Benedetto di Polirone in March 1098, Lazzarini, "Originali antichissimi," 224. Giovanni and Vitale Polani undersigned a ducal concession to the patriarch of Grado in August 1107. TTh., 1: 69–70, no. 32. Vitale signed a private document the same year. *Famiglia Zusto*, 18, no. 4. A Domenico "Paulani," who was a judge, witnessed a document made in Chioggia in March 1088. *S. Giorgio Maggiore*, 2: 160–61, no. 65. Castegnetti suggests that this may refer to the Rialtine family or a homonymous family in Chioggia. "Famiglie e affermazione politica," 635. However, this is probably a reference to a member of a separate Venetian family: the "Paulini" or Polini. See Sanudo, 39, n. 12.

5. This is Castagnetti's reasonable conclusion, based on Domenico's imperial title and a large loan he made to the state. *La società veneziana*, 1: 109.

6. *S. Giorgio Maggiore*, 3: 504–5, no. CXLIV.

7. The title *protonobelissimos* was created in the late eleventh century as a dignity of the highest order. In the twelfth century it had not yet suffered from the inflation that inevitably devalued all Byzantine titles. Cheynet, "Dévaluation des dignités," 471–75.

8. Cecchetti, *Programma*, 33–36; Cessi, *Problemi monetari*, 4. Pietro and Vitale Polani were among the undersigners of this document. In the same year Vitale Polani witnessed a private document. ASV, *Codice diplomatico veneziano*, 475.

9. Sanudo, 200, 203.

10. He witnessed an oral last testament there. *Documenti*, 1: 53–54, no. 52 (mislabeled "Rialto").

11. Ibid., 1: 64–65, no. 61.

12. Doge Pietro Polani's father and mother resided in San Luca, as did his brother Giovanni. ASV, S. Maria della Carità, b. 20 perg. Naimero, the doge's son, was also from San Luca. ASV, Mensa Patriarcale, P, no. 45; cf. *S. Giorgio di Fossone*, x, n. 1. See also Vitale Polani of San Luca: *Famiglia Zusto*, 18, no. 4. On the oft-cited opposition of the Dandolo to the election of Pietro Polani, see Chap. 2, text at n. 98.

13. ASP, Archivi privati diversi, Pergamene diverse, b. 103; Roberti, "Dei giudici veneziani," 236; Cracco, "Dandolo, Enrico," 452.

14. The tribuneship became an honorary title. Cessi, *Venezia ducale*, 1: 272–74; idem, *Le orig-*

ini del ducato veneziano, 325. Roberti, *Le magistrature giudiziare*, 37–44 argues against the view that the ducal judgeships evolved from the tribunes.

15. Castagnetti, *La società veneziana*, 1: 99–102.

16. Zordan, *Le persone nella storia del diritto veneziano prestatutario*, 192.

17. Roberti, *Le magistrature giudiziare*, 1: 45–46; Zordan, *Le persone nella storia del diritto veneziano prestatutario*, 193–96.

18. Roberti, *Le magistrature giudiziare*, 1: 44. By the end of the twelfth century ducal judges were elected rather than appointed. *Promissioni*, 3.

19. Aside from works cited above, see also Hain, *Der Doge*, 62–70; Roberti, "Dei giudici veneziani," 230–45; Mor, "Aspetti della vita costituzionale," 136–37; Fasoli, "'Comune Veneciarum,'" 81–83; Cracco, *Società e stato*, 8–11.

20. Zordan, *Le persone nella storia del diritto veneziano prestatutario*, 197; Cracco, *Società e stato*, 8.

21. Robinson, *The Papacy*, 441–42; Somerville, "Pope Honorius II, Conrad of Hohenstaufen and Lothar III," 345.

22. Kehr, "Rom und Venedig," 124.

23. Boso, *Vitae paparum*, 379; *IP*, 7/1: 34, no. 75; *IP*, 7/2: 61, no. 112. According to Dandolo, 235 n., 237 n., Honorius II deposed the patriarchs "because they were favorable to schismatics." It is possible that Grado and Aquileia, like other Venetian clergy, supported the faction in the Roman curia that would later precipitate a schism. But the schism itself did not occur until after Honorius's death. Cf. Kehr, "Rom und Venedig," 124; Cappelletti, *Le Chiese d'Italia*, 8: 234.

24. Robinson, *The Papacy*, 442–45; Morris, *Papal Monarchy*, 182–84.

25. Robinson, *The Papacy*, 384.

26. Kehr, "Rom und Venedig," 124–26.

27. Ibid.

28. *IP*, 7/2: 79, no. 4; 7/2: 186–7, no. 3; Kehr, "Rom und Venedig," 126.

29. Chalandon, *Jean II Comnène*, 1: 164–67.

30. Lane, *Venice*, 88.

31. See the letter of Gregory VII lamenting the extreme poverty of the patriarchs of Grado, Gregory VII, Reg. 2: 39.

32. For the doge's traditional rights over the election and investment of clergy, see Dandolo, 106.

33. See below, Chap. 2, text at n. 62.

34. Giovanni Polani became bishop of Castello in ca. 1133. Ughelli, *Italia sacra*, 5, col. 1240. Most authors describe him as the son of Doge Pietro Polani. However, there is no evidence for the relationship. See Cicogna, *Inscrizione*, 1: 312.

35. Some authors maintain that it was the "aristocracy" who actually nominated Dandolo, against the will of the doge. Cracco suggests that the patriarchate was a consolation prize for the faction that opposed Polani's election. "Dandolo, Enrico (patriarca)," 448. This is actually a variation on a theory put forth by W. Carew Hazlitt seventy years earlier. *History*, 1: 180. Hans Hubach suggests that the aristocracy put Polani's enemy into the patriarchate to act as a counterpoise to the doge's dynastic ambitions. "Pontifices, Clerus/Popu-

lus, Dux," 378–79. These views are based on the erroneous assumption that Enrico Dandolo or his family opposed Pietro Polani's election. See below for a discussion of this problem. Although Polani's authority was by no means despotic, like all doges he did have influence over ecclesiastical elections. There is no evidence that the "aristocracy" had any role to play in the selection of a patriarch, nor is it clear how they would formulate a majority opinion and impose it on the clergy.

36. Dandolo, 238, n. A precise date for Dandolo's election cannot be given. The *Origo*, 27, states that Dandolo had reigned as patriarch for sixty-one years at his death in 1190. That would put his election in 1129, which is the year of the deposition of his predecessor. Andrea Dandolo, 270, records his death in 1190 and places his reign at fifty years, thus putting the election in 1140. That is impossible, since he received papal confirmation of his privileges on June 12, 1135; *IP*, 7/2, 61, no. 113. Ughelli placed the election in 1130, although the gloss puts it around 1134. *Italia sacra*, 5, col. 1119. Cappelletti, *Le chiese d'Italia*, 9: 64, and Corner, *Ecclesiae venetae*, 6: 10–13, settled on 1131. Kehr suggested that earlier dates, such as 1129 and 1131, seem highly unlikely since it made little sense for the patriarch-elect to wait four to six years to receive his privileges and processional cross from the pope. "Rom und Venedig," 126. Yet, if the doge was determined before 1135 not to take a stand on the papal schism he might well have prohibited the patriarch-elect from receiving his confirmation immediately after election. On balance, though, Kehr is probably correct to place the election in 1133 or 1134.

37. See Chap. 1, text at n. 111.

38. Aside from chroniclers' references, the patriarch's youth can be inferred from the fact that he lived until ca. 1188, when contemporaries remarked on his advanced age. Dandolo, 270. See Chap. 4, text at n. 121.

39. *IP*, 7/2, 61, no. 113; Sanudo, 223 (misdated 1145); Kehr, "Rom und Venedig," 126–29; Rando, "Le strutture della chiesa locale," 650; Paschini, "I patriarchi di Aquileia," 8.

40. Rando, *Una chiesa di frontiera*, 177.

41. Dandolo, 238 n.

42. Giles Constable, *Reformation of the Twelfth Century*, 11–12; Morris, *Papal Monarchy*, 247.

43. Strictly speaking, the clergy of San Salvatore would become canons secular, since they remained in the world. However, the fluidity of the term *canons regular* allows it to encompass almost all reformed clergy. Constable, *Reformation of the Twelfth Century*, 12–13.

44. Morris, *Papal Monarchy*, 105.

45. *IP*, 7/2, 168, nos. 1 and 2; Corner, *Ecclesiae venetae*, 5: 158; Fabris, "Esperienze di vita comunitaria," 76–77; cf. Dandolo, 232, n.

46. De Gratia, *Chronicon*, 142r. Since the dispute was settled by a papal letter of May 13, 1141, it seems likely that it began in late 1139 or perhaps early 1140. *PL*, 179: 544–45, no. 474; *IP*, 7/2, 145, no. 1.

47. De Gratia, *Chronicon*, 142r. The surname of the reforming prior is a source of some confusion. Dandolo, 239, and Sanudo, 217, refer to him as Bonofilio Michiel. The fourteenth-century prior of the church, Francesco De Gratia, referred to him as Bonofilio Zusto; *Chronicon*, 142r. Letters sent to the prior by Innocent II on May 13, 1141, and by Eugenius III on Au-

gust 20, 1148, address him only as Bonofilio. *PL*, 179: 544, no. 474; ibid., 180: 1361, no. 315; *IP*, 7/2, 145, nos. 1, 2. Cicogna preferred De Gratia's recording of the surname, since the prior was writing about his own church. *Inscrizione*, 1: 312. Monticolo (Dandolo, 239, n. 3) states that the earlier papal letter, still in the ASV, was Dandolo's source for the surname, but prefers the testimony of De Gratia. De Gratia, however, is not contemporary, and the papal letter gives no surname. There was a Bonofilio Zusto who lived in San Salvatore parish, but he was not a prior of the church. Sometime between August 1140 and January 1144 he became a monk at San Giorgio Maggiore. *Famiglia Zusto*, 34–40, nos. 13, 14, 16. In February 1142, a number of parish *plebani* undersigned Pietro Polani's constitution for the procession on the feast of the Purification of the Virgin. Among them was Bonofilio Michiel of San Salvatore. Sanudo, 228; *Deliberazioni*, 1: 236, no. 1.

48. *IP*, 7/1, 235, no. 11.

49. De Gratia, *Chronicon*, 142r.

50. Fabris, "Esperienze di vita comunitaria," 96; Piva, *Il patriarcato di Venezia*, 2: 220.

51. Fabris, "Esperienze di vita comunitaria," 80. The problem of reluctant parishioners remained acute for many years. See, ASV, *Codice diplomatico veneziano*, 2614, 2866; *Famiglie Zusto*, 58–59, no. 26; Betto, *Le nove congregazioni*, 83. The most prominent residents of San Salvatore, however, were the Badoer, who almost certainly supported the reform. See below.

52. De Gratia, *Chronicon*, 142r-142v.

53. Ibid.

54. Pozzo, *I Badoeri*, 50–51.

55. Dandolo, 226; *Venetiarum historia*, 89; *IP*, 7/2, 192 (incorrectly dated to 1104); Cicogna, *Inscrizione*, 1: 237; Spinelli, "I monasteri benedettini," 111. Its mother house was the celebrated monastery of La Charité-sur-Loire, near Nevers.

56. See e.g. the will of Ugerio Badoer (Dec. 1152), ASV, S. Salvatore, b. 28, t. 55; and the donation of a vineyard in Chioggia by Urso Badoer, ASV S. Salvatore, b. 22, t. 43. See also Pozzo, *I Badoer*, 82–83, n. 38.

57. See e.g. Fabris, "Esperienze di vita comunitaria," 80; Spinelli, "I monasteri benedettini," 110.

58. For iterations of this view, see Corner, *Ecclesiae venetae*, 2: 245; Cessi, PER, 380; Kehr, "Rom und Venedig," 129; Cracco, "Dandolo, Enrico (patriarca)," 448.

59. *Benedettini in S. Daniele*, 24–25, no. 13.

60. The convent of San Danielle is often incorrectly referred to as Cistercian. See e.g. Cigogna, *Inscrizione*, 1: 309, 311; Ughelli, *Italia sacra*, 5, col. 1242; Corner, *Ecclesiae venetae*, 4: 185. On this congregation, see Spinelli, "I monasteri benedettini," 114, 128, n. 30; Santschi, *Benedettini in S. Daniele*, xv–xvi.

61. Ibid., 25–26, no. 14.

62. ASV, S. Maria della Carità, b. 20 perg. The lands were on Rio San Vidal just across the Grand Canal from the new church, which was on the site of the modern Accademia. The properties came to the doge's father, Domenico, from various debtors. After Domenico's death the properties went to Pietro Polani and his mother, Nella. Sometime before 1129,

Pietro and Nella built a "holy place" (*sancto loco*) on the land. The meaning is not clear. In June 1132, Pietro's brother Giovanni donated all of the property to S. Maria della Carità, apparently at the behest of the doge. It is not clear whether Pietro and Nella intended to give the property to the canons from the start, or whether that was decided later. Cf. Fabris, "Esperienze di vita comunitaria," 76–77.

63. Rando, *Una chiesa di frontiera*, 195–98.

64. The other three were the doge himself, Giovanni Orio, and Stefano Sanudo. There are many editions of the constitution. The best is in Sanudo, 224–28. Crouzet-Pavan gives an excellent description of the procession and its progress. *"Sopra le acque salse,"* 529–32.

65. *Atti*, 1: 57–58, no. 9. It is frequently asserted that Vitale Dandolo also served as a ducal judge in 1144. He did not. See Chap. 3, n. 19, below.

66. *S. Giorgio Maggiore*, 2: 438, no. 216; *Atti*, 1: 60, no. 10; TTh., 1: 105, no. 47.

67. According to a letter of Benintendus de Ravagnani, the chancellor of Venice, written in November 1352, Popes Innocent II, Celestine II, Lucius III, and Eugenius III wrote letters to establish peace between the patriarch and doge. *Epistola*, CV. Although there are papal privileges implying a struggle between the patriarch and bishop, no surviving letters from Innocent, Celestine, or Lucius mention any quarrel between the patriarch and the doge. Nevertheless, Kehr accepted their existence in his register. *IP*, 7/2, 21, nos. 41–43. Benintendus's letter is not only a late source but is also wretchedly confused. The papal letters are but one of the outcomes of the struggle he describes. Included also are numerous trips by the patriarch to the Roman Curia, an interdict against Venice, and the expulsion of the patriarch from Venice and the destruction of his houses. The latter is a corruption of the expulsion of the Dandolo and Badoer clans in April 1147. See below. Despite its confusion, Benintendus's testimony has some value, but it cannot be relied upon for important papal letters that do not survive or the dating of events within the space of a few years. It has clearly jumbled the story of the patriarch's later expulsion with events earlier in his reign. The papal letters seeking to calm the dispute are from Eugenius III, not his predecessors.

68. Corner, *Ecclesiae venetae*, 2: 245; Piva, *Il patriarcato di Venezia*, 2: 220.

69. Rando, *Una chiesa di frontiera*, 179.

70. *PL*, 179: 544–45, no. 474; De Gratia, *Chronicon*, 142v-143v; *IP*, 7/2, 145, no. 1; Corner, *Ecclesiae venetae*, 14: 92. Innocent did not remove San Salvatore from episcopal jurisdiction, as some authors maintain. A land tenure agreement made by the prior of the congregation in March 1153 is signed by the bishop and transacted "with the consent of our lord Giovanni Polani by the grace of God reverend bishop of Castello." ASV, S. Salvatore, b. 22, t. 43.

71. The canons' names were Peter and Cato. De Gratia, *Chronicon*, 143v; Corner, *Ecclesiae venetae*, 2: 245–46; *IP*, 7/2, 144; Fabris, "Esperienze di vita comunitaria," 81.

72. ASV, *Codice diplomatico veneziano* 4068 (March 1191); Corner, *Ecclesiae venetae*, 9: 233; Dandolo, 239; Fabris, "Esperienze di vita comunitaria," 84–85; Rando, *Una chiesa di frontiera*, 177–78.

73. *SS. Ilario e Benedetto e S. Gregorio*, 74–75, no. 22; *IP*, 7/2: 173, no. 1; Kehr, "Rom und Venedig," 129.

74. Fedalto, "La diocesi nel Medioevo," 75.

75. *PL*, 179: 835–37, no. 7; *PL*, 179: 845–46, no. 15; *IP*, 7/2: 130–31, no. 5. *IP*, 7/2: 61–62, no. 114.

76. A more precise date is not possible. See Fees, *Le monache di San Zaccaria*, 46, n. 157.

77. Benintendus de Ravagnani, *Epistola*, CV.

78. Cessi states that the ducal nominee was a "Casota Polani." PER, 380. Unfortunately, he provides no evidence to support it. This may be a confused reference to Casota Casolo, who was abbess after 1175.

79. Fees, *Le monache di San Zaccaria*, 7–8. Nella Michiel was herself elected during the dogeship of Domenico Michiel.

80. The sole source for this dispute is the letter of Benintendus de Ravagnani, CIV–CV. Benintendus claims that Dandolo bravely defended the rights of the church in the San Zaccaria matter and thereby drew the ire of the doge. Four popes and four cardinals tried to end the dispute, but none could. Finally the pope placed an interdict on Venice, and the doge responded by exiling the patriarch and destroying his houses. There are serious problems of factual error in this document. As Kehr noted, Benintendus collapsed all the events of Dandolo's reign before 1148 into the space of one event. "Rom und Venedig," 131–32. Nevertheless, despite these problems, Benintendus's report of the disputed succession at San Zaccaria seems sound. It is true that the abbess died at this time and the office did remain vacant for some time. Scholars uniformly accept the basic accuracy of Benintendus on this dispute. See e.g. Kehr, "Rom und Venedig," 132; Cessi, PER, 380; Simonsfeld, "Kurze Venezianer Annalen," 410.

81. *IP*, 7/1, 236, no. 14; *IP*, 7/2, 108, no. 3.

82. ASV, S. Zaccaria, b. 2 perg. (Feb. 1145); ASV, S. Zaccaria, b. 1 perg. (Nov. 1145).

83. *PL*, 180: 1479–80, no. 454.

84. Rösch, *Der venezianischer Adel*, 201; cf. ASV, *Codice diplomatico veneziano*, 2116. On the conversion of San Zaccaria, see Chap. 2, text at n. 123.

85. Nicol, *Byzantium and Venice*, 85–86.

86. Dandolo, 242; *Annales venetici breves*, 71; *Venetiarum historia*, 110; Simonsfeld, "Kurze Venezianer Annalen," 408; cf. Maranini, *La costituzione di Venezia*, 1: 106.

87. As evidenced by the sudden absence of Badoer from the ducal court and their subsequent expulsion with the patriarch. Dandolo, 242. The expulsion of the canons can be surmised from the testimony of the *Annales venetici breves*, 71, that "*multis clericis*" were exiled, as well as the subsequent return and persecution of Prior Bonofilio Michiel. See Chap. 2, n. 120, below.

88. In a document providing for restitution payments to Pietro Dandolo and his son Marco, Doge Domenico Morosini and his court judged that their houses had been destroyed unjustly and through no fault or crime of their own. *Famiglia Zusto*, 53, no. 23.

89. *Annales venetici breves*, 71; Dandolo, 242; *Venetiarum historia*, 110. The *Annales venetici breves* place the story of the discord and the expulsion of the patriarch, his family, and many clerics under the date April 1147. This must refer to the start of the discord between the doge and patriarch, not to the expulsion. Simonsfeld, "Kurze Venezianer Annalen," 409. In April 1147 the Normans had not yet launched their surprise attack against Corfu. No deal was struck between Venice and Byzantium until fall at the earliest.

90. Not everyone with the Dandolo surname was exiled or had his home destroyed. A minor branch of the family, probably living in San Polo parish, was not affected. Pietro Polani granted Gratone Dandolo a one-seventh share in a four-year lease of property in Constantinople that had been granted by Manuel Comnenus in March 1148. *Famiglia Zusto*, 52–56, nos. 23, 24. Gratone received the lease sometime that spring or summer; months after the Dandolo of San Luca had been exiled. Although Gratone Dandolo appears prominently in several documents in the 1160s and 1170s, his parish is never identified, nor are any references made to his kin. Nevertheless, it seems likely that he belonged to the San Polo branch of the family. *Gratone* was a very unusual name in medieval Venice. It appears in no Dandolo genealogies except for that of the San Polo Dandolo, where it appears with regularity. Barbaro, *Famiglie nobili venete*, 138v. See also ASV, Procuratori di S. Marco, Misti, b. 166; ASV, Proc. S. Marco, Misti, Diversi perg., b. 2; *Atti*, 2: 83, no. 22. It is interesting that although no Dandolo of San Polo appears in the documentary record prior to this, by the 1160s they were an important family. A Giovanni Dandolo of San Polo, for example, was the son-in-law of Doge Vitale II Michiel and even served as vice-doge in 1168. *S.S. Trinità e S. Michele*, 2: 468–70, no. 293; *S. Giorgio Maggiore*, 3: 58–59, no. 318. Perhaps they fled San Luca to San Polo around 1147 to disassociate themselves with the patriarch's closest relatives. Presumably the two branches have a common ancestor, but the connection remains unknown.

91. Kretschmayr, *Geschichte von Venedig*, 1: 246. Hain, *Der Doge*, 46–47 argued that Dandolo opposed the doge on political grounds, yet the motivations for their disputes were religious, coming directly from the Investiture Controversy that shook Germany.

92. Merores, "Der venezianische Adel," 208–9.

93. Kehr, "Rom und Venedig," 131–33. In a study published the same year, Maranini recognized the ecclesiastical nature of the dispute grounded in the ideas of Gregory VII and Bernard of Clairvaux, but he judged that it had taken on a purely political nature in Venice in the wake of the election of Pietro Polani. *La costituzione di Venezia*, 104–7.

94. See e.g. Romanin, *Storia documentata*, 2: 48; Cicogna, *Inscrizione*, 1: 241; Cessi, PER, 380; Rando, "Le strutture della chiesa locale," 652; Hubach, "Pontifices, Clerus/Populus, Dux," 378–79.

95. Cracco, "Dandolo, Enrico (patriarca)," 448. In more recent work, Cracco has moved to a more favorable view of the patriarch, stressing his sanctity and zeal for the freedom of the Church. "L'età del comune," 6.

96. Rando, *Una chiesa di frontiera*, 176–77, 201.

97. *Annales venetici breves*, 71. Doge Domenico Morosini's (1148–55) grave inscription recorded among his accomplishments: "Iste gloriosus dux fecit pacem cum ecclesia, quia ante illum magna discordia fuit inter Petrum Polanum et Henricum Dandulum patriarcham." *Venetiarum historia*, 114; cf. Sanudo, 237–38; Cicogna, *Inscrizione*, 1: 241.

98. Dandolo, *Chronica brevis*, 364.

99. Dandolo, 242.

100. See above, n. 36.

101. These include documents cited above which reveal members of the Badoer and Dan-

dolo families holding favored positions in the ducal court for many years after Polani's election. The marriage between a Dandolo and a Polani to make peace between the families is corroborated by several contemporary documents, as well. See *S. Lorenzo*, 73–74, no. 42; ASV, Mensa patriarcale, b. 93, nn. 305, 315; cf. *S. Giorgio Maggiore*, 3: 551, no. CCCIX.

102. See notes by Muratori and Pastorello in Dandolo, 242.

103. E.g. De Gratia, *Chronicon*, 142v; *Cronica veneta* (BNMV Cod. Marc. It. VII, 89 (=8381)), 19v; Sanudo, 218, states that the dispute was between the Dandolo and Badoer. For a useful discussion of the chronicle tradition of the error, see Monticolo's comments, ibid. The *Venetiarum historia*, 110, 112, gives an abbreviated version of the account in the *Chronica per extensum descripta*. Written only a few years after Dandolo's history, it predates the later copyist's omission.

104. See nn. 92–96, above.

105. Fabris, "Esperienze di vita comunitaria," 80, 96. Some authors point to a law of 1032 that forbade a doge to name his successor, thus forestalling any opportunity to found a dynasty. The election of Pietro Polani, the son-in-law of the previous doge, violated at least the spirit of that law and thus engendered the animosity of several noble families, chief of which were the Dandolo and Badoer. See e.g. Hain, *Der doge*, 15, n. 3; Merores, "Der venezianische Adel," 208–9; Maranini, *La costituzione di Venezia*, 104; Hubach, "Pontifices, Clerus/Populus, Dux," 378–79; cf. Kretschmayr, *Geschichte von Venedig*, 1: 148; Hellmann, *Grundzüge der Geschichte Venedigs*, 36. However, as Cessi has demonstrated, there was no such law. *Venezia ducale*, 2/1: 9–11.

106. Those who insist that the Dandolo and Badoer families used the patriarchate to wage war against the Polani are not even reading the erroneous passage in the *Chronica brevis* correctly. It states that it was Patriarch Enrico and the Badoer clan who opposed the doge, not the Dandolo family. Dandolo, *Chronica brevis*, 364.

107. Dandolo, 242; *IP*, 7/2, 22, no. 46; cf. Simonsfeld, "Kurze Venezianer Annalen," 409.

108. On the date of Polani's death, see Lanfranchi, in *Famiglia Zusto*, 67.

109. Dandolo, 243; Nicol, *Byzantium and Venice*, 86.

110. The pope sent a confirmation of privileges to Prior Bonofilio on August 20, 1148. *PL*, 180: 1361–63, no. 315. Not listed in *IP*.

111. A Giovanni Badoer witnessed a document in Venice in May 1149. ASV, *Codice diplomatico veneziano*, 2032. Several documents made in 1148 mention Pietro Badoer, an advocate for San Zaccaria: ASV, S. Zaccaria, b. 7 perg. (Apr. 1148); transcribed with several errors by Roberti, *Le magistrature giudiziare veneziane*, 1: 155–56, no. 13; ASV, S. Zaccaria, b. 7 perg. (May 1148); ASV, S. Zaccaria, b. 14 perg. (June 1148), transcribed with several errors by Roberti, *Le magistrature giudiziare veneziane*, 1: 156–57, no. 14. The documents do not, however, refer to events in 1148, as Pozzo suggests, but rather are testimonies concerning a case Badoer argued in 1129. *I Badoer*, 20.

112. Giovanni Badoer made his will in Constantinople in May 1148. Although he does not specifically mention having been exiled, he does instruct his brother, who acted as executor, to make a diligent investigation into his possessions in Venice and to settle all accounts there. It is clear from the will that Badoer is not certain what he still has in Venice, even making provisions for the possibility that he may not have enough to pay out all of his bequests.

He does, however, mention a house, confirming that only the Dandolo houses were destroyed. Pozzo, *I Badoer,* 118–21.

113. IP, 7/2, 22, no. 47.

114. *Promissioni,* 3, 12.

115. Hain, *Der Doge,* 49–50; Besta and Predelli, "Gli statuti civili," 25–26; Maranini, *La costituzione di Venezia,* 107–8; Zordan, *La persona nella storia del diritto veneziano prestatutario,* 219–22; Rösch, *Der venezianische Adel,* 188–89.

116. ASV, S. Zaccaria, b. 5 perg. (Mar. 1175).

117. Dandolo, 244, and *Venetiarum historia,* 112, record that to seal the peace Andrea Dandolo was married to the daughter of Naimerio Polani, the son of the doge. This is an error. In a document of September 1166, Primera identifies herself as the daughter of Giovanni Polani, who was the late doge's brother and the *consanguina* of Naimerio Polani. ASV, Mensa patriarcale, b. 93, no. 305. In a copy of this document made in 1291, the notary mistakenly substituted the word *relicta* for *filia,* thus changing Primera from the daughter of Giovanni Polani to his widow. ASV, Mensa patriarcale, b. 86. Luigi Lanfranchi relied on the later copy when he transcribed the document; ASV, *Codice diplomatico veneziano,* 2605. At some point an archivist, perhaps Lanfranchi, typed on the cover sheet of the original document, "*Primera vedova di Giovanni Polani moglie di Andrea Dandolo.*" The error has found its way into print: see *S. Giorgio Maggiore,* 3: 551, no. CCCIX. The identification of Primera as the daughter, not the widow, of Giovanni Polani is verified by several later documents. See ASV, Mensa patriarcale, b. 93, nos. 315–17.

118. A Giovanni Dandolo witnessed a document in Venice in September 1150. *Documenti,* 1: 99–100, no. 98. This Giovanni could, however, be of the San Polo branch of the family, which was not exiled. See n. 90, above. Cf. ASV, S. Zaccaria, b. 2 (Feb. 1185). The first Dandolo of San Luca appear as undersigners of a ducal act of January 1152. Sanudo, 247–48.

119. See Chap. 7, text at n. 17.

120. There are two versions of the death of Prior Bonofilio. One holds that he contracted a fever shortly after returning to Venice and subsequently died while praying for his persecutors. Corner, *Ecclesiae venetae,* 2: 246. The other tells of the prior being attacked in Venice and his clothes being torn from him. He fled to the cloister, but his persecutors violated the sanctuary in an attempt to kill him. To save his life, Michiel fled to the island of Veglia, where streams of pious penitents came to hear his wisdom and confess their sins. When his persecutors learned of this, they were enraged. Seven months later, on April 24, 1150, they assassinated Bonofilio. His tomb soon became associated with miracles. Later, Patriarch Dandolo transported the body back to Venice, where it was placed in a marble tomb behind the altar of San Salvatore. De Gratia, *Chronicon,* 145r; Corner, *Ecclesiae venetae,* 2: 246–47.

121. ASV, *Codice diplomatico veneziano,* 2147, 2162.

122. On the dispute concerning houses see ASV, *Codice diplomatico veneziano,* 2452, 2505, 2614, 2866; *IP,* 7/2: 146–48, nos. 7, 8; *PL,* 200: 118, no. 44; ibid., col. 1289, no. 1491; *Famiglia Zusto,* 58–59, no. 26; De Gratia, *Chronicon,* 148r.; Betto, *Le nove congregazioni,* 83; Rando, *Una chiesa di frontiera,* 201. On control of S. Bartolomeo, see Corner, *Ecclesiae venetae,* 1: 325; Rando, *Una chiesa di frontiera,* 257, n. 213.

123. Eugenius III confirmed the convent's conversion and placed it under the protection of the Holy See on September 26, 1151. *PL*, 180: 1479–80, no. 454; *IP*, 7/2, 178, no. 25.

124. Ughelli, *Italia sacra*, 5, cols. 1371–77.

125. ASV, S. Maria della Carità, b. 40 perg.

126. Corner, *Ecclesiae venetae*, 4: 177.

127. *CDRC*, 2: 76–79, no. 78; BNMV, lat. cl. XIV, no. 71; Dandolo, 245; Kehr, "Rom und Venedig," 135.

128. *PL*, 188: 1387–88; *CDRC*, 2: 79–80, no. 79; *IP*, 7/2: 62, no. 118; Kehr, "Rom und Venedig," 136; Piva, *Il patriarcato di Venezia*, 1: 104–5; Ferluga, "Dalmazia," 73. Hadrian reserved to the papacy the right to bestow the pallium on the archbishop of Zara.

129. *CDRC*, 3: 61, no. 55; TTh., 2: 29, no. 172.

130. *PL*, 188: 1519–20, no. 138; *CDRC*, 2: 81–84, no. 81; *IP*, 7/2: 64, no. 121.

131. *PL*, 188: 1520–21, no. 139; *IP*, 7/2: 64, no. 122.

132. On the dating of the mosaics, see Demus, *Mosaics of San Marco*, 1: 82; Dale, *Relics, Prayer, and Politics*, 54.

133. Demus, *Mosaics of San Marco*, 1: 82–83; Dale, *Relics, Prayer, and Politics*, 52–54.

134. Demus, *Mosaics of San Marco*, 1: 69.

135. Dale, *Relics, Prayer, and Politics*, 54–55. Because of subsequent restorations it is not clear that the seventh figure originally bore a cross. Demus, *Mosaics of San Marco*, 1: 68.

136. Demus, *Mosaics of San Marco*, 1: 69; Dale, *Relics, Prayer, and Politics*, 54–55; Hubach, "Pontifices, Clerus/Populus, Dux," 370–97.

137. By the same token, relations between the new doge and the Polani were probably not warm. Depicting the patriarch of Grado receiving the relics of St. Mark rather than the bishop of Castello was a direct insult to Bishop Giovanni Polani. No Polani ever served in Michiel's court.

138. One of those exiled with Patriarch Dandolo was Bonofilio Michiel, the prior of S. Salvatore.

CHAPTER 3. VITALE DANDOLO & THE REFORM OF THE VENETIAN STATE

1. See Chap. 2, text at n. 120.

2. Polani family members continued to appear in court documents signed by a large number of citizens, so it is clear that they remained important. However, after Pietro Polani no member of the family would again wear the ducal robes. The Polani were absent from court throughout the remainder of the twelfth century. The only member of the family known to have filled a position of some power was Enrico Polani, who served as one of the electors of Doge Sebastiano Ziani in 1172. *Venetiarum historia*, 122.

3. Juergen Schulz, "Houses of the Dandolo," 391–415. Many of the conclusions presented here are mine, based on Schulz's data. Responsibility for error, therefore, is also mine.

4. The extent of Domenico Dandolo's properties in San Luca can be surmised from land parcels later divided between his descendants. See ibid., 406, and below.

5. Ibid., 399.

6. This house was the only large structure on the Dandolo property. Even in the late fifteenth century, the Barbaro woodcut shows no other large building in the parish aside from this palazzo. On the location and orientation of the building, see ibid., 394–95.

7. Bono Dandolo does not appear in Barbaro's genealogy, which frequently omits those with no offspring. In July 1131 he rented an anchor to two merchants for a voyage to Greece. ASP, Archivi privati diversi, Pergamene diverse, b. 103. One year later, in July 1132, he acted as a witness for the payment of a colleganza agreement. *Documenti*, 1: 65–66, no. 62. He appears in no subsequent documents. See Chap. 1 for more on Bono Dandolo.

8. Schulz, "Houses of the Dandolo," 405–7.

9. Ibid., 393–96, 399.

10. Ibid., 399.

11. ASV, *Codice diplomatico veneziano*, 2609.

12. Marco was emancipated. He appears to have been the only son of Pietro and had therefore already taken control of his patrimony. Documents concerning the house do not refer to Pietro as deceased. In the decree of the ducal court it was judged that the palazzo had been destroyed through no fault of "Marco Dandolo and his father, Pietro Dandolo." *Famiglia Zusto*, 53, no. 23.

13. Ibid., 52–56, nos. 23–24. It is not clear why payment was not made until 1156. It may be that the lease began in 1148 but was renewed in 1152, so the payments to Marco and Pietro Dandolo would have come from the second lease. It is also possible that the investors were unable to take possession of the property in Constantinople until after the war with the Normans. If they did not arrive and acquire the lands until 1150 or 1151, payment would have been due in 1154 or 1155.

14. Schulz, "Houses of the Dandolo," 395, 399.

15. Assuming that his son, Doge Enrico Dandolo, was born in ca. 1107. Vitale himself lived until 1174. Dandolo, 261–62.

16. TTh., 1: 70, no. 32, with *Vitalis* misread as *Natalis*. See ASV, *Codice diplomatico veneziano*, 441. See also *S. Giorgio Maggiore*, 2: 211–13, no. 90.

17. Queller and Katele, "Venice and the Conquest of the Latin Kingdom," 36–39.

18. *Atti*, 1: 57–58, no. 9.

19. Vitale Dandolo is frequently referred to as a ducal judge in 1144. He was not. The error originated with Roberti, who for that year listed three judges: Giovanni Orio, Stefano Sanudo, and Vitale Dandolo. "Dei giudici veneziani," 237. Roberti cited Cecchetti, "La vita dei Veneziani," 108. Yet Cecchetti lists the three judges for 1144 as Giovanni Orio, Stefano Sanudo, and Orio Doro. On the following line, for the year 1161, Cecchetti lists Vitale Dandolo as a judge. Roberti's eye skipped when reading Cecchetti, causing him to place Dandolo in the judiciary in 1144. The widespread use of Roberti's list has caused the error to appear fre-

quently in more recent scholarship. See e.g. Cracco, "Dandolo, Enrico," 452; Rösch, *Der venezianische Adel*, 94; Castagnetti, "Il primo comune," 110 (but cf. ibid. 114).

20. In the sole surviving ducal act of Domenico Morosini, made in January 1152, Vitale signed 101st of 260. Sanudo, 247.

21. In November 1153, Vitale Dandolo was referred to with the title *iudex*, although he was not acting as a judge in the document. ASV, S. Zaccaria, b. 7 perg. After serving as a judge one was entitled to use the title for life. Roberti, *Le magistrature giudiziare*, 1:44.

22. ASV, S. Zaccaria, b. 7 perg. Dandolo contracted a rental agreement for the convent with Marco Indriomeni, a Greek master of mosaics, probably from Constantinople. Indriomeni was given a wooden house and a small plot of vacant land near San Zaccaria, in return for which he promised to pay 20 soldi annually for the land and paid up front 3 lire to purchase the house.

23. Roberti, *Le magistrature giudiziare*, 1: 66–73.

24. Rösch, *Der venezianische Adel*, 202.

25. The term coined by Cracco, "Dandolo, Enrico," 452.

26. *Historia ducum veneticorum*, 76; *Annales venetici breves*, 71; Steindorff, *Die dalmatischen Stadte*, 79–80.

27. *Famiglia Zusto*, 55, no. 24.

28. ASV, *Codice diplomatico veneziano*, 2335. They ruled against a complaint brought by Pietro Michiel of San Benedetto against his neighbor Giovanni da Ponte for building a structure that was too close to Michiel's door and blocked a foot path.

29. This relatively new practice of selecting men to serve regularly as judges can be seen in the court of Pietro Polani, who favored Giovanni Orio and Stefano Sanudo. *Atti*, 1: 54–60, nos. 8–10.

30. Lane, *Venice*, 92.

31. ASV, *Codice diplomatico veneziano*, 2355.

32. During this period of a year or so, the doge selected three other judges: Stefano Moro, Pietro Trundomenico, and Domenico Celso. First document of May 1160: *Documenti*, 1: 143, no. 143; *Deliberazioni*, 1: 239, no. 4; *Atti*, 1: 63–64, no. 12. Second document of May 1160: *Deliberazioni*, 1: 240, no. 5; *Atti*, 1: 65–66, no. 13. Third document of May 1160: *Deliberazioni*, 1: 241, no. 6; *Atti*, 1: 61, no. 11; this document is missing from Rösch's list, *Der venezianische Adel*, 92. March 1161: *S. Maria Formosa*, 16–17, no. 9. Rösch drops Domenico Celso from the list. *Der venezianische Adel*, 92.

33. Rando, *Una chiesa della frontiera*, 184.

34. Ibid., 185–86.

35. *Atti*, 1: 69, no. 14.

36. *Codice diplomatico padovano*, 2: 72–74, no. 766. The monastery was in a dispute with Chioggia.

37. Roberti, *Le magistrature giudiziare*, 1: 71, n. 1.

38. *Deliberazioni*, 2: 242.

39. *Codice diplomatico padovano*, 2: 121–22, no. 847; Rando, *Una chiesa della frontiera*, 187.

40. Sanudo, 278. For other recensions of the document, see Fees, *Reichtum und Macht*, 283–84, no. 41. The doge's signature was followed by that of Marino Michiel, who did not sign himself as a judge—likely an oversight. He was followed by Vitale Dandolo and Domenico Morosini. The latter signed himself *iudex communis.* Sebastiano Ziani and Orio Mastropiero did not serve as ducal judges in this instance because they were among those lending funds to the commune. The only Dandolo among the lenders was Gratone Dandolo, who was probably a member of the San Polo branch of the family. See Chap. 2, n. 90, above. On the importance of this loan in Venetian economic history, see Lenel, *Die Entstehung der Vorherrschaft*, 42; Monticolo, in Sanudo, 277, n. 2. The reason for the loan is not known. It could have been used to finance the ongoing war with Hungary or to support the Veronese league against Frederick I.

41. *Atti*, 1: 71, no. 15; TTh., 1: 140–44, no. 59.

42. ASV, S. Salvatore, b. 22, t. 43, no. 33.

43. The only other surviving record of a judge deciding a case alone occurred in June 1148, when Domenico Basedello ruled against San Zaccaria in a land dispute heard in the ducal court. S. Zaccaria, b. 14 perg.; published with some transcription errors by Roberti, *Le magistrature giudiziare*, 1: 156–57, no. 14.

44. *Deliberazioni*, 2: 245–47, no. 10. The judges were Sebastiano Ziani and Marino Michiel.

45. Ibid., 247–48, no. 11.

46. In the text of the document the doge mentions the presence of his judges and sapientes, yet none signs himself as such. Clearly the doge is referring to their titles of honor rather than their capacity in this proceeding.

47. ASV, *Codice diplomatico veneziano*, 2609. Rösch lists Vitale Dandolo as a judge for this date in light of this document. *Der venezianische Adel*, 92. Dandolo did sign himself as a judge, but he was not acting as such in this private transaction.

48. *Annales venetici breves*, 71; De Gratia, *Chronicon*, 148v.; Dandolo, 249. On this fire, see Dorigo, *Venezia origini*, 1: 481 and map on 478.

49. ASV, *Codice diplomatico veneziano*, 2676. A transcription of the document (with important errors) can be found in *Codice diplomatico padovano*, 2: 167, no. 927. See also *S. Giorgio di Fossone*, 29, no. X; 13–15, no. 6.

50. In September 1168, the doge made a pious donation to the convent of San Giovanni Evangelista di Torcello. It was signed by his three judges. Oddly, the document was also signed by the trio of Sebastiano Ziani, Vitale Dandolo, and Orio Mastropiero. The first names of Dandolo and Mastropiero are illegible, but the regularity of these three in court documents during Michiel's reign makes it highly unlikely that they would be anyone but Vitale and Orio. It is not clear why these three signed the donation in addition to the judges, but it does demonstrate that they still worked closely with the doge. *S. Giovanni Evangelista di Torcello*, 81–82, no. 53; *Deliberazioni*, 1: 249–50, no. 13. Dandolo acted as advocate for San Zaccaria in a simple transaction in August 1170; ASV, S. Zaccaria, b. 7 perg.

51. *Documenti*, 1: 153, no. 155.

52. ASV, *Codice diplomatico veneziano*, 2609.

53. Sanudo, 378.

54. See e.g. Cracco, "Dandolo, Enrico," 450, 452; Necker, *Dandolo*, 75–76.

55. The three brothers split their inheritance in 1181. Schulz, "Houses of the Dandolo," 397.

56. As evidenced by Giovanni Dandolo's commercial contracts discussed above as well as Andrea's service as a ducal judge in 1173 and Enrico's embassy to Constantinople in 1172.

57. On emancipation and filial subjection, see Margetic, "Il diritto," 680; Pitzorno, *Le consuetudini giudiziare*, 39. For the Florentine example, see Kuehn, *Emancipation in Late Medieval Florence*, 71, 157.

58. In an imperial privilege to Genoa, Frederick alluded to the poor relations between Venice and the German Empire. Romanin, *Storia documentata*, 2: 56.

59. Cinnamus, *Epitome*, 229–31; Nicol, *Byzantium and Venice*, 95.

60. Magdalino, *Manuel I*, 84.

61. Cinnamus, *Epitome*, 237.

62. Magdalino, *Manuel I*, 84.

63. Cinnamus, *Epitome*, 281–82.

64. Magdalino, *Manuel I*, 89.

65. Ibid., 80–81.

66. *Annales venetici breves*, 71; Dandolo, 249.

67. Dandolo, 249.

68. This is Nicol's reasonable conclusion based on the number of commercial documents executed in Constantinople between 1167 and 1171. *Byzantium and Venice*, 96.

69. *Historia ducum veneticorum*, 78; Dandolo, 250; Nicol, *Byzantium and Venice*, 97; Angold, *Byzantine Empire*, 231.

70. ASV, S. Zaccaria, b. 7 perg.

71. Magdalino, *Manuel I*, 92–93.

72. Day, *Genoa's Response to Byzantium*, 26–27.

73. Cinnamus, *Epitome*, 282; *Historia ducum veneticorum*, 78; Dandolo, 250.

74. *Historia ducum veneticorum*, 78; Dandolo, 250. According to Cinnamus, the Venetian representatives were belligerent, refusing to repay the Genoese for their losses and threatening to launch a fleet against him as they had done to his father, John. *Epitome*, 282. The Venetian sources omit mention of the attack on the Genoese Quarter and blame Manuel for luring the Venetians into his trap.

75. *Historia ducum veneticorum*, 78.

76. Cinnamus, *Epitome*, 282; *Historia ducum veneticorum*, 79; Dandolo, 250. The literature on the timing and purpose of the seizure is vast. For a useful sample, see Danstrup, "Manuel I's Coup against Genoa and Venice," 195–219, esp. 208–10; Heyd, *Histoire du commerce du Levant*, 1: 217–19; Thiriet, *La Romanie vénitienne*, 51–52; Lilie, *Handel und Politik*, 489–93; Hendy, *Studies in the Byzantine Money Economy*, 593–94; Nicol, *Byzantium and Venice*, 97–98; Magdalino, *Manuel I*, 93.

77. *Historia ducum veneticorum*, 79; Dandolo, 251.

78. E.g. Cessi, "Venice to the Eve of the Fourth Crusade," 273; Cracco, *Società e stato*, 6; Lane, *Venice*, 92.

79. All official documents of Michiel's reign are countersigned by his judges and executed with the approval of a large group of sapientes, fideles, or other "good men."

80. *Historia ducum veneticorum*, 79; Dandolo, 251; *Annales venetici breves*, 72; Da Canale, *Estoires*, 39–40.

81. Besta, "Il diritto," 232–37; Maranini, *Costituzione*, 76–77, 113–31; Cassandro, "Concetto e struttura dello stato veneziano," 37–40.

82. *Historia ducum veneticorum*, 79; Dandolo, 251.

83. Madden, "Venice and Constantinople," 173.

84. *Historia ducum veneticorum*, 79; Dandolo, 251–52.

85. ASV, *Codice diplomatico veneziano*, 2842.

86. *Historia ducum veneticorum*, 79; Dandolo, 252; *Venetiarum historia*, 120–21. Nicol postulates that Filipo Greco was selected because he "presumably knew Greek." *Byzantium and Venice*, 98–99. In this case, however, Greco was not a descriptive but a well-established surname in Venice. See Madden, "Venice and Constantinople," 175, n. 27.

87. *Historia ducum veneticorum*, 80; Dandolo, 252; *Venetiarum historia*, 121.

88. Cinnamus, *Epitome*, 283–84.

89. Pasqualo was among the many Venetians who died on the mission. In June 1172, immediately after the return of the fleet, Patriarch Dandolo consecrated his successor to the bishopric of Jesolo. ASV, *Codice diplomatico veneziano*, 2868.

90. *Historia ducum veneticorum*, 80; Dandolo, 252; *Venetiarum historia*, 121.

91. For examples of this characterization, see Madden, "Venice and Constantinople," 167–68.

92. Ibid., 175–76.

93. *Historia ducum veneticorum*, 80; Dandolo, 252. According to Cinnamus, Manuel Comnenus sent a terse and insulting letter to the Venetians scolding them for their pitiful attack on the mighty Roman Empire. *Epitome*, 285. If such a letter was indeed sent, it seems likely that Dandolo and Greco were the ones to carry it with them to Venice.

94. *Historia ducum veneticorum*, 80; 80–81, n. 6 (fragment); Dandolo, 252.

95. *Historia ducum veneticorum*, 80; Dandolo, 259; *Venetiarum historia*, 121–22.

96. Cessi, PER, 407.

97. Cracco, *Societa e stato*, 8–9.

98. Castagnetti, "Il primo comune," 106.

99. Leonardo Michiel brought only two people with him to Verona to witness his marriage to Adelasina of Lendinara on December 1, 1172. One was his kinsman, Marino, and the other was Enrico Dandolo. ASV, S. Zaccaria, B. 2 perg.

100. For a list of the eleven, see *Venetiarum historia*, 122; cf. Rösch, *Der venezianische Adel*, 107; Fees, *Reichtum und Macht*, 240–44.

101. Dandolo, 259; Sanudo, 282.

102. *Historia ducum veneticorum*, 80.

103. Dandolo, 260; Sanudo, 284.

104. Dandolo, 260.

105. Magdalino, *Manuel I*, 93–94; Madden, "Venice's Hostage Crisis," 77–78.

106. Dandolo, 260.

107. Ibid.

108. *Documenti,* 1: 251–52, no. 256.

109. Badoer served as a witness for Enrico Dandolo's collection of his brother's money in Alexandria in September 1174; *Documenti,* 1: 252–53, no. 257.

110. William of Tyre, *Historia,* 963; *Annales pisani,* 266.

111. *Documenti,* 1: 252–53, no. 257.

112. E.g. Cracco, "Dandolo, Enrico," 450–51; Crouzet-Pavan, "Quand le doge part à la croisade . . . ," 167–68.

113. The debt was due at Christmas. Romano Mairano had returned to Venice by that winter. *Documenti,* 1: 258–59, nos. 263–64.

114. Lane, *Venice,* 72.

115. *Documenti,* 1: 258–59, nos. 263–64.

116. *Historia ducum veneticorum,* 81. An exact date for the embassy is not given, but it is placed after Venetian ambassadors had been put off by Manuel Comnenus.

117. Jacoby, "Les Italiens en Égypte," 79–80.

118. Dandolo, 260; *Historia ducum veneticorum,* 81; Sanudo, 286.

119. Dandolo, 261–62.

CHAPTER 4. COMING OF AGE, 1175–1192

1. Pryor, *Geography, Technology, and War,* 88–90; idem, "Winds, Waves, and Rocks," 72, 80–82.

2. It is not clear how the vice-count was related to the future doge. The only surviving document that refers to him, dated March 1176, is an order of the procurator of San Marco concerning business dealings in Acre. *Documenti,* 1: 266–67, no. 272. Beyond his title, the document provides no other identification for this Giovanni Dandolo. Given that there were multiple men with that name in the late twelfth and early thirteenth centuries, it is not possible, as some have tried, to link this Giovanni with those mentioned in other documents. Cf. Prawer, "I Veneziani," 641; Favreau-Lilie, *Der Italiener im Heiligen Land,* 502–3. On the Venetian community in crusader Acre, see Balard, "Communes italiennes," 43–64.

3. Andrea Dandolo served as a judge in Ziani's court in November 1173, which was about the time that his brother and father were returning to Venice with Byzantine envoys. His colleagues were Orio Mastropiero and Pietro Foscarini. *Atti,* 1: 79, no. 17. Andrea served again as a judge in July 1174, the month that Enrico set sail for Alexandria. ASV, S. Zaccaria, B. 12 perg. Shortly before Enrico's return to Venice, Andrea appears again as a judge in June 1175. *Atti,* 1: 83, no. 18. Based on these appearances in the ducal court, Cracco suggests that it was Andrea who was the eldest brother and the new leader of the Dandolo clan. "Dandolo, Enrico," 452. Cracco was unaware, however, that Enrico Dandolo was absent on state business when his brother Andrea was in the doge's court and that he replaced Andrea upon his return to Venice.

4. Enrico Dandolo took his place as ducal judge in October 1176, shortly after his return

to Venice. *Atti*, 1: 85–87, no. 19. Unfortunately, no court documents survive from Ziani's reign after that date. There are, however, two sources that list the most prominent men in Ziani's court in 1177 in conjunction with the Peace of Venice; both place Enrico Dandolo among those closest to the doge. See Obo of Ravenna, in Sanudo, 481; cf. 470. Dandolo was also among the members of the doge's council chosen in 1178 to elect the next doge. *Historia Venetiarum*, 128; Sanudo, *Vitae ducum venetorum*, col. 520. The method of selecting ducal judges at this time is far from clear. It may be that the doge was still able to appoint them himself, or perhaps they were elected by the council. Cf. Besta, *Il diritto*, 171.

5. *Chronicle of Novgorod*, 48.

6. Dandolo, 260.

7. See Chap. 3, text at n. 94.

8. *Historia ducum veneticorum*, 81.

9. Roberti, *Le magistrature giudiziare*, 1: 56, n. 2.

10. *Documenti*, 1: 252–53, no. 257; Cracco, "Dandolo, Enrico," 451.

11. Roberti, *Le magistrature giudiziare*, 1: 55–56.

12. ASV, S. Nicolo di Lido, B. 9, Proc. 77. The document is transcribed in *Atti*, 1: 85–87, no. 19. While legible, the document is in poor condition. A tracing of the signature was published by Cecchetti, *Autografi*, tav. 2, no. 9. However, Cecchetti tilted it markedly to the left so as to make it appear more horizontally aligned. The computer-assisted tracing reproduced here is from the original document.

13. See n. 4, above.

14. "Et si avoit les ialç en la teste biaus et si n'en veoit gote." Villehardouin, 1: 68, sec. 67.

15. Ibid.

16. See below.

17. Tierney, "Visual Dysfunction in Closed Head Injury," 614–22; Yamamoto and Bart, "Transient Blindness Following Mild Head Trauma," 479–83; cf. Crowe et al., "Intrachiasmal Hemorrhage," 863–65.

18. It was not unusual for the elderly in the Middle Ages to lose their sight slowly to cataracts. Dandolo himself, however, attributed his blindness to a head injury, and Villehardouin noted that Dandolo's eyes were clear and bright. Villehardouin, 1: 68, sec. 67.

19. *Historia*, 538.

20. Ibid.

21. Cf. Godfrey, *1204*, 64.

22. E.g. Pears, *The Fall of Constantinople*, 233; Usseglio, *I Marchesi di Monferrato*, 2: 199; Vasiliev, *History of the Byzantine Empire*, 452–53; McNeal and Wolff, "The Fourth Crusade," 169–70; Browning, *The Byzantine Empire*, 187; Nicol, *Byzantium and Venice*, 119–20; Necker, *Dandolo*, 36.

23. Runciman, *History of the Crusades*, 3: 114.

24. E.g. Nicol, *Byzantium and Venice*, 99; Spiridonakis, *Grecs, Occidentaux et Turcs*, 105; Bartlett, *An Ungodly War*, 57; Godfrey, *1204*, 64, even attributes the story of the brawl to Villehardouin!

25. Dandolo, 262.

26. TTh., 1: 172–74, no. 65.

27. For a fuller discussion, see Madden, "Venice's Hostage Crisis," 100–104.

28. Dandolo, 262.

29. Magdalino, *Manuel I,* 95–98.

30. Madden, "Venice's Hostage Crisis," 101–2; Magdalino, *Manuel I,* 98–104.

31. Boso, *Vitae,* 437.

32. *Historia ducum veneticorum,* 82–83; Dandolo, 262–63; Boso, *Vitae,* 437.

33. *De pace veneta relatio,* Thomson, ed., 30; Balzani, ed., 12; Boso, *Vitae,* 438.

34. See Wolters, *Der Bilderschmuck des Dogenpalastes,* 164–81.

35. Fasoli, "Nascita di un mito," 473–76; Crouzet-Pavan, *Sopra le acque salse,* 961–65.

36. *Historia ducum veneticorum,* 84–89.

37. Boso, *Vitae,* 439.

38. Romuald of Salerno, *Chronicon,* 279–82.

39. See e.g. Cracco, *Societa e stato,* 48–52; Brezzi, "Le pace di Venezia," 67; Abulafia, *Two Italies,* 145–47.

40. Baldwin, *Alexander III,* 143–44.

41. Romuald of Salerno, *Chronicon,* 281. According to Romuald, Ziani did not believe anything he told the legates, but he was forced to say it by the fury of the mobs. This can safely be discounted since Romuald had no way of knowing the internal politics of the court. It is interesting to note, though, that once again the party that supported bringing Frederick to Venice is transformed in Romuald's account from the powerful to the commoners.

42. *De pace veneta relatio,* Thomson, ed., 30–31, Balzani, ed., 15.

43. Romuald of Salerno, *Chronicon,* 284; Boso, *Vitae,* 439; *De pace veneta relatio,* Thomson, ed., 31, Balzani, ed., 15; *Historia ducum veneticorum,* 83.

44. Obo of Ravenna, 481, cf. 470.

45. *De pace veneta relatio,* Thomson, ed., 31, Balzani, ed., 15.

46. Ibid.; Boso, *Vitae,* 439–40.

47. *IP,* 7/2, 168–69, nos. 5–6.

48. See Chap. 3, text at n. 49.

49. *IP,* 7/2, 149, no. 17; Concina, *Le chiese di Venezia,* 268.

50. De Gratia, *Chronicon,* 156v.

51. Da Canale, *Estoires,* 260; De Gratia, *Chronicon,* 147r.; Crouzet-Pavan, *Sopra le acqua salse,* 934.

52. Paschini, "I patriarchi di Aquileia," 132.

53. Ughelli, *Italia sacra,* 5: 66–68.

54. *PL,* 200: 1283–84.

55. Rando, *Una chiesa della frontiera,* 191. Demus suggests that "S. Giorgio" corresponds to the modern San Giorgio dei Greci. *Church of S. Marco,* 37.

56. Demus, *Church of S. Marco,* 37.

57. *IP,* 7/2, 67, no. 131; Rando, *Una chiesa della frontiera,* 191; Cappelletti, *Le chiese d'Italia,* 8: 253; Ughelli, *Italia sacra,* 5: 1129. For a useful analysis of the new jurisdictions, see Piva, *Il patriarcato di Venezia,* 1: 106–10.

58. *IP,* 7/2, 67, no. 130.

59. Ibid., 69, no. 137.

60. Ibid., no. 139.

61. The doge's letter does not survive, but its contents can be surmised from the pope's reply. Although there is no clear evidence linking Patriarch Dandolo to the idea of the merger, it is difficult to believe that it would have been championed by the doge without the patriarch's support and encouragement. It seems likely that Dandolo floated the idea in 1177 or at the Third Lateran Council and, getting nowhere, persuaded the doge to write a letter of support.

62. *IP*, 7/2 67–8, no. 133; *PL*, 200: 1284–85. The papal letter has no year, although it was written between 1178 and 1181. It is not certain, therefore, whether it was written to Doge Ziani or his successor, Orio Mastropiero.

63. Very little is known about Bishop Michiel. However, as we have seen, the Michiel and Dandolo families were friendly. There were no disputes between Castello and Grado after the accession of Michiel in 1164. Michiel may have been elderly in 1178, since he died on January 20, 1181. Corner, *Ecclesiae venetae*, 9: 365; Cappelletti, *Storia della chiesa di Venezia*, 1: 282; Piva, *Il patriarcato di Venezia*, 2: 222.

64. On the growth of the court and its authority, see Castagnetti, "Il primo comune," 92–95.

65. *Venetiarum historia*, 128; Dandolo, 266; Sanudo, *Vitae ducum venetorum*, col. 520.

66. According to Romanin, who relied on very late chronicles, each of the forty electors had to receive three votes out of the four and no more than one elector could be chosen from each family. *Storia documentata*, 2: 91.

67. Romanin provides the names of the Four: Enrico Dandolo, Stefano Vioni, Marino Polani, and Antonio Navigaioso. *Storia documentata*, 2: 91. Hodgson reproduces this list without citation. *Early History of Venice*, 331. Unfortunately, Romanin cites only "Barbaro and others" for these names. In any case, it is always perilous to rely on these late works. None of the contemporary or fourteenth-century sources provide the names of the Four, only the Forty. Even Sanudo does not give such a list in his lives of the doges. It would be very unusual for a Venetian committee to elect one of its own members to anything; that was almost never done. Orio Mastropiero was not chosen as an elector, clearly because he hoped to be elected, just as Sebastiano Ziani had remained out of the electoral group in 1172. In the same way it would not be usual for the Four to select one of their own to be an elector. It is also surprising that of the four names, only Enrico Dandolo is identifiable in the documentary record. The other three are mentioned in no surviving contemporary documents, casting further doubt on their veracity.

68. *Historia ducum veneticorum*, 89; *Venetiarum historia*, 129; Dandolo, 266; Sanudo, *Vitae ducum venetorum*, col. 520. Dandolo's name is listed sixth among the Forty.

69. Cf. Cracco, "Dandolo, Enrico," 452.

70. As evidenced by Enrico Dandolo's appointment as a ducal legate in 1184 and ambassador in 1191, as well as by Andrea Dandolo's later presence in the ducal court.

71. For an analysis of the division, see Schulz, "Houses of the Dandolo," passim, esp. 393–99, 410. The document on which Schulz relies is Museo Correr, MS P.D. C-1267, item

no. 51–bis, fol. 1 r. For the boundaries of Enrico Dandolo's property, see Schulz, "Houses of the Dandolo," 396; for the boundaries of Andrea Dandolo's lot, see ibid., 393.

72. See Chap. 5, text at n. 53.

73. Madden, "Venice's Hostage Crisis," 100–102.

74. Magdalino, *Manuel I*, 98–108; Day, *Genoa's Response to Byzantium*, 27–28.

75. E.g. Besta, "La cattura dei Veneziani," 115; Thiriet, *La Romanie vénitienne*, 53; Brand, *Byzantium Confronts the West*, 20; Ostrogorsky, *History of the Byzantine State*, 389, n. 2; Lilie, *Handel und Politik*, 516–18; Martin, "Venetians in the Byzantine Empire," 213; Borsari, *Venezia e Bisanzio*, 23–24; Nicol, *Byzantium and Venice*, 101.

76. For a complete analysis of the problem, see Madden, "Venice's Hostage Crisis," 101–2.

77. For useful treatments of the events in Constantinople, see Brand, *Byzantium Confronts the West*, 31–42; Nicol, *Byzantium and Venice*, 106–8.

78. *Documenti*, 1: 326–27, no. 331.

79. Brand, *Byzantium Confronts the West*, 196; Robbert, "Venice and the Crusades," 408–9.

80. *Venetiarum historia*, 129, 135; Dandolo, 266.

81. Since the first Venetian prisoners are parties to contracts in January 1183, Andronicus must have released them almost immediately after his assumption of the regency. See Madden, "Venice's Hostage Crisis," 103–4; Martin, "Venetians in the Byzantine Empire," 213. The documents below from the summer of 1183 suggest that the quarter was returned at the same time.

82. On the number of Venetians who returned to Constantinople, see Lilie, *Handel und Politik*, 291–93; Ferluga, "Veneziani fuori Venezia," 713.

83. E.g. ASV, *Codice diplomatico veneziano*, 3546.

84. See below.

85. *Documenti*, 1: 332–33, no. 336; ibid., 334–35, no. 338.

86. Ibid., 352–53, no. 358; see also ibid., 352–56, 359–60, 362–63, 371–74, nos. 359, 360, 361, 365, 369, 378, 379, 380.

87. Since Giovanni Dandolo was apparently still in Venice in September, when he witnessed Enrico's proxy document, it is reasonable to assume that the two traveled together to Constantinople. *Documenti*, 1: 338–39, no. 342. Indeed, there would have been little choice, as few vessels would depart the Adriatic that late in the year. Nicol maintains that Enrico Dandolo did not leave Venice until March 1184, which is impossible. *Byzantium and Venice*, 108. Enrico was already holding court in Constantinople at that time. For his part, Giovanni Dandolo was conducting business in Constantinople in February 1184. If Enrico sailed with his brother, he would have had to arrive at the end of the previous sailing season: late September or early October 1183. This conclusion is complicated, however, by the presence of another Giovanni Dandolo, who witnessed the Chioggians' acceptance of restrictions on salt sales and fugitive return procedures in February 1184. The other Venetian witness to this document was Filippo Falier, one of Enrico Dandolo's proxies. ASV, *Codice diplomatico veneziano*, 3581; Cecchetti, *Il doge*, 253–57, no. 15.

88. Domenico Sanudo, a very important man in Venice, had served regularly as a judge in the ducal court since at least June 1175: *Atti*, 1: 83, no. 18; TTh., 1: 167–71, no. 63; July 1178: *De-*

liberazioni, 1: 250–51, no. 14; March 1179: *Documenti*, 1: 236–37, no. 242; *Nuovi documenti*, 29–30, no. 27; January 1181: *Atti*, 1: 91, no. 21; *Documenti*, 1: 320–21, no. 324, (=*Deliberazioni*, 1: 252, no. 16 [misdated, Jan. 1180]); March 1181: *Atti*, 1: 95, no. 22. After the legation, by August 1185, Sanudo was back in the ducal court in Venice: *Atti*, 1: 99, no. 24 (=*Deliberazioni*, 1: 252–53, no. 17). He later served as a legate to Tyre for the Procurator of San Marco (*Documenti*, 1: 398, no. 406) and again to Constantinople (ibid., 409–10, no. 418). Pietro Ziani was the son of the late Doge Sebastiano Ziani and would himself become doge in 1205. See the thoroughly researched treatment by Fees, *Reichtum und Macht*, 23–28.

89. Roberti, *Le magistrature giudiziare*, 1: 93; Borsari, *Venezia e Bisanzio*, 57–58.

90. Cf. Brand, *Byzantium Confronts the West*, 196–97; Lilie, *Handel und Politik*, 549–50; Cracco, "Dandolo, Enrico," 451; Nicol, *Byzantium and Venice*, 108–9.

91. According to Ferluga, a ducal legate's first duty was diplomatic; settling disputes among Venetians was a secondary role. "Veneziani fuori Venezia," 705. Yet the situation is more complex. Venetians at this time used the words *nuntius, ambascitor,* and *legatus* interchangeably. See e.g. Dandolo, 250, 271, where all three terms are used without distinction. On the broader practice, see Queller, *Office of the Ambassador,* 3–5. While some *legati* conducted diplomatic activities in the imperial court, others did not. Cf. Dandolo, 271; TTh., 1: 107–9, no. 49. In the case of the legation of Dandolo, Ziani, and Sanudo, the evidence points to their primary responsibility as judges for Venetian disputes.

92. *Documenti*, 1: 338–39, no. 342.

93. Ibid., 226–27, no. 231.

94. He was in Venice in November 1173; *Atti*, 1: 79, no. 17.

95. Ibid.

96. *Atti*, 1: 89, no. 20 (Nov. 1179). Cecchetti, *Il doge*, 253–57, no. 15; ASV, *Codice diplomatico veneziano*, 3581 (Feb. 1184). Sanudo, *Vitae ducum venetorum*, cols. 522–25; Luzzatto, *I prestiti*, 12–16, no. 3; *Deliberazioni*, 253–56, no. 18 (Nov. 1187). ASV, S. Zaccaria, B. 12 perg. (Mar. 24, 1189); *Atti*, 1: 105, no. 27 (June 1189).

97. This is the impression given by the documentary evidence, which ends abruptly after 1189.

98. Minotto, *Chronik der Familie Minotto*, 1: 73–75. The will can be found in ASV, Procuratori di S. Marco de Citra, B. 323.

99. A few examples: Citing "old chroniclers," Minotto claims that Contessa brought with her to the marriage the old Minotto palace in San Luca parish on the Grand Canal. He then provides a picture of a surviving fragment from a building *in San Bartolomeo parish.* In any event, there were no stone structures there before 1200, and the Minotto did not live in San Luca. The author states absolutely that the husband of Ota was Tomà Minotto, which fits Contessa and Enrico Dandolo nicely into the Minotto family tree, but for which there is no evidence; nor does the author offer any. Minotto, *Chronik der Familie Minotto*, 1: 53–54, 75–76. The Dandolo genealogy presented on ibid., 76, is confused.

100. Aside from this proxy document, the name *Contessa* appears in no published contemporary documents and in none of the thousands of unpublished documents that I have consulted.

101. In one very late genealogy, the wife of Enrico Dandolo is given as Felicita Bembo, daughter of Pietro Bembo, a procurator of San Marco in 1143. This is found in the highly unreliable eighteenth-century continuation of Marco Barbaro's *Famiglie nobili venete* by Antonio Maria Tasca, known as *Arbori de' patritii veneti* (ASV, Miscellanea codici, serie 1, 17–23), 1: 319, 3: 177. However, Bembo's name does not appear in Barbaro's original sixteenth-century work (*Famiglie nobili venete*, 134 v.) or in the later Cappellari-Vivaro, *Campidoglio Veneto*. The latter does list Pietro Bembo as procurator in 1143 (1: 373). Bembo is still sometimes referenced as Dandolo's wife; e.g. Lombardo, "Il doge di Venezia Enrico Dandolo," 25; Da Mosto, *I Dogi*, 72. Without more reliable information, we must conclude that Felicita Bembo is a late invention.

102. See Chap. 4, text at n. 10.

103. E.g. Necker, *Enrico Dandolo*, 79–84; Bartlett, *An Unholy War*, 57; Norwich, *History of Venice*, 124; Godfrey, *1204*, 64.

104. See Villehardouin, 1: 174, sec. 173; ibid., 68, sec. 67; ibid., 2: 60, sec. 351; ibid., 172, sec. 364; Gunther of Pairis, *Hystoria*, 144; Choniates, *Historia*, 596; *Chronicle of Novgorod*, 48; Thomas of Spalato, *Historia Spalatina*, 576.

105. See Chap. 9, text at n. 39.

106. Cracco, "Dandolo, Enrico," 451.

107. See Luzzatto, *I prestiti*, 12–16, no. 3; *Deliberazioni*, 253–56, no. 18. Several documents describe Dandolo's financial activities concerning saltworks in Chioggia: *SS. Trinità e S. Michele*, 2: 411–12, no. 251 (Sept. 1188); cf. ibid. nos. CCXCVIII and CCXCIX; *S. Giorgio di Fossone*, 21–22, no. 10 (Nov. 1197). He also owned investment land on the terra firma; see ASV, *Codice diplomatico veneziano*, 4222 (Feb. 5, 1193).

108. The two shops were adjacent. Only one of the agreements has survived. *Documenti*, 1: 340–41, no. 344; (=TTh., 1: 177–78, no. 69, misdated to Feb. 1183). On the landing stages, see Maltezou, "Il quartiere veneziano," 37–39; Jacoby, "Venetian Quarter," 155–58.

109. ASV, Mensa patriarcale, B. 9, nos. 6–10. No. 10 is published by Borsari, *Venezia e Bisanzio*, 154–56.

110. "*Violentia domini imperatoris.*"

111. Schneider, "Brände in Konstantinopel," 382–403.

112. ASV, Mensa patriarcale, B. 9, no. 7.

113. The cost of the waiver was worth it. On August 19 and 20, 1203, and again on April 12 and 13, 1204, fire swept through the region. Madden, "Fires of the Fourth Crusade," 72–93.

114. *Nuovi Documenti*, 39–40, no. 35.

115. Ibid., 36–38, no. 33.

116. ASV, Mensa patriarcale, B. 94, no. 426. The Lanfranchi transcription (ASV, *Codice diplomatico veneziano*, 3700) should be used with care as it has several errors and omissions.

117. Luzzatto, *I prestiti*, 12–16, no. 3; *Deliberazioni*, 253–56, no. 18.

118. *SS. Trinità e S. Michele*, 2: 411–12, no. 251; cf. nos. CCXCVIII and CCXCIX.

119. Andrea Dandolo frequently served as a judge and signed documents immediately or shortly after the doge. *Atti*, 1: 95, no. 22 (Mar. 1181); *Documenti*, 1: 338–39, no. 342 (Feb. 1184);

S. Giorgio Maggiore, 3: 277–78, no. 486 (Oct. 1187); Luzzatto, *I prestiti,* 12–16, no. 3 (Nov. 1187); *S. Giorgio Maggiore,* 3: 282–83, no. 490 (Apr. 1188).

120. No official acts of the patriarch survive after 1183, when he was unable to sign a document because of infirmity. Corner, *Ecclesiae venetae,* 14: 109. However, his privileges were confirmed by Pope Urban III on May 31, 1186; *IP,* 7/2: 69, no. 139. The first document that mentions Dandolo's successor was the confirmation of Clement III, made on May 20, 1190; *IP,* 7/2: 70, no. 142. Cf. Dandolo, 270.

121. Cracco, "L'età del comune," 6–7.

122. Rando, *Una chiesa della frontiera,* 173.

123. Ghetti, *I patti tra Venezia e Ferrara,* 161–66; Dandolo, 272.

124. Sanudo, *Vitae ducum venetorum,* col. 526.

CHAPTER 5. THE MEDIEVAL DOGESHIP & THE ELECTION OF 1192

1. *Venetiarum historia,* 131; Dandolo, 272; Sanudo, *Vitae ducum venetorum,* col. 526.

2. *Venetiarum historia,* 131–32; Sanudo, *Vitae ducum venetorum,* cols. 526–27. The thirteen families were the Barocio, Bragadin, Dandolo, Dolfin, Falier, Foscarini, Giustinian, Michiel, Morosini, Silvo, Stornato, Ziani, and Zusto. Only one man, Domenico Silvo, served on both electoral committees.

3. Castagnetti, "Il primo comune," 110.

4. The others were the Falier, Michiel, and Morosini.

5. There were two Marino Dandolo's alive at this time. One was the son of Giovanni Dandolo of San Polo, a kinsman of Enrico Dandolo but not his nephew. He is mentioned in a document of April 1195: *SS. Trinità e S. Michele,* 2: 468–70, no. 293. In July 1207, when the other Marino Dandolo was outside of Venice, this one loaned some money to Ranieri Dandolo, the son of Enrico. ASP, Archivi privati diversi, Pergamene diverse, B. 103. There is no evidence that this Marino ever became active in politics. The other and more famous Marino Dandolo of San Luca parish became lord of Andros in 1206. In 1229 he was the choice of twenty ducal electors, the other twenty voting for Giacomo Tiepolo. Lots were cast, and Tiepolo won the throne. When the new doge went to the bedside of Pietro Ziani, however, the old doge refused to accept him, thus beginning the destructive rift between the Dandolo and Tiepolo clans. Marino Dandolo was assassinated in 1233. See, Dandolo, 282, 284, 289, 291–92. Marino's relationship to Doge Enrico Dandolo is not described by any contemporary source. According to Barbaro, Marino was the son of Andrea Dandolo and therefore the nephew of the doge. *Famiglie nobili venete,* 134 v. Most scholars have accepted this identification. E.g. Kretschmayr, *Geschichte von Venedig,* 2: 17, 35; Fotheringham, *Marco Sanudo,* 59; Lane, *Venice,* 94. In the Tasca continuation of Barbaro (*Arbori de' patritii veneti,* 177) Marino is listed as the son of Enrico himself, which must be an error. On balance it seems likely that Marino Dandolo was the son of Andrea and that it is he who served in the electoral committee of 1192.

6. Dandolo, 272; *Venetiarum historia,* 131; Sanudo, *Vitae ducum venetorum,* col. 526.

7. Cracco, "Dandolo, Enrico," 452–53; cf. idem, *Società e stato,* 54.

8. *Venetiarum historia*, 131–32; Sanudo, *Vitae ducum venetorum*, cols. 526–27.

9. For Pietro Ziani's copious overseas investments, see *Documenti*, 1: 257–58, no. 262 (Oct. 1174); 1: 275–76, no. 280 (Sept. 1176); 1: 284–86, nos. 289–90 (Mar. 1178); 1: 286–88, no. 292 (May 1178); 1: 293–94, no. 298 (Mar. 1179); 1: 295–97, nos. 300–301 (Mar. 1179); 1: 381–82, no. 388 (Aug. 1190); 1: 406–7, no. 415 (Feb. 1193). For a good outline of Pietro Ziani's career, see Fees, *Reichtum und Macht*, 23–28, 60–75. For an assessment of the Ziani family's extensive involvement in overseas commerce and investment properties, see Fees, "Die Geschäfte der venezianischen Dogenfamilie Ziani," 53–69.

10. *Nuovi Documenti*, 36–38, no. 33; 39–40, no. 35.

11. *Documenti*, 251–53, nos. 256–57.

12. See Chap. 3, text at n. 113.

13. E.g. Villehardouin, 2: 172, sec. 364; Gunther of Pairis, *Hystoria*, 144; Hugh of St. Pol, *Epistola*, Andrea, trans., 199.

14. Sanudo, *Vitae ducum venetorum*, col. 527.

15. E.g. *Venetiarum historia*, 131; Dandolo, 272; Villehardouin, 2: 172, sec. 364; Choniates, *Historia*, 538.

16. E.g. Mundo Lo, *Cruzados en Bizancio*, 78; Rousset, *Histoire des croisades*, 213; McNeal and Wolff, "The Fourth Crusade," 162; Nicol, *Byzantium and Venice*, 119; Norwich, *History of Venice*, 124; Godfrey, *1204*, 64.

17. This view is shared by Necker, *Enrico Dandolo*, 85–87.

18. Roberti, *La magistrature giudiziarie*, 1: 58, 65; Cracco, *Società e stato*, 10; Zordan, *Le persone nella storia del diritto veneziano*, 153–56; Cassandro, "Concetto caratteri," 36–37; Cessi, *Le origini del ducato*, 328.

19. Cessi, *Le origini del ducato*, 328–29; Fasoli, "Commune veneciarum," 83.

20. Zordan, *Le persone nella storia del diritto veneziano*, 157–59.

21. Maranini, *Costituzione*, 94; Zordan, *Le persone nella storia del diritto veneziano*, 156–57; Cessi, *Le origini del ducato*, 326–28. Cf. Merores, "Der venezianische Adel," 209–13; Besta, "Il diritto," 173–74.

22. Jones, *The Italian City-State*, 103–20.

23. Zordan, *Le persone nella storia del diritto veneziano*, 201–3.

24. E.g. Cracco, *Società e stato*, 38–48; Luzzatto, "Capitale e lavoro nel commercio veneziano," 99–102.

25. See Merores, "Der venezianische Adel," 213–15; Cessi, *Le origini del ducato*, 329.

26. Zordan, *Le persone nella storia del diritto veneziano*, 197–98; Cessi, *Storia della Repubblica di Venezia*, 1: 149; Marinini, *Costituzione*, 101; Castagnetti, "Il primo comune," 92–95.

27. Castagnetti, "Il primo comune," 98–102; Jones, *The Italian City-State*, 140–41.

28. The nature of the Venetian commune is a complex matter, much debated. For useful studies, see Maranini, *Costituzione*, 97–103; Cessi, PER, 372–80; idem, *Storia della Repubblica di Venezia*, 1: 148–52; Fasoli, "'Comune veneciarum,'" 93–95; Cracco, *Società e stato*, 9–11; Zordan, *Le persone nella storia del diritto veneziano*, 197–98.

29. On these various offices, see Castagnetti, "Il primo comune," 106–20.

30. *Historia ducum veneticorum,* 79. See Chap. 3, text at n. 78.

31. Besta, *Il diritto,* 171.

32. *Atti,* 1: 99–100, no. 24; *Deliberazione,* 1: 252–53, no. 17.

33. Romanin, *Storia documentata,* 2: 302–3, no. 7.

34. Castagnetti, "Il primo comune," 97.

35. Ibid., 96; Cessi, PER, 443–44. A concise, but excellent discussion of the historiography concerning earlier oaths of office can be found in Graziato's preface to *Promissioni,* vii–xv.

36. The best and most recent edition of Dandolo's promissione, and the one from which this translation is made, is in *Promissioni,* 2–4. The numbers for each clause are not in the original but are provided merely as a convenience for discussion.

37. E.g. "Under a successful buccaneer like Henry Dandolo, the office of doge threatened to become a personal monarchy." McNeill, *Venice,* 248–49, n. 45: "Enrico Dandolo behaved like a Doge of an earlier age." Nicol, *Byzantium and Venice,* 148.

38. Cracco, "Dandolo, Enrico," passim.

39. Villehardouin, 2: 172, sec. 364; cf. ibid., 1: 174–76, sec. 173.

40. Choniates, *Historia,* 538; Magoulias, trans., 295.

41. Cracco, "Dandolo, Enrico," 454.

42. See Dandolo's negotiations with Byzantium, Chap. 6, text at n. 47.

43. Maranini, *Costituzione,* 140–41.

44. The oath of Dandolo's immediate successor, Pietro Ziani (1205–29), is not related to the oath of Dandolo or Tiepolo. It is not clear why. One possibility is that it is not the oath of Pietro Ziani but an earlier oath that was misidentified by the copyist. See Pertusi, "*Quedam regalia insignia,*" 117–18, n. 336.

45. *Promissioni,* 10–20.

46. Dandolo's clause 2 is divided into Tiepolo's clauses 2 and 3 in published versions, yet that is not the case in the manuscript.

47. It should be noted that this single mention of the Minor Council is an extrapolation. It is clear from the manuscript that all councilors and a majority of the Great Council must be in agreement, but the place where Minor Council would be mentioned is effaced and illegible. Castagnetti makes the reasonable case that the words *Great Council* imply a Minor Council, so it is safe to assume that the extrapolation is correct. "Il primo comune," 126, n. 144.

48. Cessi, PER, 443.

49. See *SS. Trinità e S. Michele,* 2: 411–12, no. 251 (Sept. 1188); cf. ibid., nn. CCXCVIII and CCXCIX; ASV, *Codice diplomatico veneziano,* 4222 (Feb. 5, 1193); *S. Giorgio di Fossone,* 21–22, no. 10 (Nov. 1197).

50. On August 16, 1192, only two months after Enrico's election, Andrea Dandolo signed immediately after the doge, two judges, the judge of the commune, and two counselors. *Atti,* 1: 113, no. 30.

51. *S. Lorenzo,* 73–74, no. 42.

52. See n. 5, above.

53. Schulz, "Houses of the Dandolo," 396. The brief inventory that records this purchase

does not identify Falier beyond his name. Schulz (ibid., n. 24) hypothesized that this was the patriarch of the same name since no other Benedetto appears in Barbaro's genealogy of the Falier family. To this can be added the fact that no other Benedetto Falier appears in any published contemporary documents or in the several thousands of documents in my database. It would be difficult for a man wealthy enough to own so large a tract of land to be absent in any surviving material. The fact that the patriarchate owned vacant land in this area during the reign of Enrico Dandolo, coupled with the name of the seller, makes an extremely strong case for Schulz's identification.

54. *Documenti*, 1: 390–91, no. 398.

55. By the time of his death in 1208 Ranieri owned several properties in the Rialto markets across the Grand Canal and investment properties in Chioggia, in addition to the properties he had inherited from his father. ASP, Archivi privati diversi, Pergemene diversi, B. 103 (10/1237).

56. Sanudo, *Vitae ducum venetorum*, col. 527. Also in Barbaro, *Famiglie nobili venete*, 134v; Cappellari-Vivaro, *Famiglie venete*, 36.

57. Both candidates, however, were Venetians. One was Gervasius, the archbishop of Eraclea, the other Ludovicus, the *plebanus* of the church of San Polo in Venice. Wolff, "Politics in the Latin Patriarchate," 246–55.

58. Sanudo, *Vitae ducum venetorum*, col. 527. Barbaro does not include this daughter in his genealogy, but she does appear in the later Tasca continuation; *Arbori de' patritii veneti*, 177.

59. Usseglio, *I marchesi di Monferrato*, 1: 156.

60. Villehardouin, 2: 68, sec. 262.

61. The Tasca continuation of Barbaro (*Arbori de' patritii veneti*, 177) lists a Marino Dandolo, about which nothing else is recorded. The same genealogy records a Vitale Dandolo, who served as one of the twelve electors of the emperor in Constantinople in 1204.

62. Lane, *Venice*, 93.

CHAPTER 6. ENRICO DANDOLO'S DOGESHIP:
THE FIRST DECADE, 1192–1201

1. Roberti, *Le magistrature giudiziare*, 27–28; Hain, *Der Doge*, 52.

2. Roberti, *Le magistrature giudiziare*, 15–16.

3. Ibid., 25–26.

4. For a register of unpublished court documents from Dandolo's reign, see Madden, "Enrico Dandolo," 224–37.

5. Besta, *Il diritto*, 121; Besta and Predelli, "Gli statuti civili," 39–41.

6. *Atti*, 1: 112–13, no. 30.

7. Cracco, *Società e stato*, 54.

8. Besta, "Il diritto," 174–80; Zordan, *Le persone nella storia del diritto*, 121–27.

9. As Cracco implies, *Società e stato*, 54.

10. Besta, "Il diritto," 176–77.

11. Ibid., 179–80.

12. *Atti*, 1: 92–96, no. 22.

13. Dandolo, 273; cf. *Venetiarum historia*, 132.

14. A parish priest was required to have the approval of his parishioners and the bishop. A bishop was required to have the approval of his canons, the patriarch, and the doge. A patriarch (called simply metropolitan here) was required to have the approval of his suffragans and the doge. Besta and Predelli, "Gli statuti civili," 207–8.

15. Ibid., 205–42.

16. Dandolo, 273; cf. *Venetiarum historia*, 132.

17. Sanudo, *Vitae ducum venetorum*, col. 527; Bertaldo, *Splendor venetorum consuetudinum*, 146. The latter gives the date of the reform as 1195.

18. Besta and Predelli, "Gli statuti civili," 8–13.

19. There is some disagreement among scholars on the attribution of the codes between Enrico and Ranieri. See ibid., 19–24; Pitzorno, *Gli statuti civili*, 10–32; Cessi, "Il 'parvum statutum'," 1–7. For an overview of the debate, see Pansolli, *La Gerarchia delle fonti di diritto*, 36–38; Madden, "Enrico Dandolo," 190–97.

20. For an excellent analysis with full bibliographical references, see Stahl, "Coinage of Venice," 127–29.

21. Ibid., 129–32.

22. Stahl hypothesizes that the pennies' intrinsic value vis-à-vis the grosso led to culling of the latter. The penny was therefore discontinued to defend the grosso. Ibid., 132–33. Cf. Papadopoli, *Le monete di Venezia*, 1: 102.

23. Papadopoli, *Le monete di Venezia*, 1: 62–66; Robbert, "Venetian Money Market," 29.

24. Stahl, "Coinage of Venice," 136.

25. Stahl, "The Grosso," 264–65.

26. Da Canal, *Estoires*, 46. Da Canal lists this under the year 1202, but Queller has dated the reference to the previous year: "A Note on the Reorganization of the Venetian Coinage," 167–72.

27. Dandolo, 273. Sanudo, *Vitae ducum venetorum*, col. 527, dates the *grosso* to 1192.

28. Da Canale was the preferred source for many years. See e.g. Kretschmayr, *Geschichte von Venedig*, 1: 499; Cessi, *Problemi monetari*, xviii, n. 2; Luzzatto, "L'oro e l'argento," 262. This changed with the publication of a study by Louise Buenger Robbert, who argued for the earlier date. "Reorganization of the Venetian Coinage," 48–60. This appears to be confirmed by Stahl, "Coinage of Venice," 124–25, 132–33; idem, "The Grosso," 261–62.

29. My thanks to Alan Stahl for informing me of the continued importance of the sterling for this period. See his "Coinage and Money."

30. Stahl, "The Grosso," 265–66.

31. Lane and Mueller, *Money and Banking*, 114–15, 501.

32. ASV, *Pacta*, I., 189v–190v; an edition of the treaty can be found in Cipolla, "Note di storia veronese," 307. See also Dandolo, 272; *Venetiarum historia*, 132.

33. ASV, Miscellanea Ducali ed Atti Diplomatici, B. 6. See also Dandolo, 273.

34. According to Da Canal, who is often unreliable, the Veronese descended on Padua with a large company of knights and laid waste to much of the surrounding territory. The Paduans pleaded with the Venetians to mediate the dispute. *Estoires*, 44. Dandolo, 273, states only that "vehement disputes" between the two were settled by Enrico Dandolo. It seems likely that Andrea Dandolo took the story from Da Canal, but he does not appear to have had much confidence in its details.

35. Praga, "Zaratini e Veneziani," 53–54.

36. Dandolo, 273; cf. *Venetiarum historia*, 132.

37. Dandolo, 273; Praga, "Zaratini e Veneziani," 54; idem, *Storia di Dalmazia*, 86.

38. Brand, *Byzantium Confronts the West*, 212–13.

39. Dandolo, 268; *Venetiarum historia*, 130.

40. *Annales venetici breves*, 72; Dandolo, 273; *Venetiarum historia*, 132–33. The island of Veglia (modern Krk) may have joined Pola in rebellion. Morosini and Permarino stopped there on their trip and ordered the inhabitants to pay a certain sum, but the money was never forthcoming. In July 1196, a ducal legate, Bonofilio Dondi, arrived on the island to investigate the affair. The Count of Veglia, Bartolomeo, complained bitterly about the citizens' recalcitrance. Dondi thrice ordered the inhabitants to appear before him and pay the sum, but they refused. In the end, the legate ordered the confiscation of a long list of citizens' property. ASV, Miscellanea ducali ed atti diplomatici, B. 6. Count Bartolomeo died soon thereafter and was succeeded by his sons, Guido and Enrico. ASV, *Codice diplomatico veneziano*, 4769.

41. *Annales venetici breves*, 72; Dandolo, 273; *Venetiarum Historia*, 133.

42. The lengthy treaty, dated September 1, 1196, is in the Archivio di Stato di Pisa. A transcription is available in Venice in ASV, *Codice diplomatico veneziano*, 4497.

43. ASV, Miscellanea atti diplomatici e privati, B. 2, no. 57. The treaty is dated September 1200. See also Dandolo, 276.

44. Dandolo, 274; *Venetiarum historia*, 133. Lodovico Streit put the first embassy in the autumn of 1196 and the return legation of John Cataphloros in the summer of 1197. "Venezia e la quarta crociata," 245, n. 3. On Marino Mastropiero's relationship to Orio Mastropiero, see ASV, *Codice diplomatico veneziano*, 4489. See also, *Documenti*, 1: 415–16, no. 424; ASV, *Codice diplomatico veneziano*, 4458, 4577.

45. Zeno was among the first Venetians to return to Constantinople in 1184. He witnessed one of the rental documents negotiated by Giovanni Dandolo in March of that year: ASV, Mensa patriarcale, B. 9, no. 6. In April 1186 he was in Acre, lending money for a voyage along with Giacomo Dandolo, son of Giovanni: *Documenti*, 1: 369–70, no. 376. In November 1188, he was again in Constantinople: ibid., 364–65, no. 371. During the reign of Enrico Dandolo, Zeno moved into the ranks of the judiciary. See ASV, *Codice diplomatico veneziano*, 4218; *Documenti*, 1: 285–86, no. 290. Cf. also ASV, *Codice diplomatico veneziano*, 3209; *Deliberazioni*, 1: 250–51, no. 14.

46. Cf. Brand, *Byzantium Confronts the West*, 200; Nicol, *Byzantium and Venice*, 120–21.

47. Dandolo, 274–75; *Venetiarum historia*, 133.

48. The text of the commission is published in *Atti*, 1: 117–18, no. 32, and Kretschmayr,

Geschichte von Venedig, 1: 473. With some modifications, this translation is from Brand, *Byzantium Confronts the West*, 201–2.

49. Henry VI's confirmation of Venice's privileges is dated June 6, 1197; ASV, *Codice diplomatico veneziano*, 4549; Dandolo, 274; *Venetiarum historia*, 132, 133.

50. TTh., 1: 246–80, no. 85; Dandolo, 275; *Venetiarum historia*, 133–34; Heyd, *Histoire du commerce*, 1: 227–28; Lilie, *Handel und Politik*, 41–49; Laiou, "The Foreigner and the Stranger," 86.

51. Brand, *Byzantium Confronts the West*, 203–4; Robbert, "Venice and the Crusades," 410; Lilie, *Handel und Politik*, 41, 581; *Byzantium and Venice*, 121–23.

52. ASV, *Pacta*, I, 144r–v.; Romanin, *Storia documentata*, 2: 106; Da Mosto, *I Dogi*, 73. On the same day, the new judges were sworn in. Their oath of office survives. In its judicial scope, it is remarkably similar to the ducal promissione. ASV, *Pacta*, I, 143v.–144r.

53. ASV, Miscellanea atti diplomatici e privati, B. 2, no. 56.

54. ASV, Miscellanea ducali ed atti diplomatici, B. 6.

55. ASV, Miscellanea atti diplomatici e privati, B. 2, no. 57.

56. Romanin, *Storia documentata*, 2: 106.

CHAPTER 7. THE CRUCIBLE OF THE CRUSADE

1. Choniates, *Historia*, 538.

2. Although this alleged Venetian motto is commonly repeated, I know of no source for it, nor does any scholar I have queried on the subject over the years. The closest I have found are the words of Pope Pius II, who wrote in his Commentaries that Venetians "never think of God and, except for the state, which they regard as a deity, they hold nothing sacred, nothing holy." Pius II, of course, was not a Venetian, nor did he attribute his view to any Venetian boast. Professor Serban Marin, who has read and copied a great many Venetian manuscripts in the Marciana Library, informs me that he has never run across the motto in the manuscript sources and suggests that it originated with one of Venice's enemies. See also Queller, review of Donald M. Nicol, *Byzantium and Venice* in *Speculum* 66 (1991): 211.

3. Madden, "Outside and Inside the Fourth Crusade," 729–33.

4. See e.g. Pears, *The Fall of Constantinople*, 239–40; Ostrogorsky, *History of the Byzantine State*, 413; Vasiliev, *History of the Byzantine Empire*, 452–53; Godfrey, *1204*, 64; Fine, *Late Medieval Balkans*, 61; Nicol, *Byzantium and Venice*, 412; Brand, *Byzantium Confronts the West*, 206; Browning, *Byzantine Empire*, 197; Carile, *Per una storia dell'Impero Latino*, 54; Runciman, *History of the Crusades*, 3: 113–15. This view of Dandolo is graphically portrayed in the BBC production *The Crusades* by Terry Jones.

5. See Chap. 2, above.

6. See Chap. 1, above.

7. Villehardouin, 2: 172, sec. 364; cf. ibid., 1: 174–76, sec. 173; Robert of Clari, *Conquête*, 91, sec. 93; cf. ibid., 10, sec. 11.

8. Gunther of Pairis, *Hystoria*, 144; Andrea, trans., 97.

9. Hugh of St. Pol, *Epistola*, 814; Andrea, trans., 199.

10. Reg. 1: 336; see also ibid., 355.

11. On the question of Innocent's attitude toward Venetian participation in the crusade, see Queller, "Innocent III and the Crusader-Venetian Treaty," 31–4; *FC*, 18–20.

12. Reg. 1: 336, 343; *Gesta Innocentii*, xci.

13. This is confirmed by the words of Enrico Dandolo in the Treaty of Venice: "Ad exortationem etiam summi pontificis, qui ad hoc sepius nos paterna sollicitatione commonuit." TTh., 1: 365, no. 92.

14. According to the *Gesta Innocentii*, xc, the doge and many Venetians took the cross during Soffredo's mission. Andrea is certainly correct that this is part of a general telescoping of events in this source, since the doge was not crossed until September 1202. *Contemporary Sources*, 22.

15. Innocent, Reg. 1: 536 (539).

16. See Chap. 6, text at n. 47.

17. Soffredo was dispatched to Venice in August 1198, probably arriving there in September or October. Reg. 1: 336. Dandolo sent his envoys to Rome shortly thereafter. In his letter of December 3, 1198, Innocent reports meeting with the two men *"nuper."* Ibid. 536 (539).

18. Reg 1: 536 (539). The link between the granting of the Venetian request and the possibility of Venetian participation in the crusade was attested to by Innocent himself when he wrote, "We hope that because of this favor you will be more zealously motivated to help the province of Jerusalem." Ibid.; Andrea, trans., 24.

19. Andrea, *Contemporary Sources*, 22.

20. Reg. 1: 536 (539). This had the practical effect of rolling back Gregory VIII's prohibition, but it left intact the embargo enumerated in Canon 24 of the Third Lateran Council of 1179.

21. Dandolo, 147.

22. Romanin, *Storia documentata*, 1: 267–69, no. 9.

23. Queller and Madden, "Some Further Arguments," 438.

24. See e.g. *I diplomi arabi del R. Archivio Fiorentino*, 1: 29–30, no. 7 (ca. 1200); 1: 36–37, no. 10 (Feb. 11, 1201); 1: 48–51, nos. 14–15 (ca. 1200); 1: 55–64, nos. 17–20 (ca. 1200). See also Allmendinger, *Die Beziehungen zwischen der Kommune Pisa und Ägypten*, 61–63; Heyd, *Histoire du commerce*, 1 : 387–99; Rösch, "Der Handel Ägyptens mit dem Abendland um 1200," 243–46; Jacoby, "Supply of War Materials," 102–11. Venetians occasionally did business in Egypt after 1187, although they were much more likely to sail to Byzantium or the Crusader States. See *Documenti*, 1: 368, no. 375 (June 1190); 1: 431–32, no. 439 (June 1198).

25. Reg. 1: 336; 1: 345; 1: 346. Innocent's letter confirming the truce: Reg 2: 23–25. Maleczek, *Pietro Capuano*, 77–79.

26. *FC*, 2–5.

27. *FC*, 5–6.

28. *FC*, 6–7.

29. Villehardouin, sec. 15, 1: 18.

30. Ibid., sec. 17, 1: 20.

31. E.g. Godfrey, *1204*, 49; Bartlett, *An Ungodly War*, 58.

32. In an e-mail correspondence, Alfred Andrea noted that it would have been customary for the envoys to wear crosses, thus making plain their mission.

33. The size of the Small Council is attested to by Villehardouin, although indirectly. He states that the Great Council consisted of forty men. Villehardouin, sec. 25, 1: 26. Later he describes a meeting of both the Small and Great Councils, which consisted of forty-six men. Ibid., sec. 31, 1: 32. The size of the council suggests that it was already being elected in the *sestieri*, the six regions of the city.

34. Villehardouin, sec. 18, 1: 20–22.

35. Ibid., sec. 19, 1: 22.

36. *FC*, 11.

37. Villehardouin, sec. 21, 1: 22; *FC*, 11–12, 216 n. 11; Maleczek, *Pietro Capuano*, 107.

38. Villehardouin, secs. 20–30, 1: 22–30; *FC*, 217, n. 23.

39. Villehardouin, sec. 24, 1: 24–26.

40. *FC*, 17–18.

41. E.g. Runciman, *History of the Crusades*, 3: 114; Lane, *Venice*, 37; Godfrey, *1204*, 49–50; Nicol, *Byzantium and Venice*, 127; Maleczek, *Pietro Capuano*, 107–8.

42. See e.g. Godfrey, *1204*, 49, who assures his reader that it was not at all difficult for Venice to produce the crusade fleet, since the "Arsenal, the state-controlled-shipyard . . . was an efficient institution, well-stocked with timber and maritime spare parts, and accustomed to producing vessels to order for specific purposes." It was indeed—in the fifteenth century. Nothing like that existed in 1201. See Schulz, "Urbanism in Medieval Venice," 428.

43. See Crescenzi, *Esse de maiori consilio*, 295–305. In the thirteenth century the Great Council would grow in size, spawning the Forty (*Quarantia*), which presided over judicial matters. Lane, *Venice*, 96.

44. Villehardouin, sec. 25, 1: 26.

45. See Chap. 4, text at n. 49.

46. Cazel, "Financing the Crusades," 124.

47. Villehardouin, secs. 26–29, 1: 26–30.

48. TTh., 1: 362–73, nos. 92–93.

49. Villehardouin, sec. 30, 1: 30.

50. See Chap. 3, text at n. 118.

51. The scenario rests ultimately on a rumor that made the rounds in the crusader states after the conquest of Constantinople and then found its way into the continuation of Ernoul. Ernoul and Bernard le Trésorier, *Chronique*, 343–45. It was repeated in several later works, including the continuation of William of Tyre (RHC, Occ. 2: 251–52), the *Chronicle of Flanders* (TTh., 1: 296), the *Crusade of Constantinople* (TTh., 1: 324), and the *Chronicon Gallicum* (TTh., 1: 332).

52. Carl Hopf attempted to support the contention by claiming to have found a treaty of friendship between Venice and Egypt dated May 13, 1202; *Geschichte Griechenlands*, 1: 122. Because of his reputation, many scholars accepted Hopf's word, although it was not supported by a citation to a document. The identification was demolished by Hanotaux, "Les Vénitiens ont-ils trahi la chrétienté en 1202?" 74–102. For a discussion of the modern reluctance to abandon the false treaty, see *FC*, 235, n. 84.

53. Between 1184 and 1205 Egyptian destinations account for only 11 percent of surviving Venetian commercial voyage contracts to the East. Byzantine destinations accounted for 65 percent, with 46 percent to Constantinople alone. Queller and Madden, "Some Further Arguments," 438.

54. Villehardouin, sec. 30, 1: 30; sec. 32, 1: 32 and n. 5.

55. Ibid., sec. 31, 1: 32; *FC*, 19–20.

56. The letter is missing from the papal register. It is published by Tessier, *La quatrième croisade*, 260–61.

57. Ibid., 110.

58. See Chap. 6, text at n. 35.

59. Hóman, *Geschichte des ungarischen Mittelalters*, 1: 437; Steindorff, *Die dalmatinischen Städt*, 74–91; 121–26; Brunelli, *Storia della città di Zara*, 359–63; Cessi, *La Repubblica di Venezia e il problema adriatico*, 50–51; Sweeney, "Hungary in the Crusades," 475–76; Queller and Madden, "Some Further Arguments," 448–50.

60. Reg. 5: 103.

61. The letter does not survive, but its contents are related in Innocent's letter of February 25, 1204. Reg. 7: 18.

62. Ibid.

63. Queller and Madden, "Some Further Arguments," 446–48.

64. Robert of Clari, *Conquête*, sec. 7, 8, and sec. 11, 9–10. Such a cancellation of trade was not without precedent in Venice. Most recently, in 1188, Doge Orio Mastropiero ordered all Venetian vessels to return to the lagoon by Easter to take part in the Third Crusade. TTh., 1: 204–6; Dandolo, 270. In 1198 there was a similar, although less comprehensive, order in effect, probably in anticipation of further trouble from the Pisans, with whom Venice had recently been at war. *Nuovi Documenti*, no. 45, 51–52.

65. *Documenti*, 1: 451–52, no. 461; *Nuovi documenti*, 59–61, nos. 53–54. The last two documents record payments to investors after the *Paradise*'s return. The first is dated July 1202. The second, dated November 1202, was paid rather late, perhaps because the investor, the future doge Pietro Ziani, was out of Venice or perhaps because of a disruption of business during the crusaders' stay in the lagoon. There are no other surviving documents recording Venetian overseas trade until 1205.

66. In a forthcoming article, John H. Pryor notes that by the mid-thirteenth century large crusader transports could carry six hundred passengers. With a few exceptions, none of the Venetian transports would have been that large. If they had been, they would have needed about forty of them. "Venetian Fleet." My thanks to Professor Pryor for making a typescript manuscript available to me.

67. Pryor, "Venetian Fleet."

68. Schulz, "Urbanism in Medieval Venice," 428; Goy, *Venice*, 74.

69. See Madden, "Food and the Fourth Crusade."

70. Pryor, "Venetian Fleet." Carile calculated the Venetian crusaders to have totaled 14,600

men. *Per una storia dell'impero latino,* 90. In an earlier study, he calculated the figure to be 17,264. "Alle origini dell'Impero d'Oriente," 287–88.

71. Clari, *Conquête,* sec. 11, 9–10. This is the kind of logistical detail that Villehardouin often ignored but that stuck in Clari's mind. It appears to be a very Venetian custom, a precursor not only of the various lotteries that would become part of the ducal election process, but also of the fourteenth-century *balla d'oro* lottery for young noblemen. See, Chojnacki, "Kinship Ties and Young Patricians," 243–45.

72. On military obligations to Venice, see Settia, "L'apparato militare," 461–63.

73. E.g. *Gesta Innocentii,* cxxxviii.

74. According to Clari, the doge sent legates back with the French, who were present at an assembly of nobles at Corbie. *Conquête,* sec. 8, 8. Although Villehardouin does not mention this assembly, it would accord with the treaty's requirement that the three principals ratify it and that the other crusaders swear their own adherence to its terms. *FC,* 24.

75. *FC,* 23–31.

76. TTh., 1: 362–73, nos. 92–93.

77. Payment for the fleet was collected from individual crusaders well after their arrival in Venice. Villehardouin, sec. 57, 1: 58–60. Clari tells the story of Dandolo demanding that the envoys pay 25,000 marks immediately after signing the treaty so that he could begin construction of the fleet. The envoys agreed, so he sent ambassadors to accompany them back to France. At an assembly at Corbie the barons ratified the agreement and then paid the 25,000 marks from a bequest left by Thibaut of Champagne, funds raised by Fulk of Neuilly, and money donated by Baldwin of Flanders. *Conquête,* sec. 6, 7; sec. 8, 8. A lowly knight of Picardy, Clari is a very poor source for events before his own arrival in Venice in 1202; when it is possible to check his figures against official treaties he is almost always wrong. For example, he states that the Treaty of Venice required payment of 87,000 marks. Ibid., sec. 6, 7. Although it is possible that Venetian envoys traveled to France and attended the meeting at Corbie, they would not have been justified in requesting 25,000 marks until November 1, 1201. Also, the money raised by Fulk of Neuilly was not given to the crusaders, but went, naturally enough, to Rome. Innocent sent it directly to the Holy Land, where it was used to repair fortifications. Ernoul-Bernard, *Chronique,* 337–38. The bequest of Thibaut of Champagne was given to Boniface of Montferrat when he assumed command of the crusade. Villehardouin, sec. 43, 1: 42–44.

78. *Devastatio Constantinopolitana,* 132; *FC,* 43.

79. *FC,* 43–47.

80. *Devastatio Constantinopolitana,* 132.

81. Reg. 5: 25.

82. *Devastatio Constantinopolitana,* 132; Maleczek, *Pietro Capuano,* 128–29.

83. Although the Venetians would later refuse to accept Peter Capuano as a papal legate traveling with the crusade, they were content to recognize his authority in Venice. Peter remained in Venice from July 22 until sometime in September. He would not have done so if the Venetians had failed to accept his legatine authority from the start.

84. Villehardouin, sec. 55, 1: 56; sec. 57, 1: 58–60; *FC*, 47–48.

85. *Devastatio Constantinopolitana*, 132; Ernoul-Bernard, *Chronique*, 349; Robert of Auxerre, *Chronicon*, 261; Gunther of Pairis, *Hystoria*, 122.

86. In all Latin accounts of the crusade, Enrico Dandolo is the only Venetian who is named and the only one to have his words recorded.

CHAPTER 8. VENICE & THE DIVERSION

1. Villehardouin, sec. 57, 1: 58–60; Robert of Clari, *Conquête*, sec. 11, 9–10.

2. Robert of Clari, *Conquête*, sec. 11, 10. McNeal points out that a strict translation of *laissa* would give the opposite sense, that is, that the doge did cut off supplies. Based on the confusion of *laissa* and *lassa* elsewhere in the text and Robert's favorable words about the doge at precisely this point, McNeal believed that *lassa* was intended. In McNeal, trans., *Conquest of Constantinople*, 40, n. 22. This has become the scholarly consensus. See e.g. Setton, *Papacy and the Levant*, 1: 8; Nada Patrone, trans., *La conquista di Costantinopoli*, 136.

3. TTh., 1: 365, no. 92.

4. Villehardouin, sec. 59, 1: 60–62.

5. Ibid., sec. 60, 1: 62.

6. Ibid., sec. 61, 1: 64.

7. Robert of Clari, *Conquête*, sec. 12, 10–11.

8. Villehardouin, sec. 62, 1: 64. The marshal of Champagne does not distinguish here between various councils as he did during the negotiation of the Treaty of Venice. However, he does lay out Dandolo's arguments to his people and has him address them as "lords." Villehardouin was likely ignorant of the specifics of the process, but Dandolo would normally have discussed the situation with his Small Council before taking a proposal to the Great Council.

9. See clause 6 of the ducal promissione, Chap. 5, above.

10. The mark of Cologne weighed 238.5 grams. Robbert, "Venetian Money Market," 16.

11. Villehardouin, sec. 62, 1: 64. The Great Council is not specifically identified, but aside from the arengo, it was the only body that could approve the suspension of the debt.

12. Villehardouin, secs. 62–63, 1: 64–66.

13. Reg. 5: 103.

14. Brunelli, *Storia della città di Zara*, 368; Roberto Cessi, "Venezia e la quarta crociata," 26.

15. Lane, *Venice*, 37.

16. In essence, this was the reasoning Dandolo recounted in a letter to Innocent after the conquest of Constantinople. Reg. 7: 202.

17. Emeric was of two minds when it came to his vow. On the one hand, he asked the pope to relieve him of it. See Reg. 5: 103; 6: 7. On the other, he held out the prospect of a speedy departure for the Holy Land if the pope would consent to the coronation of his young son, thus keeping the throne from his rebellious brother. The request was finally granted, but Emeric remained in Hungary. Reg. 6: 4; 7: 57. When he died in 1204, Emeric's vow remained unfulfilled.

18. Villehardouin, sec. 60, 1: 62; sec. 62, 1: 64.

19. Robert of Clari, *Conquête*, secs. 12–14, 11–12.

20. Villehardouin, sec. 63, 1: 66.

21. On the exact date, see *FC*, 238, n. 22.

22. Villehardouin, sec. 65, 1: 66–68.

23. See Chap. 1, text at n. 105.

24. Villehardouin, sec. 66, 1: 68.

25. Ibid., sec. 68, 1: 68–70.

26. Nicol, *Byzantium and Venice*, 132. See also, Runciman, *History of the Crusades*, 3: 115; Norwich, *History of Venice*, 129.

27. *S. Giorgio Maggiore*, 2: 319, no. 145; *Atti*, 1: 52–53, no. 7; Monticolo, "Due documenti veneziani," 72–73.

28. *S. Giorgio Maggiore*, 3: 58–59, no. 318.

29. Silvano Borsari usefully addresses the question of Dandolo's authority and the relationship between the Venetian crusaders and the commune. *Studi sulle colonie veneziane in Romania*, 17–21. It is not true, however, that the mention of Dandolo and six councilors in the Pact of March 1204 was an insertion of a Venetian political organ into the Latin Empire. The Small Council remained with the vice-doge in Venice. The six councilors in Constantinople were certainly modeled on the idea of the Small Council, but they were not one in the same.

30. Nicol, *Byzantium and Venice*, 148.

31. See Chap. 3, text at n. 118.

32. Maleczek, *Pietro Capuano*, 132–34.

33. It is clear from the sources that Peter Capuano expressed his reservations about Zara to just a few people, and even then only when they sought him out. See Gunther of Pairis, 122–23; *Gesta episcoporum Halberstadensium*, 117. In a letter written three months later to the crusaders, Innocent III stated that Peter Capuano had told "some of you" (*quibusdam ex vobis*) that an attack on Zara was prohibited. Reg. 5: 160 (161). Villehardouin and Clari only learned of the papal prohibition when the army was before Zara. Villehardouin, sec. 84, 1: 84; Robert of Clari, *Conquête*, sec. 14, 14.

34. *FC*, 61–62.

35. *Gesta episcoporum Halberstadensium*, 117.

36. Gunther of Pairis, 122–23.

37. Reg. 5: 160 (161); Maleczek, *Pietro Capuano*, 133, n. 120.

38. As evidenced by his command to Martin of Pairis that he and his colleagues remain with the crusade and work to dissuade the crusaders from spilling Christian blood when the matter arose. Gunther of Pairis, 122–23.

39. *Gesta Innocentii*, chap. 85, col. 138.

40. Ibid.

41. Register 6: 48; 7: 18; 7: 200; 9: 139; Maleczek, *Pietro Capuano*, 134–35. The dating of Dandolo's refusal to allow Peter Capuano to join the crusade as legate is not precise. According to the *Gesta Innocentii*, chap. 85, col. 138, the Venetians made this decision because they feared

the legate would prohibit the attack on Zara—which would put it sometime in September 1202, after the crusade barons had agreed to go to Zara. It is unlikely that the cardinal would remain in Venice for very long after this rebuff. He was back in Rome by at least November 4, 1202, when he undersigned a papal privilege. Reg. 5: 103. I no longer believe that the Venetians were motivated by the fear that the legate would nullify the treaty between the Franks and Venetians. See *FC*, 49. Whether or not the Venetians recognized Peter Capuano was irrelevant to this question, since the Franks clearly did. In any event, the Venetians did not refuse to accept the authority of the legate, which was clearly legitimate; they simply refused to transport him with the crusade unless he renounced that authority.

42. Villehardouin, sec. 76, 1: 76.

43. ASV, S. Lorenzo, B. 21.

44. On the state of the piazza at this time, see Schulz, "La piazza medievale," 134–36.

45. Patriotic Venetian historians of the seventeenth and eighteenth centuries provided additional names, but they cannot be accepted without earlier confirmation. See e.g. Ramusio, *De bello Costantinopolitano*, 38–39.

46. *FC*, 68–69.

47. According to Pryor, the large transport vessels required perhaps approximately forty-five hundred sailors. If only half were needed, that number would decrease to around two thousand. The horse transports had a crew of about one hundred thirty each, thus requiring thirteen thousand men. The war galleys, which apparently now numbered sixty, needed at least six thousand men and probably more. "Venetian Fleet."

48. Ibid.

49. On the banner and silver trumpets, see Pertusi, "Quedam regalia insignia," 89–91.

50. Villehardouin, secs. 75–76, 1: 76–78; Robert of Clari, *Conquête*, sec. 13, 12–13.

51. Robert of Clari, *Conquête*, sec. 13, 13; Brunelli, *Storia della città di Zara*, 368; Cessi, "Venezia e la quarta crociata," 26.

52. Dandolo, 276–77; TTh., 1: 387–88, no. 96 (incorrectly dated). Kretschmayr, *Geschichte von Venedig*, 1: 288–89.

53. TTh., 1: 396–98, no. 97; *Venetiarum historia*, 134–35; *Devastatio Constantinopolitana*, 132.

54. Villehardouin, sec. 78, 1: 78.

55. Ibid., sec. 80, 1: 80. Zaran narrative sources name the heads of the delegation: Damiano de Varicassi and Berto de Matafarri. Brunelli, *Storia della città di Zara*, 375, n. 56.

56. Villehardouin, sec. 80, 1: 80.

57. Maleczek, *Pietro Capuano*, 138–39, n. 117.

58. Villehardouin, sec. 81, 1: 82; Peter of Vaux-de-Cernay, *Hystoria Albigensis*, 1: 108–9; *Gesta episcoporum Halberstadensium*, 117; *Gesta Innocentii*, chap. 85, cols. 138–39. See also Moore, "Peter of Lucedio," 243; *FC*, 244, n. 105.

59. Villehardouin, sec. 83, 1: 82–84; Peter of Vaux-de-Cernay, *Hystoria Albigensis*, 1: 109.

60. Peter of Vaux-de-Cernay, *Hystoria Albigensis*, 1: 109.

61. Villehardouin, sec. 83, 1: 82–84.

62. Ibid., sec. 84, 1: 84.

63. Thomas of Spalato, *Historia*, 576; *Gesta episcoporum Halberstadensium*, 117; *Devastatio Constantinopolitana*, 132. It is not true that Dandolo ordered the decapitations of various Zaran leaders. See *FC*, 77; Hurter, *Papa Innocenzo III*, 2: 160–61. This story originated with the late fifteenth-century writer, Lorenzo Bonincontri, in his *Historia regni utrusque Siciliae*. It does not appear in any contemporary or near-contemporary sources—even those with a strong animus against the Venetians, like Peter of Vaux-de-Cernay and Thomas of Spalato.

64. Brunelli, *Storia della città di Zara*, 369.

65. Villehardouin, secs. 88–90, 1: 88–90; Robert of Clari, *Conquête*, sec. 15, 15; *Devastatio Constantinopolitana*, 133.

66. McNeal and Wolff, "Fourth Crusade," 175; Andrea, "Conrad of Krosigk," 27, n. 74; idem, "Cistercian Accounts," 15, n. 57; Maleczek, *Pietro Capuano*, 143; *FC*, 81.

67. Reg. 5: 162.

68. *FC*, 81–82.

69. Reg. 6: 102. In Reg. 5: 160 (161), Innocent seems to equate the Venetians with the thieves in the parable of the Good Samaritan.

70. Ernoul-Bernard, *Chronique*, 350.

71. Reg. 6: 48.

72. Innocent initially demanded that the barons bind their heirs to make reparations to the king of Hungary. Because they were apparently unwilling to do this, the pope advised his legate to follow his own judgment about holding them to this requirement. Reg. 6: 48.

73. Reg. 5: 161 (162).

74. Reg. 6: 48; 6: 99.

75. Andrea, "Conrad of Krosigk," 30–41.

76. Villehardouin, sec. 91, 1: 90.

77. *FC*, 65.

78. They arrived on January 1, 1203. *Devastatio Constantinopolitana*, 133; Villehardouin, sec. 91, 1: 90; *Gesta episcoporum Halberstadensium*, 118.

79. *FC*, 33–35.

80. Reg. 5: 121 (122).

81. *Gesta Innocentii*, chap. 83, col. 132. For a more complete discussion of these events, see *FC*, 33–37.

82. Reg. 5: 121 (122); *Gesta Innocentii*, chap. 83, col. 132.

83. Villehardouin, secs. 70–72, 1: 70–74; *FC*, 63–64.

84. Villehardouin, sec. 72, 1: 72. The barons also asked the displaced papal legate, Peter Capuano, to inform the pope about the proposal when he returned to Rome and discover Innocent's will on the matter. Reg. 5: 121 (122). This is another clear sign that they were unaware of the previous attempts by Alexius and Boniface to win papal approval.

85. Villehardouin makes clear that it was only a very small group of Frankish barons who received Alexius's envoys. Sec. 72, 1: 72. The Venetians, in any event, were extremely busy with

the final preparations for the fleet's departure, while Dandolo's own attention was largely taken up by his attempt to preserve the agreement to sail to Zara.

86. Villehardouin, sec. 91, 1: 92.

87. Ibid., sec. 91–94, 1: 90–94; *Devastatio Constantinopolitana*, 133.

88. Hugh of St. Pol, *Epistola*, 812; *Chronicle of Novgorod*, 44.

89. E.g. Runciman, *History of the Crusades*, 3: 114–16; Ostrogorsky, *Byzantine State*, 415; Fine, *Late Medieval Balkans*, 61; Hellmann, *Grundzüge der Geschichte Venedigs*, 69; Browning, *The Byzantine Empire*, 187; Spiridonakis, *Grecs, Occidentaux, et Turcs*, 106; Kazhdan, s.v. "Venice."

90. Thiriet, *La Romanie vénitienne*, 70; Maleczek, *Pietro Capuano*, 116–21.

91. Charles Brand asserts that Dandolo may have negotiated with the young Alexius himself before the meeting at Zara. S.v. "Dandolo, Enrico." See also Angold, *Byzantine Empire*, 324.

92. Reg. 5: 121 (122).

93. On this topic generally, see Cheynet, *Pouvoir et contestations à Byzance*.

94. According to Andrea Dandolo, the pretender promised to pay the Venetians 30,000 silver marks, which the empire owed to Venice in compensation for the losses of 1171; 277. He appears to be confusing the original promised compensation, which totaled 1,500 gold pounds (roughly equal to 30,000 silver marks), and the amount still owed in 1202, which was between 200 and 400 gold pounds (between 4,000 and 8,000 silver marks). See Choniates, *Historia*, 538, as well as Enrico Dandolo's instructions to his envoys, Chap. 6, text at n. 48. It is likely that the young Alexius would have promised to settle Byzantium's accounts with the Venetians. Having cavalierly pledged 200,000 silver marks, he would hardly balk at an additional 8,000.

95. Brand, *Byzantium Confronts the West*, 214–18; Lilie, *Handel und Politik*, 578–93.

96. Fotheringham, "Genoa and the Fourth Crusade," 32–33.

97. *FC*, 36; Queller and Madden, "Some Further Arguments," 457–63.

98. Robbert, "Venice and the Crusades," 397–98.

99. It is common to read that relations between Venice and Constantinople were very poor in 1203. Recently, Norman Housley described them as being at a "nadir" at this time. "The Thirteenth-Century Crusades," 572. One would think that the state of war between the two after 1171 would better qualify for that status. In any case, relations in 1203 were normal in every respect, several embassies having passed between the cities in a successful attempt to hammer out the chrysobull of 1198. Diplomatic relations continued during the course of the crusade. See n. 127, below, and text at n. 127. In what may be an apocryphal story, Zancaruolo, a fifteenth-century chronicler, recorded that a Byzantine ambassador arrived in Venice while the construction of the crusade fleet was under way. He requested an alliance, but Dandolo politely declined. Thiriet sees this as evidence of courteous relations between the two powers as late as 1202. *Romanie vénitienne*, 69–70. It is possible, although troubling that Andrea Dandolo, who had official records at hand, does not mention this embassy in his history. In any case, Venetians did business freely across the Byzantine Empire, had their own prosperous quarter in Constantinople, and enjoyed generous privileges in Greek ports in 1203.

100. Choniates, *Historia*, 538; Lilie, *Handel und Politik*, 581–82; Queller and Madden, "Some Further Arguments," 454–55.

101. Madden, "Food and the Fourth Crusade."

102. Villehardouin, sec. 98, 1: 98.

103. Ibid., sec. 99, 1: 98–100.

104. *FC*, 92–94.

105. Villehardouin, sec. 108, 1: 110; *Gesta episcoporum Halberstadensium*, 118; *Venetiarum historia*, 135; Thomas of Spalato, *Historia*, 576. Andrea Dandolo, 277, and Gunther of Pairis, *Hystoria*, 125, imply that the walls were destroyed before winter. Brunelli notes that some houses that stood very near churches managed to survive. *Storia della città di Zara*, 371.

106. Brunelli, *Storia della città di Zara*, 371.

107. Reg. 5: 161 (162).

108. Dandolo and his fellow Venetians are frequently portrayed as men who gave excommunication very little thought. The truth is that Dandolo repeatedly sought absolution and the lifting of the ban after his departure from Zara. See Reg. 6:100; 6:208 (209); 7:18; 7:202; *Gesta Innocentii*, PL, 214: cxli. Indeed, it could be argued that he was more energetic in this pursuit than the Frankish barons.

109. Reg. 6: 48.

110. The date of the departure of the envoys can be surmised from later letters. Peter Capuano embarked on a voyage to the Holy Land in late April or, more likely, May 1203, after having been instructed to do so by Innocent III in a letter dated April 21. Reg. 6: 48; Andrea, *Capture of Constantinople*, 158, n. 116. He stopped off at Cyprus and then made his way to Acre, arriving in late May or June. Andrea, *Capture of Constantinople*, 159, n. 118. After his arrival he sent a letter to Innocent informing him of the mission of the Venetian envoys and requesting guidance as to what he should do if they returned. That letter does not survive. It reached Innocent before January 23, 1204, when the pope wrote a reply. Reg. 6: 208 (209). For a letter to make it aboard a convoy leaving for the West, it would have to have been written in July or August 1203 at the latest. The fact that Capuano refused to speak with the excommunicated Venetian envoys suggests that the embassy arrived sometime between the legate's formal excommunication, which was sent in April 1203, and the arrival of the pope's letter telling him to ascertain whether the Venetians were willing to receive absolution and accept Peter as legate. Ibid., 48. Clearly Peter could not discover these things if he refused to meet with the Venetians. Therefore, the envoys must have been dispatched sometime in April and have arrived before the end of the month. Peter then sailed to the Holy Land and wrote to Innocent about the matter after his arrival. Maleczek contends that the Venetian envoys to the legate were actually sent to the Holy Land, arriving there sometime during the summer of 1203. He relies in part on the testimony of the *Gesta Innocentii*, cxli, which records the arrival of Venetian envoys to the legate in the Holy Land. *Pietro Capuano*, 204. However, that embassy was a later one, which was successful in its request for absolution. See Chap. 9, text at n. 77. Nevertheless, it is possible that the Venetian envoys missed Peter Capuano at Benevento and therefore followed him to the East; possible, though unlikely. In either case the envoys would have had to depart Zara in April 1203.

111. After April 1203, Dandolo sent several sets of envoys and at least two letters request-

ing absolution. He was clearly eager to obtain absolution, so it seems reasonable to assume that this was the purpose of this embassy. Indeed, it is difficult to imagine any other purpose.

112. Evidenced by the existence of the embassy itself. There would be no reason to send envoys to Peter Capuano if the Venetians were still unwilling to accept him as papal legate. In subsequent correspondence, Enrico Dandolo referred to Capuano as a papal legate. Reg. 7: 202.

113. The letter does not survive. Its contents can be surmised from Innocent's reply, dated April 21, 1203. Reg. 6: 48.

114. Andrea, *Contemporary Sources*, 49–50.

115. Reg. 6: 100.

116. Ibid., 99, 100.

117. Ibid., 208 (209).

118. Ibid.

119. Boniface does not say explicitly that he informed the doge about the excommunication, but he does state that the doge and certain other Venetians known to him informed him about sending an envoy to Rome to seek absolution. He also states that he "knows for a fact" that the publication of the bull of excommunication would lead the Venetians to abandon the crusade and that he "received advice" to suppress the bull. This suggests pretty strongly that he spoke to Dandolo about the matter. Reg. 6: 100. It is true, however, that in an accompanying letter to the pope from Baldwin of Flanders, Louis of Blois, and Hugh of St. Pol the barons state that if the "doge and the Venetians" learned of the bull the fleet would dissolve. Ibid., 99. It seems highly unlikely, though, that news like this could be kept from the doge. In any case, Dandolo would learn the truth from his own envoys when they returned from their mission to Peter Capuano.

120. Reg. 6: 100.

121. Ibid.

122. As attested to by the letters of Boniface and the crusade barons. Ibid., 99, 100.

123. Ibid., 100.

124. Ibid., 99.

125. See the arguments of Moore in Andrea and Moore, "The Date of Reg. 6: 102," 119. See also Andrea, *Contemporary Sources*, 57–58.

126. Reg. 6: 99.

127. ASV, Miscellanea ducali ed atti diplomatici, B. 7. The exact date of the dispatch of the embassy is uncertain. The ambassadors were back in Venice before July 1203, when the Venetian government made provisions to repay their losses. Allowing for time to devise and formalize the agreement, as well as the time the ambassadors were held captive by the Zarans before returning to Venice, it seems reasonable to assume that they were dispatched in March or April, before the departure of the fleet for Corfu.

128. According to the ambassadors, "iremus in legatione de mandato vestri [Pietro Ziani] predecessoris." ASV, Miscellanea ducali ed atti diplomatici, B. 7. The plural "predecessors" refers to both Enrico Dandolo and his son.

129. Villehardouin, sec. III, I: 112–14; *Devastatio Constantinopolitana*, 133; Robert of Clari, *Conquête*, sec. 31, 31.

130. Villehardouin, sec. III, I: 112–14; *Gesta episcoporum Halberstadensium*, 118.

131. *CDRC*, 26, no. 20.

132. ASV, Miscellanea ducali ed atti diplomatici, B. 7; Brunelli, *Storia della città di Zara*, 372. Early modern chroniclers often identified Vitale Dandolo as the admiral of the crusader fleet. See e.g. Ramusio, *De bello Costantinopolitano*, 38, 135–36. The error probably stems from a misreading of the archival document above. In it, Vitale Dandolo is referred to as head of the Venetian forces in reference to an act he made in September 1203 in Arbe. At that time the crusade fleet had been in Constantinople for many months. This particular Vitale Dandolo (there were at least two alive at the time), apparently did not join the crusade. He was probably the Vitale Dandolo who stood in for Ranieri, serving as vice-doge on June 27, 1203, months after the crusade left Zara. ASV, S. Zaccaria, B. 12 perg. The substitution suggests that he was a son, grandson, or nephew of Doge Enrico Dandolo.

133. Morosini later recaptured Pago and rebuilt the fortress. Brunelli, *Storia della città di Zara*, 371.

134. ASV, Miscellanea ducali ed atti diplomatici, B. 7.

135. Dandolo, 277–78; *Venetiarum historia*, 137; Brunelli, *Storia della città di Zara*, 372.

136. Dandolo, 278. Thomas of Spoleto, 577; *Venetarum historia*, 137, claim that the Venetian squadron consisted of eighteen galleys.

137. The exact date is not certain. It would have to be between November 8, 1204, the date of the last surviving document made in Zara in the name of the king of Hungary, and July 23, 1205, the first in the name of the doge and the Venetian count. *CDRC*, 3: 49, no. 45; Brunelli, *Storia della città di Zara*, 372–73. November was too late in the year to launch a fleet. It likely occurred, then, at the beginning of the sailing season in 1205.

138. Dandolo, 278; *Venetiarum historia*, 137; Ferluga, "Veneziani fuori Venezia," 701; Brunelli, *Storia della città di Zara*, 372–73. Vitale Dandolo remained count of Zara for only a few years. By September 1208 he no longer held the position. See *CDRC* 3: 49, no. 45 (July 23, 1205); 3: 56, no. 51 (Feb. 18, 1206); 3: 79, no. 69 (Sept. 1208). It appears that he went to Constantinople, where he died in February or March 1207. He left 945 lire to Ranieri Dandolo. *Documenti*, 2: 30–31, no. 490. The *Venetiarum historia*, 137 reports that the first count of Zara was Domenico Michiel, however he was the count of Pago. See TTh., 1: 423, no. 106.

139. Brunelli, *Storia della città di Zara*, 373.

CHAPTER 9. THE CONQUEST OF CONSTANTINOPLE

1. *FC*, 96, 143–44.

2. It is sometimes suggested that Dandolo had a stranglehold on the crusade because of his control over the fleet. It is true that the day-to-day operations of the vessels would have been undertaken by Venetian captains answerable to the doge, who had himself been named leader of the Venetians when he took the cross in San Marco. However, according to the

terms of the Treaty of Venice, the fleet was at the service of the crusaders. TTh., 1: 364–65, no. 91.

3. Villehardouin, sec. 111, 1: 114.

4. Ibid., sec. 112, 1: 115; *Gesta episcoporum Halberstadensium*, 118; Clari, sec. 31, 31.

5. *FC*, 97–99.

6. *Documenti*, 1: 392–94, nos. 400–401.

7. The anonymous chronicler of Halberstadt reported that the Greeks attacked the Venetian fleet with petraries, forcing it to withdraw a safe distance. In retaliation, the crusaders devastated the island. *Gesta episcoporum Halberstadensium*, 118. Neither Villehardouin, nor Clari, nor any other eyewitness reported an altercation between the crusaders and the island's inhabitants. It is impossible to believe that something as dramatic as the bombardment of the fleet and the devastation of the island would be ignored by all of these accounts. Nicetas Choniates correctly noted that the crusaders were on Corfu for twenty days. He reported no violence, only remarking that they departed when they realized that the citadel was unassailable. *Historia*, 451. It is difficult, therefore, to accept the second-hand testimony of the *Gesta episcoporum Halberstadensium* on this matter. Andrea doubts the whole story. "Conrad of Krosigk," 43, n. 133; *Contemporary Sources*, 254, n. 65. See *FC*, 97, where we, unfortunately, accepted it.

8. *FC*, 103–4, 108.

9. Magdalino gives an excellent account of what the crusaders could see as they sailed through Marmara and the Bosporus. *Manuel I*, 119–20.

10. *FC*, 108–9.

11. Villehardouin, sec. 129, 1: 130.

12. *FC*, 106–8.

13. Villehardouin, secs. 130–31, 1: 130–32.

14. Ibid., sec. 131, 1: 132. On the identification of these "islands," see Madden, "Food and the Fourth Crusade."

15. Villehardouin, sec. 133, 1: 134; Robert of Clari, *Conquête*, sec. 40, 40; Nicetas, *Historia*, 542.

16. Villehardouin, sec. 136, 1: 136–38.

17. Hugh of Saint Pol, *Epistola*, 812; Villehardouin, sec. 137, 1: 138; Reg. 6: 210 (211).

18. Nicol, *Byzantium and Venice*, 136; Brown, "The Venetians and the Venetian Quarter," 82–83; Luzzatto, "Relazioni economiche fra oriente ed occidente," 234.

19. On the Venetian Quarter, see below.

20. Reg. 6: 210 (211).

21. Ibid.; Villehardouin, sec. 145, 1: 146.

22. *FC*, 112–13.

23. Reg. 6: 210 (211).

24. Villehardouin, sec. 145, 1: 146.

25. *Conquête*, sec. 41, 41. Clari frequently records imagined dialogue in the council of barons to explain the events he witnessed. Indeed, Clari does not appear to have even witnessed the display of the prince directly. Saying nothing of shouts and missiles, he records that ten galleys rowed directly up to the sea walls and had a rather civil discussion with the Greeks, who

claimed to know nothing at all about the young Alexius. This is pure imagination. Ville-hardouin, who was in the council, attributes the decision to display the prince on the galley solely to the barons. Sec. 145, 1: 146. Surprisingly, Clari's attribution of the scheme to Dandolo has been uncritically accepted by all authors, including Queller and myself. *FC*, 113–14.

26. Villehardouin, secs. 145–46, 1: 146–48; Robert of Clari, *Conquête*, sec. 41, 41; Reg. 6: 210 (211).

27. Robert of Clari, *Conquête*, sec. 41, 42.

28. Villehardouin, sec. 159, 1: 158; Hugh of Saint Pol, *Epistola*, 813.

29. Robert of Clari, *Conquête*, sec. 44, 43; Choniates, *Historia*, 542–43. In an excellent study, as yet still unpublished, John H. Pryor argues that Villehardouin's account of the attack on Galata is seriously defective. I have based this short synopsis on Pryor's analysis.

30. Villehardouin, sec. 162, 1: 160–62; Robert of Clari, *Conquête*, sec. 44, 43–44.

31. Villehardouin, sec. 172, 1: 174.

32. Ibid., sec. 173–74, 1: 174–76; Choniates, *Historia*, 544–45; Hugh of Saint Pol, *Epistola*, 814. According to Villehardouin, who is the only one to describe Dandolo's part in the attack, another standard of St. Mark appeared on one of the towers before the walls were occupied, although no one could say how it came to be there. The marshal of Champagne claimed to have interviewed more than forty Venetians about the course of the battle. It is suspicious, though, that two standards appear at the same time to embolden the Venetians. Perhaps in the chaos of battle the doge's standard was brought to the first captured tower before others were aware that the tower had been captured. It is also possible that a second standard was raised on the tower by a partisan of Venice or a Byzantine soldier bribed to do so. Based on a misreading of Nicetas Choniates, Queller and I mistakenly reported that the Venetians breached the wall with battering rams. *FC*, 124.

33. See e.g. Gibbon, *Decline and Fall of the Roman Empire*, 3: 2124; Mills, *The History of the Crusades*, 180.

34. E.g. McNeal and Wolff, "Fourth Crusade," 179; Godfrey, *1204*, 64.

35. Meyer, "The West's Debt to Byzantium."

36. Villehardouin states clearly that Dandolo's men leapt from the galley to plant the standard before him. Sec. 173, 1: 174–6. Since Dandolo was standing on the vessel's prow, this makes sense. In the next sentence, Villehardouin describes the Venetians' zeal at seeing on the shore the standard of St. Mark and the galley of their lord. Sec. 174, 1: 176. Nothing is said about the doge coming ashore.

37. Choniates, *Historia*, 544–45; Villehardouin, secs. 175–76, 1: 178. It is not clear how far the Venetians advanced into the city. Villehardouin only implies an advance by describing the retreat. Alberic of Trois-Fontaines claims that the Venetians advanced one-half league into the city: an absurdity. *Chronica*, 881.

38. Madden, "Fires of the Fourth Crusade," 73–74, 88.

39. Villehardouin, sec. 175, 1: 178. According to Alberic of Trois-Fontaines, whose account is somewhat jumbled, the doge sent 200 horses to Baldwin of Flanders. *Chronica*, 881.

40. *FC*, 129–34.

41. According to Nicetas Choniates, Alexius III ordered the houses outside the city walls torn down so that they could not be used for cover by the attackers. *Historia*, 541. It is not clear whether Nicetas was referring to all dwellings that flanked the walls, or just those along the land fortifications, where every attack on Constantinople before (and after) had centered. The Golden Horn was considered a safe harbor, so it may not have been thought necessary to destroy structures outside the walls flanking it. It would also be expensive, since the quays, warehouses, and shops of the Italians were situated there. The Pisans, who fought to defend Alexius III's reign, would hardly have favored the devastation of their quarter. There is no reference in any source to the destruction of these areas, nor is there evidence for it in Italian commercial transactions after 1204. A mosque that was on the water's edge in the Pisan Quarter was still standing in August 1203, when it was put to the torch by Pisans and disaffected crusaders. Madden, "Fires of the Fourth Crusade," 75–76.

42. Jacoby, "The Venetian Quarter," 154–59; Brown, "The Venetians and the Venetian Quarter," 74–82; Maltezou, "Il quartiere veneziano di Costantinopoli," 30–61.

43. E.g. Domenico, a wine merchant, who harbored Nicetas Choniates and his family after the fall of the city in 1204. Choniates, *Historia*, 588. On Venetians living outside their quarter, see Cinnamus, *Epitome*, 281–82. This posed a problem for Byzantines, not only because they did not like Latins living as Greeks, but also because it made it difficult to identify who precisely was a Venetian, and therefore a beneficiary of various legal and commercial privileges. Angold, *Byzantine Empire*, 229–30.

44. Villehardouin, sec. 191, 1: 194; Robert of Clari, *Conquête*, sec. 55, 55–56; Gunther of Pairis, *Hystoria*, 142; Reg. 7: 152.

45. Reg. 6: 210 (211); Villehardouin, sec. 193, 1: 196.

46. Villehardouin, sec. 193, 1: 196; Robert of Clari, *Conquête*, sec. 56, 56; *FC*, 136–37.

47. Villehardouin, secs. 194–95, 1: 196–200.

48. Oikonomides, "La décomposition de l'Empire byzantin," 16–17; Cheynet, *Pouvoir et contestations*, 461.

49. Villehardouin, sec. 196, 1: 200.

50. Madden, "Vows and Contracts in the Fourth Crusade," 442.

51. *FC*, 143.

52. Choniates, *Historia*, 553; *Devastatio*, 135. For the dating of the riot and fire, see Madden, "Fires of the Fourth Crusade," 74, n. 12.

53. Choniates, *Historia*, 552; Hubaldus of Pisa, 32.

54. Choniates, *Historia*, 552.

55. *FC*, 144–45.

56. Madden, "Fires of the Fourth Crusade," 74–77; *FC*, 145.

57. Madden, "Fires of the Fourth Crusade," 77–88.

58. Villehardouin, sec. 205, 1: 210.

59. Since the fire was set at the Mitaton mosque in the Pisan Quarter, the flames moved in a southerly direction, bypassing the Venetian Quarter to the northwest. See the plot of the devastation in Madden, "Fires of the Fourth Crusade," 90–93.

60. *FC,* 148–50.

61. Villehardouin, sec. 211, 2: 10.

62. *FC,* 154–56.

63. Choniates, *Historia,* 560; Villehardouin, sec. 216, 2: 14; sec. 226, 2: 25; *Devastatio,* 135–36.

64. *FC,* 155–67.

65. Choniates, *Historia,* 565–66; *FC,* 166–67; Hendrickx and Matzukis, "Alexios V," 126.

66. The date is given by Baldwin, who places the meeting the day before the murder of Alexius, which occurred on February 8. Reg. 7: 152.

67. Choniates, *Historia,* 567–68; Reg. 7: 152; *FC,* 167–69.

68. Several of his companions were captured by the crusaders. Choniates, *Historia,* 568. Baldwin of Flanders omits this incident from his relation of events.

69. *FC,* 168–69.

70. Choniates, *Historia,* 564; Villehardouin, sec. 223, 2: 22; Robert of Clari, *Conquête,* sec. 62, 61–62; *Devastatio,* 136; Alberic of Trois-Fontaines, *Chronica,* 883; *FC,* 170–71. According to Gunther of Pairis, Mourtzouphlus concealed the murder and sent messengers in Alexius IV's name to the crusader camp asking the leaders to come to the palace to receive their rewards. They were about to do so, but Dandolo urged them not to walk into a trap because of their love of money. He feared just what had happened: Mourtzouphlus had murdered Alexius and was now attempting to do the same to the crusade's leaders. *Hystoria,* 144–45. Since no other source mentions this episode, Andrea reasonably concludes that it is probably erroneous or a figment of Gunther's artistic imagination. *Capture of Constantinople,* 165, n. 166.

71. Madden, "Vows and Contracts in the Fourth Crusade," 460–61.

72. Villehardouin, sec. 224, 2: 22–24; Reg. 6: 101; *FC,* 173–75.

73. Some have assumed that because the excommunication remained in effect, the Venetians were well aware of it and simply did not care. See e.g. Maleczek, *Pietro Capuano,* 145; Nicol, *Byzantium and Venice,* 147; Setton, *Papacy and the Levant,* 1: 9.

74. The letter does not survive, although some of its contents can be surmised from the papal response. Reg. 7: 18. Presumably, the doge's letter was sent along with two other letters dispatched to the pope at this time, one from Alexius IV and the other from the crusade barons. Reg. 6: 209 (210), 210 (211).

75. Reg. 7: 18; Andrea, trans., *Contemporary Sources,* 97–98.

76. *Gesta Innocentii,* cxli. The Venetian envoys must have sailed to the Holy Land and returned quickly, within the space of a few months. In a letter written to the pope in or around June 1204, Dandolo reported that he and the Venetians had already been absolved by the legate. Reg. 7: 202.

77. Villehardouin, secs. 232–33, 2: 32–34; Robert of Clari, *Conquête,* sec. 69, 69.

78. The Venetian point of view concerning Alexius's outstanding debt is attested to in the Pact of March. TTh., 1: 446, 449, nos. 119, 120. See also, Carile, "Partitio," 126; *FC,* 175.

79. Even after the sack of Constantinople, Greeks would greet a Latin by making the sign of the cross with their fingers and proclaiming, "Ayos phasileos marchio" (Holy Emperor the Marquis). Gunther of Pairis, *Hystoria,* 157. On or around March 3, city officials expelled

the last remnants of Latins from Constantinople to guard against possible espionage or sabotage attempts. Acropolita, *Annales*, 9; Hendrickx and Matzukis, "Alexios V," 124. For a detailed examination of the Byzantine perspective with full references, see *FC*, 186–88, 191–92.

80. As they, in fact, attempted to do. *Devastatio*, 137; Choniates, *Historia*, 572.

81. Fotheringham, *Marco Sanudo*, 22–24; Lock, *Franks in the Aegean*, 142.

82. There are two texts of the treaty, one in the name of Dandolo, the other in the names of the Frankish leaders. TTh., 1: 444–52, nos., 119–20. An English translation of the copy in the papal register (Reg. 7: 205) can be found in Andrea, *Contemporary Sources*, 140–44.

83. It is not true, as it is common to read, that the first division was considered to be monies owed only to Venice. The treaty explicitly defines it as a sum owed to both the Franks and the Venetians. TTh., 1: 446; Carile, "Partitio," 126. For examples of this error, see: Finlay, *History of Greece*, 3: 265–66; Nicol, "The Fourth Crusade and the Greek and Latin Empires," 285; idem, *Byzantium and Venice*, 141; McNeal and Wolff, "Fourth Crusade," 182; Brand, *Byzantium Confronts the West*, 254; Setton, *Papacy and the Levant*, 1: 12; Godfrey, *1204*, 120.

84. Alexius had paid half of the promised 200,000 marks shortly after his ascension to the throne. Robert of Clari, *Conquête*, sec. 56, 56. Additional payments trickled in, but these were very small. When Dandolo met with Mourtzouphlus, he demanded 5,000 pounds of gold, the equivalent of 100,000 silver marks. The cost of the extension of the Treaty of Venice is revealed by the later treasure division, wherein the Franks gave to the Venetians 50,000 marks out of their share to reflect the initial three-to-one division. Villehardouin, sec. 254, 2: 59. Thus, when the booty was divided, the first 200,000 marks was initially divided equally, with 100,000 going to each side and the transfer of 50,000 from the Franks to the Venetians representing the payment of all Alexius's debts.

85. In addition to the treaty, see Villehardouin, sec. 235, 2: 36.

86. Fotheringham, "Genoa and the Fourth Crusade," 34.

87. Prawer, "The Italians in the Latin Kingdom," 225.

88. Some historians have viewed the exemption as evidence that Dandolo crafted a treaty that benefitted only Venice. E.g. Nicol, *Byzantium and Venice*, 141. It is hard to see how placing all Venetian-held territories under the jurisdiction of the emperor was a victory for the Venetians. In any case, the question of the exemption was academic, since Dandolo personally received no territories in the partition.

89. Villehardouin, sec. 237, 2: 38.

90. *Devastatio*, 137.

91. Robert of Clari, *Conquête*, sec. 71, 70.

92. Villehardouin, sec. 238, 2: 38; Robert of Clari, *Conquête*, sec. 71, 70–71; Reg. 7: 152; *FC*, 177–79.

93. Villehardouin, sec. 239, 2: 40.

94. Ibid., sec. 240, 2: 40–42.

95. Ibid., sec. 241, 2: 42; Choniates, *Historia*, 569.

96. Villehardouin, sec. 242, 2: 245; Robert of Clari, *Conquête*, sec. 74, 73; Reg. 7: 152.

97. Robert of Clari, *Conquête*, sec. 74, 73–74; Villehardouin, sec. 242, 2: 42–44; Reg. 7: 152;

Choniates, *Historia*, 568–69; Ernoul-Bernard, *Chronique*, 372; Anonymous of Soissons, *De terra Iherosolimitana*, 160.

98. Robert of Clari, *Conquête*, secs. 75–76, 75–76; Choniates, *Historia*, 569–70.

99. For a detailed account of the military operations as well as the internal dynamics behind the surrender of Constantinople, see *FC*, 181–92.

CHAPTER 10. THE VENETIANS IN THE LATIN EMPIRE, 1204–1205

1. On the sack of Constantinople, see *FC*, 193–98.

2. Choniates, *Historia*, 588.

3. For an inventory, see Lorenzetti, *Venezia e il suo estuario*, 212–23.

4. On the tetrarchs, see Müller-Wiener, *Bildlexikon*, 267 and references.

5. Choniates, *De signis*, 651–54.

6. For an excellent introduction to the early history of the horses, see Borelli Vlad and Guidi Toniato, "The Origins and Documentary Sources of the Horses of San Marco," 127–36.

7. Dandolo, 280; *Venetiarum historia*, 142.

8. See, BNMV, Cod. It. VII, 517 (=7883). Subsequent chroniclers and genealogists often repeated the story; e.g. Cappellari-Vivaro, *Famiglie venete*, 2: 35.

9. E.g. Da Mosto, *I Dogi*, 74; Concina, *A History of Venetian Architecture*, 63.

10. See e.g. BNMV, Cod. It. VII, 89 (=8381), 25r., (a 1410 edition of the 1380 chronicle of Enrico Dandolo); BNMV, Cod. Lat., X 136 (=3026), 32v. (a fourteenth-century chronicle, incorrectly attributed to Enrico Dandolo).

11. Villehardouin, sec. 251, 2: 55.

12. Ibid., sec. 259, 2: 64. According to later Venetian tradition, Dandolo's palace was on the Augusteion. Ramusio, *De bello Constantinopolitano*, 136. Jean Longnon postulated that this referred to part of the Great Palace. *L'Empire latin*, 50, n. 2. While this is consistent with the tradition (which may after all be false), it supposes that Boniface of Montferrat would have been willing to share his accommodations with the doge. It seems much likelier that the palace in question was the patriarchal complex, which was also on the Augusteion.

13. Villehardouin, secs. 249–50, 2: 50–52.

14. Ibid., sec. 252, 2: 56; Robert of Clari, *Conquête*, sec. 81, 80–81. According to the *Devastatio*, 137, three large towers were filled with silver.

15. Villehardouin, sec. 253, 2: 56–58. Ernoul-Bernard heard that the Venetians secretly put much of the booty on their ships under cover of darkness, thus cheating the French. *Chronique*, 375. While Venetians were probably just as guilty of concealing booty as other members of the crusade, there is no hint from any eyewitness source, or any other source save Ernoul-Bernard, that they depleted the pool by spiriting treasure away. Both Robert of Clari and the author of the *Devastatio* blame the rich knights, not the Venetians. Modern writers who view Venice in the worst possible light, not surprisingly, find Ernoul-Bernard reliable on this point. E.g. Brand, *Byzantium Confronts the West*, 263; Godfrey, *1204*, 130.

16. Robert of Clari noticed that the rich treasure was quickly reduced to silver, although he accused the guards and the rich knights of stealing the more precious items. *Conquête*, secs. 81, 98; 79–81, 95–96. The time for theft, however, was before the booty had been brought together and placed under close scrutiny. Gems and other costly items could not be divided into twenty-, ten-, or five-mark allotments, but would instead have to be sold to Greek or Latin merchants. Cf. Choniates, *Historia*, 594.

17. Villehardouin, sec. 254, 2: 58; *FC*, 199.

18. Villehardouin, sec. 254, 2: 58.

19. *Devastatio*, 137, 149.

20. For a more detailed analysis of the booty acquired at Constantinople, see *FC*, 199–200.

21. Villehardouin, sec. 256, 2: 62; Robert of Clari, *Conquête*, sec. 94, 92. Both authors refer to a parliament that adjourned without a decision. Clari reports that they convened for an additional two weeks before finally settling on the electors. Villehardouin states that after the first meeting they decided to meet on another day to choose the electors, and he then describes the contention between the two parties. Villehardouin is probably referring to formal parliaments, whereas Clari counts any meeting at which leaders argued over the matter as a parliament.

22. Gunther of Pairis, *Hystoria*, 157.

23. Villehardouin, sec. 262, 2: 68.

24. Ibid., sec. 256, 2: 62.

25. Ibid., secs. 257–58, 2: 62–64.

26. Gerland, *Geschichte des lateinischen Kaiserreiches*, 4; Fotheringham, *Marco Sanudo*, 22.

27. Robert of Clari, *Conquête*, sec. 94, 92; Reg. 7: 152.

28. The only source for this is Robert of Clari, *Conquête*, sec. 94, 92. As in his report of the lottery in Venice, Clari's level of detail about a comparatively minor matter suggests that he had good information about an event that, for whatever reason, stuck in his mind. Never one for numbers, though, Clari states that the Franks and Venetians chose ten electors each, rather than six. He may be wrong on other details as well, but the method he describes is without question typically Venetian.

29. Carile, *La cronachistica veneziana*, 497, 501, 506, 519, 524, 528.

30. Sec. 260, 2: 66.

31. *De bello Constantinopolitano*, 136.

32. See Chap. 8, n. 133.

33. Luzzatto, *I prestiti*, 8–11, no. 2.

34. TTh., 1: 249, no. 85; Nicol, *Byzantium and Venice*, 154. Querini also did business in Constantinople; ASV, Cancellaria inferiore, b. 178, no. 5 (May 1189).

35. Robert of Clari, *Conquête*, sec. 93, 91; Gerland, *Geschichte des lateinischen Kaiserreiches*, 3–4.

36. *Historia*, 596.

37. Da Canal, *Les estoires de Venise*, 60; Dandolo, 279; Carile, *La cronachistica veneziana*, 343, 363, 401, 411, 431, 466, 479, 510; Thiriet, "Les chroniques vénétiennes," 265.

38. Usseglio, *I marchesi di Monferrato*, 2: 242–43.

39. Robert of Clari, *Conquête*, sec. 95, 92–93; Villehardouin, sec. 259, 2: 64–66.

40. Da Canal has Dandolo declining the throne when the Frankish barons offered it to him. *Les estoires de Venise*, 60. Andrea Dandolo, who had a much clearer grasp of the electoral procedure, reports that a Frankish elector nominated Dandolo; in return, a Venetian elector nominated Baldwin, whom they all agreed upon. Dandolo, 279. Later chronicles asserted that the Frankish electors consisted of four French and two Lombards. When the election was held the four French electors voted for Baldwin of Flanders, the two Lombards for Boniface of Montferrat, five of the six Venetians for Enrico Dandolo, and one Venetian, Pantaleone Barbo, remained silent. Since the French favored Dandolo over Boniface, and the Lombards favored the doge over Baldwin, it seemed that Dandolo would be elected. Just then, however, Barbo arose and said that if they elected the doge the French soldiers would leave and the empire would be defenseless. This persuaded the Venetians to change their votes to Baldwin, and the others followed suit. Carile, *La cronachistica veneziana*, 343, 363, 401, 411, 431, 466, 479. Another Venetian chronicle, attributed to Nicolò Trevisan, reports that all the Venetian electors voted for Dandolo on the first ballot, while all the Franks chose Baldwin. Then Ottavio Querini stood up and gave the same speech usually attributed to Pantaleone Barbo, after which the Venetians switched their votes to Baldwin. Ibid., 510; Thiriet, "Les chroniques vénétiennes," 265.

41. Carile, *Per una storia*, 184.

42. Choniates, *Historia*, 596–97. A few months later, Dandolo was able to persuade Emperor Baldwin to cease his war against Boniface of Montferrat simply by sending some messengers. The emperor "did not want to alienate the doge of Venice." Villehardouin, sec. 295, 2: 102.

43. Fotheringham, "Genoa and the Fourth Crusade," 36–37.

44. Villehardouin, sec. 260, 2: 66; Robert of Clari, *Conquête*, sec. 95, 93.

45. Robert of Clari, *Conquête*, sec. 96, 93–95; Villehardouin, sec. 263, 2: 68–70; Reg. 7: 152.

46. The date can be surmised from a letter from Dandolo to the pope informing him of the absolution of the Venetians. Reg. 7: 202. The undated letter was certainly written after the fall of the city on April 12, since it describes events up to that point. It does not mention the imperial election of Baldwin of Flanders or the patriarchal election of Thomas Morosini, so it may have been written before those events took place. It was not sent, however, until after the patriarchal election, for the two envoys who bore it were charged with acquiring the pope's confirmation of the election. See ibid., 203, 206. Since the doge's correspondence was part of a letter-writing campaign by the crusade leaders to gain the pope's confirmation of the Pact of March, this letter was probably written at the same time as the others. Baldwin's letter was written before early July, when he left Constantinople. Ibid., 201. The absolution arrived sometime before that.

47. *Gesta Innocentii*, cxli.

48. Reg. 7: 127.

49. Ibid., 202.

50. Andrea, *Contemporary Sources*, 129.

51. Ibid.

52. Reg. 7: 207.

53. *Gesta Innocentii*, cxli.

54. Reg. 8: 126; Andrea, *Contemporary Sources*, 167.

55. Reg. 7: 18.

56. Ibid., 202. It is impossible to be more precise on the relationship between Navigaioso and Dandolo.

57. The envoy's instructions are apparent in the pope's reply, dated January 29, 1205. Ibid., 206.

58. Andrea, *Contemporary Sources*, 146.

59. Ibid., 147. Innocent is referring to several letters from the barons extolling Dandolo and the Venetians and stressing how important they were to the continued well-being of the empire. See Reg. 7: 201; cf. Reg. 7: 203.

60. Reg. 7: 206; Setton, *Papacy and the Levant*, 1: 15.

61. Fedalto, "Il patriarcato latino di Costantinopoli," 414; Carile, *Per una storia*, 219–20.

62. Reg. 7: 203.

63. In a letter to the clergy of Constantinople, Innocent juxtaposed the moods of the two groups of envoys. The Venetian clerics *humiliter postularunt*, while the ambassadors of the doge *cum instantia requiente*. Reg. 7: 203; Andrea, *Contemporary Sources*, 137, n. 560.

64. *Devastatio*, 137. The appeal and contest is also mentioned by Innocent III; Reg. 7: 203.

65. Reg. 7: 203.

66. This is the implication of Innocent's report, ibid.

67. Ibid., 201.

68. Ibid., 203. Innocent relates that the appeal and challenge were withdrawn, but does not say that he had any part in it. Given his desire to patch things up with the Venetians, though, it seems likely.

69. Ibid.; see also Innocent's letters to Ranieri Dandolo of February 8, 1205: TTh., 1: 534–38, no. 134; and March 30, 1205, TTh., 1: 538–39, no. 135, neither of which appears in the papal register. In the latter, Innocent tells Ranieri that he is confirming Thomas Morosini "to please your father."

70. *Gesta Innocentii*, chap. 98, col. cxliii; Reg. 8: 19–24; Wolff, "Politics in the Latin Patriarchate," 230–31.

71. Reg. 8: 21; 8: 25; TTh., 1: 538–39, no. 135. In fact, though, Innocent and his successors played a prominent role in the selection of subsequent patriarchs of Constantinople, twice appointing them directly. Wolff, "Politics in the Latin Patriarchate," 229–30; Hussey, *Orthodox Church*, 188.

72. Reg. 8: 26.

73. On June 13, 1157, Hadrian IV gave to Grado authority over all Venetian churches in the Byzantine Empire. Fedalto, "Il patriarcato latino," 413–16.

74. TTh., 1: 551–53, no. 146; Wolff, "Politics in the Latin Patriarchate," 234–36.

75. TTh., 1: 547–51, nos. 144, 145.

76. Morosini's written oath to this effect does not survive. It is attested to by later events.

See, Reg. 9: 130; 11: 76; 12: 105; Borsari, *Studi sulle colonie veneziane*, 99–105.

77. Reg. 12: 140.

78. The canons took their oaths on May 8 and May 14, TTh., 1: 547–51, nos. 144, 145; Morosini on May 15, TTh., 1: 551–53, no. 146.

79. The letter is not in the register. See Wolff, "Politics in the Latin Patriarchate," 229 and appendix II.

80. Reg. 8: 62.

81. "Politics in the Latin Patriarchate," 232.

82. Wolff, "Greeks and Latins," 324; Lamma, *Comneni e Staufer*, 1: 302.

83. Villehardouin, secs. 283–86, 2: 92–94.

84. The ambassadors are named in the treaty dated August 12, 1204. TTh., no. 123, 512–15. Villehardouin does not mention the two Venetian ambassadors on this embassy, but he does record that two went on a second embassy to Boniface near the end of the month. Villehardouin, sec. 296, 2: 104. Carile is probably correct that this was a simple error, confusing the Venetian presence on the two embassies. "Partitio," 146–47.

85. Fotheringham, *Marco Sanudo*, 31–32.

86. E.g. Nicol, *Byzantium and Venice*, 149; Longnon, *L'empire latin*, 59–60; Godfrey, *1204*, 136; Borsari, *Il dominio veneziano in Creta*, 12–13; Thiriet, *La Romanie vénitienne*, 75–76; Bury, "Lombards and Venetians in Euboia," 312. Gerland suggested that Dandolo hoped that the money would cause Boniface to renege on his promise to Villehardouin and put his trust in his arms, thus keeping the Franks in disarray while Venice prospered. *Geschichte des lateinischen Kaiserreiches*, 26.

87. TTh., no. 123, 512–15. The security receipt in which Boniface acknowledged receiving the 1,000 silver marks is available in Cervellini, "Come i veneziani acquistarono Creta," 274–75.

88. TTh., no. 123, 512–15.

89. This is further confirmed by the fact that none of Boniface's territories appears in the Treaty of Partition. See below.

90. Shortly after Dandolo's death, a successor to his authority in Byzantium was elected by the Venetians of Constantinople. See TTh., 1: 566–69, no. 157. Doge Pietro Ziani, however, later took Crete and the title.

91. Villehardouin, sec. 293, 2: 100–102; Choniates, *Historia*, 600.

92. Villehardouin, sec. 295–96, 2: 102–4; Carile, "Partitio," 149–51.

93. These sentiments are expressed throughout Clari's account.

94. This, indeed, was true for later Venetian chroniclers as well. See Dandolo, 280; *Venetiarum historia*, 143; Cervellini, "Come I veneziani acquistarono Creta," 274–77. Sanudo claimed that Crete came to Boniface as an inheritance from his mother and was purchased by Dandolo for 10,000 silver marks. *Vitae ducum venetorum*, col. 531.

95. Fotheringham, *Marco Sanudo*, 34.

96. Villehardouin, sec. 298, 2: 106.

97. Ibid., sec. 299, 2: 106.

98. Ibid. Asia Minor was apportioned to the emperor in the Treaty of Partition. Carile, "Partitio," 217–18.

99. See the arguments laid out below.

100. Fotheringham, "Genoa and the Fourth Crusade," 42.

101. The pope's letter of protest over the attack was dated November 4, 1204. Reg. 7: 147.

102. Ibid.

103. Fotheringham, *Marco Sanudo*, 41.

104. Ibid., 41–44.

105. Jacoby, "Venetian Presence," 149.

106. *Historia*, 595. Nicol is incorrect, therefore, when he states that the partition "lists numerous towns, ports, islands and provinces which were nothing but names to the crusaders." *Byzantium and Venice*, 142.

107. Choniates records the difficult negotiations, yet lampoons the crusaders in his description of them dividing not only the current empire, but all of the ancient Roman world as well. *Historia*, 595. The Treaty of Partition proves otherwise.

108. Robert of Clari, *Conquête*, sec. 105, 100–101.

109. Villehardouin, sec. 302, 2: 110; Fotheringham, *Marco Sanudo*, 35–36; Carile, "Partitio," 155–58.

110. Carile, "Partitio," 159–61; Fotheringham, *Marco Sanudo*, 36–38; Nicol, *Byzantium and Venice*, 149–50; Borsari, *Studi sulle colonie veneziane*, 22–25.

111. Dandolo's successor in Constantinople, Marino Zeno, took the title immediately after his election in May or June 1205. TTh., 1: 558–61, no. 154. The title was not transferred to Doge Pietro Ziani until 1206 or 1207. See Epilogue.

112. Acropolita, *Opera*, 1: 13.

113. See e.g. Oikonomides, "La décomposition de l'empire," 13–22, who argues that the omitted regions of the Partition Treaty were areas in rebellion against Constantinople in 1204. Aside from the fact that all of the omitted areas correspond to properties that were accorded to either Boniface of Montferrat or the emperor by virtue of his exchange with the marquis, it is important to note that when the Partition Treaty was written the vast majority of the empire was in rebellion against Constantinople. That is, after all, why the crusaders had to conquer it.

114. Carile, "Partitio," 152–53; Longnon, "Frankish States in Greece," 236–37.

115. Carile, "Partitio," 152–53.

116. Longnon, "Frankish States in Greece," 237–40.

117. Villehardouin, sec. 314 and n. 2: 122.

118. Ibid., sec. 306, 2: 114; Robert of Clari, *Conquête*, sec. 108, 103.

119. Hendrickx and Matzukis, "Alexius V," 130, n. 1.

120. Choniates, *Historia*, 608–9; Villehardouin, sec. 306, 2: 114; Robert of Clari, *Conquête*, sec. 109, 103–4.

121. Robert of Clari, *Conquête*, sec. 109, 104.

122. Villehardouin, sec. 307, 2: 116; Gunther of Pairis, *Hystoria*, 165.

123. See e.g. Kretchmayr, *Geschichte von Venedig*, 2: 3; Cracco, "Dandolo, Enrico," 456–57; Nicol, *Byzantium and Venice*, 153.

124. TTh., 1: 571–74, no. 160.

125. He had, in fact, been thinking about it for some time. Witness his request to Innocent that because of feebleness of age and a body broken by labor he be relieved of his crusading vow. Reg. 7: 206.

126. They departed in April. Villehardouin, secs. 376–77, 2: 184–86.

127. Reg. 8: 126. The wording of the letter is not precise on this point. Innocent recounts that Peter dispensed of the crusading vow for "all crusaders who remain in the defense of Constantinople from the preceding March to the next." It is possible, as Andrea suggests, that this refers to the period stipulated in the Pact of March, namely, March 1204 to March 1205. *Contemporary Sources*, 165, n. 640. This seems unlikely, though. Peter Capuano would not have taken so bold an action—one that would earn him the bitter rebuke of the pope—without good reason. To prevent the loss of the army would be a good reason; the confirmation of the crusaders' Pact of March arrangement would not. In a letter to the king of France, Innocent described the legate's action as a consequence of the war against Ioannitsa, which would put it in March 1205. Reg. 8: 125. Villehardouin, sec. 377, 2: 184, describes how Peter did everything he could to stop the departure of the crusaders in April 1205. Taken together, these suggest strongly that the legate issued the dispensation in March 1205 for those who would remain an additional year.

128. FC, 202.

129. Villehardouin, secs. 335–36, 2: 144–46; sec. 340, 2: 150. See also the letter of Henry of Flanders to the West. Pokorny, "Zwei unedierte Briefe," 200.

130. Villehardouin, secs. 347–50, 2: 156–60; Choniates, *Historia*, 614–15.

131. Villehardouin, sec. 344, 2: 144.

132. Ibid., sec. 351, 2: 160. Settia makes the point that Venetians must have had cavalry and infantry forces of their own given that Dandolo led them to Adrianople. "L'apparato militare," 489–50. He is certainly correct that Venetians were involved in land-based warfare at times, particularly after 1204. However, in this case it seems unlikely that the doge led a Venetian army. If so, why did he not leave with the emperor? Villehardouin implies that Dandolo remained behind to await the arrival of additional Frankish troops, which he then led to Adrianople.

133. Villehardouin, secs. 355–63, 2: 164–72; Choniates, *Historia*, 615–16; Pokorny, "Zwei unedierte Briefe," 200; Longnon, *L'empire latin*, 78–79.

134. Villehardouin, secs. 364–66, 2: 172–76.

135. Choniates, *Historia*, 617.

136. Villehardouin, secs. 369–75, 2: 178–84. On Rodosto, see Lilie, *Handel und Politik*, 209–20; Borsari, *Venezia e Bisanzio*, 40; Jacoby, "Venetian Presence," 151.

137. Villehardouin, secs. 376–79, 2: 184–88; Longnon, *L'empire latin*, 80; Ravegnani, "La Romània veneziana," 187–88.

138. Ignoring the expiration of service, Nicol characterizes the departing crusaders as "hopelessly demoralized," thus fleeing because "the crusade had been in vain." *Byzantium and Venice*, 152.

139. Villehardouin, secs. 384–85, 2: 192–94. According to Robert of Clari, Dandolo and the Venetians opposed the elevation of Henry unless they were given the icon of the Virgin in Hagia Sophia purportedly painted by St. Luke. *Conquête*, sec. 114, 107. McNeal discounts this because the dispute over the icon did not erupt until after Henry's coronation. *Conquest of Constantinople*, 126–27, n. 132. Still, Dandolo may have struck a deal with Henry at Rodosto, a deal that only later went sour.

140. Villehardouin, sec. 386, 2: 194. On the Venetian garrison, see Jacoby, "Venetian Presence," 155.

141. Villehardouin, secs. 387–88, 2: 196–98.

142. Ibid., sec. 388, 2: 198, reports only that Dandolo became ill. Nicetas Choniates, who appears to have had good information about events at this time, describes the doge's malady more fully. *Historia*, 617.

143. Ibid.

144. Villehardouin, sec. 388, 2: 198. The date of Dandolo's death is frequently given as May 29 or June 1, 1205. Cf. Fees, *Reichtum und Macht*, 250; Kretschmayr, *Geschichte von Venedig*, 1: 472, n. 37/1. The first date is a result of a misreading of Villehardouin, who places it between the return to Constantinople and May 29. The second date comes from Dandolo, 281. There is no reason, however, to prefer a fourteenth-century chronicle to the testimony of Villehardouin, who was there. Gerland argued that the doge must have died after June 5, since his death is not mentioned in a letter of that date from Henry of Flanders. *Geschichte des lateinischen Kaiserreiches*, 57, n. 3. However, as Fotheringham noted, Henry said nothing at all about the Venetians in his letter, which could easily have been drafted before the doge's death. *Marco Sanudo*, 45.

145. On Dandolo's tomb, see Gallo, "La tomba di Enrico Dandolo," 270–83. In an unpublished study, delivered at the Twenty-first Annual Byzantine Studies Conference in 1995, Thomas Dale suggested that the tomb was in the south gallery near the nineteenth-century stone inscription of Dandolo's name. He further hypothesized that the famous Deesis mosaic nearby was executed as part of an overall program to honor the doge during the years of the Latin Empire. Together, these were part of the "Chapel of the Venetians" in Hagia Sophia later mentioned by Sanudo. My thanks to Professor Dale for kindly allowing me to consult this intriguing study.

EPILOGUE: BIRTH OF A MARITIME EMPIRE

1. See Chap. 9, text at n. 91.

2. TTh., 1: 558–61, no. 154; 1: 567–68, no. 157.

3. In addition to those cited below, see also Cessi, "Venezia e la quarta crociata," 50; Zakythinos, "La conquête de Constantinople," 150–52; Cracco, "Dandolo, Enrico," 456–57; Maltezou, "Venetian *habitores*," 233–41.

4. Wolff, "Oath of the Venetian Podestà," 545; Thiriet, *La Romanie vénitienne*, 92–93. Barbaro states that the Venetians considered the proposal in 1224. Wolff believes it happened earlier than that.

5. See the carefully worded report of Marino Zeno to the doge, TTh., 1: 567–68, no. 157. In everything, Zeno remained obedient to the government of Venice. See also Jacoby, "The Latin Empire," 532.

6. *Venetiarum historia,* 144.

7. This is from the report of Marino Zeno, which was to be a written version of the messengers' relation. TTh., 1: 567–68, no. 157.

8. Ibid.

9. *Venetiarum historia,* 144.

10. As Lane wrote, "Overshadowed by his father, Ranieri Dandolo is not generally considered one of the heroes of Venetian history. His name is not on the list of doges, but should be on a list of those who established the tradition of behavior which gave viability to the Venetian political system. In that list, the non-doges, those who gracefully accepted second place, are as important as those who filled the highest office successfully." *Venice,* 94.

11. TTh., 1: 567–68, no. 157.

12. See Borsari, *Studi sulle colonie,* 26–27, which has full references.

13. TTh., 1: 569–71, no. 159.

14. The decree does not survive, but its contents are made evident by subsequent events and documents as well as the reports of later chroniclers. Fotheringham, *Marco Sanudo,* 49; Wolff, "Oath of the Venetian Podestà," 550.

15. See *Atti,* 2: 23–25, nos. 1–2; TTh., 1: 558–61, no. 154; 1: 566–69, no. 157; 1: 566–71, no. 159; 2: 18, no. 169.

16. TTh., 1: 569–71, no. 159. It is possible that because Crete had not been apportioned to the Venetians in the Treaty of Partition the doge saw no reason for the podestà to relinquish what he had not received. Nevertheless, the sale of Crete does transfer the island to Enrico Dandolo and the Venetians—not Venice. TTh., 1: 513, no. 123.

17. Fotheringham, *Marco Sanudo,* 51–52.

18. For a good analysis, see ibid., 52–54.

19. Andrea Dandolo, who frequently relied on state records, does not mention Crete as a destination of this expedition, focusing instead on the capture of Vetrano. Dandolo, 282–83. See also *Venetiarum historia,* 146.

20. Dandolo, 283; Fotheringham, *Marco Sanudo,* 54–55, 81.

21. Da Canal, *Estoires,* 69–70.

22. The latter interpretation would be consistent with Andrea Dandolo's testimony. Dandolo, 283.

23. Ranieri Dandolo was back in Venice in December 1206, when he witnessed the will of his aunt, Primera Polani. ASV, S. Lorenzo, B. 21.

24. Fotheringham, *Marco Sanudo,* 51.

25. *Venetiarum historia,* 147; Dandolo, 283; Fotheringham, *Marco Sanudo,* 81–83.

26. Zeno used the title for the last time in a document of 1206; TTh., 2: 18, no. 169. In a document of February 1207, Zeno referred to the doge rather than himself as "*dominator quarte*

partis et dimidie Imperii Romanie." TTh., 2: 4: no. 164 (misdated to 1206). The first reference to the doge with the title appears in a pact between Venice and Pisa of August 1206. ASV, Miscellanea ducali ed atti diplomatici, B. 7. However, it was written in Pisa by a Pisan notary, so it may have reflected their familiarity with Enrico Dandolo's title in Constantinople, rather than Pietro Ziani's in Venice. The following month, in September 1206, a Venetian notary referenced the doge with the title. Ibid. In the ducal court, however, the title was apparently not used at all in 1206 or 1207. See *Atti*, 2: 25–38, nos. 2–5. It first appears there in a document of February 1208. Ibid., 2: 39–41, no. 7.

27. The title was used by Venetian doges until 1358. Lazzarini, "I titoli dei dogi," 300.

28. Later chroniclers gave the date for embarkation as April 7, 1207. Fotheringham, *Marco Sanudo*, 81. However, the commander of the fleet, Ranieri Dandolo, was still in Venice in June 1207, when he received a bequest from a kinsman, probably a cousin, Vitale Dandolo. *Documenti*, 2: 30–31, no. 490.

29 ASP, Archivi privati diversi, Pergamene diverse, B. 103.

30. Fotheringham, *Marco Sanudo*, 83–84.

31. Enrico Pesacatore delivered the body to the Venetians with full honors. According to Andrea Dandolo, Ranieri was buried in the church of S. Giorgio at Candia. Dandolo, 283–84. Ogerio, a Genoese chronicler contemporary with the event, recorded that three galleys were sent to convey the body back to Venice, but they were overtaken by Benvenuto, son of Alamanno Costa, who seized the body and took it with him to Syracuse. *Annales Genuenses*, 109–10.

32. Fotheringham, *Marco Sanudo*, 84.

Bibliography

PRIMARY SOURCES

Unpublished

Archivio di Stato, Padua (ASP)

Archivi privati diversi
    Pergamene diverse, B. 103.

Archivio di Stato, Venice (ASV)

Cancelleria inferiore
    B. 106, no. 8.
    B. 178.
Codice diplomatico veneziano. 31 vols.
Mensa patriarcale
    B. 9, nos. 6–10.
    B. 86.
    B. 93, nos. 305, 315–17.
    B. 94, no. 426.
Miscellanea atti diplomatici e privati
    B. 2, nos. 56, 57.
Miscellanea codici
    Serie 1, 17–23: Marco Barbaro. *Arbori de' patritii veneti.* An eighteenth-century contin-
        uation by Antonio Maria Tasca of Barbaro's *Famiglie nobili venete.* A copy is also
        available on the reference shelves of the reading room in the ASV.
    Serie 3, 31–34: Girolamo Alessandro Cappellari-Vivaro. *Famiglie venete (Campidoglio
        Veneto).*
Miscellanea ducali ed atti diplomatici
    B. 6.
    B. 7.

Pacta

    T. 1.

Procuratori di S. Marco de Citra

    B. 323.

Procuratori di S. Marco, Misti

    Diversi perg., b. 2.

    B. 166.

S. Lorenzo

    B. 21.

S. Maria della Carità

    B. 20 perg.

    B. 40 perg.

S. Nicolò di Lido

    B. 9, Proc. 77.

S. Salvatore

    B. 22, t. 43.

    B. 28, t. 55.

S. Zaccaria

    B. 1 perg.

    B. 2 perg.

    B. 5 perg.

    B. 7 perg.

    B. 12 perg.

    B. 14 perg.

    B. 35 perg.

    B. 2.

Biblioteca Apostolica Vaticana, Rome

Cod. Vat. Lat. 6085. Contains a sixteenth-century copy of the *Chronicon Monasterii S. Salvatoris* by Francisco De Gratia. The original is in ASV, S. Salvatore, B. 3. An eighteenth-century copy is available at the Biblioteca del Museo Correr, Venice, Cod. Cicogna 2088. The chronicle was published in 1766, but is extremely rare.

Biblioteca Nazionale Marciana, Venice (BNMV)

Cod. Marc. It. VII 89 (=8381).

Cod. Marc. It. VII 516 (=7882).

Cod. Marc. It. VII 517 (=7883).

Cod. Marc. It. VII 551 (=7281).

Cod. Marc. Lat. X 136 (=3026).

Cod. Marc. Lat. XIV 71.

Österreichische Nationalbibliothek, Vienna

Fondo ex Foscarini

Cod. 6155–56: Marco Barbaro. *Famiglie nobili venete.* A holograph of book 3 of Barbaro's *Origine e discendenze delle famiglie patrizie.* For medieval families, this is far superior to the Tasca continuation available in the ASV.

Published

Acropolita, Georgius. *Opera.* Edited by Peter Wirth. 2 vols. Stuttgart: B. G. Teubner, 1978.

Alberic of Trois-Fontaines. *Chronica.* Edited by P. Scheffer-Boichorst. In *MGH, SS,* 23: 631–950.

Albert of Aachen. *Historia Hierosolymitanae expeditionis.* RHC, Occ., vol. 4.

Annales pisani. In *MGH, SS,* 19: 236–66.

Annales venetici breves. Edited by H. Simonsfeld. In *MGH, SS,* 14: 69–72.

Anonymous of Bari. *Ignoti civis Barensis, sive Lupi Protospatae chronica ab anonymo auctore Barensi.* Edited by Lodovico Antonio Muratori. In *RIS,* vol. 5: 145–57. Milan, 1724.

Anonymous of Soissons. *De terra Iherosolimitana et quomodo ab urbe Constantinopolitana ad hanc ecclesiam allate sunt relique.* Edited by Alfred J. Andrea. In Alfred J. Andrea and Paul I. Rachlin, "Holy War, Holy Relics, Holy Theft: The Anonymous of Soissons's *De terra Ihersolimitana,* An Analysis, Edition, and Translation," *Historical Reflections* 18 (1992): 157–75.

Atti originale della cancelleria veneziana, Gli. Edited by Marco Pozza. 2 vols. Venice: Il Cardo, 1994–96.

Benedettini in S. Daniele (1046–1198). Edited by Elisabeth Santschi. Venice: Comitato per la pubblicazione delle fonti relative alla storia di Venezia, 1989.

Benintendus de Ravagnani. *Epistola Domini Benintendi de Ravagnanis Cancellarii Venetiarum in commendationem per illustrissimum Dominum Andream Dandalum Inclytum Venetiarum Ducem editarum.* Edited by Ester Pastorello. In *RIS,1* vol. 12, pt. 1: CIV–CV. Bologna: Nicola Zanichelli, 1938.

Bertaldo, Giacomo. *Splendor venetorum consuetudinum.* Edited by Francisco Schupfer. Bologna: Monti, 1901.

Bilanci generali. Edited by Enrico Besta. 2 vols. Venice: Visentini Cav. Federico, 1912.

Boso. *Vitae paparum.* In *Le liber pontificalis.* Edited by L. Duchesne, 2: 351–446. Paris: E. Thorin, 1886–92. Reprint, Paris: E. de Boccard, 1955.

Choniates, Nicetas. *Historia.* Edited by Jan-Louis van Dieten. 2 vols. In *Corpus fontium historiae byzantinae.* Vol. XI/1. Berlin: De Gruyter, 1975. English translation: *O City of Byzantium, Annales of Niketas Choniates.* Translated by Harry J. Magoulias. Detroit: Wayne State University Press, 1984.

———. *De signis.* Edited by Jan-Louis van Dieten. In *Corpus fontium historiae byzantinae.* Vol. XI/1. Berlin: De Gruyter, 1975.

Chronicle of Novgorod, 1016–1471, The. Translated by Robert Michell and Nevill Forbes. In Camden Third Series, Vol. 25. London: Camden Society, 1914. A more recent translation of the section relevant to the crusade can be found in Jared Gordon. "The Novgorod Account of the Fourth Crusade." *Byzantion* 43 (1973): 297–311.

Cinnamus, John. *Epitome rerum ab Ioanne et Alexio Comnenis gestarum.* Edited by Augustus Meineke. (*Corpus scriptorum historiae byzantinae.*) Bonn, 1836.

Codex diplomaticus regni Croatiae, Dalmatiae, et Slavoniae. Edited by Tadija Smiciklas. 16 vols. Zagreb: Academia Scientiarum et Artium Slavorum Meridionalium, 1904–.

Codice diplomatico padovano. Edited by Andrea Gloria. 3 vols. Venice, 1877–81.

Comnena, Anna. *Alexiade.* Edited by Bernard Leib. 3 vols. Paris: Société d'édition "Les Belleslettres," 1937–45. English translation: *The Alexiad of Anna Comnena.* Translated by E. R. A. Sewter. London: Routledge, 1969.

Constantine Porphyrogenitus. *De administrando imperio.* Edited by Gy. Moravscik. Translated by R. J. H. Jenkins. (*Corpus fontium historiae byzantinae*, 1.) Washington, D.C.: Dumbarton Oaks, 1967.

Da Canal, Martin. *Les Estoires de Venise: Cronaca veneziana in lingua francese dalle origini al 1275.* Edited by Alberto Limentani. Florence: Leo S. Olschki, 1972.

Dandolo, Andrea. *Chronica brevis.* Edited by Ester Pastorello. In *RIS*, vol. 12, pt. 1: 351–73. Bologna: Nicola Zanichelli, 1938.

———. *Chronica per extensum descripta.* Edited by Ester Pastorello. In *RIS*, vol. 12, pt. 1: 1–327. Bologna: Nicola Zanichelli, 1938.

Deliberazioni del Maggior Consiglio di Venezia. Edited by Roberto Cessi. 3 vols. Bologna: Nicola Zanichelli, 1931–50.

Devastatio Constantinopolitana. Edited and translated by Alfred J. Andrea. In "The *Devastatio Constantinopolitana*, a Special Perspective on the Fourth Crusade: An Analysis, New Edition, and Translation." *Historical Reflections* 19 (1993): 131–49.

Diplomi arabi del R. Archivio Fiorentino, I. Edited by Michele Amari. 2 vols. Florence: F. Le Monnier, 1863–67.

Documenti del commercio veneziano nei secoli XI–XIII. Edited by Raimondo Morozzo della Rocca and Antonio Lombardo. 2 vols. Rome: Istituto storico italiano per il Medio Evo, 1940.

Documenti relativi alla storia di Venezia anteriori al mille. Edited by Roberto Cessi. 2 vols. Padua: Gregoriana, n.d. Reprint, Venice: Deputazione di storia patria per le Venezie, 1991.

Documenti sulle relazioni delle città toscane coll'Oriente cristiano e coi Turchi fino all'anno MDXXXI. Edited by Giuseppe Müller. Florence: M. Cellinie, 1879. Reprint, Rome: Società multigrafica editrice, 1966.

Ernoul and Bernard le Trésorier. *Chronique.* Edited by Louis de Mas Latrie. Paris: J. Renouard, 1871.

Famiglia Zusto. Edited by Luigi Lanfranchi. Venice: Comitato per la pubblicazione delle fonti relative alla storia di Venezia, 1955.

Fulcher of Chartres. *Historia Hierosolymitana.* Edited by Heinrich Hagenmeyer. Heidelberg: C. Winter, 1913.

Geoffrey of Malaterra. *De rebus gestis Rogerii Calabriae et Sicilae Comitis et Roberti Guiscardi Ducis fratris eius.* Edited by E. Pontieri. In *RIS*, vol. 1. Bologna, 1927.

Geoffrey of Villehardouin. *La conquête de Constantinople.* Edited by Edmond Faral. 2 vols. Paris: Société d'édition "Les Belles-lettres," 1938–39.

Gesta episcoporum Halberstadensium. In *MGH, SS,* 23: 73–123.

Gesta Innocentii III. In *PL,* 214: xviii–ccxxviii.

Gunther of Pairis. *Hystoria Constantinopolitana.* Edited by Peter Orth. Hildesheim: Weidmann, 1994. English translation: *The Capture of Constantinople: The* Hystoria Constantinopolitana *of Gunther of Pairis.* Edited and translated by Alfred J. Andrea. Philadelphia: University of Pennsylvania Press, 1997.

Historia ducum veneticorum. Edited by H. Simonsfeld. *MGH, SS,* 14: 72–89.

Hubaldus of Pisa. *Das Imbreviaturbuch des Erzbischöflichen Gerichtsnotars Hubaldus aus Pisa.* Edited by Gero Dolezalek. Cologne: Böhlau, 1969.

Hugh of St. Pol. *Epistola.* In *Annales Coloniensis maximi, MGH, SS,* 17: 812–14. Also in TTh., 1: 304–11. The best version of the letter, which takes into account all its various forms, is provided in the English translation by Alfred J. Andrea, *Contemporary Sources for the Fourth Crusade,* 186–201.

Innocent III. *Die Register Innocenz' III.* Edited by Othmar Hageneder et al. Graz: H. Böhlaus, 1964–. Five volumes to date, numbered according to register year.

Italia pontificia sive repertorivm privilegiorvm et letterarvm a Romanis pontificibvs ante annvm MCXXXXVIII. Edited by Paul F. Kehr. Vol. 7. Berlin: Weidmannos, 1923.

John the Deacon. *Cronaca veneziana.* Edited by Giovanni Monticolo, 57–171. Rome: Forzani e C. Tipografi del Senato, 1890.

Lazzarini, Vittorio. "Originali antichissimi della cancelleria veneziana." *Nuovo Archivio Veneto* 8 (1904): 199–229.

Lupus Protospatharius. *Annales.* Edited by H. Pertz. In *MGH, SS,* 5: 51–63.

Monk of the Lido. *Historia de translatione Magni Nicolai.* In RHC, Occ., vol. 5.

Nuovi documenti del commercio veneto nei secoli XI–XIII. Edited by Antonino Lombardo and Raimondo Morozzo della Rocca. Venice: Deputazione di storia patria per le Venezie, 1953.

Obo of Ravenna. In Marino Sanudo, *Le vite dei dogi.* Edited by Giovanni Monticolo. In *RIS,* vol. 22, pt. 4, 455–84. Città di Castello, 1900.

Ogerio. *Annales Genuenses.* In *Annali genovesi di Caffaro e dei suoi continuatori,* edited by E L. T. Belgrano and C. Imperiale di Sant'Angelo, 2: 69–154. 5 vols. Genoa: Fonti per la storia d'Italia, 1890–1929.

Orderic Vitalis, *Historiae Ecclesiasticae.* In *PL,* 188, cols. 17–982.

Origo Civitatum Italie seu Venetiarum (Chronicon Altinate et Chronicon Gradense). Edited by Roberto Cessi. Rome: Tipografia del Senato, 1933.

Pace Veneta relatio, De. The best edition is included in Rodney M. Thomson, "An English Eyewitness of the Peace of Venice, 1177." *Speculum* 50 (1975): 21–32. The older version is edited by Ugo Balzani. In *Bullettino dell'Istituto Storico Italiano* 10 (1891): 7–16.

Peter of Vaux-de-Cernay. *Petri Vallium Sarnaii monachi hystoria Albigensis.* Edited by Pascal Guébin and Ernest David Lyon. 3 vols. Paris: Champion, 1926–39.

Pokorny, Rudolf. "Zwei unedierte Briefe aus der Frühzeit des lateinischen Kaiserreichs von Konstantinopel." *Byzantion* 55 (1985): 180–209.

Promissioni del doge di Venezia dalle origini alla fine del duecento, Le. Edited by Gisella Graziato. Venice: Comitato per la pubblicazione delle fonti relative alla storia di Venezia, 1986.

Raimbaut de Vaqueiras. *The Poems of the Troubadour Raimbaut de Vaqueiras.* Edited by Joseph Linskill. The Hague: Mouton, 1964.

Ramusio, Paolo. *De bello Costantinopolitano et imperatoribus Comnenis per Gallos, et Veneto restitutis.* . . . Venice: Marc. Ant. Brogiolum, 1634.

Robert of Auxerre. *Chronicon.* In *MGH, SS,* 26: 219–76.

Robert of Clari. *La Conquête de Constantinople.* Edited by Philippe Lauer. Paris: Edouard Champion, 1924. English translation: *The Conquest of Constantinople.* Translated by Edgar H. McNeal. New York: Columbia University Press, 1936. Reprint, 1966. Italian translation: *La conquista di Costantinopoli.* Translated by Anna Maria Nada Patrone. Genoa: n.p., 1972.

Romuald of Salerno. *Chronicon.* Edited by C. A. Garufi. In *RIS,* vol. 7, pt. 1, 3–297. Città di Castello, 1914.

S. Giorgio di Fossone. Edited by Bianca Strina. Venice: Comitato per la pubblicazione delle fonti relative alla storia di Venezia, 1957.

S. Giorgio Maggiore. Edited by Luigi Lanfranchi. Venice: Comitato per la pubblicazione delle fonti relative alla storia di Venezia, 1968–.

S. Giovanni Evangelista di Torcello. Edited by Luigi Lanfranchi. Venice: Il Tridente, 1948.

S. Lorenzo. Edited by Franco Gaeta. Venice: Comitato per la pubblicazione delle fonti relative alla storia di Venezia, 1959.

S. Lorenzo di Ammiana. Edited by Luigi Lanfranchi. Venice: Alfieri, 1947.

S. Maria Formosa. Edited by Maurizio Rosada. Venice: Comitato per la pubblicazione delle fonti relative alla storia di Venezia, 1972.

SS. Ilario e Benedetto e S. Gregorio. Edited by Luigi Lanfranchi and Bianca Strina. Venice: Comitato per la pubblicazione delle fonti relative alla storia di Venezia, 1965.

SS. Secondo ed Erasmo. Edited by Eva Malipiero Ucropino. Venice: Comitato per la pubblicazione delle fonti relative alla storia di Venezia, 1958.

SS. Trinità e S. Michele Arcangelo di Brondolo. Edited by Biancha Lanfranchi Strina. Venice: Comitato per la pubblicazione delle fonti relative alla storia di Venezia, 1981–.

Sansovino, Francesco. *Venetia città nobilissima et singolare.* Venice: Steffano Curti, 1663.

Sanudo, Marino. *Le vite dei dogi.* Edited by Giovanni Monticolo. In *RIS,* vol. 22, pt. 4. Città di Castello, 1900. This edition ends with the reign of Sebastiano Ziani (1172–78). For subsequent doges see the older edition: *Vitae ducum venetorum.* Edited by Lodovico Antonio Muratori. In *RIS,* vol. 22. Milan, 1733.

Thomas of Spalato. *Historia Spalatina.* Edited by L. de Heinemann. *MGH, SS,* 29: 570–98.

Translatio Isidori. In RHC, Occ., vol. 5.

Trattati con Bisanzio, 992–1198, I. Edited by Marco Pozza and Giorgio Ravegnani. Venice: Il Cardo, 1993.

Urkunden zur älteren Handels- und Staatsgeschichte der Republik Venedig. Edited by G. L. Fr. Tafel and G. M. Thomas. 3 vols. Vienna: Kaiserlich-königlichen Hof- und Staatsdruckerei, 1856–57. Reprint, Amsterdam: Hakkert, 1964.

Venetiarum historia vulgo Petro Iustiniano Iustiniani filio adiudicata. Edited by Roberto Cessi and Fanny Bennato. Venice: Deputazione di storia patria per le Venezie, 1964.

William of Apulia. *La Geste de Robert Guiscard.* Edited by Marguerite Mathieu. Palermo: Bruno Lavagnini, 1961.

William of Tyre. *Historia rerum in partibus transmarinis gestarum.* In *Corpus Christianorum, Continuatio medievalis.* Vol. 63A. Edited by R. B. C. Huygens. Turnhout: Brepols, 1986.

SECONDARY LITERATURE

Abulafia, David. *The Two Italies. Economic Relations between the Norman Kingdom of Sicily and the Northern Communes.* Cambridge: Cambridge University Press, 1977.

Allmendinger, Karl-Heinz. *Die Beziehungen zwischen der Kommune Pisa und Ägypten im hohen Mittelalter: Eine rechts- und wirtschafts-historische Untersuchung.* Wiesbaden: Steiner, 1967.

Andrea, Alfred J. "Cistercian Accounts of the Fourth Crusade: Were They Anti-Venetian?" *Analecta Cisterciensia* 41 (1985): 3–41.

———. *Contemporary Sources for the Fourth Crusade.* Leiden: E. J. Brill, 2000.

———. "Conrad of Krosigk, Bishop of Halberstadt, Crusader and Monk of Sittichenbach: His Ecclesiastical Career, 1184–1225." *Analecta Cisterciensia* 43 (1987): 11–91.

Andrea, Alfred J., and John C. Moore. "The Date of Reg. 6: 102: Pope Innocent III's Letter of Advice to the Crusaders." In *Medieval and Renaissance Venice,* edited by Ellen E. Kittell and Thomas F. Madden, 109–23. Urbana: University of Illinois Press, 1999.

Angold, Michael. *The Byzantine Empire, 1025–1204: A Political History.* 2d ed. New York: Longman, 1997.

Balard, Michel. "Communes italiennes, pouvoir et habitants des états francs de Syrie-Palestine au XIIe siècle." In *Crusaders and Muslims in Twelfth-Century Syria,* edited by Maya Shatzmiller, 43–64. Leiden: E. J. Brill, 1993.

Baldwin, Marshall Whithed. *Alexander III and the Twelfth Century.* Glen Rock, N.J.: Newman Press, 1968.

Bartlett, W. B. *An Ungodly War: The Sack of Constantinople and the Fourth Crusade.* Stroud, Gloucestershire: Sutton, 2000.

Bellavitis, Giorgio, and Giandomenico Romanelli. *Venezia.* Rome: Laterza, 1985.

Berto, Luigi Andrea. "Pietro IV Candiano, un doge deposto perché era troppo virtuoso o perché era troppo autoritario?" *Studi Veneziani,* n.s. 40 (2000): 163–68.

Besta, Enrico. "La cattura dei Veneziani in Oriente per ordine dell'imperatore Emanuele Comneno e le sue consequenze nelle politica interna ed esterna del Comune di Venezia." *Antologia Veneta* 1 (1900): 35–46, 111–23.

———. "Il diritto e le leggi civili di Venezia fina al dogado di Enrico Dandolo." *Ateneo Veneto* 20/2 (1897): 290–320; 22/1 (1899): 145–84, 302–31; 22/2 (1899): 61–93, 202–48. Also published as *Il diritto e le leggi civili di Venezia fino al dogado di Enrico Dandolo.* Venice: Visantini Cav. Federico, 1900.

Besta, Enrico, and Riccardo Predelli. "Gli statuti civili anteriori al 1242 editi per la prima volta." *Nuovo Archivio Veneto,* n.s. 1 (1901): 5–117, 205–300.

Betto, Bianca. *Le nove congregazioni del clero di Venezia (sec. XI–XV).* Padua: Antenore, 1984.

Bianchi, Guido. "Il patriarca di Grado Domenico Marango tra Roma e l'Oriente." *Studi Veneziani* 8 (1966): 9–125.

Borsari, Silvano. "Il crisobullo di Alessio I per Venezia." *Annali dell' Istituto Italiano per gli studi storici* 2 (1970): 111–31.

———. *Il dominio veneziano in Creta nel XIII secolo.* Naples: Fauso Fiorentino, 1963.

———. "L'organizzazione dei possessi veneziani nell'Impero bizantino nel XII secolo." In *Studi albanologici, balcanici, bizantini e orientali in onore di Giuseppe Valentini, S. J.* Florence: Leo S. Olschki, 1986.

———. *Studi sulle colonie veneziane in Romania nel XIII secolo.* Naples: University of Naples, 1966.

———. *Venezia e Bisanzio nel XII secolo. I rapporti economici.* Venice: Deputazione di storia patria per le Venezie, 1988.

Brand, Charles M. *Byzantium Confronts the West, 1180–1204.* Cambridge, Mass.: Harvard University Press, 1968.

———. S.v. "Dandolo, Enrico." In *Oxford Dictionary of Byzantium.* Oxford: Oxford University Press, 1991.

Brezzi, Paolo. "Le pace di Venezia del 1177 e le relazioni tra la Repubblica e l'Impero." In *Venezia dalla prima crociata alla conquista di Costantinopoli del 1204,* 49–70. Florence: G. C. Sansoni, 1965.

Brown, Horatio F. "The Venetians and the Venetian Quarter in Constantinople to the Close of the Twelfth Century." *Journal of Hellenic Studies* 40 (1920): 68–88.

Browning, Robert. *The Byzantine Empire.* Rev. ed. Washington, D.C.: Catholic University of America Press, 1992.

Brunelli, Vitaliano. *Storia della città di Zara dai tempi più remoti sino al 1409 compilata sulle fonti e integrata da tre capitoli sugli usi e costumi.* 2d ed. Trieste: Lint, 1974.

Bury, John B. "The Lombards and Venetians in Euboia (1205–1303)." *Journal of Hellenic Studies* 7 (1886): 309–52.

Cappelletti, Giuseppe. *Le chiese d'Italia.* 21 vols. Venice: Giuseppe Antonelli, 1844–70.

———. *Storia della chiesa di Venezia dalla sua fondazione sino ai nostri giorni.* 6 vols. Venice: n.p., 1849–50.

Carile, Antonio. *La cronachistica veneziana (secoli XII–XVI) di fronte alla spartizione della Romania nel 1204.* Florence: Leo S. Olschki, 1969.

———. "Alle origini dell'Impero d'Oriente: analisi quantitativa dell'esercito crociato e ripartizione dei feudi." *Nuova Rivista Storica* 56 (1972): 284–314.

———. "Partitio Terrarum Imperii Romanie." *Studi Veneziani* 7 (1965): 125–305.

———. *Per una storia dell'Impero Latino di Costantinopoli (1204–1261).* Bologna: Pàtron, 1978.

Cassandro, Giovanni. "Concetto caratteri e struttura dello stato veneziano." *Rivista di Storia del Diritto Italiano (Milan)* 36 (1963): 23–49. Also published in *Bergomum* 38/2 (1964): 33–55.

Castagnetti, Andrea. "Famiglie e affermazione politica." In *Storia di Venezia*, 1: 613–44. Rome: Istituto della Enciclopedia italiana, 1992.

———. "Insediementi e 'populi.'" In *Storia di Venezia*, 1: 577–612. Rome: Istituto della Enciclopedia italiana, 1992.

———. "Il primo comune." In *Storia di Venezia*, 2: 81–130. Rome: Istituto della Enciclopedia italiana, 1995.

———. *La societá veneziana nel Medioevo.* 2 vols. Verona: Libreria universitaria editrice, 1992–93.

Cazel, Jr., Fred A. "Financing the Crusades." In *A History of the Crusades,* edited by Kenneth M. Setton, 6: 116–49. Madison: University of Wisconsin Press, 1989.

Cecchetti, Bartolomeo. *Autografi, bolle ed assise dei dogi di Venezia.* Venice: P. Naratovich, 1881.

———. *Il doge di Venezia.* Venice: P. Naratovich, 1864.

———. *Programma dell'I. R. Scuola di Paleografia in Venezia. Pubbl. alla fine dell'anno scolastico, 1861–1862.* Venice: Tipografia del commercio, 1862.

———. "La vita dei Veneziani fino al sec. XIII." *Archivio Veneto* 2 (1871): 63–123.

Cervellini, G. B. "Come i veneziani acquistarono Creta." *Nuovo Archivio Veneto,* n.s. 16 (1908): 262–78.

Cessi, Roberto. *Le origini del ducato veneziano.* Naples: A. Morano, 1951.

———. "Il 'parvum statutum' di Enrico Dandolo." *Archivio Veneto,* ser. 5, 62 (1958): 1–7.

———. "Politica, economia, religione." In *Storia di Venezia*, 2: 69–476. Venice: Centro internazionale delle arti e del costume, 1957.

———. *La repubblica di Venezia e il problema adriatico.* Naples: Edizioni scientifiche italiane, 1953.

———. *Storia della repubblica di Venezia.* 2 vols. Milan: Giuseppe Principato, 1968.

———. *Venezia ducale.* 2 vols. Venice: Deputazione di storia patria per le Venezie, 1963–65.

———. "Venezia e la quarta crociata." *Archivio Veneto,* ser. 5, 48–49 (1959): 1–52.

———. "Venice to the Eve of the Fourth Crusade." In *Cambridge Medieval History,* vol. 4, pt. 1, 251–73. Cambridge: Cambridge University Press, 1966.

———, ed. *Problemi monetari veneziani fino a tutto il secolo XIV.* Padua: A. Milani, 1937.

Cessi, Roberto, and Annibale Alberti. *Rialto: L'isola, il ponte, il mercato.* Bologna: Nicola Zanichelli, 1934.

Chalandon, Ferdinand. *Essai sur le règne d'Alexis Ier Comnène (1081–1118).* Paris: A. Picard, 1900. Reprint, New York: Burt Franklin, 1972.

———. *Jean II Comnène (1118–1143) et Manuel I Comnène (1143–1180).* 2 vols. Paris: A. Picard, 1912. Reprint, New York: Burt Franklin, 1971.

Cheynet, Jean-Claude. "Dévaluation des dignités et dévaluation monétaire dans la seconde moitié du XIe siècle." *Byzantion* 53 (1983): 453–77.

———. *Pouvoir et contestations à Byzance (963–1210).* Paris: Publications de la Sorbonne, 1990.

Chojnacki, Stanley. "Kinship Ties and Young Patricians in Fifteenth-Century Venice." *Renaissance Quarterly* 38 (1985): 240–70.

Cicogna, Emanuele Antonio. *Delle inscrizioni veneziane*. 6 vols. Venice: Giuseppe Picotti, 1824–53.

Cipolla, Carlo M. "Note di storia veronese. VII. Trattati commerciali e politici del sec. XII inediti o imperfettamente noti." *Nuovo Archivio Veneto* 15 (1898): 288–352.

Claar, Maximilian. *Die Entwickelung der venetianischer Verfassung von der Einsetzung bis zur Schliessung del Grossen Rates (1172–1297)*. Munich: H. Lüneburg, 1895.

Classen, Peter. "La politica di Manuele Comneno tra Federico Barbarossa e le città italiane." In *Popolo e stato in Italia nell'età e la lega Lombarda*, 265–79. Turin: Deputazione subalpina di storia patria, 1970.

Concina, Ennio. *Le chiese di Venezia: L'arte e la storia*. Udine: Magnus, 1995.

———. *A History of Venetian Architecture*. Translated by Judith Landry. Cambridge: Cambridge University Press, 1998.

Constable, Giles. *The Reformation of the Twelfth Century*. New York: Cambridge University Press, 1996.

Corner, Flaminio. *Ecclesiae Venetae antiquis monumentis nunc etiam primum editis illustratae ac in decades distributae*. 13 vols. Venice: Iohannes Bapt. Pasquali, 1749.

Cracco, Giorgio. "Chiesa e istituzioni civili nel secolo della quarta crociata." In *La chiesa di Venezia nei secoli XI-XIII*, edited by Franco Tonon, 11–30. Venice: Studium cattolico veneziano, 1988.

———. S.v. "Dandolo, Enrico." In *Dizionario biografico degli Italiani*. Rome: Istituto della Enciclopedia italiana, 1960–.

———. S.v. "Dandolo, Enrico (patriarca)." In *Dizionario biografico degli Italiani*. Rome: Istituto della Enciclopedia italiana, 1960–.

———. "L'età del comune." In *Storia di Venezia*, 2: 1–30. Rome: Istituto della Enciclopedia italiana, 1995.

———. *Società e stato nel medioevo veneziano*. Florence: Leo S. Olschki, 1967.

Crescenzi, Victor. *Esse de maiori consilio. Legittimità civile e legittimazione politica nella Repubblica di Venezia (secc. XIII–XVI)*. Rome: Istituto storico italiano per il Medio Evo, 1996.

Crouzet-Pavan, Elisabeth. "'Quand le doge part à la croisade. . . .'" In *Guerre, pouvoir, et noblesse au Moyen âge: Mélanges en l'honneur de Philippe Contamine*, edited by Jacques Paviot and Jacques Verger, 167–74. Paris: Presses de l'Université de Paris–Sorbonne, 2000.

———. *"Sopra le acque salse": Espaces, pouvoir et société à Venise à la fin du Moyen âge*. Rome: Ecole française de Rome, 1992.

———. *Venise triomphante: les horizons d'un mythe*. Paris: Albin Michel, 1999.

Crowe, N. W., T. P. Nickles, B. T. Troost, and A. D. Elster, "Intrachiasmal Hemorrhage: A Cause of Delayed Post-traumatic Blindness." *Neurology* 39 (1989): 863–65.

Da Mosto, Andrea. *I dogi di Venezia nella pubblica e privata*. Milan: A. Martello-Giunti, 1977.

Dale, Thomas E. A. *Relics, Prayer, and Politics in Medieval Venetia: Romanesque Painting in the Crypt of Aquileia Cathedral*. Princeton: Princeton University Press, 1997.

Danstrup, J. "Manuel I's Coup against Genoa and Venice in the Light of Byzantine Commercial Policy." *Classica et Mediaevalia* 10 (1948): 195–219.

Darù, Pierre. *Histoire de Venise*. 2 vols. Brussels: Société typographique belge, 1838.

Day, Gerald W. *Genoa's Response to Byzantium, 1155–1204: Commercial Expansion and Factionalism in a Medieval City*. Urbana: University of Illinois Press, 1988.

Demus, Otto. *The Church of San Marco in Venice: History, Architecture, Sculpture*. Washington, D.C.: Dumbarton Oaks, 1960.

————. *The Mosaics of San Marco*. 2 vols. Chicago: University of Chicago Press, 1984.

Diehl, Charles. *Venise: Une république patricienne*. Paris: E. Flammarion, 1915.

Dorigo, Wladimiro. *Venezia origini. Fondamenti, ipotesi, metodi*. 3 vols. Milan: Electa, 1983.

Dusa, Joan. *The Medieval Dalmatian Episcopal Cities: Development and Transformation*. New York: Peter Lang, 1991.

Errera, Carlo. "I crociati veneziani in Terra Santa dal concilio di Clermont alla morte di Ordelafo Falier (=1118)." *Archivio Veneto* 38 (1889): 237–77.

Fabris, Antonio. "Esperienze di vita comunitaria: I canonici regolari." In *La chiesa di Venezia nei secoli XI–XIII*, edited by Franco Tonon, 73–107. Venice: Studium cattolico veneziano, 1988.

Fasoli, Gina. "'Comune Veneciarum.'" In *Venezia dalla prima crociata alla conquista di Costantinopoli del 1204*, 71–102. Florence: G. C. Sansoni, 1965.

————. "Nascita di un mito." In *Studi storici in onore di Gioacchino Volpe per il suo 80 compleanno*, 1: 455–79. 2 vols. Florence: G. C. Sansoni, 1958.

Favreau-Lilie, Marie-Luise. *Die Italiener im Heiligen Land vom ersten Kreuzzug bis zum Tode Heinrichs von Champagne (1098–1197)*. Amsterdam: Hakkert, 1989.

Fedalto, Giorgio. "La diocesi nel Medioevo." In *Patriarcato di Venezia*, edited by Silvio Tramontin, 49–90. Padua: Libreria Editrice, 1991.

————. "Il patriarcato latino di Costantinopoli (1204–1261)." *Studia Patavina* 18 (1971): 390–464.

Fees, Irmgard. "Die Geschäfte der venezianischen Dogenfamilie Ziani." In *Venedig und die Weltwirtschaft um 1200*, edited by Wolfgang von Stromer, 53–69. Stuttgart: Jan Thorbecke, 1999.

————. *Le monache di San Zaccaria a Venezia nei secoli XII e XIII*. Translated by Ilva Fabiani. Venice: Centro Tedesco di Studi Veneziani, 1998.

————. *Reichtum und Macht im mittelalterlichen Venedig: Die Familie Ziani*. Tübingen: Max Niemeyer, 1988.

Ferluga, Jadran. "La Dalmazia fra Bisanzio, Venezia e l'Ungheria." *Studi Veneziani* 12 (1970): 63–83.

————. "L'impero bizantino nel giudizio dei Veneziani fino alla IV crociata." *Rivista Storica Italiana* 105 (1993): 5–35.

————. "Veneziani fuori Venezia." In *Storia di Venezia*, 1: 693–722. Rome: Istituto della Enciclopedia italiana, 1992.

Fine, John V. A. *The Late Medieval Balkans: A Critical Survey from the Late Twelfth Century to the Ottoman Conquest*. Ann Arbor: University of Michigan Press, 1987.

Finlay, George. *A History of Greece from Its Conquest by the Romans to the Present Time, B.C. 146 to A.D. 1864*. Edited and revised by Henry F. Tozer. 7 vols. Oxford: Clarendon Press, 1877.

Folda, Jaroslav. "The Fourth Crusade, 1201–1203: Some Reconsiderations." *Byzantinoslavica* 26 (1965): 277–90.

Fotheringham, John Knight. "Genoa and the Fourth Crusade." *English Historical Review* 25 (1910): 26–57.

————. *Marco Sanudo: Conqueror of the Archipelago.* Oxford: Clarendon Press, 1915.

Francès, E. "Alexis Comnène et les privilèges octroyés à Venise." *Byzantinoslavica* 29 (1968): 17–23.

Gallo, Rudolfo. "La tomba di Enrico Dandolo in Santa Sofia à Constantinople." *Rivista Mensile della Città di Venezia* 6 (1927): 270–83.

Geary, Patrick J. *Furta Sacra: Thefts of Relics in the Central Middle Ages.* Rev. ed. Princeton: Princeton University Press, 1990.

Gerland, Ernst. *Geschichte des lateinischen Kaiserreiches von Konstantinopel.* 1905. Reprint, Darmstadt: Wissenshaftliche Buchgesellschaft, 1966.

Ghetti, Bernardino. *I patti tra Venezia e Ferrara dal 1191 al 1313 esaminati nel loro testo e nel loro contenuto storico.* Rome: Ermanno Loescher, 1907.

Gibbon, Edward. *The Decline and Fall of the Roman Empire.* Edited by J. B. Bury. 3 vols. New York: Heritage Press, 1946.

Godfrey, John. *1204: The Unholy Crusade.* Oxford: Oxford University Press, 1980.

Goy, Richard J. *Venice: The City and Its Architecture.* London: Phaidon, 1997.

Grubb, James S. "When Myths Lose Power: Four Decades of Venetian Historiography." *Journal of Modern History* 58 (1986): 43–94.

Hain, Arnold. *Der Doge von Venedig seit dem Sturze der Orseoler bis zur Ermordung Vitale Michiel.* Königsberg: Hartungsche, 1883.

Hanotaux, Gabriel. "Les Vénitiens ont-ils trahi la chrétienté en 1202?" *Revue historique* 4 (1877): 74–102.

Hazlitt, W. Carew. *History of the Origin and Rise of the Venetian Republic.* 2 vols. London: Adam & Charles Black, 1915.

Hellmann, Manfred. *Grundzüge der Geschichte Venedigs.* Darmstadt: Wissenschaftliche Buchgesellschaft, 1981.

Hendrickx, Benjamin, and Corinna Matzukis. "Alexios V Doukas Mourtzouphlus: His Life, Reign, and Death (?–1205)." *Hellenika* 31 (1979): 108–32.

Hendy, Michael F. *Studies in the Byzantine Money Economy, 300–1453.* Cambridge: Cambridge University Press, 1985.

Heyd, Wilhelm. *Histoire du commerce du Levant au Moyen Age.* 2 vols. 1885. Reprint, Amsterdam: Adolf M. Hakkert, 1959.

Hocquet, Jean Claude. *Denaro, navi e mercanti a Venezia: 1200–1600.* Rome: Il Vetro, 1999.

Hodgson, Francis Coterell. *The Early History of Venice from the Foundation to the Conquest of Constantinople A.D. 1204.* London: George Allen, 1901.

Hóman, Bálint. *Geschichte des ungarischen Mittelalters.* 2 vols. Berlin: W. de Gruyter, 1940–43.

Hopf, Carl. *Geschichte Griechenlands.* In *Encyclopädie*, vols. 85–86. Edited by J. S. Ersch and J. G. Gruber. Leipzig: J. F. Gieditsch, 1867–68.

Housley, Norman. "The Thirteenth-Century Crusades in the Mediterranean." In *New Cambridge Medieval History*, vol. 5, edited by David Abulafia, 569–89. Cambridge: Cambridge University Press, 1999.

Hubach, Hans. "Pontifices, Clerus/Populus, Dux. Osservazioni sul più antico exempio di autorappresentazione politica della società." In *San Marco: aspetti storici ed agiografici. Atti del convegno internazionale di studi*, edited by Antonio Niero, 370–97. Venice: Marsilio, 1996.

Hurter, Friedrich. *Storia di Papa Innocenzo III.* Translated by T. Giuseppe Gliemone. 4 vols. Milan: A. Arzione, 1857–58.

Hussey, Joan M. *The Orthodox Church in the Byzantine Empire.* Oxford: Clarendon Press, 1986

Jacoby, David. "Les Italiens en Égypte aux XIIe et XIIIe siècles: du comptoir à la colonie?" In *Coloniser au Moyen Age*, edited by M. Balard and A. Ducellier, 76–89. Paris: Armand Colin, 1995.

———. "The Latin Empire of Constantinople and the Frankish States in Greece." In *New Cambridge Medieval History*, Vol. 5, edited by David Abulafia, 525–42. Cambridge: Cambridge University Press, 1999.

———. "The Supply of War Materials to Egypt in the Crusader Period." *Jerusalem Studies in Arabic and Islam* 25 (2000): 102–32.

———. "The Venetian Presence in the Latin Empire of Constantinople (1204–1261): The Challenge of Feudalism and the Byzantine Inheritance." *Jahrbuch der österreichischen Byzantinistik* 43 (1993): 141–201.

———. "The Venetian Quarter of Constantinople from 1082 to 1261: Topographical Considerations." In *Novum Millennium: Studies on Byzantine History and Culture Dedicated to Paul Speck*, edited by Claudia and Sarolta Takács, 153–70. Aldershot: Ashgate, 2001.

———. "Venetian Settlers in Latin Constantinople (1204–61): Rich or Poor?" In *Ricchi e poveri nella società dell'Oriente grecolatino*, edited by Chryssa A. Maltezou, 181–204. Venice: Instituto ellenico di studi bizantini e postbizantini di Venezia, 1998.

Janin, Raymond. *Constantinople byzantine. Développement urbain et répertoire topographique.* 2d ed. Paris: L'institut français d'études byzantines, 1964.

Jones, Philip J. *The Italian City-State: From Commune to Signoria.* Oxford: Clarendon Press, 1997.

Kazhdan, Alexander. S.v. "Venice." In *The Oxford Dictionary of Byzantium.* Oxford: Oxford University Press, 1991.

Kehr, Paul F. "Rom und Venedig." *Quellen und Forschungen aus italienischen Archiven und Bibliotheken* 19 (1927): 1–180.

Kretschmayr, Heinrich. *Geschichte von Venedig.* 3 vols. Gotha: F. A. Perthes, 1905–34.

Kuehn, Thomas. *Emancipation in Late Medieval Florence.* New Brunswick, N.J.: Rutgers University Press, 1982.

Laiou, Angeliki. "The Foreigner and the Stranger in Twelfth-Century Byzantium: Means of Propitiation and Acculturation." In *Fremde der Gesellschaft*, edited by Marie Theres Fögen, 71–97. Frankfurt am Main: V. Klostermann, 1991.

Lamma, Paolo. *Comneni e Staufer: Ricerche sui rapporti fra Bisanzio e l'Occidente nel secolo XII.* 2 vols. Rome: Istituto storico italiano per il Medio Evo, 1955–57.

Lane, Frederic C. *Venice: A Maritime Republic.* Baltimore: Johns Hopkins University Press, 1973.

Lane, Frederic C., and Reinhold C. Mueller. *Money and Banking in Medieval and Renaissance Venice.* Vol. 1, *Coins and Moneys of Account.* Baltimore: Johns Hopkins University Press, 1985.

Lanfranchi, Luigi, and G. G. Zille. "Il territorio del ducato veneziano dall'VIII al XII secolo." In *Storia di Venezia,* 3–65. Venice: Centro internazionale delle arti e del costume, 1957.

Lazzarini, Vittorio. "I titoli dei dogi di Venezia." *Nuovo Archivio Veneto,* n.s. 5 (1903): 271–313.

Lenel, Walter. *Die Entstehung der Vorherrschaft Venedigs an der Adria.* Strassburg: K. J. Trübner, 1897.

Lewis, Archibald R. *Naval Power and Trade in the Mediterranean, A.D. 500–1100.* Princeton: Princeton University Press, 1951.

Lilie, Ralph-Johannes. *Byzantium and the Crusader States, 1096–1204.* Rev. ed. Translated by J. C. Morris and Jean E. Ridings. Oxford: Oxford University Press, 1994.

———. *Handel und Politik zwischen dem byzantinischen Reich und den italienischen Kommunen Venedig, Pisa und Genua in der Epoche der Komnenen und der Angeloi (1081–1204).* Amsterdam: Adolph M. Hakkert, 1984.

Lock, Peter. *The Franks in the Aegean, 1204–1500.* New York: Longman, 1995.

Lombardo, Antonino. "Il doge di Venezia Enrico Dandolo e la prima promissione ducale." *Archivi e Cultura* 10 (1976): 25–35.

Longnon, Jean. *L'empire latin de Constantinople et la principauté de Morée.* Paris: Payot, 1949.

———. "The Frankish States in Greece, 1204–1261." In *A History of the Crusades,* edited by Kenneth M. Setton, 2: 235–74. Philadelphia: University of Pennsylvania Press, 1962.

Loredan, Alvise. *I Dandolo.* Varese: dall'Oglio, 1981.

Lorenzetti, G. *Venezia e il suo estuario.* Milan: Bestetti & Tumminelli, 1926. Reprint, Rome: Istituto poligrafico dello stato, 1956.

Luzzatto, Gino. "Capitale e lavoro nel commercio veneziano dei secoli XI e XII." In *Studi di storia economica veneziana,* 89–116. Padua: Cedam, 1954.

———. "L'oro e l'argento nella politica monetaria veneziana dei secoli XIII–XIV." In *Studi di storia economica veneziana,* 259–70. Padua: Cedam, 1954.

———. *I prestiti della Repubblica di Venezia (Sec. XIII–XV).* Padua: A. Draghi, 1929.

Madden, Thomas F. "The Chrysobull of Alexius I Comnenus to the Venetians: The Date and the Debate." *Journal of Medieval History* 28 (2002): 23–41.

———. *A Concise History of the Crusades.* Lanham, Md.: Rowman & Littlefield, 1999.

———. "Enrico Dandolo: His Life, His Family, and His Venice before the Fourth Crusade." Ph.D. diss., University of Illinois at Urbana–Champaign, 1993.

———. "The Fires of the Fourth Crusade in Constantinople, 1203–1204: A Damage Assessment." *Byzantinische Zeitschrift* 84–85 (1991–92): 72–93.

———. "Food and the Fourth Crusade." In *How They Made War in the Age of the Crusades,* edited by John H. Pryor. Aldershot: Ashgate, forthcoming.

———. "Outside and Inside the Fourth Crusade." *International History Review* 17 (1995): 726–43.

———. "Venice and Constantinople in 1171 and 1172: Enrico Dandolo's Attitude towards Byzantium." *Mediterranean Historical Review* 8 (1993): 166–85.

———. "Venice's Hostage Crisis: Diplomatic Efforts to Secure Peace with Byzantium between 1171 and 1184." In *Medieval and Renaissance Venice,* edited by Ellen E. Kittell and Thomas F. Madden, 96–108. Urbana: University of Illinois Press, 1999.

———. "Vows and Contracts in the Fourth Crusade: The Treaty of Zara and the Attack on Constantinople in 1204." *International History Review* 15 (1993): 441–68.

Magdalino, Paul. *The Empire of Manuel I Komnenos, 1143–1180.* Cambridge: Cambridge University Press, 1993.

Maleczek, Werner. "Das Kardinalskollegium unter Innocenz II und Anacletus II." *Archivum Historiae Pontificiae* 19 (1981): 27–78.

———. *Pietro Capuano: Patrizio amalfitano, cardinale, legato alla quarta crociata, teologo (1214).* Translated by Fulvio Delle Donne. Rev. ed. Amalfi: Centro di cultura e storia amalfitana, 1997.

Maltezou, Chrysa A. "Il quartiere veneziano di Costantinopoli (Scali marittimi)." *Thesaurismata* 15 (1978): 30–61.

———. "Venetian *habitores, burgenses* and Merchants in Constantinople and Its Hinterland (Twelfth–Thirteenth Centuries)." In *Constantinople and Its Hinterland,* edited by Cyril Mango and Gilbert Dagron, 233–41. Aldershot: Variorum, 1993.

Manfroni, Camillo. *Storia della marina italiana dalle invasioni barbariche al Trattato di Ninfeo (anni di c. 400–1261).* Livorno, R. Accademia navale, 1899.

Maranini, Giuseppe. *La costituzione di Venezia dalle origini alla Serrata del Maggior Consiglio.* Venice, 1927. Reprint, Florence: La nuova Italia, 1974.

Maretto, Paolo. *L'edilizia gotica veneziana.* 2d ed. Venice: Filippi Editore, 1978.

Margetic, Lujo. "Il diritto." In *Storia di Venezia,* 1: 677–92. Rome: Istituto della Enciclopedia italiana, 1992.

Martin, M. E. "The Chrysobull of Alexius I Comnenus to the Venetians and the Early Venetian Quarter in Constantinople." *Byzantinoslavica* 39 (1978) 19–23.

———. "The Venetians in the Byzantine Empire before 1204." *Byzantinische Forschungen* 13 (1988): 201–14.

McNeal, Edgar H and Robert Lee Wolff. "The Fourth Crusade." In *A History of the Crusades,* edited by Kenneth M. Setton, 2: 153–85. Philadelphia: University of Pennsylvania Press, 1962.

McNeill, William H. *Venice: The Hinge of Europe, 1081–1797.* Chicago: University of Chicago Press, 1974.

Merores, Margarete. "Der venezianische Adel. Ein Beitrag zur Sozialgeschichte." *Vierteljahrschrift für Sozial- und Wirtschaftsgeschichte* 19 (1926): 193–237.

Meyer, Karl E. "The West's Debt to Byzantium." *New York Times,* March 30, 1997.

Mills, Charles. *The History of the Crusades.* Philadelphia: Lea & Blanchard, 1844.

Minotto, Demetrius. *Chronik der Familie Minotto beiträge zur Staats- und Kulturgeschichte Venedigs.* 3 vols. Berlin: A. Asher, 1901–6.

Monticolo, Giovanni. "La costituzione del doge Pietro Polani (febbraio 1143, 1142 more veneto) circa la processio scolarum." In *Atti dell'Accademia nazionale dei Lincei, rendiconti. cl. sc. mor. st. filosof.,* 91–133. Rome: Tipografia della R. Accademia dei Lincei, 1901.

———. "Due documenti veneziani del secolo dodicesimo." *Nuovo Archivio Veneto* 19 (1900): 56–75.

———. "Il testo del patto giurato dal doge Domenico Michiel al comune di Bari." *Nuovo Archivio Veneto* 18 (1899): 96–140.

Moore, John C. "Peter of Lucedio (Cistercian Patriarch of Antioch) and Pope Innocent III." *Römische Historische Mitteilungen* 29 (1987): 221–49.

Mor, Carlo Guido. "Aspetti della vita costituzionale veneziana fino alla fine del X secolo." In *Le origini di Venezia*, 121–40. Florence: G. C. Sansoni, 1964.

Morris, Colin. *The Papal Monarchy: The Western Church from 1050 to 1250.* Oxford: Oxford University Press, 1989.

Mueller, Reinhold C. "The Procurators of San Marco in the Thirteenth and Fourteenth Centuries: A Study of the Office as a Financial and Trust Institution." *Studi Veneziani* 13 (1971): 105–220.

Muir, Edward. "Idee, riti, simboli del potere." In *Storia di Venezia*, 2: 739–60. Rome: Istituto della Enciclopedia italiana, 1995.

Müller-Wiener, Wolfgang. *Bildlexikon zur Topographie Istanbuls: Byzantion, Konstantinupolis, Istanbul bis zum Beginn des 17. Jahrhunderts.* Tübingen: Ernst Wasmuth, 1977.

Mundo Lo, Sara de. *Cruzados en Bizancio: la cuarta cruzada a la luz de las fuentes latinas y orientales.* Buenos Aires: Universidad de Buenos Aires, 1957.

Muratori, Saverio. *Studi per una operante storia urbana di Venezia.* Rome: Istituto poligrafico dello stato, 1959.

Necker, Karl-Hartmann. *Dandolo: Venedigs kühnster Doge.* Vienna: Böhlau, 1999.

Nicol, Donald M. *Byzantium and Venice: A Study in Diplomatic and Cultural Relations.* Cambridge: Cambridge University Press, 1988.

———. "The Fourth Crusade and the Greek and Latin Empires, 1204–1261." In *Cambridge Medieval History.* Vol. 4, pt. 1, 275–324. Cambridge: Cambridge University Press, 1966.

Niero, Antonio. "Patriarcato di Grado, diocesi lagunari, patriarcato di Venezia." In *Archivi chiesa locale. Studi e contribute,* edited by Francesca Cavazana Romanelli and Isabella Ruol, 93–101. Venice: Studium cattolico veneziano, 1993.

Noble, Peter. "Eyewitnesses of the Fourth Crusade—the War against Alexius III." *Reading Medieval Studies* 25 (1999): 75–89.

Norden, Walter. *Der vierte Kreuzzug in Rahmen der Beziehungen des Abendlandes zu Byzanz.* Berlin: E. Beck, 1898.

Norwich, John Julius. *A History of Venice.* New York: Alfred A. Knopf, 1982.

Oikonomides, Nicolas. "La décomposition de l'Empire byzantin à la veille de 1204 et les origines de l'Empire de Nicée: A propos de la 'Partitio.'" In *XVe Congrès international d'études byzantines: Rapports et co-rapports,* 1: 3–28. 2 vols. Athens: Comité d'organisation du congrès, 1979–81.

Ortalli, Gherardo. "Il ducato e la 'civitas Rivoalti': tra carolingi, bizantini e sassoni." In *Storia di Venezia*, 1: 725–790. Rome: Istituto della Enciclopedia italiana, 1992.

————. "Venezia dalle origini a Pietro II Orseolo." In *Storia d'Italia*, edited by Giuseppe Galasso, 341–438. Turin: UTET, 1980.

Ostrogorsky, George. *History of the Byzantine State*. Translated by Joan Hussey. Rev. ed. New Brunswick, N.J.: Rutgers University Press, 1969.

Pansolli, Lamberto. *La gerarchia delle fonti di diritto nella legislazione medievale veneziana*. Milan: A. Giuffré, 1970.

Papadopoli, Nicolò. *Le monete di Venezia*. 4 vols. Venice: Libreria Emiliana, 1893–1919.

Paschini, Pio. "I patriarchi di Aquileia nel secolo XII." *Memorie Storiche Forogiuliese* 10 (1914): 1–36, 113–81.

Pears, Edwin. *The Fall of Constantinople, Being the Story of the Fourth Crusade*. New York: Harper & Bros., 1886.

Pertusi, Agostino. "La contesa per le reliquie di S. Nicola tra Bari, Venezia e Genova." *Quaderni Medievali* 5 (1978): 6–56.

————. "*Quedem regalia insignia*. Ricerche sulle insegne dei poteri dei dogi di Venezia nel medioevo." *Studi Veneziani* 7 (1965): 3–123.

————. "Venezia e Bisanzio nel secolo XI." In *La Venezia del mille*, 117–60. Florence: G. C. Sansoni, 1965.

Pitzorno, Benvenuto. *Le consuetudini giudiziare veneziane anteriori al 1229*. Venice: Premiata tipografica Emiliana, 1910.

————. *Gli statuti civili attributi ad Enrico Dandolo*. Perugia: Guerra, 1913.

Piva, Vittorio. *Il patriarcato di Venezia e le sue origini*. 2 vols. Venice: Studium cattolico veneziano, 1938–1960.

Pozza, Marco. *I Badoer. Una famiglia veneziana dal X al XIII secolo*. Padua: Aldo Francisci, 1982.

Praga, Giuseppe. *Storia della Dalmazia*. Padua: Cedam, 1954.

————. "Zaratini e Veneziani nel 1190: La battaglia di Trani." *La Rivista Dalmatica* 8 (1925): 47–54.

Prawer, Joshua. *The Crusaders' Kingdom: European Colonialism in the Middle Ages*. New York: Praeger, 1972.

————. *Histoire du royaume latin de Jérusalem*. 2 vols. Paris: Éditions du Centre National de la Recherche Scientifique, 1969.

————. "The Italians in the Latin Kingdom." In *Crusader Institutions*, 217–49. Oxford: Oxford University Press, 1980.

————. "I Veneziani e le colonie veneziane nel Regno latino di Gerusalemme." In *Venezia e il Levante fino al secolo XV*, 625–56. Florence: Leo S. Olschki, 1973.

Pryor, John H. *Geography, Technology, and War: Studies in the Maritime History of the Mediterranean, 649–1571*. Cambridge: Cambridge University Press, 1988.

————. "Winds, Waves, and Rocks: The Routes and the Perils Along Them." In *Maritime Aspects of Migration*, edited by Klaus Friedland, 71–85. Cologne: Böhlau, 1989.

————. "The Venetian Fleet for the Fourth Crusade and the Diversion of the Crusade to Constantinople." Forthcoming.

Queller, Donald E. "L'évolution du rôle de l'Ambassadeur: les pleins pouvoirs et la traité de 1201 entre les Croisés et les Vénitiens." *Le Moyen Age* 19 (1961): 479–501.

———. "Innocent III and the Crusader-Venetian Treaty of 1201." *Medievalia et Humanistica* 15 (1963): 31–4.

———. "A Note on the Reorganization of the Venetian Coinage by Doge Enrico Dandolo." *Rivista Italiana di Numismatica e Scienze Affini* 67 (1979): 167–72.

———. *The Office of Ambassador in the Middle Ages.* Princeton: Princeton University Press, 1967.

———. Review of Donald M. Nicol, *Byzantium and Venice. Speculum* 66 (1991): 210–13.

Queller, Donald E., and Irene B. Katele. "Venice and the Conquest of the Latin Kingdom of Jersualem." *Studi Veneziani,* n.s. 12 (1986): 15–43.

Queller, Donald E., and Thomas F. Madden. *The Fourth Crusade: the Conquest of Constantinople.* 2d ed. Philadelphia: University of Pennsylvania Press, 1997.

———. "Some Further Arguments in Defense of the Venetians on the Fourth Crusade." *Byzantion* 62 (1992): 433–73.

Rando, Daniela. "Le struttura della Chiesa locale." In *Storia di Venezia,* 1: 645–75. Rome: Istituto della Enciclopedia italiana, 1992.

———. *Una chiesa di frontiera: Le istituzioni ecclesiastiche veneziane nei secoli VI–XII.* Bologna: Il Mulino, 1994.

Ravegnani, Giorgio. "La Romània veneziana." In *Storia di Venezia.* 2: 183–231. Rome: Istituto della Enciclopedia italiana, 1995.

Riley-Smith, Jonathan. "The Venetian Crusade of 1122–1124." In *I comuni italiani nel regno crociato di Gerusalemme,* edited by B. Z. Kedar and G. Airaldi, 337–50. Genoa: Università di Genova, 1986.

Robbert, Louise Buenger. "Reorganization of the Venetian Coinage by Doge Enrico Dandolo." *Speculum* 49 (1974): 48–60.

———. "The Venetian Money Market, 1150–1229." *Studi Veneziani* 13 (1971): 3–94.

———. "Venice and the Crusades." In *A History of the Crusades,* edited by Kenneth M. Setton, 5: 379–451. Madison: University of Wisconsin Press, 1985.

Roberti, Melchiorre. "Dei giudici veneziani prima del 1200." *Nuovo Archivio Veneto,* n.s. 8 (1904): 230–45.

———. *Le magistrature giudiziare veneziane e i loro capitolari fino al 1300.* 3 vols. Padua: Tipografia editrice del seminario, 1906–11.

Robinson, Ian S. *The Papacy, 1073–1198: Continuity and Innovation.* Cambridge: Cambridge University Press, 1990.

Romanin, Samuele. *Storia documentata di Venezia,* 3d ed., 10 vols. Venice: Libreria Filippi, 1972–75.

Rösch, Gerhard. "Der Handel Ägyptens mit dem Abendland um 1200." In *Venedig und die Weltwirtschaft um 1200,* edited by Wolfgang von Stromer, 235–56. Stuttgart: Jan Thorbecke, 1999.

———. *Venedig und das Reich: Handels- und verkehrspolitische Beziehungen in der deutschen Kaiserzeit.* Tübingen: Max Niemeyer, 1982.

——. *Der venezianische Adel bis zur Schließung des Großen Rats: Zur Genese einer Führungsschicht.* Sigmaringen: Jan Thorbecke, 1989.

Rousset, Paul. *Histoire des croisades.* Paris: Payot, 1957.

Runciman, Steven. *A History of the Crusades.* 3 vols. Cambridge: Cambridge University Press, 1952–54.

Schneider, A. M. "Brände in Konstantinopel." *Byzantinische Zeitschrift* 41 (1941): 382–403.

Schulz, Juergen. "The Houses of the Dandolo: A Family Compound in Medieval Venice." *Journal of the Society of Architectural Historians* 52 (1993): 391–415.

——. "La piazza medievale di San Marco." *Annali di architettura* 4 (1992): 134–56.

——. "Urbanism in Medieval Venice." In *City States in Classical Antiquity and Medieval Italy,* edited by Kurt Raaflaub, Anthony Molho, and Julia Emlen, 419–45. Stuttgart: Franz Steiner, 1991.

Settia, Aldo A. "L'apparato militare." In *Storia di Venezia,* 2: 461–505. Rome: Istituto della Enciclopedia italiana, 1995.

Setton, Kenneth M. *The Papacy and the Levant (1204–1571).* Vol. 1. Philadelphia: American Philosophical Society, 1976.

Simonsfeld, H. "Kurze Venezianer Annalen." In *Neues Archiv der Gesellschaft für Ältere Deutsche Geschichtskunde zur Beförderung einer Gesammtausgabe der Quellenschriften Deutscher Geschichten des Mittelalters,* 1: 397–410. Hanover: Hahnsche Buchhandlung, 1876.

Somerville, Robert. "Pope Honorius II, Conrad of Hohenstaufen and Lothar III." *Archivum Historiae Pontificiae* 10 (1972): 341–46.

Spinelli, Giovanni. "I monasteri benedettini fra il 1000 ed il 1300." In *La chiesa di Venezia nei secoli XI–XIII,* edited by Franco Tonon, 109–33. Venice: Studium cattolico veneziano, 1988.

——. "I primi insediamenti monastici lagunari nel contesto della storia politica e religiosa veneziana." In *Le origini della chiesa di Venezia,* edited by Franco Tonon, 151–66. Venice: Studium cattolico veneziano, 1987.

Spiridonakis, Basile G. *Grecs, Occidentaux et Turcs de 1054 à 1453: Quatre siècles d'histoire de relations internationales.* Thessaloniki: Institute for Balkan Studies, 1990.

Spufford, Peter. *Money and Its Uses in Medieval Europe.* Cambridge: Cambridge University Press, 1988.

Stahl, Alan M. "Coinage and Money in the Latin Empire of Constantinople." *Dumbarton Oaks Papers* 55 (2001): 197–206.

——. "The Coinage of Venice in the Age of Enrico Dandolo." In *Medieval and Renaissance Venice,* edited by Ellen E. Kittell and Thomas F. Madden, 124–40. Urbana: University of Illinois Press, 1999.

——. "The Grosso of Enrico Dandolo." *Revue belge de Numismatique* 145 (1999): 261–68.

Steindorff, Ludwig. *Die dalmatinischen Stadte im 12. Jahrhundert: Studien zu ihrer politischen Stellung und gesellschaftlichen Entwicklung.* Cologne: Böhlau, 1984.

Storia di Venezia. Rome: Istituto della Enciclopedia italiana, 1992–.

Streit, Ludwig. "Venezia e la quarta crociata." Translated by R. Fulin. *Archivio Veneto* 16 (1878): 50–94, 239–71.

Sweeney, James Ross. "Hungary in the Crusades, 1169–1218." *International History Review* 3 (1981): 467–81.

Tassini, Giuseppe. *Curiosità veneziane ovvero origini delle denominazioni stradali di Venezia.* 9th ed. Edited by Lino Moretti. Venice: Filippi Editore, 1988.

Tessier, Jules. *La quatrième croisade: La diversion sur Zara et Constantinople.* Paris: Ernest Laroux, 1884.

Thiriet, Freddy. "Les chroniques vénétiennes de la Marcienne et leur importance pour l'histoire de la Romanie gréco-vénitienne." *Mélanges d'archéologie et d'histoire: Ecole Française de Rome* 66 (1954): 241–92.

———. *La Romanie vénitienne au Moyen Age: Le développment et l'exploitation du domaine colonial vénetien.* Paris: E. De Boccard, 1959.

Tierney, D. W. "Visual Dysfunction in Closed Head Injury." *Journal of the American Optometric Association* 59 (1988): 614–22.

Tramontin, Silvio. "Fondazione e sviluppo della diocesi." In *Patriarcato di Venezia,* edited by Silvio Tramontin, 21–46. Padua: Gregoriana, 1991.

Tuilier, André. "La date exacte du chrysobulle d'Alexis Ier Comnène en faveur des Vénitiens et son contexte historique." *Rivista di studi bizantini e neoellenici* 4 (1967): 27–48.

Tůma, Oldřich. "The Dating of Alexius's Chrysobull to the Venetians: 1082, 1084, or 1092?" *Byzantinoslavica* 42 (1981): 71–85.

———. "Some Notes on the Significance of the Imperial Chrysobull to the Venetians of 992." *Byzantion* 54 (1984): 358–66.

Ughelli, Ferdinand. *Italia sacra,* 2d ed. Edited by Niccolo Coleti. 10 vols. Venice: Sebastiano Coleti, 1717–22. Reprint, Nendeln, Liechtenstein: Kraus Reprint, 1970.

Uhlirz, Mathilde. "Venezia nella politica di Ottone III." In *La Venezia del mille,* 31–43. Florence: G. C. Sansoni, 1965.

Usseglio, Leopoldo. *I marchesi di Monferrato in Italia ed in oriente durante i secoli XII e XIII.* 2 vols. Milan: Miglietta, 1926.

Vasiliev, A. A. *History of the Byzantine Empire, 324–1453.* Madison: University of Wisconsin Press, 1952.

Violante, Cinzio. "Venezia fra papato e impero nel secolo XI." In *La Venezia del mille,* 47–84. Florence: G. C. Sansoni, 1965.

Vlad, L. Borelli, and A. Guidi Toniato. "The Origins and Documentary Sources of the Horses of San Marco." In *The Horses of San Marco,* edited by Guido Perocco; translated by Valerie Wilton-Ely and John Wilton-Ely, 127–36. London: Thames & Hudson, 1979.

Vryonis, Speros. *Byzantium and Europe.* London: Thames & Hudson, 1967.

Wolff, Robert Lee. "Greeks and Latins before and after 1204." *Ricerche di storia religiosa* 1 (1957): 320–34.

———. "The Latin Empire of Constantinople." In *A History of the Crusades,* edited by Kenneth M. Setton, 2: 187–233. Philadelphia: University of Pennsylvania Press, 1962.

————. "A New Document from the Period of the Latin Empire of Constantinople: The Oath of the Venetian Podestà." *Annuaire de L'Institut de Philologie et d'Histoire Orientales et Slaves* 12 (1953): 539–73.

————. "Politics in the Latin Patriarchate of Constantinople, 1204–1261." *Dumbarton Oaks Papers* 8 (1954): 225–303.

Wolters, Wolfgang. *Der Bilderschmuck des Dogenpalastes: Untersuchungen zur Selbstdarstellund der Republik Venedig im 16. Jahrhundert.* Wiesbaden: Franz Steiner, 1983.

Yamamoto, L. G. and R. D. Bart, Jr. "Transient Blindness Following Mild Head Trauma: Criteria for a Benign Outcome." *Clinical Pediatrics* 27 (1988): 479–83.

Zakythinos, Denis A. "La conquête de Constantinople en 1204, Venise et le partage de l'Empire Byzantin." In *Venezia dalla prima crociata alla conquista di Costantinopoli del 1204*, edited by Vittore Branca, 137–56. Florence: G. C. Sansoni, 1965.

Zordan, Giorgio. *Le persone nella storia del diritto veneziano prestatutario.* Padua: Cedam, 1973.

————. "I vari aspetti della comunione familiare di beni nell Venezia dei secoli XI–XII." *Studi Veneziani* 8 (1966): 127–159.

Index